Religion and Psychology: Mapping the Terrain

Religion and Psychology: Mapping the Terrain is a thorough and incisive survey of the current state of the relationship between religion and psychology from the leading scholars in the field. The issues addressed are:

- the psychology–theology dialogue in the West
- psychological perspectives on non-Western religions
- psychology, religion and gender studies
- perspectives on modernity and post-modernity
- psychology "as" religion
- empirical, cultural and social scientific approaches
- international perspectives

An essential resource for students and researchers in the area of psychology of religion, this collection systematically examines the whole range of ways in which the psychology/religion debate has developed.

Diane Jonte-Pace teaches in the department of Religious Studies at Santa Clara University and is the editor of *Religious Studies Review*. **William Parsons** teaches Religious Studies at Rice University.

Religion and Psychology: Mapping the Terrain

Contemporary dialogues, future prospects

Edited by Diane Jonte-Pace and William B. Parsons

London and New York

First published 2001
by Routledge
11 New Fetter Lane, London EC4P 4EE

Simultaneously published in the USA and Canada
by Routledge
29 West 35th Street, New York, NY 10001

Routledge is an imprint of the Taylor & Francis Group

Typeset in Times by Taylor & Francis Books Ltd
Printed and bound in Great Britain by Clays Ltd, St Ives plc

British Library Cataloguing in Publication Data
A catalogue record for this book is available from the British Library

Library of Congress Cataloging in Publication Data
A catalog record has been requested for this title

ISBN 0–415–20617–0 (hbk)
ISBN 0–415–20618–9 (pbk)

**To our students, for nourishing this project,
and our colleagues, for making it possible**

Contents

Contributors

G. William Barnard is Associate Professor at Southern Methodist University. He teaches in the areas of comparative religion and the social-scientific study of religion. He is the author of *Exploring Unseen Worlds: William James and the Philosophy of Mysticism* (SUNY Press 1997) and the co-editor of *Crossing Boundaries: Essays on the Ethical Status of Mysticism* (Seven Bridges Press 2000).

Jacob A. Belzen has degrees in psychology, philosophy, and history. He holds an endowed chair at the University of Amsterdam in the psychology of religion. He serves in several international scholarly organizations. He is the editor of *Hermeneutical Approaches in Psychology of Religion* (Rodopi 1997).

Lucy Bregman is Professor of Religion at Temple University. She has authored several books on psychology, death and spirituality in contemporary life. These include *Death in the Midst of Life: Perspectives on Death from Christianity and Depth Psychology* (Baker Book House 1992) and *Beyond Silence and Denial: Death and Dying Reconsidered* (Westminster John Knox 1999).

Don Browning is Alexander Campbell Professor of Religious Ethics and the Social Sciences at the University of Chicago. He is currently director of the Lilly Endowment project for Religion, Culture, and Family. His recent books have been *A Fundamental Practical Theology* (Fortress Press 1991), and, with Bonnie Miller-McLemore, Pam Couture, Bernie Lyon, and Robert Franklin, *From Culture Wars to Common Ground: Religion and the American Family Debate* (Westminster John Knox 1997).

Donald Capps is William Harte Felmeth Professor of Pastoral Theology at Princeton Theological Seminary. His recent books include *Men, Religion, and Melancholia* (Yale University Press 1997), *Living Stories* (Fortress Press 1998), *Social Phobia* (Chalice Press 1999), and *Jesus: A Psychological Biography* (Chalice Press 2000).

Jeremy R. Carrette is Lecturer in Religious Studies at the University of Stirling, Scotland, UK. He is the editor of *Religion and Culture by Michel Foucault* (UK: Manchester University Press and USA: Routledge 1999) and the author of *Foucault and Religion: Spiritual Corporality and Political Spirituality* (Routledge 2000).

Volney P. Gay is Professor and Chair of Religion, Professor of Psychiatry, and Professor of Anthropology at Vanderbilt University. He is a Training and Supervising Analyst at the St. Louis Psychoanalytic Institute. He serves on the editorial boards of several scholarly journals. He is also Vice-Chair of the Committee on Research and Special Training, American Psychoanalytic Association, and Chair of the the Liddle-Hymowitz Fund of the American Psychoanalytic Association. His last book, *Freud on Sublimation* (SUNY Press 1992), won the Heinz Hartmann Award from the New York Psychoanalytic Institute. His forthcoming book, *The Objects of Psychoanalysis,* will be published by SUNY Press.

Luis O. Gómez holds appointments in the Departments of Psychology and Asian Languages and Cultures at the University of Michigan. His interests span Buddhism in India, early Zen and Pure Land, and the psychology of religion. Professor Gómez has published in the area of Indian Buddhism and is editor of several books, including *Land of Bliss* (University of Hawaii Press 1996). He is also a clinical psychologist at the University of Michigan's Psychological Clinic.

Susan E. Henking is Associate Professor of Religious Studies and Interim Dean of the Faculty at Hobart and William Smith Colleges. She is co-editor of *Que(e)rying Religion: A Critical Anthology* (with Gary David Comstock of Wesleyan University; Continuum 1997) and author of a variety of work on the history of American sociology, feminist perspectives in religious studies, and the intersection of religious studies with lesbian and gay studies. In addition, she is series editor of the AAR book series, *Teaching Religious Studies*.

Diane E. Jonte-Pace is Associate Professor of Religious Studies and Acting Associate Dean at Santa Clara University. She serves as chair of the editorial board of *The Religious Studies Review*. Her publications include *Speaking the Unspeakable: Religion, Misogyny, and the Uncanny Mother in Freud's Cultural Texts*, forthcoming from the University of California Press.

Jeffrey J. Kripal is the Vira I. Heinz Associate Professor of Religion at Westminster College. His publications include *Kali's Child: The Mystical and the Erotic in the Life and Teachings of Ramakrishna* (University of Chicago Press 1995), which won the American Academy of Religion's History of Religions Prize, and *Vishnu on Freud's Desk: A Reader in Psychoanalysis and Hinduism* (Oxford University Press 1998), which he co-edited with T.G. Vaidyanathan of Bangalore, India.

Bonnie J. Miller-McLemore is Professor of Pastoral Theology at Vanderbilt University Divinity School. Her most recent publications include *Also a Mother: Work and Family as Theological Dilemma* (Abingdon 1994), a co-authored book, *From Culture Wars to Common Ground: Religion and the American Family Debate* (with Don S. Browning, Pamela D. Couture, Brynolf Lyon and Robert Franklin; Westminster John Knox 1997), and a co-edited book, *Feminist and Womanist Pastoral Theology* (with Brita L. Gill-Austern; Abingdon 1999).

Kathleen V. O'Connor is a trained historian, psychologist and psychotherapist. Formerly at the University of Sydney, currently she teaches the psychology of religion at the Catholic Institute of Sydney, conducts a private practice and supervises the training of psychologists. She has published on religion, personality, and mental health and is on the editorial boards of *The International Journal for the Psychology of Religion* and *Mental Health, Religion and Culture*.

William B. Parsons is Associate Professor of Religious Studies at Rice University. He is the author of *The Enigma of the Oceanic Feeling* (Oxford 1999) and numerous articles in edited books and journals, including *The Journal of Religion*.

Jonathan Shear, Affiliated Associate Professor of Philosophy at Virginia Commonwealth University, was a Fullbright Scholar in philosophy of science. For the past thirty-eight years his work has focused on the significance of basic meditation experiences for questions of Western philosophy and psychology. Recent publications include *The View From Within: First-Person Approaches to the Study of Consciousness*, co-edited with Francisco Varela (UK: Imprint Academic 1999), and *Models of the Self*, co-edited with Shaun Gallagher (UK: Imprint Academic 1999). He is Managing Editor of *The Journal of Consciousness Studies*.

Bernard Spilka, Professor Emeritus at the University of Denver, is author, co-author and editor of a number of books and many other publications. He is a past-President of the Psychology of Religion Division of the American Psychological Association and recipient of its William James Award.

David M. Wulff is Professor of Psychology at Wheaton College, Norton, Massachusetts. He is the author of *Psychology of Religion: Classic and Contemporary* (Wiley, 2nd edn 1997) and is a past president of Division 36, Psychology of Religion, of the American Psychological Association.

Introduction

Mapping religion and psychology

William B. Parsons and
Diane Jonte-Pace

What is the relation of psychology to religion? Does psychology attack, critique, and challenge religion? Or does psychology collaborate with religion in promoting mental and spiritual wholeness? Do psychological models contain implicit cultural assumptions and visions of personhood and relationality that interfere with its ability to study and interpret religion objectively? Has a modern or even postmodern psychological worldview replaced a pre-modern religious worldview? How can we describe the terrain where psychology and religion intersect?

The scholars contributing to this volume each map a portion of this terrain. Unlike ordinary maps, which are schematic pictures of space, these essays offer both cartographies and chronologies of the intersections between psychology and religion. The contributors to this volume describe how and where psychology has encountered religion earlier in this century and in recent decades: they look back to the past. At the same time, they look forward: a major aim of the contributions is to provoke sustained debate over future directions for the field. The essays thus represent and "map" the parameters of distinct approaches and dialogues found in that domain which designates the intersection between religion and psychological studies.

Framing the debate: "and," "of," "in dialogue with"

Even a cursory historical overview reveals that the domain which is the subject of this volume has been circumscribed by various designations. There is good reason for this fact. The differences between psychological models utilized, the religious responses evoked, and the inclusion of internationally based scholars and religious professionals who locate themselves and their institutions in multiple social settings (the clinic, the seminary, the church, and the university) have invariably led to specialization, segmentation, and the development of distinct approaches and arenas of dialogue. Indeed, the perspectives have become so diverse that it is questionable whether the multiplicity of dialogues and approaches gathered here can be said to constitute a single "field"; that, for example, what has been called the psychology "of" religion should be marked as a single field apart from those enterprises that champion more religiously toned, dialogical approaches. On the other hand, it is important to note that there have been numerous attempts to create cohesion (a singular "field") out of the chaos of multiplicity and diversity. "Religion and the human sciences," "religion and culture studies," "pastoral psychology," "practical theology," "religion and personality," "religion, person, and culture" – these are some of the designations that have been used to characterize the domain that this volume maps in graduate programs in universities and seminaries over the last few decades.

The categories utilized in this volume do not necessarily preclude other ways of framing the intersection between psychology and religion. Indeed, as we shall see, the contributors sometimes disagree on precisely how it is that this domain should be framed and "mapped." Nevertheless, in order to encompass the various cartographies and chronologies found in this volume, the editors have preferred to utilize the broad designation "religion and psychological studies" (or RPS). As opposed to other designations, this terminology does not privilege either term. Rather, the designation has the advantage of being both inclusive – recognizing that diversity and dialogue have come to characterize the intersection between psychology and religion – and neutral, for it understands that its participants champion differing, sometimes opposed, intellectual agendas.

In soliciting contributions from leading scholars, the editors sought to avoid imposing any conceptual schema that might prejudice their remarks. Subsequently, the editors found that the finished essays fall almost seamlessly into two major enterprises associated with the field. In order to reflect this, we have specified within the inclusive designation "religion and psychological studies" the more restrictive subsets: "psychology of religion" and "religion in dialogue with psychology."

Historically, the origins of the interaction between psychology and religion are usually located in the period 1880–1930. During this period the field was commonly known as the psychology "of" religion. It assumed a method ("psychology"), a series of cultural phenomena ("religion"), and a specific relation between the two: the psychology of religion referred to the analysis of the psychological meanings, origins, and patterns in religious ideation and practice. It found expression in the depth psychologies of Freud and Jung, the descriptive surveys and pragmatic evaluations of William James, the folk-psychological forays of Wilhelm Wundt, and the diverse studies authored by related scholars in Europe and North America (e.g., William E. Hocking, James Leuba, Pierre Janet, Theodore Flournoy, Frederick Meyers, R.M. Bucke, James Pratt, etc.). Topics that commanded interest varied from prayer, conversion, the paranormal, and mysticism, to the broad array of issues connected with the comparative study of religion and the relation between religion and society.

Since that time, the field has expanded in several ways. With regard to advances within psychological theory, the field has incorporated the virtual explosion of metapsychological advances found throughout the course of the century: the development of experimental and empirical approaches; the mid-century projects initiated by ego-psychologists, object-relations theorists, proponents of phenomenology, existentialism, and humanistic psychology; and the more recent advances of transpersonal psychology, sociobiology and neurocognition. As with many other academic enterprises, the field has also become more interdisciplinary, integrating social scientific partners such as sociology, anthropology and political theory in order to illuminate religious phenomena. The latter have proven useful in linking issues regarding religion and individual biography to the wider historical and socio-cultural surround. More recently, those in the field have had to take account of postmodern analyses and the rise of gender studies and related cultural modes of reflection. The latter have ignited epistemological and cultural self-reflection concerning the normative, apologetic and ethnopsychological dimensions of psychological theory, calling into question its supposed value-neutral and objective stance *vis-à-vis* religion.

In a fundamental sense all interpretative forays within the field can be referred to as engaging in the intellectual discipline known as the psychology of religion. Our second major subset, "Religion in dialogue with psychology", is thus not to be understood as wholly separate from the first. The two categories are not mutually exclusive, often drawing on the same body of theory, engaging common issues and generally overlapping to the extent that blurs sharp distinctions between them. On the other hand, the contributions that make up our second section can be characterized as exhibiting a marked difference in perspective from the first. Psychology is used not simply to explore and interpret religious phenomena. It is utilized to further, through dialogue, the very aims of religion, be they conceived of as the primordial, the theological, or the sacred unconscious. Religion is understood as a category *sui generis* that maps an area of human subjectivity extending beyond the conceptual parameters of secular psychology. The rubric "religion in dialogue with psychology" aptly captures this difference in perspective.

Dialogical enterprise of various kinds has long animated RPS. The essays which comprise the second section of the volume engage three distinct dialogical enterprises, each of which has a definitive history within the field. The most familiar of these is the psychology–theology dialogue. The apex of the latter is usually located in the period between 1950 and 1970. During this time theologians and religious philosophers like Paul Tillich, Martin Buber, and Reinhold Niehbuhr were culturally significant moral figures. In the aftermath of the Second World War, with the onset of modernity and what appeared at that time to be a cultural trend towards secularization, questions of ultimate concern became an existential, intellectual, and cultural priority. But in their efforts to reframe matters of faith, religious intellectuals could not dispense with psychology. The depth-psychologies of Freud and Jung were exciting and popular. As noted above other psychologies (ego-psychology, humanistic psychology and existentialism) and psychologists (e.g., Erik Erikson, Carl Rogers, Rollo May) were meeting with cultural acceptance and approval. The various psychologies of that time were, as Tillich's "correlational method" made abundantly evident, American culture's way of formulating central existential questions about the nature and condition of the human spirit. At the same time, psychological analyses of religion went so far as to undercut religious claims to transcendence and cast suspicion on the conceptual categories of theological discourse: faith, morality, sin, redemption. This intellectual and cultural atmosphere made the dialogue between psychology and theology necessary, fruitful, and particularly creative. Paradigmatically represented by the collected essays, under the editorship of Peter Homans, in the University of Chicago volume *The Dialogue Between Theology and Psychology* (1968), the general nature of the dialogue and the debates it created affected many of the classic works in religious studies of this era: Paul Tillich's *The Courage to Be* (1952), Paul Ricoeur's *Freud and Philosophy* (1970), Gordon Allport's *The Individual and His Religion* (1950). Central issues included the relation between unconscious determinants and the conscious avowal of religious tenets and practices, the psychological meaning of heteronomy and the heteronomous God, the developmental infrastructure of morality and faith, the nature of mature religious sentiments, the psycho-social dynamics of religious relationships, and the value of a "hermeneutics of suspicion." This period also saw the birth of significant social institutions: pastoral psychology emerged as a cultural force, as did the role of the pastoral counselor.

With the waning of Protestant culture, the visibility and hegemony of the dialogue between psychology and theology has declined. However, the psychology–theology dialogue is still very much extant, having expanded and engaged a wider spectrum of issues with theoretical aplomb. Indeed, over the past few decades voices from mainstream Protestantism have been joined by increasing representation from Catholic, Jewish, and African-American perspectives.

More recently, another arena of dialogue, the psychology–comparativist dialogue, has reached maturity. The origins of this dialogue go back to the formation of the field at the turn of the century. At that time several related factors converged to create a sustained interest in Eastern religions: the influx of Eastern adepts and their practices; the impact of the World Parliament of Religions (1893); the translation of Eastern texts (e.g., Max Müller's *Sacred Books of the East*); the formation of university positions in comparative religions, and the cultural dissemination of Eastern worldviews by socially prominent sympathizers (e.g., Emerson, Paul Carus, the Theosophists); William James's accounts of Buddhist and Hindu mysticism; Sigmund Freud's correspondences with Girindrasekhar Bose and Romain Rolland's "oceanic feeling;" C.G. Jung's exchanges with Richard Wilhelm, D.T. Suzuki, Heinrich Zimmer and commentaries on Taoist, Buddhist and

Hindu texts; and James Bisset Pratt's sojourns to India and the Far East. All these are testimonies to the strength of the emerging psychology–comparativist dialogue.

In the 1950s and 1960s the psychology–comparativist dialogue was spurred on by social unrest and the gaze eastwards. The seeming disillusionment with the heteronomy of the Judeo-Christian tradition and the rise of the Beat and Hippie generations, a new cadre of socially prominent Buddhist and Hindu sympathizers (e.g., Aldous Huxley, Allen Ginsberg, Richard Baker, Timothy Leary, etc.), and the development of the human potential movement all contributed to the surging popularity of Eastern religions. Zen and its colorful proponents (notably D.T. Suzuki, Shin'ichi Hisamatsu, Shunryu Suzuki) as well as Hindu gurus like Maharishi Mahesh Yogi (Transcendental Meditation) and A.C. Bhakytivedanta Swami Prabhupada (Hare Krishna) made a strong impact on the Western cultural scene. Like their theological counterparts of this period, comparativists included psychological perspectives in their works. A notable example is Mircea Eliade, who in his *Myths, Dreams and Mysteries* (1960) utilized the depth-psychologies of Freud and Jung to enhance the phenomenological study of comparative religions, as is the oeuvre of Joseph Campbell, utilizing as it does a Jungian approach to discerning the universal significance and meaning of myths. Psychologists followed suit, as is exemplified in Jung's conversation with the noted Buddhist scholar Shin'ichi Hisamatsu, Erich Fromm's collaboration with D.T. Suzuki and Richard DeMartino, the surge of experimental studies on meditation and the engagement of existential and humanistic psychologists with Eastern worldviews.

The efforts of the above have flowered in contemporary comparativist and psychological scholarship. One can point to the Indologist Wendy Doniger's attempt to synthesize depth-psychology with historical and philological studies for the interpretation of Hindu myths and symbols, and Luis Gomez's careful evaluation of Jungian approaches to the texts of Indian Buddhism (Wendy Doniger O'Flaherty 1980; Gomez 1995). Psychologically informed anthropological works on Eastern religions (e.g., Stanley Kurtz's *All the Mothers Are One*, 1992; Gananath Obeyesekere's *The Work of Culture*, 1990) have further contributed to the dialogue, while psychological studies on Buddhism (e.g., Wilber *et al.*'s *Transformations in Consciousness*, 1986; Jeffrey Rubin's *Psychotherapy and Buddhism*, 1996) and Hinduism (e.g., Jeffrey Kripal's *Kali's Child*, 1995; Sudhir Kakar's *The Inner World*, 1981) continue the trend towards interdisciplinary sophistication.

Certainly the psychology–comparativist dialogue depends on many of the same originative psychological and culture theorists utilized by those in the psychology–theology dialogue. At the same time, just as the psychology–theology dialogue has concentrated on issues germane to the Judeo-Christian tradition, particularly Protestantism, the psychology–comparativist dialogue has afforded the field the opportunity to develop new ways of thinking about religion commensurate with its subject matter. The cultural relativity of conceptions of self, world and other; the differing aims conceptions of self, world and other; the differing aims and conceptions of health and maturity of healing enterprises East and West; the relativity of developmental themes and gender solutions; the possible existence of a "contemplative line of development" and the complexity of saintly eroticism and mysticism – these are but some of the many themes that presently engage studies in the psychology–comparativist dialogue.

The final dialogical enterprise stems from analyses of the socio-historical effects of psychology, particularly the ways in which, in its efforts to understand and analyze religion, psychology has acted "like a religion." This enterprise, which we, following Vitz (1977) and Van Herik (1984), call psychology as religion, is often utilized for the purpose of organizing and expressing the existential search for wholeness, numinous experiences, and individuation. It seeks not simply to interpret religious phenomena but quite intentionally offers itself as a modern, unchurched way to map one's religiosity. Like the psychology–theology and psychology–comparativist dialogues, this approach developed out of a complex interaction between powerful cultural forces and seminal psychological theoreticians of the past. As Michel de Certeau reminds us, it was as far back as the seventeenth century that a form of generic and psychological religiosity began to emerge. Religion was no longer confined only to particular religious institutions. Rather, one finds the notion of an "Absolute," framed in generic terms as "an obscure, universal dimension of man, perceived or experienced as a reality (*un réel*) hidden beneath a diversity of institutions, religions, and doctrines" (de Certeau 1992: 14). Around the turn of the century many psychologists studying religion gave further impetus to this movement. William James's championing of immediate religious experience, construal of religion as essentially individualistic and even unchurched (James 1936); Carl Jung's similar stress on the individual and his view of the church and its inventory of myths and symbols as derivative, defining them as "codified and dogmatized forms of original religious experience" (Jung 1977: 6); Richard Maurice Bucke's attempt to insert a psychological mysticism into culture at large (Bucke 1993) – all these point to an emerging psychological way of framing, expressing and monitoring one's religiosity.

Certainly other social movements in the beginning of this century, such as Mesmerism, Theosophy, Neopaganism, New England Transcendentalism, and New Thought further contributed to a cultural acceptance of the development of an unchurched, psychological form of spirituality. With the development of humanistic and then transpersonal psychology as found operating in the works of theorists like Abraham Maslow, Stanislav Grof, and Ken Wilber, and the promotion of unchurched, psychological spirituality by contemporary popular authors like M. Scott Peck, the case has become clear. Large segments of the population now configure their religiosity in overtly psychological ways; psychology as religion is a cultural reality.

Maps

In asking each scholar to contribute to this volume we put to them but one question: what they perceived to be the present status of the field and the probable paths for its future. We have endeavored to let the contributors present their own views on the contemporary status and likely or hoped for future of RPS from the perspectives they represent. In that sense the essays represent fresh, original attempts to map religion and psychological studies. At the same time, the individual contributions which make up this collection are not meant to, and indeed cannot, exhaust the complex and multiple theoretical perspectives which currently animate the field. Limitations of space prohibit total representation; the essays presented here can only begin a conversation that we hope will be taken up by unrepresented others.

The editors have found it appropriate to organize the essays in Part I, "Psychology of religion," under three headings. Each heading reflects the general orientation and approach of the essays in question. In the first, "Empirical and cultural approaches," David Wulff describes the major phases of the history of the field, outlining the pastoral and theological backgrounds of some early psychologists of religion; noting the concern to expose the "irrationality" of religion in the backgrounds of others; and exploring the systematic descriptive approaches of still others. He points out a dramatic decline in the scholarship in the field in the period between the wars, tracing a recovery from that decline in the emergence of empirical perspectives and depth psychological interpretations in the post-war years. Bernard Spilka follows by giving us a thorough overview and assessment of the major forms of empirical approaches found within the psychology of religion. In surveying the central issues, research strategies, goals and successes of empirical approaches, Spilka links the future of the field to the continued development of objective–empirical methods. Jacob Belzen counters by surveying past and present European contributions to the psychology of religion. While noting the prevalence of empirical and mechanistic–experimental approaches within the psychology of religion, Belzen argues for the value of an interdisciplinary, cultural, and hermeneutical psychological approach to religion.

In "Perspectives on modernity and post-modernity," Susan Henking leads off by drawing attention to the socio-cultural and historical context that serves to manufacture alternate understandings of the nature and future of RPS. Henking argues for a demythologization of the field, the critical reflection on the sites of its manufacture, and the mapping of a future which highlights the role of RPS as a form of cultural criticism. Asking "What is our present?" Kathleen O'Connor offers a consideration of modernity, and of the dynamics of certainty–uncertainty and belief–unbelief, for psychology and religion. Volney Gay similarly seizes on the theme of modernity. Focusing his analysis on that aspect of the field which champions the use of social scientific methodology and reductionism, Gay argues for the use of information theory to correct the errors wrought by modern interpreters of religion. Jeremy Carrette ends this sub-section by bringing to bear post-structuralist critiques of the foundations of psychology, arguing that the future of the field should proceed with respect to overcoming its "disciplinary amnesia" and the development of a "history of the present."

In "Psychology, religion and gender studies," Diane Jonte-Pace begins by providing an overview of feminist contributions to the psychology of religion. Concentrating on studies of morality, ritual, and God imagery, and dividing such studies into three kinds of projects (analytic, critical and inclusive), Jonte-Pace shows how these endeavors developed in the work of Freud, Jung, the object-relations theorists and the post-structuralists, examining the impact of feminist theory on the field. Don Capps takes the analysis further by arguing that gender studies, by grounding RPS in everyday struggles, is a welcome antidote to the prevalence of social scientific and theological–ethical theorizing in the field. Capps then goes on to argue for sustained research on a specific aspect of psychology, religion and gender studies: male melancholia.

In Part II, "Religion in dialogue with psychology," we have located the essays in the three sub-sections described earlier. Don Browning initiates the reflections on "Theology and psychology in the West" by surveying salient historical developments in practical theology and in the field as a whole. Browning argues that the continued success of RPS is dependent on grounding itself in critical hermeneutical theory. Bonnie Miller-McLemore follows by highlighting the impact of feminist scholarship on pastoral and practical theology, arguing for its importance in assessing the contemporary nature of and future possibilities for the field as a whole. Luis Gómez finishes up the section through a meditation on history, culture and the alternate ways in which psychology and religion frame the value of madness and ritual.

In "Comparative studies: psychological perspectives on non-Western religions," William Parsons opens the proceedings by arguing that "the psychology–comparativist dialogue" is and has been a legitimate enterprise within RPS. Surveying depth-psychological, humanistic and experimental forays into Eastern religions, he argues that such analyses have moved from early twentieth-century reductive, orientalist beginnings through mid twentieth-century halting attempts at collaboration to a contemporary split between a leveling discourse and an interdisciplinary dialogue that is respectful of real differences, taking into account as it does comparative research, culture studies, and the legitimacy of alternate modes of construing self, world and Other. Jeffrey J. Kripal specifies the analysis further by concentrating on depth-psychological treatments of Hindu mythology and mysticism. Noting in particular the contributions of Sudhir Kakar, Kripal shows how new developments in psychoanalysis have emerged which suggest the emergence of a bona fide, non-reductive, dialogical collaboration with proponents of Eastern religions. Jonathan Shear ends this section by surveying past and contemporary experimental analyses of meditation, arguing that such studies must take into account the claims made in Eastern textual sources that meditation can lead to potentially transformational and mystical modes of consciousness.

Finally, in "Psychology 'as' religion," G. William Barnard begins by providing us with an analysis of the multiple historical sources responsible for the cultural emergence of psychologies that act "like" a religion. Through an analysis of sources from Mesmerism and the researches of William James and Carl Jung to transpersonal psychology and the New Age, Barnard argues that scholarly engagement with this form of religio-cultural expression is a legitimate and cutting-edge enterprise. Continuing the analysis, Lucy Bregman traces the theme of psychology as religion into an arena of contemporary cultural concern: the death awareness movement. Contrasting psychological and traditional religious modes of engaging loss and mourning, Bregman evaluates the adequacy of the popular and clinical literature on death which pervades the movement.

Futures

In assembling the essays for publication, the editors were not surprised to find what can be framed as two central conclusions of the contributors' efforts. First, the contributors almost unanimously agree that the field is rich and vibrant, more varied and more sophisticated than ever. Second, the contributors concur that there is no single future, no one definitive path, for RPS. The essays reveal multiple conceptions of the status of the field and multiple prescriptions for its future growth. The contributors to this volume champion a variety of psychological models and predict increasing attention to a broad spectrum of diverse issues: sustained critical reflection on methods in experimental and empirical research; an array of epistemological and cultural issues associated with gender studies; the field's reflection in popular psychology and popular religiosity; an increasing analysis of the sites of secularization; the articulation of a new dialogical relation with other social sciences, comparative studies and culture studies; an increasing focus on critical hermeneutics and postmodern reflection.

Given the liminal and interdisciplinary nature of RPS, such diversity is to be expected. RPS has long been noted by its proponents as a creative discipline that is betwixt and between all others, demanding acquaintance with and dialogue between multiple viewpoints. In that sense this book does not aim at dogmatic statement, nor does it promote a unified agenda. Rather, it embodies what Nietzsche once said about the aphoristic spirit: it is a book for chewing. The editors assume that transcendence of given frameworks and the development of new vistas of reconceptualization will be the inevitable outcome of the reflections offered in this volume. It is our collective hope, then, that those reading it will be spurred on to formulate new responses and reflect on new directions for the field; to challenge, through communication and collaboration, the segmentation and divisiveness that one all too often finds among its participants.

References

Allport, G.W. (1950) *The Individual and His Religion*, New York: Macmillan.

Bucke, R.M. (1993) *Cosmic Consciousness*, New York: Citadel Press.

de Certeau, M. (1992) "Mysticism," *Diacritics* 22: 11–25.

Eliade, M. (1960) *Myths, Dreams and Mysteries*, New York: Harper & Row.

Erikson, E. (1958) *Young Man Luther*, New York: W.W. Norton.

Gómez, L. (1995) "Oriental wisdom and the cure of souls: Jung and the Indian East," in D. Lopez Jr (ed.), *Curators of the Buddha: The Study of Buddhism under Colonialism*, 197–250. Chicago: The University of Chicago Press.

Homans, P. (ed.) (1968) *The Dialogue Between Theology and Psychology*, Chicago: The University of Chicago Press.

James, W. (1936) *The Varieties of Religious Experience*, New York: The Modern Library.

Jung, C. (1977) *Psychology and Religion*, New Haven: Yale University Press.

Kakar, S. (1981) *The Inner World*, New Delhi: Oxford University Press.

Kripal, J. (1995) *Kali's Child*, Chicago: The University of Chicago Press.

Kurtz, S. (1992) *All the Mothers Are One*, New York: Columbia University Press.

Obeyesekere, G. (1990) *The Work of Culture*, Chicago: The University of Chicago Press.

O'Flaherty, W. Doniger (1980) *Women, Androgynes and Other Mythical Beasts*, Chicago: The University of Chicago Press.

Ricoeur, P. (1970) *Freud and Philosophy*, New Haven: Yale University Press.

Rubin, J. (1996) *Psychotherapy and Buddhism*, New York: Plenum Press.

Tillich, P. (1952) *The Courage to Be*, New Haven: Yale University Press.

Van Herik, J. (1984) " 'Thick description' and the psychology of religion," in F. Reynolds and B. Moore (eds), *Anthropology and the Study of Religion*, 56–74. Chicago: Center for the Scientific Study of Religion.

Vitz, P. (1977) *Psychology as Religion*, Grand Rapids: William B. Eerdmans.

Wilber, K., Engler, J. and Brown, D. (eds) (1986) *Transformations in Consciousness*, Boston: Shambhala.

Part I
Psychology of religion

Section 1

Empirical and cultural approaches

1 Psychology of religion

An overview

David M. Wulff

If we set aside "religious psychology" – the psychology that, in varying degrees, is implicit in the historic religious traditions – the psychology of religion constitutes the oldest form of encounter between psychology and religion. It is also the easiest to define. Strictly conceived, psychology of religion comprises the systematic application of psychological theories and methods to the contents of the religious traditions and to the related experiences, attitudes, and actions of individuals. In this configuration, "religion" is understood not as a system of reflection or scholarship that might actively engage in dialogue with psychology but as a domain of human ideation and activity that may – without its consent – be taken as the object of systematic psychological investigation. In contrast to religious psychology, which remains uncritically submerged in a specific religious worldview, the psychology of religion stands in principle outside of all religious tradition. It is thus often thought to call into question the entirety of the religious life, including the fundamental conviction of having made connection with some higher order.

The impulse toward reinterpretation and reform

Historically, however, the psychology of religion has seldom been carried out at such remove from religious commitment. Rather than conceiving of the field as a disinterested science, most of the earliest proponents saw it as a means of advancing certain religious agendas or of justifying religion as a whole. Whereas the psychology of religion was in some measure yet another expression of the burgeoning, nineteenth-century interest in applying scientific methods in the human realm, it was also a manifestation of the reform-minded Progressive movement and in particular the Social Gospel. Some of the leading figures in the field started out in theology, found it unexpectedly problematical, and then shifted to psychology as a base for reconstructing their conceptions of religion. Their ultimate goal was to make religion compatible with twentieth-century understandings and serviceable to a society that had been profoundly disrupted by the momentous and ramifying changes of industrialization.

Stanley Hall, for example, who, as the founding president of Clark University, established the Clark school of the psychology of religion, had earlier prepared for the ministry. But the increasingly liberal views he developed during his studies at Union Theological Seminary and his work on the streets of New York City finally led him to psychology instead. His interest in religion remained strong, however, expressed first in his studies of conversion and religious development and, later, in his reflections on the figure of Christ. The objective of religion, Hall was to conclude, is not contact with some transcendent realm but adjustment in the human one. His last work in the field, *Jesus, the Christ, in the Light of Psychology* (1917), was intended to convince others of this humanistic point of view.

George Coe, another major contributor in the inaugural period, underwent a similar evolution. At first he expected to follow his father into the Methodist ministry, but his theological studies at Boston University left him troubled by theology's apparent incompatibility with both scientific method and historical criticism. He shifted, then, to the study of philosophy and world religions and finally to psychology. According to the functional view of religion that emerged out of Coe's reading of Walter Rauschenbusch and others prominent in the Social Gospel movement as well as his involvement in settlement work and local political reform, the essence of religion lies in the heightening and fostering of personal and social values. Having concluded from his early studies of conversion and mystical experience that the Christian tradition is one sided in its emphasis on feeling, Coe gave the rest of his professional life to promoting his social theory of religious education, in the department of Religious Education and Psychology that he established at Union Theological Seminary and through a series of books that profoundly influenced several generations of liberal religious educators (Wulff 1999).

Unlike Hall and Coe, Edward Scribner Ames (1910) followed through on his theological education by becoming a preacher. Yet he, too, was deeply influenced by the Social Gospel movement (see Ames 1959) and saw psychology as a way of liberating religion from dogmatic authority and transforming it into a non-theological, adventurous, and scientifically respectable way of dealing with social problems (Ames 1929). As a professor of philosophy at the University of Chicago and concurrently a minister of the University Church of the Disciples of Christ, Ames saw the church as "a kind of laboratory for cultivation and observation of the living processes of religion, while the university was a place for their systematic study" (96).

Although in Europe the psychology of religion never threatened to displace theology as it did in the United States early in the twentieth century, even on the Continent the new field was perceived by some as either an alternative to theology or a means of revolutionizing it. The Swiss psychologist Theodore Flournoy, for example, was another early contributor who started off in theological studies; but he dropped out after only a semester and turned to medicine instead. Much like Coe, he found theology to be filled with unnecessary intellectual difficulties (Le Clair 1966: xvii). Later on, when Flournoy (1903b) published a collection of brief religious autobiographies, he concluded that emancipation from traditional theological doctrine is for some people a prerequisite for the development of an inner religious life. In the classic principles that he laid down for the psychology of religion, Flournoy (1903a) carefully excluded theological presuppositions, most notably assumptions about the nature of the religious object. At the same time he advocated the broadest possible application to religion of the diverse perspectives of psychology. In his subsequent case study of "Cécile Vé," Flournoy (1915) further illustrated how a deepening faith can become increasingly alienated from traditional religious forms at the same time that he demonstrated the possibility of a non-reductionistic psychological understanding of exceptional religious experience.

Georges Berguer, who was the leading figure in a French eclectic tradition inspired by Flournoy and centered in Geneva, not only completed his theological studies but also became a pastor and then a professor in a Protestant school of theology. Yet, like the others introduced here, he saw psychology as an invaluable aid for reinterpreting religious history, symbols, and experience. Noting in particular the regrettable mythologizing of the life of Jesus, Berguer (1923) argued that what is ultimately asked of Christians is not dutiful belief in certain miraculous events but a dying and rebirth of the individual self. Thus, for Berguer, psychology offered a means of promoting a deeper and truer faith.

The critique of religion as irrational

There were other early contributors, on both sides of the ocean, who were far less interested in reinterpreting religion than in demonstrating its irrationality. One such psychologist of religion was James Henry Leuba, who, as a young man, immigrated to the United States from Switzerland and eventually wrote a doctoral dissertation on conversion under Stanley Hall's direction. Leuba is best known for his questionnaire investigations of belief in God and immortality among scientists and historians. He found that traditional religious belief tended to be low among these scholars, especially among those most knowledgeable about biological and psychological processes and eminent in their respective fields. Having noted the sheer improbability and pettiness of much religious content, Leuba (1925) set about demonstrating that mystical experiences can be accounted for in terms of basic principles of psychology and physiology, both normal and pathological. Yet even Leuba (1950), who especially regretted the inhibitory effects of conservative religious views on scientific progress, postulated a spiritual urge in humankind and proposed the founding of non-theistic religious societies.

In the inaugural period of the field – that is, from the 1890s to the 1920s – it was Sigmund Freud who was most famously thoroughgoing in his critique of religion. Equating it with fervent belief in a father-god and careful observance of obligatory ritual, Freud viewed religion as an effort to reclaim, in moments of vulnerability, the protective care of the seemingly omniscient and omnipotent father of early childhood. The longing for the father, which Freud said was the origin of every form of religion, is marked by deep ambivalence, however, given the vicissitudes of the Oedipus complex. That is to say, the beloved father eventually becomes an object of resentment, fear, and guilt as well. Thus, only through obedient submission to the will of God can the devotee restore the long-lost relationship with the infantile father. Observing religious ritual's seemingly compulsive character and the devotee's proneness to feelings of guilt and to fear of divine retribution, Freud concluded that religion is a defensive maneuver akin to neurosis, a wish-fulfilling illusion that is dangerous for individuals and society alike. Only by abandoning religion and relying instead on science and reason, declared Freud (1961), can humankind grow into maturity and escape the oppressiveness of a society that operates through religious sanctions and rewards.

Systematic descriptive approaches

If the dominant trend in the early psychology of religion was toward the criticism and reconstruction of religion, there were nevertheless concurrent impulses toward more disinterested perspectives. William James, too, had undertaken a critique and evaluation of religion in his monumental *The Varieties of Religious Experience* (1902), in an effort to justify religion in the eyes of his fellow intellectuals; yet he inexorably combined this agenda with two others: an empathic–descriptive exploration of religious experience and an explanatory account of it. These three agendas effectively established the fundamental trends in the field ever since: (1) systematic description of religious experience, ideation, and practice, both ordinary and exceptional; (2) theories of the origin and meaning of religious content and expression, in individual lives and in the human species as a whole; and (3) research on the fruits – the personal and social correlates – of the varieties of religious attitudes and experiences.

Both in James's day and in ours, the *Varieties* has been most highly regarded for the striking descriptive material that James carefully assembled to make religious experience accessible to the understanding of outsiders. Convinced as he was that ordinary piety is little more than imitation and dull habit, he features excerpts from personal documents written by persons – some famous, others not – who were subject to exceptional religious experiences. To help the reader understand such experiences, James places them in their personal and historical contexts, compares them to analogous and often non-religious phenomena that are more familiar and better understood, and adds his own incisive yet sympathetic comments that help to drive home the crucial point or distinction he wishes to make. Himself a professed outsider to such experiences, James hoped through the testimony he gathered to make transparent their inner meaning and logic, if not also their value, for individuals as well as for society.

Among those who greatly admired James's sympathetic approach but took exception to his emphasis on extreme and even pathological cases was James Pratt, who completed a dissertation on the psychology of religious belief under James at Harvard. Likewise accenting description, Pratt (1920) championed the value of ordinary piety and explored with exceptional sensitivity such phenomena as religious beliefs, symbols, and ritual, all of which James was inclined to dismiss. And just as Pratt valorized the gradual and imperceptible "moral" type of conversion over James's "merely emotional" type, so he found greater value in commonplace mild mystical experiences than in the rarer – and in Pratt's view, dangerous – extreme forms that James favored. An authority on Eastern religious traditions who was thoroughly acquainted with the international literature on the psychology of religion, Pratt offered a rare model for systematic work in this field.

A precarious field in decline

In Europe, the decade during which Pratt labored on his *Religious Consciousness* (1920) produced several other classic works in the descriptive tradition, including Rudolf Otto's *The Idea of the Holy* (1950), Friedrich Heiler's *Prayer* (1932), and, from the Dorpat school of the psychology of religion, founded at Dorpat University in Estonia, Karl Girgensohn's (1930) weighty tome on the psychic structure of religious experience (Wulff 1985). But the ominously shifting social and political climates in both the United States and Europe were shortly to bring the promising inaugural period of the psychology of religion to a close. In America, the devastation of World War I and the subsequent economic crises dealt a death blow to Progressivism and fostered a resurgence of fundamentalism. In both Europe and the United States, the highly influential dialectical theology of Karl Barth and Emil Brunner succored a postliberal theocentric perspective that discouraged the interest in religious consciousness that the psychology of religion had promoted. More than that, it unequivocally rejected the field as offensively reductionistic (Wulff 1997, 1998).

Religious experience was shut out from the side of psychology as well. The behaviorist movement, which caught fire in the 1920s and rapidly spread through academic circles in the United States, ruled out of order any serious discussion of subjective states. Following the model of the natural sciences, the behaviorists limited themselves to objectively observable behavior and developed mechanistic and deterministic theories for explaining it. A field that had never been hospitable to the study of religion now made such work far more difficult, though David Trout's *Religious Behavior* (1931) demonstrated that, with strategic compromises, it was not utterly impossible.

It must be emphasized that the psychology of religion was a precarious undertaking from the beginning, especially given the small number of scholars who were drawn to it and the virtual absence of academic positions in the field. It was the paucity of both contributors and subscribers that eventually forced Hall to discontinue his *Journal of Religious Psychology*, which appeared erratically from 1904 to 1915 (Wulff 1998: 188n). Journals abroad faced similar difficulties. Taking into account, then, the hostile religious and psychological climates that emerged in the 1920s, the profound effects of the worldwide economic depression in the 1930s, and finally the rise of National Socialism and the massive destructiveness of World War II, it is not difficult to understand why scholarship in what had always been a marginal field sharply declined.

A revival in defense of religion: the empirical literature

Along with other fields interested in subjective experience, the psychology of religion underwent a gradual revival in the 1950s, as behaviorism's domination of psychology gradually receded. A major impetus for this revival came from the work of Gordon Allport, whose incursions into the field, like James's before him, significantly added to its visibility and prestige. As a humanistic personality psychologist, Allport (1950) was interested in the uniquely integrative role that the religious sentiment, in its mature forms, can play in the lives of individuals. But as a deeply religious person himself, Allport was also disturbed by the evidence that piety is often associated with negative social attitudes.

To resolve these conflicting impressions, Allport adopted a distinction, made earlier by Adorno and his associates (1950), between two forms of religious orientation: an *intrinsic* one that takes religion seriously as an end in itself and an *extrinsic* one that treats religion as a means toward personal and social ends. The first of these orientations, Adorno *et al.* had suggested, is associated with ethnocentric attitudes, whereas the second one is generally opposed to them. Allport and Ross (1967) developed questionnaire items to measure the two orientations and then to establish their relationships to various social attitudes.

The Allport–Ross Religious Orientation scales did not produce as clear a pattern of relationships as Allport had hoped, partly because of certain persistent psychometric problems with the scales (Burris 1999; Kirkpatrick and Hood 1990) but also because the Intrinsic items tend to correlate positively with conservative Christian views, which are associated in turn with conservative social attitudes (Wulff 1997). The scales have nevertheless been widely used in the psychology of religion, more than any other measures of religiousness. They have also been translated into several

European languages, adapted for younger respondents, and – in the form of individual representative items – inserted into current Gallup polls.

Like Allport himself, proponents of the Allport–Ross scales have generally viewed the Intrinsic scale as a measure of religiousness at its best. Others, having noted that the scales correlate with measures of social desirability, have been more circumspect, suggesting that high scorers may be persons who, perhaps unconsciously, are trying to give a good impression (Leak and Fish, 1989). Sharing the suspicion that the intrinsic orientation is less genuine than it represents itself to be, and preferring a more existential definition of religion than the Allport–Ross scales embody, Daniel Batson set about to develop a third alternative, the quest orientation, which reflects "an open-ended, responsive dialogue with existential questions raised by the contradictions and tragedies of life" (Batson *et al.* 1993: 169). The Quest scale he developed, Batson argues, incorporates three of the facets of the mature religious sentiment that Allport (1950) had characterized in his writings – complexity, tentativeness, and doubt – but left out of his scales.

Through a series of quasi-experimental studies, Batson found evidence, first, that the intrinsic orientation is associated with insistent helpfulness whereas the quest orientation is associated with greater sensitivity to the expressed wishes of the needy person; and, second, that the prosocial behavior of those high on the Intrinsic scale is motivated less by compassion for others and a desire to avoid feelings of guilt or shame than by a need to feel good about oneself and to be thought well of by others (Batson 1990; Batson *et al.* 1993). Researchers using Batson's Quest scale or an augmented version of it have found that the Quest orientation shows a more consistent relationship than the Intrinsic one to a variety of socially relevant variables, including level of moral judgment (Sapp and Jones 1986), the valuing of equality (Luce *et al.* 1987), and non-discriminatory attitudes (McFarland 1989). On the other hand, in the burgeoning empirical literature on religion and mental health, the Intrinsic scale tends to be positively correlated with measures of mental health whereas the Quest scale shows, if anything, a modest association with personal distress, including negative attitudes toward death (Wulff 1997: 248–9).

While research on religious orientation is in various ways representative of the empirical approach in the psychology of religion, especially its current interest in establishing a positive pattern of correlates between religiousness or "spirituality" and mental health, it does not constitute the whole of this substantial literature. Alternate measures of religiosity are sometimes used (Hill and Hood 1999) and still others are under development (Hutsebaut 1996). Topics of investigation encompass a broad range of phenomena, including religious development at various stages of life, conversion, meditation, mysticism, and coping processes (Hood *et al.* 1996). Findings in this literature are far from consistent, however, and many issues remain under debate, including the adequacy of the various measures and the need for grounding research in more adequate theories. There is some interest in identifying the neurophysiological underpinnings of exceptional religious experience, but speculation of this sort is mainly found outside of formal psychology-of-religion circles (e.g., d'Aquili and Newberg 1999; see also Wulff 2000a).

The contemporary empirical perspective has been promoted mainly by researchers trained in psychology – typically, social psychology. Anxious to gain the attention and respect of mainstream psychologists – attention to religion as a significant variable in human lives, respect for the research carried out by psychologists of religion – proponents of the empirical approach have aspired to as rigorous a science as the character of religion will allow (Batson 1977; Hood *et al* 1996). Toward the same ends, some have conducted their research within one or another theoretical framework developed apart from religion, notably attribution theory (Spilka *et al.* 1985), attachment theory (Kirkpatrick 1992), and coping theory (Pargament 1997). Most researchers, however, have proceeded in the fashion of "dust-bowl empiricism," simply correlating indicators of religiousness with demographic, social-attitude, and personality variables without the guidance of theory-derived hypotheses.

Interpretive perspectives: the meaning of religious content

Those who have come into the psychology of religion by way of religious studies typically conceive of the field as one of the sciences of religion (*Religionswissenschaften*) rather than a specialization within psychology. They correspondingly decline to follow the empirical approach and opt instead for one or another of the interpretive perspectives. Just as the empirical outlook can be traced back to the Clark school, so the interpretive approach has roots going back to James and Freud in the early twentieth century and, before them, to a tradition of reflection extending from Feuerbach and Hume, in the nineteenth and eighteenth centuries, back to the early Greek rationalists (Wulff 1997). Whereas the empirical approach is inherently a psychology of religious *persons* and is therefore focused on individual differences in piety, the interpretive perspective is foremost a psychology of religious *contents* and thus seeks out the *meaning* of the images, objects, stories, and rituals that together compose the religious traditions. Even when this content is idiosyncratically appropriated or transformed in individual lives, the accent remains on its meaning, not the range of its variations.

Much of the interpretive literature even today centers on reviewing, elaborating, and critiquing the views of the classic interpreters, especially Freud and Jung. James is also periodically revisited, as a wellspring of insights into individual religious experience and its consequences (Capps and Jacobs 1995). Yet given his disdain for religious symbols and rituals, James offers his readers little for interpreting specific contents. Thus it has been the depth psychologists, mainly, who have animated the interpretive literature.

Although Freud's views of religion are still affirmed and applied by occasional researchers, his interpretations are more often criticized, frequently becoming themselves the subject of psychological analysis. His narrowly patriarchal configuration of religion and his thoroughgoing rejection of it have been explored in terms of his personal history, his connection with the Jewish world, and the broader historic context in which he lived (e.g., Wallace 1984). Other critics have argued, however, that whatever limitations Freud's views may have suffered, there are nevertheless essential insights to be found in his work. These insights they have sought to appropriate and develop in a number of directions.

Foundations for a revised and more positive psychoanalytic view of religion were laid down by several of the British object relations theorists, notably Harry Guntrip (1956) and Donald Winnicott (1971). Whereas Freud took religion to be a regressive and stultifying effort to reclaim the illusory security of infancy, the object relations theorists argued that religion, by offering a sense of cosmic connection and validation, serves as a kind of psychotherapy that – as long as it resists neurotic distortion – promotes better and more satisfying interpersonal relationships. Furthermore, whereas Freud traced the dynamics of religion exclusively to the Oedipal father, the object relations theorists ascribed to the pre-Oedipal mother an equal if not more important role and allowed that still other caretakers might also be influential in the shaping of individual religious sensibilities. By ascribing to religious feelings and images a far more complex derivation than Freud offered, the object relations theorists provide a framework that is not only more adequate for understanding particular individuals but also more encompassing of the world's religious traditions.

Object relations theory similarly helps to recontextualize the discussion of the ontological status of religious content. Whereas Freud distinguished only two realms of human ideation, an infantile, autistic one (to which he consigned religious ideation) and a mature, reality-oriented one (preeminently the world of science), Winnicott posited an illusory, intermediate area of experience, the contents of which aid human beings of all ages to bridge inner and outer realities. Just as the young child gradually comes to recognize and accept objective reality with the help of cherished transitional objects – the ubiquitous blankets and teddy bears – so adults continue to make the world humanly inhabitable through continuing elaboration of the intermediate sphere, in the diverse forms of human culture, including religion.

From this perspective, then, religion is not something to be outgrown, but a potentially vital resource for the fullest realization of human ideals. As the outcome of creative human imagining, however, this "illusionistic world" is peculiarly subject to distortion, either through autistic elaborations ungrounded in reality or through literalistic misinterpretations, which transform the playfully conceived symbol into reified and obligatory doctrine or ritual (Pruyser 1983). Perhaps most idiosyncratic in its construction is the individual God representation, the adaptive value of which has been explored by Rizzuto (1979). From her own clinical practice, Rizzuto concludes that the formation, modifications, and uses of the God representation are often highly revealing of an individual's relations with primary objects and other significant people. They are also said to testify to the character of a person's evolving self-representations.

Like the British object relations theorists, ego psychologist Erik Erikson (1963) located the ontogenetic origins of religion in the early mother–child relationship. He agreed, moreover, that these origins testify not to religion's immaturity, as Freud would have it, but to its association with the most fundamental needs and longings of the human species. For each of the eight developmental stages, Erikson said, there is some institution or societal element that, having evolved in intimate association with the human life cycle, is poised to support the successful unfolding of that stage and the preservation of its peculiar strength or virtue. For the first, infancy stage that element is religion: through its formulations and shared rituals, religion universalizes the first stage's heritage of trust and mistrust and confirms the first and most basic virtue, hope, and its mature derivative, faith. That is not the whole of the story, however, for religious tradition also provides support for the attainment of wisdom, the vital virtue of the last stage, old age. While acknowledging that the religious traditions have exploited human-kind's infantile past and that individual religious faith is vulnerable in various ways to pathological distortion, Erikson doubts that many human beings can afford to pass by the resources it provides for growth into full maturity.

Starting with a rather different set of presuppositions and positing a sharply contrasting dynamic, C.G. Jung was yet another depth psychologist who viewed religion as inextricably and vitally bound up with essential human dispositions. Jung hypothesized that underlying the personal unconscious familiar to the psychoanalysts is a deeper-lying region, the collective unconscious, whose structural elements, the archetypes, are said to represent the forms and patterns of experience of countless human generations and their pre-human ancestors. These archetypes dispose us, Jung says, to have these experiences anew, and to represent and preserve them in the form of various mythical images and ideas. There is in the collective unconscious, moreover, a fundamental tendency toward the progressive differentiation of its contents and the integration of them into consciousness; Jung called this lifelong process of striving toward psychic balance and wholeness "individuation." Throughout history, Jung (1969) says, it has been the religious traditions that have chiefly facilitated the realization of the self, the archetype of wholeness, which is commonly symbolized by images associated with divinity.

Jung's analytical psychology was first of all a system of psychotherapy, a means of guiding and promoting the individuation process, especially among those who found themselves incapable of meaningful relationship with religious tradition. Jung employed it, too, as a framework for diagnosing the ills of contemporary society and for interpreting the terrible destructiveness of the world wars and the continuing potential for mass annihilation that is our inheritance. And from Jung onward, analytical psychology has proved itself invaluable as an instrument for exploring the history of religions and for interpreting a great diversity of symbols, rituals, and experiences, in both Eastern and Western religious contexts. It has also, to be sure, been the subject of much critical reevaluation (see Wulff 1997: 461–71).

Jung's postulating of an inherent process of self-realization was echoed on the other side of the ocean by some of the best-known American humanistic psychologists, who together have contributed to the psychology of religion yet another set of well-known interpretive perspectives. Allport, we have already noted, contributed a portrait of the mature religious sentiment, which he characterizes – in mainly cognitive terms – as an effective working hypothesis that is well differentiated yet integrated, autonomously dynamic, unifyingly comprehensive, and consistently directive. Allport's subsequent distinguishing of intrinsic and extrinsic religious orientations served to contrast the mature sentiment in some of its aspects with less sincere and hence less genuine forms.

Other humanistic psychologists likewise offered visions of contrasting types of religious outlook that have implications for personal growth. German expatriate Erich Fromm (1950) delineated two fundamental types of religious traditions: authoritarian traditions, which, by enjoining obedient submission to a reigning transcendent power, foster feelings of diminution, guilt, and sorrow; and humanistic traditions, which, centered in humankind and its strengths, promote self-realization and a corresponding attitude of joy. Rollo May (1957) draws a similar contrast between religion that functions as a refuge for weakness and religion that serves as a source of strength. Drawing on his research on self-actualizing people, Abraham Maslow (1964) distinguishes "peakers" – persons who have intensely personal religious, or peak, experiences and use them for personal growth and fulfillment – and "non-peakers," who, if they have ever had such experiences, repress rather than incorporate them into their lives. Convinced that the religious traditions themselves tend by and large to suppress peak experiences, Maslow envisioned a new humanistic psychology that would promote them.

Like the empirical approaches, though usually more explicitly, the interpretive psychologies of religion tend to offer a mix of criticism and defense or advocacy. Criticism, when it is not thoroughgoing (as it is in the case of Freud, for example), is generally aimed at ordinary piety, especially the more orthodox or conservative forms. Defense or advocacy is usually of more individual, experience-centered, and humanistic forms. In this respect the interpretive traditions represent a liberal trend that can be traced to the field's very beginnings. Contemporary empirical approaches, in contrast, are often – though certainly not always – enlisted in defense of more traditional or even conservative forms of religiosity. Rather than seeking to reinterpret religion, empirical psychologists of religion have set about to establish scientifically its positive values in human functioning.

Prospects for the future

The long-standing disposition to criticize or promote religion is partly responsible for the field's precarious status within both religious studies and psychology. Scholars of religion are understandably wary of any disposition to reduce religion to a simple formula and then to explain it away, in effect, in terms of some psychological mechanism. Psychologists, in contrast, because they are frequently disdainful of religion, tend to be suspicious of any theory or study that appears to valorize or promote it. As this essay suggests, both groups are to some degree justified in their attitudes. Psychologists of religion rarely proceed as disinterested investigators; they act, rather, to promote certain perspectives on religion – whether positive or negative – that are rooted in their own sensibilities and experience. Perhaps it cannot be otherwise, for the very questions one begins with require a prior judgment about the nature of religion and its objects, a judgment that is ultimately personal. It may also be institutional, if psychology of religion is incorporated into a theological education, especially as the foundation for religious education and pastoral care.

We have also to deal with differences in views of what psychology is about, differences that are likewise grounded in the personal equation. Contrary to the dream of those who anticipated the emergence over time of a unified psychology, the field has become evermore fractionated and specialized, to the point that it is more accurate to call it "the psychological studies" (Koch and Leary 1985). It has been common to read such diversity as a sign of the field's immaturity. In the framework of contemporary philosophy of science, however, today's conspicuous pluralism may be seen as evidence of health and potential creativity. Roth (1987) advises psychologists and other social scientists to adopt the viewpoint of methodological pluralism, according to which one's frame of reference and methods are ultimately determined on pragmatic grounds. Meanwhile, various scholars are subjecting many of the existing fields of psychology to critical reanalysis in terms of their underlying agendas (Fox and Prilleltensky 1997) while others anticipate new and more adequate possibilities (Kvale 1992).

Such possibilities would greatly enrich the psychology of religion as well. However, without a significant increase in institutional support through the creation of academic positions and graduate programs in the field, the psychology of religion cannot hope to progress much beyond the point it has reached thus far. Whether adequate support will ever be forthcoming is impossible to predict, but the prospects for it might well be improved if today's proponents took a critical new look at the field and readdressed a number of fundamental issues, including the questions of assumptions, methods, and goals, especially in the context of today's unprecedented religious pluralism and the climate of postmodernism (Wulff 2000b). Needed, too, is a frank consideration of the role that personal religious perspectives and agendas have played – and continue to play – in shaping work in the field. Reconstituted as a genuinely disinterested field that is broadly informed by the best scholarship in both psychology and religious studies, the psychology of religion might at last find the support it needs to fulfill its considerable promise.

References

Adorno, T.W., Frenkel-Brunswik, E., Levinson, D.J., and Sanford, R.N. (1950) *The Authoritarian Personality*, New York: Harper and Brothers.

Allport, G.W. (1950) *The Individual and His Religion: A Psychological Interpretation*, New York: Macmillan.

Allport, G.W. and Ross, J.M. (1967) "Personal religious orientation and prejudice," *Journal of Personality and Social Psychology* 5: 432–43.

Ames, E.S. (1910) *The Psychology of Religious Experience*, Boston: Houghton Mifflin.

—— (1929) *Religion*, New York: Holt.

—— (1959) *Beyond Theology; The Autobiography of Edward Scribner Ames*, Chicago: University of Chicago Press.

Batson, C.D. (1977) "Experimentation in psychology of religion: An impossible dream," *Journal for the Scientific Study of Religion* 16: 413–18.

—— (1990) "Good Samaritans – or priest and Levites? Using William James as a guide in the study of religious prosocial motivation," *Personality and Social Psychology Bulletin* 16: 758–68.

Batson, C.D., Schoenrade, P., and Ventis, W.L. (1993) *Religion and the Individual: A Social-Psychological Perspective*, New York: Oxford University Press.

Berguer, G. (1923) *Some Aspects of the Life of Jesus from the Psychological and Psycho-Analytic Point of View*, trans. E.S. Brooks and V.W. Brooks, New York: Harcourt, Brace.

Burris, C.T. (1999) "Religious Orientation Scale (Allport and Ross, 1967)," in P.C. Hill and R.W. Hood, Jr (eds) *Measures of Religiosity*, 144–51, Birmingham, AL: Religious Education Press.

Capps, D. and Jacobs, J.L. (eds) (1995) *The Struggle for Life: A Companion to William James's The Varieties of Religious Experience*, West Layfayette, IN: Society for the Scientific Study of Religion.

d'Aquili, E.G. and Newberg, A.B. (1999) *The Mystical Mind: Probing the Biology of Religious Experience*, Minneapolis, MN: Fortress Press.

Erikson, E.H. (1963) *Childhood and Society* (2nd edn), New York: W.W. Norton.

Flournoy, T. (1903a) "Les principes de la psychologie religieuse," *Archives de Psychologie* 2: 33–57.

—— (1903b) "Observations de psychologie religieuse," *Archives de Psychologie* 2: 327–66.

—— (1915) "Une mystique moderne. (Documents pour la psychologie religieuse)," *Archives de Psychologie* 15: 1–224.

Fox, D. and Prilleltensky, I. (eds) (1997) *Critical Psychology: An Introduction*, London: Sage.

Freud, S. (1961) "The future of an illusion," in *The Standard Edition of the Complete Psychological Works of Sigmund Freud*, vol. 21, trans. J. Strachey, 1–56, London: Hogarth Press and the Institute of Psycho-Analysis.

Fromm, E. (1950) *Psychoanalysis and Religion*, New Haven, Conn.: Yale University Press.

Girgensohn, K. (1930) *Der seelische Aufbau des religiösen Erlebens: Eine religionspsychologische Untersuchung auf experimenteller Grundlage* (2nd edn), corrected and supplemented by W. Gruehn, Gütersloh: C. Bertelsmann.

Guntrip, H. (1956) *Mental Pain and the Cure of Souls*, London: Independent Press.

Hall, G.S. (1917) *Jesus, the Christ, in the Light of Psychology* (2 vols.), New York: Doubleday, Page.

Heiler, F. (1932) *Prayer: A Study in the History and Psychology of Religion*, trans. S. McComb, New York: Oxford University Press.

Hill, P.C. and Hood, R.W., Jr (eds) (1999) *Measures of Religiosity*, Birmingham, AL: Religious Education Press.

Hood, R.W., Jr, Spilka, B., Hunsberger, B., and Gorsuch, R. (1996) *Psychology of Religion: An Empirical Approach* (2nd edn), New York: Guilford.

Hutsebaut, D. (1996) "Post-critical belief: A new approach to the religious attitude problem," *Journal of Empirical Theology* 9, 2: 48–66.

James, W. (1902) *The Varieties of Religious Experience: A Study in Human Nature*, London: Longmans, Green.

Jung, C.G. (1969) "Psychology and religion," in *The Collected Works of C.G. Jung*, vol. 11 (2nd edn), 3–105, H. Read, M. Fordham and G. Adler (eds), trans. R.F.C. Hull, Princeton, N.J.: Princeton University Press.

Kirkpatrick, L.A. (1992) "An attachment-theory approach to the psychology of religion," *International Journal for the Psychology of Religion* 2: 3–28.

Kirkpatrick, L.A. and Hood, R.W., Jr (1990) "Intrinsic-extrinsic religious orientation: The boon or bane of contemporary psychology of religion?" *Journal for the Scientific Study of Religion* 29: 442–62.

Koch, S. and Leary, D.E. (eds) (1985) *A Century of Psychology as Science*, New York: McGraw-Hill.

Kvale, S. (1992) *Psychology and Postmodernism*, London: Sage.

Leak, G.K. and Fish, S. (1989) "Religious orientation, impression management, and self-deception: Toward a clarification of the link between religiosity and social desirability," *Journal for the Scientific Study of Religion* 28: 355–9.

Le Clair, R.C. (ed.) (1966) *The Letters of William James and Theodore Flournoy*, Madison: University of Wisconsin Press.

Leuba, J.H. (1925) *The Psychology of Religious Mysticism*, New York: Harcourt, Brace.

—— (1950) *The Reformation of the Churches*, Boston: Beacon Press.

Luce, T.S., Briggs, S.R., and Francis, J.C. (1987) "Religiosity and Rokeach's Value Survey: A comparison in three samples," paper presented at the convention of the American Psychological Association, New York, N.Y., August.

McFarland, S.G. (1989) "Religious orientations and the targets of discrimination," *Journal for the Scientific Study of Religion* 28: 324–36.

Maslow, A.H. (1964) *Religions, Values, and Peak-Experiences*, Columbus: Ohio State University Press.

May, Rollo (1957) "The relation between psychotherapy and religion," in J.E. Fairchild (ed.), *Personal Problems and Psychological Frontiers: A Cooper Union Forum*, 168–87, New York: Sheridan House.

Otto, R. (1950) *The Idea of the Holy: An Inquiry into the Non-Rational Factor in the Idea of the Divine and Its Relation to the Rational* (2nd edn), trans. J.W. Harvey, London: Oxford University Press.

Pargament, K.I. (1997) *The Psychology of Religion and Coping: Theory, Research, Practice*, New York: Guilford Press.

Pratt, J.B. (1920) *The Religious Consciousness: A Psychological Study*, New York: Macmillan.

Pruyser, P.W. (1983) *The Play of the Imagination: Toward a Psychoanalysis of Culture*, New York: International Universities Press.

Rizzuto, A.-M. (1979) *The Birth of the Living God: A Psychoanalytic Study*, Chicago: University of Chicago Press.

Roth, P.A. (1987) *Meaning and Method in the Social Sciences: A Case for Methodological Pluralism*, Ithaca: Cornell University Press.

Sapp, G.L. and Jones, L. (1986) "Religious orientation and moral judgment," *Journal for the Scientific Study of Religion* 25: 208–14.

Spilka, B., Shaver, P., and Kirkpatrick, L.A. (1985) "A general attribution theory for the psychology of religion," *Journal for the Scientific Study of Religion* 24: 1–20.

Trout, D.M. (1931) *Religious Behavior: An Introduction to the Psychological Study of Religion*, New York: Macmillan.

Wallace, E.R., IV (1984) "Freud and religion: A history and reappraisal," *Psychoanalytic Study of Society* 10: 115–61.

Winnicott, D.W. (1971) *Playing and Reality*, London: Tavistock.

Wulff, D.M. (1985) "Experimental introspection and religious experience: the Dorpat school of religious psychology," *Journal of the History of the Behavioral Sciences* 21: 131–50.

—— (1997) *Psychology of Religion: Classic and Contemporary* (2nd edn), New York: John Wiley and Sons.

—— (1998) "Rethinking the rise and fall of the psychology of religion," in Arie L. Molendijk and Peter Pels (eds), *Religion in the Making: The Emergence of the Sciences of Religion*, 181–202, Leiden: Brill.

—— (1999) "George Albert Coe," in J.A. Garraty and M.C. Carnes (eds), *American National Biography*, vol. 5, 136–8, New York: Oxford University Press.

—— (2000a) "Mystical experience," in E. Cardeña, S.J. Lynn, and S. Krippner (eds), *Varieties of Anomalous Experience: Examining the Scientific Evidence*, 397–440, Washington, D.C.: American Psychological Association.

—— (2000b) "On the current status of the psychology of religion in the United States," in C. Henning and E. Nestler (eds), *Religionspsychologie Heute*, 13–28, Frankfurt am Main: Peter Lang.

2 Psychology of religion

Empirical approaches

Bernard Spilka

For over a century, the psychology of religion has been torn between mainstream psychology and religion, one a realm with empirical scientific aspirations, the other basically reliant on the non-empirical. Shadows of the science versus religion debate further cloud this relationship. Nevertheless, most psychologists now recognize the importance of religion in both individual and cultural life. Understanding personal faith has thus become a significant research venture, a meaningful subfield of social psychology (Dittes 1969). Within this framework, the role of empirical methodology is often a source of controversy. The present paper is an effort to clarify such issues while noting background influences to mute or soften efforts to create a scientific psychology of religion.

Methodological concerns in the psychology of religion

Basic issues

Objectivity and subjectivity

A scientific viewpoint stresses the empirical which is often defined as the gaining of "knowledge from events which are publicly observable" (Arnoult 1972: 200). Rarely are things as simple as definitions imply. The terms "knowledge" and "publicly observable" carry a great deal of freight with them (Colodny 1970; Feigl and Maxwell 1962). One theme central to their comprehension concerns what may be called objective-empirical versus subjective-empirical approaches. The former will be emphasized here. Various combinations of these procedures are also in use. The objective orientation relies on standardized measuring instruments and/or the use of experimental methods; the subjective, more on procedures variously labeled phenomenological, humanistic, and existential (Wulff 1997). This objective–subjective distinction overlaps with Allport's (1942) nomothetic vs idiographic classification. The former is modeled after the physical and biological sciences, seeking lawful relationships and exacting operational definitions utilizing quantified group data. In contrast, an idiographic outlook stresses clinical methods, emphasis on the individual, and a claimed qualitative perspective. The assertions and terminology of advocates of each of these positions are, to some degree, problematic, yet both orientations can be employed to advantage, though possibly for different purposes. The crucial task is to determine which is most likely to provide the most valid and useful information for a scientific psychology of religion. Even the phrase, "scientific psychology of religion" confronts matters of purpose and application that further complicate the study of individual faith. This is a sphere replete with hidden agendas.

This last assertion is premised on the fact that religion elicits a great deal of feeling and emotion. Regardless of the methodology employed, realization of the scientific ideal is often dubious, for *sub rosa* presuppositions may be subtly introduced into research, and remain unrecognized by the workers themselves. The classic volumes by Rosenthal (1966) and Rosenthal and Rosnow (1969) for psychology-in-general have been supplemented by analyses in the psychology of religion that reveal similar masking functions (Kirkpatrick and Hood 1990). Frequently many years pass before partiality and prejudice become evident.

The "hidden agenda" theme in the objective–subjective distinction can be traced to Aristotle and Plato; however, many philosophical streams have historically contributed to this dichotomy. Of special import here is the centuries-long submergence of Aristotelian empiricism by religious power. Though only one among a multitude of forces, it is a significant one, that may underlie attempts to validate subjective judgment via claims of expertise. Too frequently, the latter is justified by little more than authority that is irrelevant to the issues being investigated. Such considerations may be particularly pertinent when objective-empirical efforts are applied to religion. The hypothesis may be entertained that subjective-empirical methodology is more congenial to conservative religionists than to their liberal peers. The latter may be more willing to embrace objective-empirical techniques.

Simply put, as Shaklee (1958) stated, there is an "optional stopping" in theory construction, and probably in chosen research methodology, the reasons for which may not be initially evident to either investigators or readers.

Holism and reductionism

Central to the objective–subjective dichotomy is the classic debate of holism versus reductionism. Critiques of reductionism by those advocating phenomenological or clinical outlooks should be taken seriously. Similarly, objectivist criticisms of what appear to be ambiguous linguistic referents cannot be ignored. The problem is to distinguish what is naive reductionism and naive holism from their more solid expressions. I would suggest that sophisticated forms must derive from theoretical positions that logically connect the concepts in question, result in testable hypotheses, utilize verifiable measures, and eventuate in exacting data. The panic cry of reductionism often leveled against statistical techniques is essentially vacuous. These can be applied at all levels of analysis. In like manner, knee-jerk rejection of holistic notions is no more sound. Efforts stressing social interaction, cognition, and integration with emotion and motivation strive toward an holistic perspective. To understand the human as a whole is a long-term aim; all forms of analysis necessarily fall short of fully representing whatever religious phenomena are studied. Currently many feel they cannot work toward such an end by abandoning objective science for sophisticated interpretation unless it is independently and objectively verified.

Holism validly argues for an hierarchy of levels that may be analyzed. This is, of course, an ideal situation, for workers employ the approach that is most congenial to them, and rarely coordinate with others who use alternate techniques. Granted the obvious existence of emergent properties at different analytic levels, to assume the complete independence of such levels is naive. Whether labeled reductionistic or holistic, the final criteria for data gathered at any analytic level must be the ability to (1) make observations public, (2) confirm their replicability, and (3) demonstrate their predictive accuracy within a solid theoretical framework.

Operational definitions

The key to these disputes centers about the issue of operational definition. This refers to the procedures used to establish meaning (Margenau 1954). Just as religion is a complex subject, so is its measurement. Confining ourselves to individual religion, we are referring to behavior, experience, intellect, and belief. Few investigators have studied more than one of these facets of personal religion. Ultimately, all need to be integrated so that religion as a total human phenomenon may be fully understood.

The relative ease of scale construction, administration and scoring has endeared them to empirically oriented psychologists. These instruments strongly convey the impression of providing maximum information with minimal effort. The fact that they are standardized in presentation and scoring does not gainsay the necessity of careful scrutiny of every aspect of their conceptualization and creation. For example, unintentional distortion might be introduced by response sets. To illustrate, there is reason to believe that social desirability and acquiescence may combine in the same direction to affect assessments of popular measures of intrinsic faith, but operate in opposite directions with extrinsic faith (Spilka and Amaro 1981). Any good work on psychometrics can point to a variety of other problems encountered with these devices: to wit, what happens to the assumptions underlying error scores when different groups are studied.

Sampling and context influences

Measurement techniques mean very little when examined outside of the context in which they are employed. Brown (1987) shows how sensitive objective tests dealing with religion are to the nuances of instructions plus cues from the testing situation. As a rule, these matters receive little attention.

Not surprisingly, a number of problems plague the samples studied. Since most researchers are affiliated with educational institutions, college students are easiest to procure. They may be described well in terms of age, sex, ethnic group, and religious affiliation, factors rarely seen as pertinent to the hypotheses being tested. The range of responses to religious items reduces as variation in personal religious importance narrows, whether this be toward either the liberal or the conservative end of the spectrum. Such restriction necessarily lowers test reliability and validity. Parallel lowering of inter-item correlations may also mean that chance variations acquire a false significance that may defy cross-validation in new samples.

The content and goals of an empirical psychology of religion

In limited fashion, the above discussion attempts to delineate the major issues and arguments that circumscribe methodology and measurement in the psychology of religion. The aim is to realize the goals of psychological science and science *per se*. The objective-empirical approach seems to best meet this end, and is stressed here. Indeed, difficulties abound with objective-empirical methodology, some of which are noted here. Problems of the subjective-empirical approach are also pointed out; however, with proper controls, it is felt that these can better meet the criteria of objective-empirical science than is currently true. The following section thus examines methodology in the psychology of religion in objective-empirical terms.

Research in the psychology of religion: approaches

The empirical study of religious expression began over a century ago (Barnes 1892). The stage was then set for the use of questionnaires and surveys, a methodology that has essentially ruled the field to the present day. Statistical-correlational approaches also dominate the literature as the numbers provided by items and scales are readily manipulated statistically. These methods have become increasingly abstruse, sophisticated, and often rather formidable to many psychologists of religion.

Empirical methods are tools that need be placed in the context of theory, thus the framework for conceptualizing research is of primary importance. Unfortunately, influential ideas may not be easily transformed into operational equivalents. This problem is nowhere more evident than in the abstraction, spirituality. The term is loosely used, yet many have created scales to assess this quite complex notion. Most, if not all, tap some aspect of religiosity or orthodoxy. Meaningful directions toward operationalizing multidimensional schemes have been advanced by Helminiak (1996), Feingold (1994), and LaPierre (1994). They have yet to result in scales.

Categorical approaches

Some scholars have constructed typological frameworks that are amenable to measurement. Despite the implication that such classes connote qualitative variations, they often mask underlying continuities: for example, classifying respondents as religiously intrinsic or extrinsic is often distinguished by little more than expedient cut-offs on scale scores, frequently medians or means.

Designating individuals in terms of theological orientation also assumes sharp distinctions between various identifications. For example, Bridges (1989), in an impressive work, categorized those he interviewed as Fundamentalist, Pentecostal, Holiness, Evangelical, Process, Feminist, and Liberation oriented. Analysis of his measures resulted in a simple liberal–conservative breakdown, as overlap among the categories within each of the groupings was considerable.

Two additional shortcomings of the qualitative–categorical approach must be noted. First, the complexity of religion challenges the creation of exclusive categories. They become relatively crude devices. To speak of a person as a liberal religionist simply because that individual belongs to a sociologically or theologically defined liberal church or denomination tells us essentially nothing about that specific person's religious behavior, beliefs, or experiences. In other words, the use of categories is apt to lose significant information. This recommends alternative ways of organizing and utilizing data.

Continuous approaches: religion as trait

Instead of classifying people, this perspective recognizes the continuous nature of the variables in question, e.g. degree of conservatism or liberalism, strength of belief, etc. A dimension is identified, and an ordered scale is produced. Ideally, the task is to make an instrument that is unidimensional. This is where techniques such as factor analysis are used.

Fine examples of the use of factor analysis are numerous in the empirical psychology of religion (Hood *et al.* 1996). A particularly good illustration is Kirkpatrick's (1989) cross-validation of factor-analytic findings with multiple samples, item analysis, and the use of external criteria to demonstrate the multidimensionality of Allport and Ross' (1967) and Feagin's (1964) extrinsic religious items.

Empirical assessment of religious content

Religious behavior

In general, psychologists of religion aver that behavior is the most convincing indicator of religious motivation and commitment. The responses people make are also easily observed and measured, and the most widely employed of these are self-reports of attendance at religious services. Even though some doubt attends these estimates, the assumption is that the more people are involved in institutional behavior, the more religious they are. Overall, the evidence supports such a contention, as attendance correlates highly and positively with religious beliefs, importance, and experience (Hood *et al.* 1996; Stark and Glock 1968).

Simply going to services does not distinguish religious habit or utilitarian involvement from true intrinsic dedication. Attendance is a good "marker," but needs to be supplemented by other indicators, not all of which may be behavioral. Still, there are additional response possibilities, e.g. saying grace, keeping dietary laws, engaging in prayer, Bible reading, subscribing to religious publications, or making donations for church-supported missionary, charitable, family, or pastoral activities. Clearly, the behavioral side of personal faith is quite complex. Given the number of possible actions, one wonders if these form a unidimensional scale or might be multidimensional in nature.

Religious beliefs and attitudes

Religious beliefs are often regarded as the core of faith. In line with this supposition, psychologists of religion have constructed hundreds of attitude and belief questionnaires over the past century. When these judge degree of adherence to church tenets, they may be termed fundamentalism, orthodoxy, or conservatism–liberalism. Such designations overlap with sociological assessments of the doctrines of the religious bodies studied. Virtually every aspect of religious belief of which one can conceive has been evaluated by scales. They have also been employed with every group from children to the aged, and from laity to clergy.

The data gathered using attitude and belief surveys tell us how people understand and interpret their faith. These findings can then be theoretically and analytically related to external criteria. For example, images of God have been shown to correlate differentially with prejudice (Spilka and Reynolds 1965). Within the sphere of religion, the consonance of God images to patterns of prayer behavior has also been demonstrated (Fairchild *et al.* 1993). Such efforts reveal how people strive to maintain consistency and avoid dissonance among their beliefs.

A number of large sample studies examining the religious beliefs of many thousands of respondents have been undertaken. Though basically descriptive in nature, this work provides invaluable insights into the religious life and personalities of those participating (Benson and Eklin, 1990; Roof 1993; Roof and McKinney, 1987). It also offers sociological entrée into the thinking of collectives and changes in society and culture, factors which understandably affect individuals.

Religious experience

To many believers, the essence of religion is to be found in the deep, meaningful experiences that accompany the practice of one's faith. Though mysticism has been conceptualized in somewhat different terms, for our purposes it may be placed under the broad rubric of experience *per se*. Despite the oft stated emotional cry that such experiences "can't be put in words," or are beyond the realm of the natural, the task is to treat this realm empirically and as objectively as possible. The work of Ralph Hood, probably the world's foremost researcher in this area, demonstrates how amenable experience is to measurement and experimental manipulation (Hood 1995; Hood *et al.* 1996).

The objective assessment of these religious encounters has been realized via rigorous construction of defining criteria, the creation of reliable measures that detail experiential content and process, studies of their physiological concomitants, and the activation of such experiences in a variety of experimental settings (Hood *et al.* 1996). Recently, neuropsychology has contributed to the study of religious experience, as such has been observed among epileptics during stimulation of the temporal lobe and limbic system (Ramachandran and Blakeslee 1999).

As significant as religious belief and behavior are to the psychologist of religion, the complexities of experience are especially intriguing. Theoretical speculation has spanned almost the entire gamut of psychological thought from motivation and cognition to the realms of social, developmental, and clinical psychology. For almost a century, psychoanalytic thought has been applied to experience in general, and religious experience in particular (Hood 1995; Parsons 1999; Pruyser 1968). Conceptually fertile, these ideas merit much more objective-empirical research and verification than has appeared to date.

Religious knowledge

Very little research has examined religious knowledge – of scripture, ritual, or the doctrines of one's faith. Indirectly, such may represent religious motivation, or simply intellectual interest.

Religious knowledge, along with indices of belief, behavior, and experience, has been descriptively employed to characterize religious groups and people in general (Stark and Glock 1968). It has probably not been utilized more because the other domains already discussed offer easier means of assessing the topics studied by psychologists of religion.

Some trends and issues in measuring personal religion

Dimensions of personal religion

An attempt has been made above to delineate, somewhat puristically, the major features of personal faith. Even though measures in these areas continue to be constructed and refined, the most widely employed questionnaires combine elements from all of these realms. Broad schemas of personal religious orientation are thus defined. For approximately four decades, this kind of research has focused on Gordon Allport's intrinsic (I) and extrinsic (E) faith perspectives (Hood *et al.* 1996).

Since their conceptualization, research using various I and E scales has dominated the research literature. Questions still exist concerning what these devices actually measure (Kirkpatrick and Hood 1990). Emphasizing Intrinsic faith, Gorsuch (1994) claims religious motivation is being assessed. He recognizes the complexity of such motivation, indicating additional possibilities for further specification. Kirkpatrick's (1989) denotation of two kinds of extrinsic religion opens that door to motivational explanation. Pargament (1992) continues this trend, interpreting both I and E as motivational in nature. The fact that these scales have been related to a broad spectrum of theoretically meaningful variables for some time suggests the appropriateness of a meta-analytic review of findings with these measures.

Claiming that existing I and E scales overlook key elements proposed by Allport, Batson and his students have constructed indices of what he terms a Quest orientation. The latest version is composed of three scales designed to assess "readiness to face existential questions without reducing their complexity ... self criticism and perception of religious doubts as positive, ... and openness to change" (Batson *et al.* 1993: 169). Questions have also been raised about what this tri-partite instrument actually measures (Wulff 1997). Though more testing is desirable, this approach provides a fuller picture of the domain of personal faith.

The issue of curvilinearity

The general use of linear correlation and regression procedures has obscured the likelihood that religious variables might relate in a curvilinear fashion. In a number of instances, non-linear associations have been observed and confirmed (Wulff 1997).

Though explanations have been theorized for these findings, there is need to consider the inherent complexity of religious variables and confounding with demographic indicators. Deficiencies in scaling may also result in a false curvilinearity. When potential sources of confounding are eliminated and pertinent theoretical sources evaluated, we will be in a better position to determine the true significance of curvilinearity. While this process is being pursued, the greater conservatism of linear over curvilinear analysis should be considered a research strength, not a weakness.

Experimental and laboratory studies of religion

In 1985, DeConchy wrote that "well-controlled experimental studies are rare in the psychology of religion" (95). Experimentation seems alien to religious thinking, hence theoretical frameworks that lead to such appraisal are uncommon (DeConchy 1985). Batson (1977) further sees ethical and practical barriers to the widespread use of experimentation. Asher and Yeatts (1979), however, claim experimental studies are necessary. Batson's alternative is the quasi-experiment which attempts to employ real-life circumstances. For example, observations may be made over time preceding and following significant events. These designs are based on clear designations of independent and dependent variables and, hopefully, a well-formulated framework. Though the use of experimental and quasi-experimental methods is slowly increasing, their potential has yet to be adequately exploited.

Utilizing subjective-empirical methods

Projective techniques

A variety of projective measures are regularly utilized in the psychology of religion. These are mostly employed with children. Godin and Coupez (1957) developed a set of religious projective pictures on which descriptive data were accumulated from children in Europe. Graebner (1964) created a set of simple drawings which he used in combination with questions to elicit ideas about God, but this also received limited usage. For over fifty years, a number of researchers have asked children to draw pictures of God, and either make up stories or answer open-ended questions that offer insight into cognitive processes in religion (Harms 1944; Pitts 1976). Tamminen (1991: 165) supplemented what he termed a "projective photograph measure" with fill-in sentences. Ozorak (1993) had young adults both write stories in response to pictures and do a sentence completion task.

These approaches provide much information, but the critical problem is selecting and organizing the data to test hypotheses in a reliable and valid manner. Again, interpreters may choose responses that support expectations and ignore that which seems irrelevant or even counters presumptions. Such bias, *à la* Rosenthal (1966), is very difficult to avoid, hence independent judges and demanding instructions are a necessity in this work.

Interview procedures: problems and potential

Volumes have been written on literally every aspect of the interview, especially as it is used in clinical and counseling work. Unfortunately, when it is employed as a research tool a certain vagueness prevails that defies the exactitude scientific research requires. Appropriately, Elkind and his associates (1964, 1968) detail their semi-clinical interview which is based on a series of clearly stated questions. This is associated with a training program using well-defined scoring criteria, and the use of a number of judges for cross-checking. As little as possible is left to individual idiosyncrasies and bias.

Another issue concerns interview structure. All degrees of rigor are found in the literature, from open, unstructured formats in which skilled interviewers take their cues from respondents to more common, relatively structured frameworks where specific queries are used to elicit responses.

Though much fascinating information is elicited by interviews, it is not always evident how that reported was selected. One may also ask whether interviewees are led to produce certain responses. Psychology has long noted the shaping of verbal reactions by subtle reinforcements. In addition, cross-validation infrequently occurs. We are rarely informed about how the data are recorded. In most instances, it appears that the interviewer simply writes down what seems pertinent, opening the door to fortuitous selection. The total process has the potential of leaving unquestioned the weaknesses of subjectivity. Obviously, this need not be so, but seldom are the necessary precautions undertaken or, if carried out, fully elucidated.

Despite such challenges, the interview method is an invaluable tool with respondents of all ages, but especially with children. Unless strictly and precisely conducted, interviews must be considered a better source of hypotheses than a basis for their confirmation.

An interesting variant for older research participants is the use of open-ended questions which allow those queried to answer as they desire, though often in limited ways. The doubts phrased above are still applicable.

Prospects and conclusions

Gorsuch (1988) has noted that "the purpose of psychological science is to increase objectivity" (218). Given the emotional involvement that accompanies religion, total objectivity may be the impossible dream. Nevertheless, objective-empirical principles should at least serve as guides for research in the psychology of religion. There can be no doubt that this approach has been successful in providing valid and useful information (Gorsuch 1984, 1988). What have been termed subjective-empirical methods should be held to the standards demanded by objective-empiricism. Otherwise, findings must be suspect, though they may be helpful for theory construction and hypothesis formulation. Philosophical, psychological, and psychometric questions may be phrased relative to both objective and subjective approaches; however, for the advancement of psychological science, the former appears to be in the strongest position to prevail. Progress in objective-empirical research design and measurement has been considerable and continues at a rapid pace. Unless there is some major paradigm shift, which at this time seems unlikely, the future for the psychology of religion as a scientific venture apparently lies in exploiting objective-empirical methodology.

References

Allport, G.W. (1942) *The Use of Personal Documents in Psychological Science*, Bulletin No. 49, New York: Social Science Research Council.

Allport, G.W. and Ross, J.M. (1967) "Personal religious orientation and prejudice," *Journal of Personality and Social Psychology* 5: 432–43.

Arnoult, M.D. (1972) *Fundamentals of Scientific Method in Psychology*, Dubuque, IA: W.C. Brown.

Asher, W. and Yeatts, J.R. (1979) "Can we afford not to do true experiments in psychology of religion?" *Journal for the Scientific Study of Religion* 18: 86–9.

Barnes, E. (1892) "Theological life of a California child," *Pedagogical Seminary* 2: 442–8.

Batson, C.D. (1977) "Experimentation in the psychology of religion: An impossible dream," *Journal for the Scientific Study of Religion* 16: 413–18.

Batson, C.D., Schoenrade, P., and Ventis, W.L. (1993) *Religion and the Individual*, New York: Oxford.

Benson, P.L. and Eklin, C.H. (1990) *Effective Christian Education: A National Study of Protestant Congregations*, Minneapolis, MN: Search Institute.

Bridges, R.A. (1989) "Preliminary steps towards the construction of a theologically-based questionnaire," unpublished PhD dissertation, Iliff School of Theology–University of Denver Joint Program.

Brown, L.B. (1987) *The Psychology of Religious Belief*, London: Academic.

Colodny, R.G. (ed.) (1970) *The Nature and Function of Scientific Theories*, Pittsburgh, PA: University of Pittsburgh Press.

DeConchy, J.-P. (1985) "Non-experimental and experimental methods in the psychology of religion: A few thoughts on their implications and limits," in L.B. Brown (ed.), *Advances in the Psychology of Religion*, New York: Pergamon, 76–112.

Dittes, J.E. (1969) "The psychology of religion," in G. Lindzey and E. Aronson (eds), *The Handbook of Social Psychology*, vol. 5, Reading, MA: Addison-Wesley, 602–59.

Elkind, D. (1964) "Piaget's semi-clinical interview and the study of spontaneous religion," *Journal for the Scientific Study of Religion* 4: 40–47.

Elkind, D., Spilka, B., and Long, D. (1968) "The child's conception of prayer," in A. Godin (ed.), *From Cry to Word*, Brussels, Belgium: Lumen Vitae, 51–64.

Fairchild, D., Roth, H., Milmoe, S., Gotthard, C., Fehrmann, L., Richards, S., Kim, B.H., Sedlmayr, J., Carley, B., Pan, P., and Spilka, B. (1993) "God images and prayer behavior: consonance in the psychology of religion," paper presented at the joint Convention of the Rocky Mountain and Western Psychological Associations, Phoenix, AZ.

Feagin, J.R. (1964) "Prejudice and religious types: a focused study of Southern Fundamentalists," *Journal for the Scientific Study of Religion* 4: 3–13.

Feigl, H. and Maxwell, G. (eds) (1962) *Scientific Explanation, Space and Time*, vol. III of *Minnesota Studies in the Philosophy of Science*, Minneapolis, MN: University of Minnesota Press.

Feigl, H. and Scriven, M. (1956) *The Foundations of Science and the Concepts of Psychology and Psychoanalysis*, vol. I of *Minnesota Studies in the Philosophy of Science*, Minneapolis, MN: University of Minnesota Press.

Feingold, B. (1994) "Spirituality: A credible scientific approach?" paper presented at the first international Prevention: The Key to Health for Life conference, Charlestown, WV, October.

Godin, A. and Coupez, A. (1957) "Religious projective pictures: A technique of assessment of religious psychism," *Lumen Vitae* 12(2): 260–74.

Gorsuch, R.L. (1984) "Measurement: The boon and bane of investigating religion," *American Psychologist* 39: 228–36.

—— (1988) "Psychology of religion," *Annual Review of Psychology* 39: 201–21.

—— (1994) "Toward motivational theories of intrinsic religious commitment," *Journal for the Scientific Study of Religion* 28: 348–54.

Graebner, O. (1964) "Child concepts of God," *Religious Education* 59: 234–41.

Harms, E. (1944). "The development of religious experience in children," *American Journal of Sociology* 50: 112–22.

Helminiak, D. (1996) *The Human Core of Spirituality*, Albany, NY: State University of New York Press.

Hood, R.W. Jr (1995) "The facilitation of religious experience," in R.W. Hood, Jr (ed.), *Handbook of Religious Experience*, Birmingham, AL: Religious Education Press, 568–97.

Hood, R.W. Jr, Spilka, B., Hunsberger, B., and Gorsuch, R.L. (1996) *The Psychology of Religion: An Empirical Approach*, New York: Guilford.

Kirkpatrick, L.A. (1989) "A psychometric analysis of the Allport–Ross and Feagin measures of intrinsic–extrinsic religious orientation," in M.L. Lynn and D.O. Moberg (eds), *Research in the Social Scientific Study of Religion*, vol. 1, Greenwich, CT: JAI Press, 1–31.

Kirkpatrick, L.A. and Hood, R.W. Jr (1990) "Intrinsic–extrinsic religious orientation: The boon or bane of contemporary psychology of religion?" *Journal for the Scientific Study of Religion* 29: 442–62.

Kubie, L.S. (1959) "Psychoanalysis and scientific method," in S. Hook (ed.), *Psychoanalysis, Scientific Method, and Philosophy*, New York: New York University Press, 57–77.

LaPierre, L.L. (1994) "A model for describing spirituality," *Journal of Religion and Health* 33: 153–61.

Margenau, H. (1954) "On interpretations and misinterpretations of operationalism," *Scientific Monthly* 79: 209–10.

Ozorak, E.W. (1993) "Religion and Relationships: A Projective Assessment," paper presented at the Annual Convention of the American Psychological Association, Toronto, Canada.

Pargament, K.I. (1992) "Of means and ends: Religion and the search for significance," *International Journal for the Psychology of Religion* 2: 201–29.

Parsons, W.B. (1999) *The Enigma of the Oceanic Feelings: Revisioning the Psychoanalytic Theory of Mysticism*, New York: Oxford University Press.

Pitts, V.P. (1976) "Drawing the invisible: children's conceptualization of God," *Character Potential* 8: 12–24.

Pruyser, P. (1968) *A Dynamic Psychology of Religion*, New York: Harper & Row.

Ramachandran, V.S. and Blakeslee, S. (1999) *Phantoms in the Brain*, New York: William Morrow.

Roof, W.C. (1993) *A Generation of Seekers*, New York: HarperCollins.

Roof, W.C. and McKinney, W. (1987) *American Mainline Religion: Its Changing Shape and Future*, New York: HarperCollins.

Rosenthal, R. (1966) *Experimental Effects in Behavioral Research*, New York: Appelton-Century-Crofts.

Rosenthal, R. and Rosnow, R.L. (eds) (1969) *Artifact in Behavioral Research*, New York: Academic.

Scheffler, I. (1967) *Science and Subjectivity*, Indianapolis, IN: Bobbs-Merrill.

Shaklee, A.B. (1958) "Optional stopping and the theory maker," *Psychological Reports* 4: 17.

Spilka, B. and Amaro, A. (1981) "A signal detectability validation of measures of Intrinsic–Extrinsic, Committed–Consensual Faith," Convention of the Society for the Scientific Study of Religion, Baltimore, MD, 30 October 1981.

Spilka, B. and Reynolds, J.F. (1965) "Religion and prejudice: A factor-analytic study," *Review of Religious Research* 6: 163–8.

Stark, R. and Glock, C.Y. (1968) *American Piety: The Nature of Religious Commitment*, Berkeley, CA: University of California Press.

Tamminen, K. (1991) *Religious Development in Childhood and Youth*, Helsinki: Suomalainen Tiedeakatemia.

Wulff, D. (1997) *Psychology of Religion: Classic and Contemporary Views* (2nd edn), New York: Wiley.

3 The future is in the return

Back to cultural psychology of religion

Jacob A. Belzen

Waves and forces in psychology

The fate of the psychology of religion has varied depending on time and place: whereas in the United States the most popular period for the psychology of religion seems to have been in the first two decades of this century, the situation in several European countries has been strikingly different. And even today, in many places interest in psychology of religion is clearly increasing, yet the emerging picture of the field is far from homogeneous. To delineate the reasons for these differing developments would be a task for serious and detailed historical scholarship, and cannot be undertaken here. And yet, while I wish to avoid simple generalizations about the development of so hybrid an enterprise as the psychology of religion in the twentieth century, I think that we do not err in stating that the early and prominent interest in psychology of religion had something to do with religion's dominant social position at the time psychology emerged. Almost all "founding fathers" of different psychologies around and shortly after 1900 published on religion (for an excellent review of these works, see Wulff 1997).

In a way, this is all too understandable: as religion is an affair of human beings and important to many, psychology – in so far as it is a human science – can, even has to, deal with it. Religion can be approached from a variety of psychological perspectives: psychoanalytic, behavioristic, cognitive, humanistic, and so on. Yet, as religion lost at least in Europe much of its societal influence, psychology lost much of its interest in religion; other concerns were put on the agenda (by "customers" such as the Pentagon, big industries, and others). In addition to this development, however, there is the often noticed but little understood phenomenon of a seemingly anti-religious attitude among professional psychologists. For example, in the 1960s and 1970s, in the Netherlands, a country with the second highest "psychology density" in the world, it was a courageous act for students and/or professionals of psychology to admit to an interest in religion, let alone to be religious.

Today, as indicated already, things are changing again: interest in religion, and especially in its spiritual dimension, is increasing in contemporary psychology. There are a number of factors responsible for this. In part, it is a "cohort effect": the antipathy towards religion is decreasing because the generation of its advocates is retiring (younger colleagues and students are more apt be interested in religious phenomena, perhaps because their youth was less spoiled by religion than the older generation's). In part, it is the effect of scholars known for their religious sympathies finding courage to publish on the topic again. To a certain extent, the renewed interest is another clear effect of market forces in psychology: religion is being put on the agenda again as a result of a number of loosely related developments.

1   There is an increasing realization, not the least among health insurance companies, that religion can be positively correlated with mental health and subjective wellbeing.
2   The process of globalization and cultural impact of immigration and pluralism has, despite the forces of secularization, made it abundantly clear that religion is a very important element in most non-Western parts of the world. In dealing with these other "cultures," whether in trade or war or otherwise, one can no longer afford to disregard religious traditions, sentiments and customs.
3   The large numbers of refugees and immigrants confront the civil services (mental health care, integration programs, etc.) with the importance of religion in the lives of these individuals and groups. In light of such data, psychology has recognized the social need to find out more about religiosity's impact on the general populace. It is revealing that in recent years quite a number of substantial publications, especially from clinical psychological perspectives, written by and intended for psychologists, have endeavored to do just that (Pargament 1997; Shafranske 1996).

When is psychological research into religion really psychology of religion?

At this point, however, a critical question can and should be asked. Does or will the kind of attention devoted to religion for the reasons elaborated above yield any substantial contribution to the psychology of religion? When research is done from the perspective of a new psychological theory does this result in any more insight into religion? Or is it "just" the application of that new theory to religion? In other words: it may be an additional validation of that particular theory, rather than an effort to obtain insight in the particularity of religion. When proceeding in the way just indicated, is one not in danger of "just" finding in the "case" of religion what had been established already in a number of other (non-religious) samples?

Of course, these questions touch upon the definition of the psychology of religion. Very liberally, one could state that any research on religion from a psychological perspective may be called psychology of religion. Although this need not be denied, I wonder whether the aim of psychology of religion should not be to investigate psychologically the specificity of what religion is and "does." I will return to this problematic question.

First, a few more observations must be made on the historical development of the psychology of religion, understood as any psychological research on religion. When this type of research waned in psychological institutes, or among psychologists, this did not imply that psychological interest in religion was lost. In all kinds of institutes for theology and for religious studies, in circles of pastoral care and of training for the ministry, a lively interest in psychology continues. Not all of this should be called psychology of religion (Belzen 1995, 1996), however. This present volume is only one indication of the fact that psychology of religion, broadly understood as any psychological research on religion, is only one section of the broader field of "religion and psychology". Although deeply interested in psychology of religion, scholars from the aforementioned institutes are usually neither professional psychologists nor involved in empirical research. Moreover, they often have been serious critics of the discipline, offering frequent complaints about the meager results produced by the so-called empirical psychology of religion in the research conducted by professional psychologists. Performed correctly with current methods and techniques, these findings are often not very exciting. This surely is one of the reasons why the (admittedly more speculative) reasonings from psychoanalytical perspectives enjoy more popularity in departments of religious studies. However, and this is a very important point, disappointment with academic psychology has not only been articulated in relation to its analysis of religion, but has also been voiced in relation to its understanding of other topics characterizing the human being as well, such as love, art, fantasy, etc. This "lack of relevance" (Giorgi 1976) may seem to contradict the appeal of this essay to "return to psychology", i.e. to enlarge the section "psychology of religion" within the larger field of "religion and psychological studies". Yet this contradiction can be resolved if we manage to settle the question of what kind of psychology the psychology of religion should employ in order to achieve meaningful results.

What kind of psychology to turn to?

Tautological as it may sound, it must be stated even among psychologists, who all too often erroneously consider any research on religion to be theology, that psychology of religion is, by its nature, a branch of psychology: it works with theories and concepts, methodology and techniques from some more general psychological theory. Problematic, or at least short-sighted, however, is the simple application of psychological reasoning to religion. Here we cannot avoid the problem of the definition of religion, so let us devote a few thoughts to it (some readers may have been waiting for it all along!). Not in the least because of the globalization mentioned above, awareness is dawning, even among Western psychologists, that "religion", however defined, is not one and the same all over the world. Religion is a term used to designate a multifarious and multiplex phenomenon. The very term may be ill fated when used in such analysis as it is a term coined by Western, Christian thinkers and replete with Western, Christian connotations. Paradoxically, but understandably from a historical perspective, even the rise of psychology (of religion) itself has, instead of broadening perspectives and understandings, contributed to narrowing the current understanding of religion in the West (Belzen 1999a). All too often, religion is understood after the model of some property inherent to the human being, of a personality trait, or a sentiment. This inflated, psychologized understanding of religion – unintentionally fostered by such masterpieces as James' *Varieties* – are concordant with the "cult of the individual" that has characterized Western thought since the Renaissance. And it is not just characteristic of the Western psychological approach to religion, but to most other topics as well (e.g. emotion, sexuality, cognition, and the like). In brief, Western psychology tends to have forgotten that the majority of human actions and experiences are mediated: they are carried out by a body and situated and constituted by a culture at a certain stage of its historical development.

Currently, however, an increasing number of scholars, even in psychology, are becoming aware of the mediated character of human functioning. (I shall not enter into a discussion of the embodied mediation of psychic functioning, as the treatment of its cultural mediation is complex enough already.) Although the schools of psychology linked to this perspective (hermeneutical, narrative, semiotic, critical, feminist and ecological psychology) are still on the edge of the so-called "main stream", there is a rapidly growing wing of psychology striving for a different orientation than the experimental and mechanistic one that has dominated the last decades. These psychologists find methodologies, methods and techniques like phenomenology, hermeneutics, "grounded theory", ethnomethodology, field studies, case studies, and so on, more suited to explore domains characteristic of the human being than methodological behaviorism, laboratory research or "cognitive science". In emphasizing that there is a movement striving for an approach other than the mechanistic experimental, let me evoke historical continuity: many past figures in the psychology of religion have also been aware of the cultural character of the phenomena they desired to explore. While space prohibits detailed illustrations, it will suffice to point to Wilhelm Wundt. Wundt, whom many consider to be the founder of academic psychology, as he established the first "psychological laboratory" (Leipzig, 1879), wrote that psychology can only turn to experiment as an auxiliary method if it seeks to examine the "elementary psychic processes"; but if it seeks to study the higher psychic processes it has to consult other sciences for orientation (Wundt 1900–1909). His own suggestion was that psychologists should consult history. The study of the higher psychic processes, to which religiosity belongs, Wundt called "cultural psychology". With Wundt, and with many psychologists of the first generation, one still found a recognition that religion is first and foremost a cultural phenomenon. Today (perhaps one should say: after Foucault), people increasingly realize that not only human sexuality but many branches of action and experience, including religiosity, are culturally constituted. These branches of action and experience, if they are present in a certain culture, will bear the characteristics of the "forms of life" (Wittgenstein) that evoked, facilitated and structured them. Therefore, a phenomenon like "conversion" will be found with some religious "forms of life", but not with others; if present, it will display a particular form, meaning and structure in one culture, but another form, meaning and structure in another culture (for an empirically based example of an approach led by this insight, cf. Belzen 1999b).

Introduction of cultural psychology

Briefly put, then, the psychology of religion should not just rejoice in the current increase of attention to religion among psychologists, but beware of the deception caused by former unreflective applications of "mainstream" psychology to religion. For the study of many phenomena, particularly the scientific research of so heterogeneous and multifarious a phenomenon as religion, psychology should orient itself toward the older "cultural psychology" which is nowadays undergoing a resurgence in a variety of alternative venues (Belzen 1997). To explain this proposal, let us take a brief look at what "cultural psychology" currently stands for (for instructive recent overviews see: Cole 1996; Shore 1996; Markus *et al.* 1996; cf. also Goldberger and Veroff 1995; Matsumoto 1994, 1996; Ratner 1991; Shweder 1991; Valsiner 1999). As with so many challenging approaches, it is still easier to define cultural psychology in a negative sense (what it is opposed to) than to say what it positively stands for. But let me attempt a preliminary circumscription by mentioning a few of its elements (cf. also Belzen 1999c). Stated rather simply, cultural psychology does not search inside the human being to investigate belief, feeling, reasoning and behavior, but rather tries to understand how the specific "form of life" the person is embedded in constitutes and constructs feelings, thoughts and conduct. Cultural psychologists try to counterbalance the prevailing bias in psychology according to which psychological phenomena have their origin in intra-individual processes. They stress that psychological phenomena (such as attitudes, emotions, motives, perceptual outlook, forms of reasoning, memory, and so on) are not just shaped by a surrounding culture, but are constituted by and rooted in particular cultural interactions. Culturally different settings require different activities, leading to different (cognitive) abilities. Thus, to refer to just one example, it was found that arithmetic problem-solving occurs differently, leading to different results, in different situations. Lave *et al.* (1984) found that whereas 98 per cent of problems were correctly solved by subjects when engaged in grocery shopping, only 59 per cent of an equal kind of questions were answered correctly by the same subjects when tested in a classroom. Further, they argue that problem-solving is not a disembodied mental activity, but belongs to, and is specific to, the kind of situation the subject is involved in. Likewise, emotions are not just the same ones, differing in degree across cultures, they are different in different cultures: i.e. some emotions exist in some cultures and not in others. Emotions are characterized by beliefs, judgments, and desires, the content of which are not natural, but are determined by the systems of cultural belief, values and mores of particular communities. They are no natural responses elicited by natural features which a situation may possess. Rather, they are socio-culturally determined patterns of experience and expression which are acquired and subsequently feature in specifically social situations (Armon Jones 1986). Research in cross-cultural psychology has produced abundantly striking examples of this kind.

Accepting that culture is a major shaping force in self-definition, conduct, and experience, requires a different kind of research than is usual in mainstream psychology of religion. The particular religious "form of life" the human being is embedded in can no longer be neglected in favor of the search for assumed inherent and invariable psychic structures. On the contrary, as is clear from the example of grocery shopping, it is necessary to study people engaging in their particular "form of life", not to take them out of it by submitting them to experiments, tests or questionnaires in the "laboratory". Accordingly, researchers have to turn to participant observation, analysis of personal documents, interview and other ecologically valid techniques. Further, it becomes necessary to study not the isolated individual, but also the beliefs, values and rules that are prevalent in a particular situation, together with the patterns of social relatedness and interaction that characterize that situation. In any case, it is erroneous to try to study the "individual mind" as such.

To be more concrete, when analyzing different types of religiosity, one could consider employing several recent developments compatible with a cultural psychological approach. A few examples are given below to illustrate the scope and substance of these developments.

When investigating populations where religiosity is inseparable from cultural tradition, renewed attention to the notion of "activity", as elaborated for instance in the cultural historical Russian tradition after Leontiev (1979, 1981), Luria (1971, 1976) and Vygotsky (1978, 1991) might be helpful. Pierre Bourdieu (1977, 1990) offers parallel reasoning, developed from studying such (sub)cultures as the Berbers in Morocco.

When dealing with forms of religiosity that are the result of the subject's more or less conscious choices, as in the case of adult conversions or switches to another faith, or with religiosity that in general is not learned as a child and where, for example, cognitive aspects like meaning-giving are far more important than being embedded in a local community, narrative psychology (e.g. Howard 1991; Sarbin 1986, 1993) may be fruitful to analyze the meaning that specific activities have for these believers.

To assess the impact of individual life history and its dynamic aspects, psychoanalytic approaches that stress the importance of the local symbolic system might prove valuable (Clement and Kakar 1993; Kakar 1982; Vergote 1988).

Let me elaborate briefly on the thinking behind these examples. First, the notion that psychological phenomena depend on practical activities has a long tradition, ranging from Marx and Engels to Dewey and contemporary thinkers like Bourdieu. Religious people very often cannot explain on a cognitive level why they perform as they do, for example, in rituals. Most often they have no knowledge of the "official" rationales for certain conduct. Accordingly, Roman Catholics cannot account for their behavior during Mass, nor can Buddhists explain the reasons for experiencing grief as they do (Obeyesekere 1985). Yet people perform perfectly in accordance with the expectations of their religious (sub)culture, often with a competence and to an extent that a foreigner will never learn to manage. Religion regulates conduct, although this conduct cannot be conceived of as the conscious following of rules. People's conduct, in the broadest sense, including their perception, thinking, emotion, needs, etc., is regulated according to a scheme or structure that is not consciously known. This scheme is not even primarily *really?* cognitive but is something belonging to the body. People act not because they know consciously what to do. Rather, it is as if their body knows for them. Affect, for example, is not the result of properly knowing how to feel – it is ruled by an immediate corporeal structure. Bourdieu (1990) calls this structure "habitus" – it is this structure that generates and structures people's actions. Although these structures are personally embodied, they are not individual: they characterize the (sub)culture and are derived from the patterns in the participant's conduct. They belong to both the individual and a (sub)culture; in fact, they are precisely the nexus between an individual and a cultural institution. Unlike Western secularized societies, religion in most cultures is not just a specific practice performed on specific occasions. In such cultures, religion is transmitted through practice,

without raising to the level of discourse. The child mimics other people's actions rather than "models." Body praxis speaks directly to motor function, in the form of a pattern of postures that is both individual and systematic, being bound up with a whole system of objects, and charged with a host of special meanings and values.

(Bourdieu 1990: 73–4)

The same applies to those Western subcultures where religion still is predominantly a shaping and integrating force. To give just one example: it is because he carries, in his body, the habitus of an Indian Hindu that a believer thinks, reacts, feels and behaves as an Indian Hindu, in fact is an Indian Hindu, and not because he would know the specifics of the doctrine, the ethical rules or the rituals. The believer usually is not aware of these specifics. Not being individual, the habitus is itself structured by social practices: its dispositions are durably inculcated by the possibilities and impossibilities, freedoms and necessities, opportunities and prohibitions inscribed in the objective conditions. It is in social practices that the habitus can be observed at work: being (re)produced and producing conduct itself.

Second, to whatever extent the habitus operates in unconscious or non-cognitive ways, the conduct that results does mean something both to the actor and to other cultural participants. This meaning is rooted in both personal life history and culturally available meanings. Analysis of activity must take into account the "forms of life" that are the context of meaning. This culturally available meaning can only be traced and analyzed at the level of text: words, proverbs, stories, myths, articulated symbols. However true it may be that without the analysis of activity, cultural psychology is only telling half of the story (Ratner 1996), it remains true that cultural knowledge, symbols, concepts and words, laid down in and maintained by linguistic conventions, stimulate and organize psychological phenomena. Here narrative psychology can be seen as an obvious ally in any analysis of religiosity. It points out that in the course of their life, people hear and assimilate stories which enable them to develop "schemes" which give direction to their experience and conduct, schemes with whose help they can then make sense out of a potential stimulation overload. To each developing story, and in every situation with which they are confronted, people bring an acquired catalogue of "plots" which is used to make sense out of the story or situation (Mancuso and Sarbin 1983). Herein lies the possibility of applying narrative psychology to religious phenomena (cf. Belzen 1996, 2000). For, whatever religion may be besides this, it is in any case also a reservoir of verbal elements, stories, interpretations, prescriptions and commandments which in their power to determine experience and conduct and in their legitimization possess narrative character. Clifford Geertz's definition of religion, which is most widely disseminated in cultural psychology, points to the central importance of "stories", of linguistically transmitted and given reality:

> a religion is a system of symbols which act to establish powerful, perva-
> sive and long-lasting moods and motivations in men by formulating
> conceptions of a general order of existence and clothing those concep-
> tions with such an aura of factuality that the moods and motivations
> seem uniquely realistic.

(1973: 90)

In order to effect a connection with narrative psychology, one need only take the word "symbols" in this definition and give it more precise content with the aid of "stories and practices" (in this connection one must realize that both practices and "conceptions" again employ stories to explain and legitimate themselves). In other words: people who, among the various culturally available life forms, have also been introduced to, or have appropriated, a religious life form, have at their disposal a system of interpretation and conduct which (narratively) prefigures reality for them. Thus, in every situation, expectations, interpretations and actions can be brought to bear which have been derived from a religious horizon of understanding and which, under certain circumstances, confirm and reinforce this understanding. Indeed, precisely those persons and groups are considered deeply devout who succeed, with the greatest frequency, spontaneously and persistently to activate this religious horizon of understanding and who are in a position (despite the paradoxes they are confronted with) to overcome their own problems of religious interpretation and to act in harmony with the system of interpretation and conduct they have appropriated as well as with the "stories" that have been handed down to them.

Third, in some psychoanalytic circles (notably in France and in those that orient themselves towards developments there) there is an awareness of the impact of culture that seems contrary to much vulgarized psychoanalytic reasoning. There is a recognition that supra-individual entities like societies and/or entire cultures are not just repeating the phases and mechanisms that psychoanalytic theorizing claims to have discovered when studying patients. Instead, structurally informed analysts emphasize the importance of what Lacan called the "symbolic order" or the *discours de l'Autre*. This symbolic order predates the individual and will persist when the individual has left it. Yet the individual is already represented in this order before birth, even if only by the name that will be given. Lacan clearly gave primacy to the cultural order when he articulated his dictum: "man talks, yet because the symbol has made him man" (1966: 242). Psychic development is the result of culture: there is no natural (in the sense of innately preconceived) growth, according to Lacan. The structure of the psyche as such (not just its culturally variable contents) is dependent on culture, on forces from "outside". The constitution of the subject, the "psychic birth" (after natural birth) is dependent on (aware of the separateness of) the "other" (usually the mother); in order to achieve a first – imaginary – image of itself, the child (in the "mirror phase") needs someone else to pass down this image. Most important for cultural psychology, self-consciousness, in Lacan's view, only emerges thanks to language: it is because of identification with the "discourse of the other" that the human being becomes a participant in culture, able to say "I" and – later – to speak in its own name. Subjectivity is constituted and marked by cultural givens. Because of the entrance into the cultural symbolic order (preeminently language), needs are transformed into desires, which are therefore not naturally given, but a product of culture.

In this sense, it is impossible to conceive of a human instinct that would not be marked by cultural references that define it. Even sexual instincts are never merely natural forces: the strata of meanings deposited in them invariably condition the strategies of satisfaction as well as the pitfalls of suffering and discontents. That human beings desire, and the way in which they want to satisfy that desire, is the consequence of cultural signifiers that direct human desire. Thus, just as Freud defined the drive as psychic labor because of the intrinsic unity with the corporeal, culture also imposes labor, shaping the psychic realm.

Ricoeur (1965) also tried to show that "desire" cannot be conceived of without an "Other", and that Freud developed his second topical model precisely because of his realization that libido is confronted with a non-libidinal variable that manifests itself as culture (188). Although it must be admitted that, in this branch of psychoanalysis, emphasis is perhaps one-sided on language, stories and symbols, there is recognition of the cultural embeddedness of the individual life history, and awareness that for a psychological understanding of meaningful action and experience it is therefore necessary to apply a double perspective: the perspective of the meaning shared by a cultural community in general as well as that of the personal meaning which can only be understood in terms of the individual life history. Even a deviation can be thus interrogated as to its meaning, since in deviating from the surrounding order it can be seen as a manifestation of the psychic conflict underlying it. I deliberately say "can be" since not every deviation points to psychopathology and, on the other hand, the (apparent) absence of conflict need not indicate psychic health. Psychology cannot determine in advance a person's health and sickness and will only make statements after having examined a concrete individual against the background of culture and life history.

Concluding remarks

Not much of this type of reasoning has been received in the psychology of religion thus far. If psychologists turn to research on religion, it is usually from a more conventional theoretical point of view, and with application of traditional research methods. Although such research is published in respected psychological journals, it is rare that it provides substantial insight into the religion and religiosity of the investigated subjects. Even when the number of publications by psychologists is increasing, this type of research is in danger of being criticized (again) by those in the broader field of "religion and psychological studies", for reasons outlined in the beginning of this essay. Therefore, for a psychology of religion that strives for insight into the psychic particularities of any religion, the vista of cultural psychology is going to be vital. Moreover, it is this approach that promises to do justice to the phenomena under consideration: a cultural psychological approach will take into account the specific form of religion in which some (sub)sample of subjects is involved. Granted, the results obtained will not be valid for every person and/or group in every religion, but this is precisely an aim that should be abolished in psychology (not just in psychology of religion)! As there exists no religion-in-general, but only specific forms of life that go all under the label "religious", and as psychology should not strive for insight into elements of psychic functioning universal for all subjects, regardless of time and place, psychology should try to detect how a specific religious form of life constitutes, involves and regulates the psychic functioning of the persons involved.

As I would not like to discuss my own efforts in cultural psychology of religion, let us take a brief look at a body of work that does not present itself under the label "cultural psychology", but which has developed in a direction clearly compatible with it: namely, the approach advocated by Antoine Vergote, the Francophone founder of the Center for Psychology of Religion at the University of Leuven (Belgium). Vergote's work is characterized by a remarkably interdisciplinary approach: he draws on cultural anthropology, history and sociology, psychoanalysis and philosophy (subjects he studied in both Leuven and Paris, where he went into Lacanian psychoanalysis). When confronted with the task of defining his object of study, he does not commit the fallacy of trying to develop a psychological definition of religion, but he turns to the cultural sciences, e.g. to Clifford Geertz' well-known definition of religion. Accordingly, the task for psychology of religion is to develop or to make use of an approach that will yield insight into the psychic processes that are involved in and determined by this culturally given religion.

Next, a delimitation of the subject to be studied is needed; for psychology of religion is not studying "religion" in general (whatever that may be), but some concrete phenomenon, belonging to a particular religious form of life (be it stigmata, worship of ancestors, or whatever). Usually, Vergote's publications deal only with aspects of the Christian faith in its Roman Catholic version, or, even more concretely, in its Belgian context. It is on this point that some criticize him for employing overgeneralizing language. These critics may be correct to some extent, although they apparently forget his purposive restrictions. In one of his major publications, Vergote attempts a study of "belief", which he considers to be one of the most important elements in and specific for the Christian faith. Before starting his psychological research, he offers a brief account of what "to believe" means in Christianity (1996: 187, 191). Proceeding in this way, he distances himself from any effort to write a psychology of religion in general, as he is not writing on religion in general; he is not even writing on the Christian religion in general, but only on one of its aspects: faith. As in his well-known *Guilt and Desire* (1988), he defends the position that "by nature" the human being is neither religious nor irreligious; the human being can only become a religious or irreligious person because of culturally available meanings: "what is studied by psychology is the effect of psychic archeology on the process by which the individual appropriates the symbolic system of religion" (1996: 26). It is psychology's task to bring to light (latent) meanings and motivations in experienced religion, and to investigate how these relate organically to each other and form the structure of personal religiosity. Therefore, it is just as revealing to study the process by which a person develops into an unbeliever as to study the oscillations between belief and unbelief.

As I suggested above, this is just one example of a current European oeuvre (too little known in the United States) that would be compatible with an interdisciplinary cultural psychological approach to religion. And it is here that I see a future for psychology of religion, and the possibility of coming up with meaningful results and interpretations: in selecting some specific phenomenon from a religious form of life, taking account of its particular psychic impact, using concepts and methods from currently evolving cultural psychological theorizing. Psychology of religion for many decades has been in danger of being a field that ruminates endlessly, in teaching and publications, on the admittedly sometimes great works of the past (by James, Pratt, Freud, Jung and many others). It has been in danger of losing contact with psychology at large, and of being "just" a partner in a dialogue with theology and/or religious studies. Yet to be and to remain psychology of religion, it must be or become psychology (again): psychology of religion should return to psychology. This process is currently developing. I pointed out earlier the increase in publications on religion by psychologists. I would also like to refer to a recent Editor's Note in *The International Journal for the Psychology of Religion* (1999: 1), expressing the wish that the field may influence psychology "as a whole". Yet psychology of religion should be aware of which kind of psychology it is going toward: if it is to those parts of mainstream psychology that are criticized as lacking relevance, it will share the fate of this kind of psychology. If, however, psychology of religion aligns itself to such psychologies as are striving to understand the peculiarities of the human being constituted and situated historicoculturally, clouds as big as a hand may expand into a rain that will yield rich harvests.

References

Armon-Jones, C. (1986) "The thesis of constructionism," in R. Harré (ed.), *The Social Construction of Emotions*, 32–56, Oxford: Blackwell.

Belzen, J.A. (1995/1996) "Sketches for a family portrait of psychology of religion at the end of modernity," *Journal of Psychology of Religion* 4/5: 89–122.

—— (1996) "Beyond a classic? Hjalmar Sunden's role theory and contemporary narrative psychology," *International Journal for the Psychology of Religion* 6: 181–99.

—— (1997) "The historicocultural approach in the psychology of religi\ perspectives for interdisciplinary research," *Journal for the Scientific Study* ω *Religion* 36(3): 358–71.

· —— (1998) "The psychology of religion in Europe: a contextual report," *Pastoral Psychology* 46(3): 145–62.

—— (1999a) "Paradoxes. An essay on the object of psychology of religion," in J.G. Platvoet and A.L. Molendijk (eds), *The Pragmatics of Defining Religion. Contexts, Concepts, and Contests*, 93–122, Leiden: Brill.

—— (1999b) "Religion as embodiment: cultural psychological concepts and methods in the study of conversion among Bevindelijken," *Journal for the Scientific Study of Religion* 38(2): 235–52.

—— (1999c) "The cultural psychological approach to religion: contemporary debates on the object of the discipline," *Theory and Psychology* 9: 229–56.

—— (2000) "Religion, culture and psychopathology. Cultural psychological reflections on religion in a case of manslaughter in The Netherlands," *Pastoral Psychology* 48: 415–35.

Bourdieu, P. (1977) *Outline of a Theory of Practice*, New York: Cambridge University Press.

—— (1990) "Belief and the body," in P. Bourdieu, *The Logic of Practice*, 66–79, Cambridge: Polity Press (originally published in French as *Le sens pratique*, 1980).

Clement, C. and S. Kakar (1993) *La folle et le saint*, Paris: Editions du Seuil.

Cole, M. (1996) *Cultural Psychology. A Once and Future Discipline*, Cambridge: Belknap Press/Harvard University Press.

Geertz, C. (1973) *The Interpretation of Cultures*, New York: Basic Books.

Giorgi, A. (1976) "Phenomenology and the foundations of psychology," in W.J. Arnold (ed.), *Conceptual Foundations of Psychology: Nebraska Symposium on Motivation, 1975*, 281–408, Lincoln/London: University of Nebraska Press.

Goldberger, N.R. and Veroff, J.B. (eds) (1995) *The Culture and Psychology Reader*, New York/London: New York University Press.

Hood, R.W., Spilka, B., Hunsberger, B., and Gorsuch, R. (1996) *The Psychology of Religion: An Empirical Approach*, 2nd edn, New York: Guilford.

Howard, G.S. (1991) "Culture tales. A narrative approach to thinking, cross cultural psychology and psychotherapy," *American Psychologist* 46: 187–97.

Kakar, S. (1982) *Shamans, Mystics, and Doctors: A Psychological Inquiry into India and its Healing Traditions*, Boston: Beacon.

—— (1991) *The Analyst and the Mystic: Psychoanalytic Reflections on Religion and Mysticism*, Chicago: University of Chicago Press.

Lacan, J. (1966) *Ecrits*, Paris: Seuil.

Lave, J., Murtaugh, M., and de la Rocha, O. (1984) "The dialectic of arithmetic in grocery shopping," in B. Rogoff and J. Lave (eds), *Everyday Cognition. Its Development in Social Context*, 67–94, Cambridge: Harvard University Press.

Leontiev, A. (1979) "The problem of activity in psychology," in J. Wertsch (ed.), *The Concept of Activity in Soviet Psychology*, 37–71, Armonk, NY: Sharpe.

—— (1981) *Problems of the Development of the Mind*, Moscow: Progress.

Luria, A.R. (1971) "Towards the problem of the historical nature of psychological processes," *International Journal of Psychology* 6: 259–72.

—— (1976) *Cognitive Development: Its Cultural and Social Foundations*, Cambridge: Harvard University Press.

Mancuso, J.C. and Sarbin, T.R. (1983) "The self-narrative in the enactment of roles," in T.R. Sarbin and K.E. Scheibe (eds), *Studies in Social Identity*, 233–53, New York: Praeger.

Markus, H.R., Kitayama, S., and Heiman, R.J. (1996) "Culture and basic psychological principles," in E.T. Higgins and A.W. Kruglanski (eds), *Social Psychology*, 857–913, New York/London: Guilford Press.

Matsumoto, D. (1994) *People. Psychology from a Cultural Perspective*, Pacific Grove, Ca.: Brooks/Cole.

—— (1996) *Culture and Psychology*, Pacific Grove, Ca.: Brooks/Cole.

Obeyesekere, G. (1981) *Medusa's Hair*, Chicago: University of Chicago Press.

—— (1985) "Depression, Buddhism and the Work of Culture in Sri Lanka," in A. Kleiman and B. Good (eds), *Culture and Depression: Studies on the Anthropology and Cross-Cultural Psychiatry of Affect and Disorder*, 134–52, Berkeley: University of California Press.

Pargament, K.L. (1997) *The Psychology of Religion and Coping. Theory, Research, Practice*, New York/London: Guilford Press.

Ratner, C. (1991) *Vygotsky's Sociohistorical Psychology and its Contemporary Applications*, New York: Plenum.

—— (1996) "Activity as a key concept for cultural psychology," *Culture and Psychology* 2: 407–34.

Ricoeur, P. (1965/1970) *Freud and Philosophy. An Essay on Interpretation*, New Haven, Conn.: Yale University Press.

Sarbin, T.R. (ed.) (1986) *Narrative Psychology: The Storied Nature of Human Conduct*, New York: Praeger.

—— (1993) "The narrative as the root metaphor for contextualism," in S.C. Hayes L.J. Hayes, H.W. Reese and T.R. Sarbin (eds), *Varieties of Scientific Contextualism*, 51–65, Reno, NV: Context Press.

Shafranske, E.P. (ed.) (1996) *Religion and the Clinical Practice of Psychology*, Washington: American Psychological Association.

Shore, B. (1996) *Culture in Mind. Cognition, Culture and the Problem of Meaning*, Oxford: Oxford University Press.

Shweder, R.A. (1991) *Thinking Through Cultures. Expeditions in Cultural Psychology*, Cambridge, MA: Harvard University Press.

Valsiner, J. (1999) *Culture and Human Development*, London: Sage.

Vergote, A. (1988) *Guilt and Desire: Religious Attitudes and their Pathological Derivatives*, New Haven, CT: Yale University Press (originally published 1978).

—— (1996) *Religion, Belief and Unbelief. Psychological Study*, Amsterdam/Leuven: Rodopi/Leuven University Press (originally published 1983).

Vygotsky, L.S. (1978) *Mind in Society: The Development of Higher Psychological Processes*, ed. and transl. M. Cole, Cambridge: Harvard University Press.

—— (1991) "Imagination and creativity," *Soviet Psychology* 29: 73–88 (originally published 1931).

Wulff, D.M. (1997) *Psychology of Religion. Classic and Contemporary*, 2nd edn, New York: Wiley.

Wundt, W. (1900–1909) *Völkerpsychologie, eine Untersuchung der Entwicklungsgesetze von Sprache, Mythos und Sitte (Folk Psychology: An Investigation of the Laws of Development of Language, Myth and Mores)*, Leipzig: Engelmann.

Section 2

Perspectives on modernity and post-modernity

4 Does (the history of) religion and psychological studies have a subject?[1]

Susan E. Henking

Historian of psychology Roger Smith (1988) has asked: "Does the history of psychology have a subject?" In elaborating his answer to this question, Smith identified several possible candidates for that subject:

1   the history of psychology as an area of study (or perhaps as a discipline);
2   the objects that this history studies (i.e., its subject matter);
3   the subject that does the writing (i.e., the authorial self).

(Smith 1988: 148)

Extending Smith's discussion, one may understand psychology's subject as the discipline and as the range of human subjectivities construed and, indeed, constructed by the diverse traditions and practices of the field – experimental, theoretical, authorial, clinical and otherwise. Similarly, Danziger (1994) notes that a critical history of the field might affect three aspects of psychology: its conception of its subject matter, its understanding of its practices, and the nature of its social contribution (479). In raising the question of whether the history of psychology has a subject and in linking critical history to a reframing of psychology, Smith and Danziger each push psychology to widen its purview and point to the complex entanglements of the history of human subjectivity with human subjectivity itself (Smith 1998).

Reframing religion and psychological studies (RPS) by asking an analogous question requires asking what our object of study is, who or what the subjects of our work are, what the practices of our discipline and specialty are, and, indeed, who "we" are as authorial (and teacherly) subjects. Such questions push the boundaries of religion and psychological studies, asking us to renew the enterprise arising in the interstices between the academic study of religion and the academic study of human subjectivity, sometimes labeled the human sciences.

To comprehend this renewed enterprise requires teasing apart a series of historical linkages, epistemological conundrums, and theoretical underpinnings, each of which contributes to the shaping of the field. Mapping a renewed religion and psychological studies is, thus, an exercise in theorizing, in taking a position, in creating and sustaining communal forms in particular ways. It is also an exercise in historical reflection. Recognizing intellectual disciplines as social authorizing practices and locating them within history and culture is part of this endeavor. Indeed,

> As scholars of social authorizing practices, we fail to fulfill our role as public intellectuals when we decline to demonstrate consistently that such a thing as society, text, nation, ethnicity, tradition, intuition, gender, myth, or even religion, is "not a natural or god-given entity, but is a constructed, manufactured, even in some cases invented object, with a history of struggle and conquest behind it."
>
> (McCutcheon 1997a: 459, citing Said 1996: 33)

In other words, mapping a renewed religion and psychological studies requires critical reflection on its manufacture.

Such reflection has ordinarily emphasized that religion and psychological studies resides at the intersection of two intellectual domains. Today, each of these domains is in creative flux (sometimes known as crisis). Reframing religion and psychological studies requires responding to the many cross-currents evident within the histories of both the academic study of religion and academic reflection on human subjectivity. It requires pondering: is our field a hybrid? a jointly defined field? a misfit? a conversation? And it requires attending to thorny issues at the very center of contemporary theory and culture, including those raised in resisting both the metaphysical claims of religion and the cultural authority of positivist epistemologies. As religious studies moves beyond its religious past in a fashion which "may have more to do with developing our skills for naturalistic and explanatory theorizing than many scholars of religion have so far realized" (McCutcheon 1997b: xi–xii), so psychology is becoming an increasingly "polycentric" (Danziger 1994: 479) framing of human subjectivities. As psychology reaches out to engage contemporary debate regarding the nature of "science," religious studies must find its way within the context of both the cultural authority of religion and contemporary interpretations of *Religionswissenschaften*, including those aspects of the academic study of religion which emerged with the rise to dominance of positivist social science.

While marginal to historically dominant modes of academic study of religion (McCutcheon 1997b: 21), the naturalistic (reductionistic) approach is central to (and indeed, strongly criticized as hegemonic within) the wider academy. Navigating the methodological and theoretical tension between a religious studies still seeking a route beyond metaphysics and a psychology whose hegemonic positivism is under criticism from within is a requisite of the reframing of religion and psychological studies. Such reframing requires rejection of naive scientist or objectivist approaches as well as avoidance of the naturalizing of socially constructed disciplines. Religion and psychological studies, that is, must come fully to grips with current challenges to epistemology while simultaneously avoiding the quagmire of non-reductionist religiosity. Accomplishing this requires critical reflection upon our origin myths and renewed intellectual engagement with dialogue partners which push us beyond the narrow confines of religion and psychological studies as we have heretofore understood it.

Looking backwards: origin myths and the manufacture of RPS

"To write the history of a discipline is to state what the discipline is, and this, in the social sciences, is often highly contentious" (John Burrow as cited in Smith 1998: 5). Current debate regarding the nature of objectivity makes it apparent that the biographical, historical and cultural embeddedness of intellectual work is methodologically important (Stone 1998). Like other fields, religious studies mythologizes its disciplinary history and must struggle with the complexities of presentist and historicist accounts of its origins (Henking 1993; Jones 1977: 291–2; Jones 1983; Samelson 1974; Stocking 1969; Vande Kemp n.d.: 4). Likewise, understandings of the history of psychology and of the human sciences more broadly have undergone significant change as they move toward a more "critical" history (Furumoto 1989; Smith 1998).

The "subdiscipline" or "dialogical field" of religion and psychological studies has faced – and continues to face – similar difficulties and opportunities. Like other fields, it has rationalized its present form by narrating its history. And, it has reconstructed its theoretical agenda by reflecting anew on past and future. In 1987, for example, Peter Homans published an entry in the *Encyclopedia of Religion* which offered what became an influential narration of the history of the "psychology and religion movement" in the United States. Homans began by attending to "definition and context." He wrote:

> it is essential to clarify at the outset the meaning of the terms *psychology* and *religion*. They are not cognate or parallel terms. *Psychology* denotes a science or method for the study of subjective states. On the other hand, *religion* refers to a series of historical and cultural expressions or phenomena and not to a method or science.
>
> (Homans 1987: 66)

Having distinguished in this way between the two phenomena, Homans noted that the psychology and religion movement "does not refer to a particular method for the study of religious expressions ... [but] an intellectual movement in which different disciplines are mixed" (1987: 66). Thus, the history of religion and psychological studies was entangled, for Homans, with its then contemporary form.

Having set the scene, Homans turned to an examination of the movement from the point of view of its development and history. In doing so, he emphasized historical and cultural connections between religion and psychology across time. Homans' story began with what he labeled "Psychology of Religion, 1885–1930," associated with names like James, Leuba and Starbuck, focused on topics like conversion and adolescence, and connected to the emergence of psychology within higher education and the church. This approach, he argued, declined in significance in the 1930s, and a dialogical interaction between psychoanalysis, existentialism and theology associated, for example, with Paul Tillich, emerged and achieved dominance. A shift to a transitional period occurred in the 1960s; this period was followed, in the 1970s and 1980s, by what Homans labels the segmentation of the movement. Homans depicted these decades, contemporaneous with his essay, as a time when "theological, historical-anthropological, and social scientific orientations coexist within their own clusters of allied disciplines and subdisciplines. In this period, very different writers with very different audiences work simultaneously in very different institutional settings" (68).

In telling this story, Homans depicted several types of interaction between religion and psychology. Central to this narrative theorization of the field are notions of secularization (and differentiation) as well as the framing of a relationship between two different areas of inquiry under various rubrics – dialogue, competition, historical interaction, and the like. Homans is not alone in his myth-making.

This tale of religion and psychological studies is reiterated – and contested – elsewhere. Others, for example, offer narrations which emphasize integration of the two fields (Vande Kemp n.d.) or extend the narrative to the work of pre-Jamesians (Spilka 1987). Many emphasize a decline of attention in the mid 1930s, sometimes citing Homans' work in doing so (Byrnes 1984: 15–16). Still others offer alternative periodizations of interactions between religion and psychology, focusing on particular arenas such as psychotherapy (Vande Kemp 1985) or psychoanalysis (Michel 1984), or argue for linkages between religion and wider aspects of psychology (Vande Kemp 1998), or respond to contemporary historiography's rejection of grand narrative by turning their attention to a more detailed examination of a single era (Taves 1999) or theme (Hoopes 1989).

Of particular note are works which enable us to see the lacunae in dominant narratives. While not directed specifically at Homans' article, the *Encyclopedia of Religion* itself has been criticized for its limited "Chicago" approach (McMullen 1989; McCutcheon 1997b: 139–44). Beyond this, historians of psychology, of religious studies, and of their interaction point us in additional directions. An early work by Misiak and Staudt (1954), for example, offers a discussion of Catholicism and psychology, thereby reminding us to reflect on the overwhelming emphasis upon Protestantism characteristic of the Homans narrative. In doing so, Misiak and Staudt (1954) also remind us of the broader global context within which intellectual work takes place by examining an array of international data from Belgium, the Netherlands, and elsewhere. Byrnes (1984) offers an alternative nudge away from American Protestant emphases by noting the links of James' work to Asian Studies (10ff.). Moreover, an array of scholarship extends Homans' emphasis upon institutions to elaborate on the crucial role of organizations in the history of our field. In particular, Misiak and Staudt (1954) discuss the role of the American Catholic Psychological Association, founded in 1948, which later becomes "Psychologists Interested in Religious Issues," Division 36 of the American Psychological Association. This division of the APA was renamed "Psychology of Religion" (Vande Kemp 1998: 205; Vande Kemp, n.d. See also Belzen 1999: 247, n. 2). Its history stands over against that of "Person, Culture and Religion" which operates within the American Academy of Religion.

Such work reminds us that a "history of struggle and conquest" (McCutcheon 1997a: 459) underlies much of the history of religion and psychological studies, that some analyses risk enhancing the isolation of our purportedly dialogical field, and that histories may reinforce contemporary trends. It raises the possibility that fragmentation (or segmentation) of religion and psychological studies is a product of religious difference. It raises, as well, the possibility that nationalisms affect theoretical and disciplinary formulations. And it reminds us that history as a grand narrative has been increasingly challenged as its entanglement with the (history of) human subjectivities becomes a matter of critical debate (Smith 1998). Most crucially, it makes apparent that the future of religion and psychological studies can be limited by – and enhanced by – institutions of disciplinarity; strategies which locate religion and psychological studies within either psychology or religious studies limit the multidisciplinary and interdisciplinary potential of the academic study of religion, the academic study of human subjectivities, and religion and psychological studies *per se*.

In sum, histories of religion and psychological studies both narrate and manufacture, establishing the limits of the present and future in (re)constructing the past. Homans' narrative thus stands as an example of the potential and the risk of history in shaping academic inquiry. As Roger Smith has put it, "when the narrative brings the story into the present ... it is not possible to claim truth for any current position. The history cannot avoid being an intervention in contemporary argument about the nature of the human sciences" (Smith 1998: 11).

Reframing the historical: interventions, definitions and contexts

Demythologizing religion and psychological studies requires us to understand history as much more messy than Homans' narrative makes apparent. Indeed, as Kurt Danziger has put it, "The way in which a scholarly (or any other) community relates to its own history depends on the way in which tradition is mobilized to support an ongoing pattern of community life"

(Danziger 1994: 471). Reconsidering the history of the field permits us to ask anew, "What is (or are) the relation(s) between religion and psychological studies?" In reflecting on this question from a metatheoretical perspective, one is pushed to (re)examine the theoretical underpinnings of two phenomena and to consider anew fruitful relations between them. As we move into the twenty-first century, we may ask, then, what the relation between religious studies and the academic study of human subjectivities (sometimes labeled the human sciences) might be.

In approaching this question, we might adopt a modified form of Homans' (1987) approach and begin with "definitions and contexts." As noted above, Homans' history was founded upon "definitions and contexts" which involved arguing that psychology and religion "are not cognate or parallel terms" (1987: 66). In the late 1990s, this perspective was increasingly challenged as we have come to understand both psychology and religion as historical and cultural phenomena and to understand both as methods, sciences, or forms of academic inquiry. As we enter the twenty-first century we may, thus, ask what understandings of religion and psychological studies emerge as we move beyond Homans' argument that religion and psychology are neither parallel nor cognate to an understanding of them as, indeed, parallel phenomena. To answer this query requires renewed reflection on the academic study of religion, on psychological studies, and on the "and" which conjoins these two enterprises.

The academic study of religion

Debate about the nature of religion (including the referent of the term) (Eliade and Tracy 1980; Clarke and Byrne 1993; Saler 1993) and the academic study of religion is not new. Nor is it settled. Indeed, "religion" may be the "centrally contested concept"[2] of the academic study of religion. Both explicitly and implicitly, the literature of the field asks: "What is religion?" Equally importantly, the literature inquires: "How should we understand religion?" The many texts which constitute the academic study of religion offer a wide array of answers (and types of answer) to these questions. And many more offer meta-reflection on these answers, distinguishing between those who care for and those who oppose religion (Wilken 1989), between theology and religious studies, between non-reductionist and reductionist theoretical models, interpretive and explanatory perspectives as well as humanistic and social scientific studies. Much of the backdrop of the field involves arguing for or against the legitimacy of these various approaches. Histories of the academic study of religion as well as sweeping theorizations of its domain disagree regarding its disciplinary status (e.g., is it disciplinary, interdisciplinary, or about a subject matter rather than a method and hence a "field"?), the place of methodology (e.g., its importance relative to data; whether the field ought have a single method or many; and whether any particular method is appropriate), the status of empathic involvement versus detached observation, the adoption of social scientific versus humanistic approaches, and the reducibility versus the irreducibility of religion (Vernoff 1983: 109–10; see also Capps 1995; McCutcheon 1999; Preus 1987; Sharpe 1986).

While the academic study of religion may be understood as a widely inclusive endeavor incorporating these many approaches beneath its umbrella, "religious studies" might refer to a perspective which emphasizes the need to understand and explain religion as a human endeavor and experience. From this perspective it is axiomatic "that 'religion could be understood without benefit of clergy' and without needing 'commitments about its causes *different* from the assumptions one might use to understand and explain other realms of culture' (Preus 1987: x)" (McCutcheon 1997b: ix). Adopting such an approach means, of course, that "the self-evidence of religion as a unified, personal, and socially autonomous phenomenon needs to be held up to critical examination" (McCutcheon 1997b: xi). And, in considering the field which seeks to understand the phenomena of religion, it means that the "dream of a unified, autonomous study of religion must be dropped in favor of an interdisciplinary model" (McCutcheon 1997b: 5, citing Arthur McCalla).

This perspective limits the range of religious studies by eliminating religious enterprises themselves from its purview as other than its subject matter and favoring the development of a (secular) academic approach to understanding the phenomena of religion. As such, the academic study of religion is parallel to the academic study of psychology. Moreover, this argument is oriented toward an understanding of the historical and cultural embeddedness of academic work. While religious studies is not religion, neither is it removed from culture or history.

Psychological studies: the academic study of human subjectivity

Though institutionalized in significantly different ways, psychology, like the academic study of religion, is an academic endeavor which is polycentric. Indeed, according to Byrnes (1984), "by 1940 it was fairly clear that the goal of making psychology *the* science of human nature was unattainable. Psychology could be only one of a number of studies dealing with human behavior, its motives and causes" (9–10). As Roger Smith reminds us, " 'Psychology' is the generic sign of a cluster of competing would-be disciplines. Psychology has had (and continues to have) a protean character, differing with specific, local circumstances" (Smith 1988: 156).

As such a polycentric field, psychology is engaged in multiple disputes regarding its identity as a "natural" or as a "human" science. And, certainly, the meaning of science, while assumed by some, has been and is being interrogated by an array of insiders whose use of history and contemporary philosophical work has moved beyond celebration to criticism and reconstruction of science and of the "psychological subject" (Bayer and Shotter 1998; Danziger 1997; Smith 1998: 7–10).

In Homans' narration of the "psychology and religion movement," the term psychology "denotes a science or method for the study of subjective states" (1987: 66); psychology, here, is quite definitively differentiated from phenomena of history and culture. Contemporary critical approaches to psychology resist both construals. Such work argues for a move beyond any narrow construal of psychology to an understanding of the academic study of human subjectivities which we might, using shorthand, label the "human sciences" (Smith 1998). Like religious studies, this view of psychology recognizes its historical and cultural embeddedness as well as the complex epistemological and methodological debate swirling around psychology in the 1990s. Like the academic study of religion, the academic study of human subjectivities is in creative crisis as we enter the twenty-first century.

Varieties of connections: of, as, and

Religion and psychological studies has been an umbrella which shelters an array of connectors between two domains: psychology *of* religion, religion *as* psychology and psychology *as* religion, for example. As Judith Van Herik has noted: "Areas with an "and" in their titles require definition because the "and" serves to specify neither which is the method and which the datum in a particular instance nor which, if either, contains the topic" (Van Herik 1984: 66).

Though sometimes understood (and functioning) as undifferentiated, religion and psychological studies has also been construed as the intersection of two broad and messy areas of academic reflection. In the past, for example, I have moved from Homans' (1987) historical argument to identify three types of relevant scholarship (Henking, 1993). Like psychology *of* religion, *social scientific interpretations of religion* involve the adoption of theoretical and methodological stances characteristic of the social sciences in order to investigate religious phenomena. *Dialogical* work involves a conversation between the two enterprises of religion and the social sciences in an effort to translate, integrate or differentiate between the two phenomena. (As understood here, dialogical work occurs between theology and the social sciences.) A third type of work, emphasizing *historical and cultural connections* between the two enterprises, moves beyond ahistorical dialogue as well as the hierarchy implicit in social scientific interpretations of religion.

Whether construed narrowly or more inclusively, "[i]nterest in the so-called 'psychology of religion' appears to be reviving" (Belzen 1999: 229). And yet, contemporary debate regarding religion and psychological studies remains unresolved. As Jacob Belzen recently wrote:

> in spite of its lengthy history, the psychology of religion is a problematic enterprise and many of its basic questions – what kind of scholarship, if

any, is it; what is its place in academia; what is it about – still await answers. To some observers, research on religion is a field of applied psychology ... Others, however, strongly opposed to this view, argue that the psychology of religion belongs to theoretical psychology ... As with other significant psychological research focusing on a specific domain (e.g., art, literature, sport, war and peace), there is no clear institutional unity among people involved in the psychology of religion. They are found in departments of philosophy, psychiatry, anthropology, religious studies and in the various specialized departments of psychology.

(Belzen 1999: 231)

The field is rife with historical disagreement regarding the object of its study, its purpose, its philosophical basis, in large part because the academic study of religion and the human subject are each rife with equally divisive, long-standing and theoretically significant debate. With disagreement and debate come both the potential for productive work and the risk of failure.

Asking, then, whether (the history of) religion and psychological studies has a subject raises a variety of possibilities. In this situation of creative crisis, religious studies might be understood to be one among many forms of the academic study of human subjectivities. Second, one might utilize the conceptual, methodological and other apparatuses of the critical human sciences to understand religion. Likewise, the conceptual, methodological and other apparatuses of religious studies might expand the potential of the critical human sciences. Thus, a dialogue between these two academic enterprises might involve efforts to translate, integrate or differentiate the two phenomena. And one might emphasize historical and cultural connections between the two enterprises.

The umbrella of religion and psychological studies, that is, shelters an ever widening array of (parallel) secular enterprises. At the center of each of these possibilities lie the epistemological, theoretical, methodological and cultural concerns which are central to religious studies and to the academic study of human subjectivities. As Belzen puts it: "Religion as a cultural phenomenon is always more than can be conceived of within any, necessarily partial, psychological perspective" (Belzen 1999: 246). Religious studies requires a critical religion and psychological studies for an adequate understanding of its subject. Similarly, given the cultural importance of religion, critical psychology's efforts to understand the individual and the social world increasingly must benefit from the expertise of religious studies and, hence, religion and psychological studies.

Triangulations: situating RPS in wider conversations

The metaphor of dialogue – of conversation – runs throughout much of contemporary discussion of religious studies (Berling 1993) and has figured much within debate regarding interdisciplinary and multidisciplinary thinking. While there are many potential contributors to the history and culture of the contemporary academy and, thus, to the conversation between the academic study of religion (religious studies) and the academic study of human subjectivities (psychological studies), I will discuss two which are entangled within contemporary United States culture: the contributions of feminisms and related intellectual endeavors, and the place of the academy within wider public discourse. Both psychology and religious studies are faced with central challenges emerging from the civil rights movement, from feminisms, from the changing place of the academy in culture – challenges which are simultaneously political, theoretical, and intellectual. Such challenges call religious studies, psychology, and religion and psychological studies to renewed understandings.

The place of feminism and related matters

In discussing the changing shape of historical inquiry within psychology, Kurt Danziger (1994) emphasizes the move beyond "feminist empiricism" to a deeper critique and reconstruction of the discipline informed by feminist critique of science. Likewise, Laurel Furumoto (1989) points to the crucial role of feminism in challenging traditional histories of psychology. In the academic study of religion, feminisms of various sorts have contributed to the reshaping of the field substantially in recent decades. Here, the dominant voice has been theological, in feminist, mujorista, lesbian/gay/queer and other identity-based forms of religious reflection. More recently, religious studies is beginning to be challenged by feminists raising questions about how to undertake a non-theological religious studies within a context which recognizes and validates previously marginalized persons and perspectives within the field (Henking 1996; Comstock and Henking 1997). This has included work on figures within the canon of religious studies as well as constructive theoretical and historical work (a very different enterprise than constructive theology). Indeed, the impact of feminism, for example, has been labeled a paradigm shift within the academy and within religious studies (Christ 1987; Gross 1996).

Feminisms and other justice-oriented (and identity-based) intellectual and political challenges call for a remaking of the psychological subject (Bayer and Shotter 1998), the religious studies subject, and the subject of religion and psychological studies (see Jonte-Pace in this volume). Feminism has also called for a remaking of the academy – of particular disciplines, of pedagogy, and of the institution itself (e.g., Langland and Gove 1983; O'Barr 1989; Minnich *et al.* 1988). In this, feminist studies, alongside an array of other new intellectual perspectives and institutional forms which entered the academy in recent decades, have called for renewed attention to the epistemologies which underlie intellectual work (Minnich 1990). As a result, the disciplines – including those which meet in the conversation once called "religion and psychological studies" – are sites of confrontation, crisis and creativity (Nelson and Gaonkar 1996).

Religion and psychology in the academy

All of these issues – religious studies, psychologies, and the remakings of our subjects associated with feminisms and related matters – interact in various ways within our culture. Recent decades which saw the rise of such important intellectual and political challenges have also been accompanied by upheavals and responses within and without higher education. Debate rages on regarding the nature of the academy, the place of religion in American culture, and the role of psychology in our lives – in intellectual work, on television, in polling booths and demonstrations, in clinics and religious institutions.

One crucial site of this ongoing cultural upheaval – and the conversation which is religion and psychological studies – is the academy. Thus, an important part of a renewed religion and psychological studies involves contemporary critical discourse regarding the academy. Two aspects of such discussions merit particular attention, viz., those which attend to the role of the academic as public intellectual and as teacher. Both discussions are aspects of the culture shaping religious studies and the academic study of human subjectivities too frequently taken for granted as we seek to comprehend our work.

As Russell McCutcheon has noted:

> Outside of small numbers of readers and writers, few members of our own society – and few members of the academy – know what we [religious studies intellectuals] do or know who we are, let alone are influenced in their public decisions by our scholarship. When one examines books written by those who advocate an increased role for religious commitment (most often this turns out to be a particular form of Protestant Christian commitment) in the affairs of the nation, it is as if the academic study of religion – even in its earlier incarnation as comparative religion – has never existed or made any significant contribution to the human sciences. It is as if we had nothing to add to public affairs whatsoever and that theologians are the only commentators on "religion" who have a role to play in helping to decide issues of law, justice, and social welfare.
>
> Given the tools that scholars of religion routinely employ in their wide-ranging studies, I believe we have a vital role to play in public affairs but it is a role that is rather different from the one championed by many current writers.
>
> (McCutcheon 1997a: 444)

And what is that role? As McCutcheon puts it, the role of the religious studies (or other academic) professional as public intellectual involves "the active business of uncloaking the ahistoric rhetoric that makes its appearance in public debates," allowing forces within our culture to "authorize the local as universal and the contingent as necessary" (ibid.: 451, 454). A similarly controversial role for the public intellectual awaits those who seek to critically reflect upon the role of psychology (and science more broadly) in our lives. Uncritical acceptance of the authority of science – like ahistorical religious certainties – merits the attention of scholars of social authorizing practices. The appropriate role for the public intellectual is a critical role. And the student of a renewed religion and psychological studies stands at a particularly important juncture – helping us to understand the complex intertwining of expertise and authority circulating in our culture around "religion," "psychology," and "science."

Such reflections remind us to reflect on where religious studies and the human sciences take place and why. This raises the question of where we publish our scholarship, what conferences we attend (or don't), what we read and to whom we listen as well as the question of the relation of clinic, religious institution, and other sites of work. It raises, moreover, the vexed question of the relation of religious studies to the humanities and/or social sciences and the question of the allocation of subject matters to departments of psychology or religious studies.

A significant portion of our engagement with publics beyond the academy takes place within the context of the classroom. Contemporary reflection on pedagogy abounds – from critical, feminist, and related political perspectives – and in the form of sessions at professional conferences, book series, and new journals (e.g., hooks 1994; Giroux and McLaren 1994). Both the religious studies classroom and the psychology classroom have been the subject of substantial reflection.[3]

Links between the history of disciplines and the classroom are not new – certainly the making of any academic endeavor is, in part, the making of a lineage of scholars and teachers (Grimes 1995: 40–41). Triangulating with concerns of pedagogy in a reflective way is also not new. The longer history of a concern for teaching and its relation to religion and psychological studies is attested to both by historical links between RPS and religious education and by particular courses offered at key institutions such as the University of Chicago. In 1956–7, for example, the University of Chicago Divinity School offered, under the rubric of an area of study then known as "Religion and Personality," a course entitled "Teaching Religion in Colleges and Universities." The course, taught by Perry LeFevre, was described in the *University of Chicago Course Announcement* as follows:

> Designed to help students intending to teach, regardless of their fields of specialization: philosophy of teaching, teaching methods, the learning process, and curriculum content and organization are considered in the light of the theological foundations of higher education, the interrelationships of disciplines, and the existence situation of the college student.

In the decades since this course was offered, feminism has renewed its presence in American culture and faced backlashes within and without the academy, the crucial place of teaching in higher education has been recognized, and culture wars have redefined public discourse about higher education. Meanwhile, religion and psychological studies has flourished at the University of Chicago – and been dissolved. What is our future?

The future of religion and psychological studies

My preferred future is one which recognizes and engages with the exciting critical work being pursued within psychology, which is fully interdisciplinary (and even multidisciplinary), and which is engaged with central aspects of religious studies. That future, I suspect, will continue to be multiple; its best work, I believe, will be at the center of the efflorescence of theoretical work within religious studies and psychology. As we undertake this work, we must become part of the key theoretical and metatheoretical debates within religious studies and the academic study of what it means to be human. To do so, we must be located in the centrally marginal position characteristic of the best (and the worst) of interlocutors.

To be our best, rather than our worst, like religious studies and like psychology and the human sciences more broadly, we will have to face squarely the epistemological challenges of the changing faces of scholarship. Certainly, attending to such epistemological challenges will mean listening seriously to those of feminist and other critical theoreticians from within and beyond religious studies and, in our case, from within and beyond psychology and other human sciences, including cultural studies.[4] Facing the epistemological will also mean facing the historical in different ways than we have yet. Our prospects require us to think retrospectively as well, challenging the ways our current sense of our field's history is itself celebratory rather than critical (Danziger 1994: 471). In this, "[t]he quest for methodological integrity yields to the desire to understand" (Homans 1968: 10).

As we accomplish this, we must rethink our disciplinary myths – of secularization and Protestant origins, of differentiation and tension, of objectivity and subjectivity, of cultural criticism both for and against religion. As we move forward, mapping and manufacturing are conjoined enterprises – and religion and psychological studies becomes a major player in the intellectual and political work of the culture in which we are embedded, the culture which is the academy and public life. The social authorizing practices of both religion and psychology must be subjected to critical inquiry. As we undertake this work, we can reconstruct the social contributions of our field as well. We can, that is, regain the courage of cultural criticism which is our heritage from Freud, from Jung, from feminists and others and, in doing so, favor the secular and seek meaning in the worlds in which we work and live.

Notes

1 I am indebted to Betty M. Bayer for exposing me to wider notions of psychology and for help in thinking through this paper. This includes pointing me to the work of Roger Smith and Kurt Danziger. I am also indebted to Diane Jonte-Pace and Bill Parsons for their patience, editorial advice, and the original request to participate in a panel which led to this paper.

2 I am indebted to Donald N. Levine of the University of Chicago's Department of Sociology for this phrase. I heard him use it many years ago in class and have remembered it ever since.

3 Thus, for example, both fields support a journal focused on teaching: *Teaching Theology and Religious Studies* and *Teaching Psychology*.

4 The implied argument of this chapter is that those aspects of the academic study of religion which adopt a wide definition of religion and move beyond *sui generis* notions involve a religious studies which is cultural studies. After submitting the chapter, I encountered Timothy Fitzgerald's (2000) book, *The Ideology of Religious Studies*, which makes an analogous argument.

References

Bayer, B.M. and Shotter, J. (eds) (1998) *Reconstructing the Psychological Subject*, London: Sage.

Belzen, J.A. (1999) "The cultural psychological approach to religion," *Theory and Psychology* 9(2): 229–55.

Berling, J.A. (1993) "Is conversation about religion possible? (And what can religionists do to promote it?)" *Journal of the American Academy of Religion* 61(1): 1–22.

Byrnes, J.F. (1984) *The Psychology of Religion*, New York: Free Press.

Capps, W.H. (1995) *Religious Studies: The Making of a Discipline*, Minneapolis: Fortress Press.

Christ, C. (1987) "Toward a paradigm shift in the academy and religious studies," in Christie L. Farnham (ed.) *The Impact of Feminist Research in the Academy*, Bloomington: University of Indiana Press, pp. 53–76.

Clarke, P.B. and Byrne, P. (1993) *Religion Defined and Explained*, New York: St. Martin's Press.

Comstock, G.D. and Henking, S.E. (eds) (1997) *Que(e)rying Religion: A Critical Anthology*, New York: Continuum.

Danziger, K. (1994) "Does the history of psychology have a future?" *Theory and Psychology* 4(4): 467–84.

—— (1997) *Naming the Mind: How Psychology Found Its Language*, London: Sage.

Eliade, M. and Tracy, D. (eds) (1980) *What is Religion? An Inquiry for Christian Theology*, New York: Seabury Press.

Fitzgerald, T. (2000) *The Ideology of Religious Studies*, New York: Oxford University Press.

Furumoto, L. (1989) "The new history of psychology," *G. Stanley Hall Lecture Series* 9: 5–34.

Giroux, H.A. and McLaren, P. (eds) (1994) *Between Borders: Pedagogy and the Politics of Cultural Studies*, New York: Routledge.

Grimes, R.L. (1995) *Marrying and Burying: Rites of Passage in a Man's Life*, Boulder, CO: Westview Press.

Gross, R. (1996) *Feminism and Religion: An Introduction*, Boston: Beacon Press.

Henking, S.E. (1993) "Placing the social sciences: cases at the intersection of the histories of disciplines and religions," *Religious Studies Review* 19(2): 116–24.

—— (1996) "The open secret: dilemmas of advocacy in the religious studies classroom," in Patricia Meyer Spacks (ed.) *Advocacy in the Classroom: Problems and Possibilities*, New York: St Martin's Press, pp. 245–59.

Homans, P. (1968) *The Dialogue Between Theology and Psychology*, Chicago: University of Chicago Press.

—— (1987) "The psychology and religion movement," in Mircea Eliade (ed.), *Encyclopedia of Religion*, New York: Macmillan, vol. 12, pp. 66–74.

hooks, b. (1994) *Teaching to Transgress: Education as the Practice of Freedom*, New York: Routledge.

Hoopes, J. (1989) *Consciousness in New England: From Puritanism and Ideas to Psychoanalysis and Semiotic*, Baltimore: Johns Hopkins University Press.

Jones, R.A. (1977) "On understanding a sociological classic," *American Journal of Sociology* 83(2): 279–319.

—— (1983) "The new history of sociology," *Annual Review of Sociology* 9: 447–69.

Langland, E. and Gove, W. (eds) (1983) *A Feminist Perspective in the Academy: The Difference It Makes*, Chicago: University of Chicago Press.

McCutcheon, R.T. (1997a) "A default of critical intelligence? The scholar of religion as public intellectual," *Journal of the American Academy of Religion* 65(2): 443–68.

—— (1997b) *Manufacturing Religion: The Discourse on Sui Generis Religion and the Politics of Nostalgia*, Oxford: Oxford University Press.

—— (ed.) (1999) *The Insider/Outsider Problem in the Study of Religion: A Reader*, London and New York: Cassell.

McMullen, N. (1989) "The *Encyclopedia of Religion*: a critique from the perspective of the history of the Japanese religious traditions," *Method and Theory in the Study of Religion*, 1: 80–96.

Michel, S. (1984) "American conscience and the unconscious: psychoanalysis and the rise of personal religion, 1906–1963," *Psychoanalysis and Contemporary Thought* 7(3): 387–421.

Minnich, E. (1990) *Transforming Knowledge*, Philadelphia: Temple University Press.

Minnich, E., O'Barr, J., and Rosenfeld, R. (eds) (1988) *Reconstructing the Academy: Women's Education and Women's Studies*, Chicago: University of Chicago Press.

Misiak, H. and Staudt, V.M. (1954) *Catholics in Psychology: A Historical Survey*, New York: McGraw Hill.

Nelson, C. and Gaonkar, D.P. (eds) (1996) *Disciplinarity and Dissent in Cultural Studies*, New York: Routledge.

O'Barr, J.F. (1989) *Women and a New Academy: Gender and Cultural Contexts*, Madison: University of Wisconsin Press.

Preus, J.S. (1987) *Explaining Religion: Criticism and Theory from Bodin to Freud*, New Haven: Yale University Press.

Said, E. (1996) *Representations of the Intellectual*, New York: Vintage.

Saler, B. (1993) *Conceptualising Religion: Immanent Anthropologists, Transcendent Natives and Unbounded Categories*, Numen Supplement Series vol. 56, Boston: Brill Academic Press.

Samelson, F. (1974) "History, origin myth and ideology: 'discovery' of social psychology," *Journal for the Theory of Social Behavior* 4: 217–31.

exton, V. S. (1986) "Psychology of religion: some accomplishments and challenges," *Journal of Psychology and Christianity* 5(2): 79–83. Cited here as reprinted in H. Newton Maloney (ed.), *Psychology of Religion: Personalities, Problems, Possibilities*, Grand Rapids, Michigan: Baker Book House, pp. 37–43.

Sharpe, E.J. (1986) *Comparative Religion: A History*, 2nd edn, La Salle, Illinois: Open Court.

Smith, R. (1988) "Does the history of psychology have a subject?" *History of the Human Sciences* 1(2): 147–77.

—— (1998) "The big picture: writing psychology into the history of the human sciences," *Journal of the History of the Behavioral Sciences* 34(1): 1–13.

Spilka, B. (1987) "Religion and science in early American psychology," *Journal of Psychology and Theology* 15(1): 3–9.

Stocking, G. (1969) "On the limits of 'presentism' and 'historicism' in the historiography of the behavioral sciences," in G. Stocking (ed.), *Race, Culture and Evolution: Essays on the History of Anthropology*, New York: Free Press, pp. 1–12.

Stone, J.R. (ed.) (1998) *The Craft of Religious Studies*, New York: St Martin's Press.

Taves, A. (1999) *Fits, Trances, and Visions: Experiencing Religion and Explaining Experience from Wesley to James*, Princeton: Princeton University Press.

Vande Kemp, H. (n.d.) "Historical perspective: religion and clinical psychology in America," in Peter J. Verhagen and Gerrit Glas (eds) *Psyche and Faith: Beyond Professionalism* (Proceedings of the first international symposium of the Christian Association of Psychiatrists, Psychologists and Psychotherapists (CVPPP) in the Netherlands), Zoetermeer: Uitgeverij Boekencentrum, pp. 3–35.

—— (1985) "Psychotherapy as a religious process: a historical heritage," *The Psychotherapy Patient* 1(3): 135–46.

—— (1998) "Christian psychologies for the twenty-first century: lessons from history," *Journal of Psychology and Christianity* 17(3): 197–209.

Van Herik, J. (1984) " 'Thick description' and psychology of religion," in Robert L. Moore and Frank E. Reynolds (eds), *Anthropology and the Study of Religion*, Chicago: Center for the Scientific Study of Religion, pp. 56–74.

Vernoff, C.E. (1983) "Naming the game: a question of the field," *Council on the Study of Religion Bulletin* 14(4): 109–10.

Wilken, R.L. (1989) "Who will speak *for* the religious traditions?" *Journal of the American Academy of Religion* 57(4): 699–718.

5 What is our present?

An Antipodean perspective on the relationship between "psychology" and "religion"

Kathleen V. O'Connor

Introduction

For over two decades I have been preoccupied with the relationship between "psychology" and "religion", particularly as it has been inscribed in what has traditionally been called "the psychology of religion". Throughout this time, this general issue, and possible responses to it, seemed central to me for a number of reasons and I am under no illusion that these reasons were as much personal and shaped by my cultural context as they were academic. The more obvious ones concerned some apprehension and understanding of prevailing notions about "psychology" as a science in the context of debates about epistemology, methodology and causation in the natural and social sciences, as well as some understanding of "religion", both as a cultural and personal phenomenon in human existence and experience, and as an object of psychological inquiry. My concerns here focused particularly on the interplay between theory and method, and on how one might conceptualize, ground and carry out a psychological investigation of religion in the late twentieth century. Less obvious reasons, no doubt related to and embedded in the more obvious, concerned how one could think about a possible future (or futures) for this field of inquiry.

At the beginning of the third millennium, against a background of debates, for example concerning the epistemological status of both psychology as a science and religious experience as a way of knowing; more openness among psychologists of religion to religious pluralism and to investigating both between- and within-group religious differences; attempts to clarify the focus and meaning of psychological research attendant upon the so-called death of the modern subject; an increased readiness to investigate gendered ways of knowing in relation to religion in the context of recent philosophical, cultural and psychoanalytical inquiries about the experiences of women; together with what appears to be a growing willingness among psychologists themselves to consider the ideological issues underlying their own theoretical perspectives and research objectives, I am now even more preoccupied with the centrality of the issue concerning the relationship between "psychology" and "religion" than I was in the early 1970s. Inescapably, as we begin the next millennium these new developments both challenge and engage psychologists in the tasks of developing new frameworks for understanding the relationship between "psychology" and "religion" and new ways of approaching and doing research in different cultural contexts. Inevitably, speculations about the future can only proceed within the context of those activities.

In thinking through the relationships between "psychology" and "religion" in the context of this paper I employ the provocative, useful and tantalizing question: "What is our present?" I do this for a number of reasons: (1) to provide a perspective on the historical heritage; (2) to construct a framework within which to locate and explore the problematic; and (3) to provide a context for thinking about the future. To this end the question serves as a vehicle to explore the relationship between cultural-historical issues and the personal orientations and commitments of researchers that shaped and continue to shape research and the development of different forms of discourse in "the psychology of religion" this century.

Some historical realities and generalities

My initial preoccupation with the relationship between "psychology" and "religion" emerged and took shape as a result of my attempts in the 1970s to get a grasp on "the field of study" that had captivated my interest as a psychologist in Australia. This odyssey began in a psychology department markedly unsympathetic to the study of religion, and in a religious context deeply suspicious of psychology, and continued in quite different cultural, intellectual and attitudinal surrounds during various periods of study and research in England and Belgium. As I studied the Anglo-Australasian, European and North American literatures, I became increasingly aware of a number of realities. Foremost was the widespread and rather optimistic assumption that religion and religious phenomena could be investigated by the same scientific methods used to study other human experience and behavior in psychology, an assumption, I would argue, that remains today, however modified and qualified, as a motivating variable among psychologists who have preserved, or are developing, an interest in research at the interface between "psychology" and "religion".

Other realities readily observed were: the enormous diversity of orientations, methods and content foci evident in the research literature; the complex of influences outside psychology; endless statements and conflicting claims about the field's origins; frequent references to crises in the field; periodic calls to theoretical reconstruction; struggles to establish theoretical foundations; the diverse applied interests and objectives of researchers; seemingly endless debates about the nature and scope of the area of study, its objectives and methods; issues about the identity of the enterprise and what to call it; and, at critical times, doubts about the efficacy and relevance of research. Despite – perhaps because of – the inherent ethnocentrism, parochialism and the peculiarly Christo-centric focus of most reported studies at that time, it was evident in countries where this "field of study" had emerged that its development and evolution was largely shaped by prevailing and particular theoretical, methodological, contextual and personal factors. Although throughout the course of the century it was evident that there had been quite serious attempts to establish a consensus regarding the scope and nature of the enterprise and to formulate and construct adequate research paradigms in different regional settings, the relationship between "psychology" and "religion" remained unclear and uneasy. These observations are by no means unique, and both researchers and historians in the field in North America, in Europe, in England and Australia have commented on and accounted for these phenomena at different times. National reviews of research in *The International Journal for the Psychology of Religion* since its inception in 1991 have also highlighted these issues.

In the development of my own consciousness, thinking and research orientation in Australia I also became increasingly aware that one could not begin to think about the relationship between "psychology" and "religion" and research in the "psychology of religion" apart from a consideration of the particular cultural and micro-cultural contexts in which it is found, and, just as importantly, without taking historical-cultural and personal perspectives on its origins and evolution. When one surveys the current international scene it is evident that diversity is here to stay (cf. O'Connor 1997) and, with regard to this expected pluriformity, my own current thinking is provoked by two related preoccupations. One concerns a deeper examination of the broader historical, philosophical, cultural and contextual issues influencing the development of particular stances and discourses amongst psychologists to "psychology" and to "religion". A second issue concerns the role of more personal factors and positions, commitments and agendas (implicit and explicit ideological issues) in the development of research perspectives, projects and discursive practices within the psychology of religion.

In considering the relationship between "psychology" and "religion" from the vantage point of the late twentieth century, the influences noted above coalesce for me around a consideration of the interplay between the broad historical options evident concerning psychologists' responses to modernity on the one hand, and the more personal implications of the range and nature of prevailing cultural commitments concerning "religion" and "psychology" on the other. My aim in the next section is to develop a framework within which to explore these interrelationships further.

What is our present?

There is a form of reflection that can be traced at least through the last two hundred years of philosophy – across the philosophical spectrum from Kant, Hegel and Nietzsche to more recent scholars like Habermas, Ricoeur and Foucault – which is preoccupied with a single question, one that remains the same although approaches to it, and answers proposed, constantly change: "What is our present?" To ask a question like this about the present in the context of a discussion on the relationship between "psychology" and "religion" is neither as abstract nor as irrelevant as might appear. Although in the work of philosophers this question could be viewed as a heuristic device to address the issues of the day, or as an organizing principle within which to view and construe their life work, or in general philosophy as constituting some form of ontological or metaphysical inquiry into the "Being" of the present, this question is proposed at this point in this paper rather as a way of evoking a range of more pedestrian but nonetheless timely questions that are both general and more specific in nature and relevance: What are things like for us today? In what kinds of situations do we find ourselves? What kinds of issues or conundrums confront us? What constraints or oppressions bind us? How did we get to this point? What are the implications and challenges? How do we move from here? (adapted from May 1993). Undoubtedly many answers can be given to questions like these that are provoked by a consideration of our present, and many avenues to satisfying answers might be taken. It seems to me, however, that despite differences in the questions addressed to the present and in the pathways taken in our efforts to understand it (personal explorations as well as disciplinary routes which have their own defining features and outcomes), they have important things in common. They are all attempts to articulate, in "different regions of our present" (May 1993: 2) and in different realms of our experience and range of activities, how the human subject entered into "language games" (Wittgenstein 1958, 1969) and "games of truth" (Foucault 1988). Concerning these domains, "the questions of what we hold to be true and how we came to do so" (May 1993: 2), and how we talk about and communicate these in relation to ourselves and others in the ordinary course of our lives, and within the disciplinary and work contexts and constraints we operate and work within, are important clues in understanding and attempting to articulate what our present is. However, although undoubtedly pivotal, the importance of these questions seems to me to lie far beyond simply naming the present. May captured the implication of this point well when he argued that:

> The significance of these questions is not confined to their relevance for comprehending our situation. In fact, what is at stake in the questions of what we hold true and how we came to do so is the conduct of our lives. How we understand what we have come to accept about the world and about ourselves, the context in which we place our various knowledges

of things, determines not only the theoretical underpinnings of our epistemology but also the political and ethical commitments of our practice.

(May 1993: 2)

Looking anew at the relationship between "psychology" and "religion" with the aid of the sorts of lenses referred to here, lenses that have been employed widely in philosophical, cultural and feminist studies for quite some time now, seems appropriate and timely. To gain any kind of international perspective we need to know more, not only about what has been done in the field internationally from historical surveys, but why we asked the questions we did, why we took the perspectives and selected and used the methods we did, why we focused on particular topics and how we talked about and framed our research; and, just as importantly, what we did about, or with, the findings of our projects. We need to be more explicit in talking about the dilemmas we struggle with and the ways in which our own horizons changed and shifted, and about the meanings of research for our subjects and the communities of which our subjects are representatives. A consideration of the ideological, political and ethical aspects of our theorizing and practice seems to me to be well overdue. While it is not possible to do this comprehensively within the context of this paper, I do want to begin to open up the issue by reviewing some controversies around "naming the present".

On "naming the present"

David Tracy captured well the dilemma facing researchers across diverse disciplines today when he remarked that "we live in an age that cannot name itself" (Tracy 1990: 66). For some, as he noted:

we are still in an age of modernity and the triumph of the bourgeois subject. For others, we are in a time of the levelling of all traditions and await the return of the repressed traditional and communal subject. For yet others, we are in a post-modern moment where the death of the subject is now upon us as the last receding wave of the death of God.

(ibid.)

Whether one agrees or not with this observation or these namings of the present (modernity, anti-modernity and post-modernity respectively), we are enabled to locate the issues of diversity in the field of "psychology of religion" (with reference to both "psychology" and "religion") as much as its history, in a broader context of debate since these three conflicting namings of the present are at the heart of what Tracy proposes as "the conflict of interpretations in that place which was once construed as the center of history – Western, including Western Christian theological culture" (1990:

66). In effect, the very existence of the conflict on how to name itself, and the inescapable reality of cultural and religious pluralism, demonstrates that the Western, masculine, Christian center can no longer maintain its former unquestioned pre-eminence. Perhaps it has been the case, however, that psychologists of religion have been somewhat slower than others to acknowledge this reality (cf. Hutch 1982) and come to terms with its implications for theorizing and for research. More positively, however, a consideration of debates about naming the present offer a way of consider-ing anew the relationship between "psychology" and "religion", and of exploring across the field internationally the differential mechanisms of adaptation and resistance evident in contemporary change and challenges to accepted scientific and religious certitudes and truths.

Modernity and debates about "naming the present"

Debates about the nature of "modernity" are endless. In reviewing some of the literature on "modernity", several perspectives are evident that differentially take "time" and "history" as points of departure – a broad cultural approach, another linking "modernity" with "Enlightenment" and its particular intellectual projects, and yet another more general and qualitative in nature denoting an historical time consciousness. In philoso-phy debates have most often focused on the relationship of rationality and modernity as epitomized in Descartes' quest for a knowledge that was self-evident to reason, and in Kant's critical "revolution" in the spheres of epistemology, ethics and aesthetic judgement. In this context the concepts of "modernity" and "Enlightenment" have been used interchangeably, whether by those thinkers who seek to sustain the "Enlightenment project", or by those who consider it a closed chapter in the history of ideas (cf. Tracy 1990; Norris 1995). In aesthetics, "modernity" has been considered a category in the most general sense of denoting a particular experience of time, as in Baudelaire's descriptive use of the phrase "modern life". This historical dimension – "the fact that this way of experiencing time emerges only at a particular moment, within particular kinds of society" (Osborne 1997: 347) – ties it closely to the sociological study of cultural forms and processes such as the city, industrialization, secularization and bureaucracy, which have come to constitute the subject matter of sociology (cf. Osborne 1997; Luhmann 1998). In more general usage, "modernity" has been taken to refer to the quality, experience, or period of the "modern". In this sense it "highlights the novelty of the present as a break or rupture with the past, opening out into a rapidly approaching and uncertain future" (Osborne 1997: 346). In this broad sense it has been associated with ideas of innovation, progress and fashion, and counterposed to those of antiquity, the classical and tradition. But one of the recognized difficulties of using the term "modern" as a category of historical periodization is that its meaning changes relative to the time and place of the classification. This difficulty is evident from the emergence of the concept "modern" to designate "the present" and the cyclical opposition of "old and new" in Western culture. "Modernity" plays at the least a dual role as a category of periodization:

> it designates the contemporaneity of an epoch to the time of its classification, but it registers this contemporaneity in terms of a qualitatively new, self-transcending temporality which has the simultaneous effect of distancing the present from even that most recent past with which it is thus identified.
>
> (Osborne 1997: 348)

Osborne claims that it is "this paradoxical doubling or inherently dialectical quality which makes 'modernity' both so irresistible and so problematic a category". In that it has no fixed, objective referent, "it is the product, in the instance of each utterance, of an act of historical self-definition through identification and projection which transcends the order of chronology in the construction of a meaningful present" (Osborne 1997: 348–9). Effectively, the logical structure of the process of change is abstracted from its concrete historical determinants: that is, it has been rendered ahistorical. It is this sense of "modernity" as a ceaselessly renewed act of historical self-definition and projection which underlies Habermas's reformulation of the idea of "modernity" as an "incomplete project". However, whereas the content of such acts of self-definition is always relative to the historical location and projects of the actors concerned, both Habermas (1987) and his "postmodern" opponents tend to fix the meaning of "modernity" through its historical association with the Enlightenment. For them "modernity" is equivalent to the incomplete project of the Enlightenment (Osborne 1997; Teigas 1997). Although this fixing of "modernity" may have merit for focusing debate, for example, on to a specific intellectual or social project, it runs the risk of obscuring the broader cultural-historical dimensions and structure of the concept of "modernity". To this extent I agree with Teigas, who identifies this notion of "modernity" with a restricted view of human history, and with Osborne, who argues that this fixing not only represses "the fluidity, formality and paradoxical dynamics" of "modernity", but that it is altogether reflective of "the wider historical process of colonialism during which a specific (European) present was imposed as the measure of social progress on a global scale" (1997: 349).

Similar parallels are noted in the religious domain. In theological circles, "modernism" was a general descriptive term for "the manifold crisis in the doctrine and discipline of the Church" (Aubert 1975: 969) at the end of the nineteenth and beginning of the twentieth centuries. Although in religious circles its use can be traced to the sixteenth century to characterize the tendency to esteem the "modern age" more highly than "antiquity", in the nineteenth century its use in a religious sense extended beyond distinguishing one historical period from another, or a historical time consciousness.

Among Protestants, the term "modernism" was typically used to distinguish the anti-Christian tendencies of the modern world and also the radicalism of liberal theology. Within Catholicism, however, it was initially identified with the movement urging reform of the Church and its doctrines in the sense of adapting them to modern needs. In time, however, the term "modernism" was often applied without distinction to all who refused to adopt a strictly conservative standpoint (cf. Encyclical *Pascendi* of Pius X 1907). When reduced to this technical-political usage, the notion of "modernism" effectively became ahistorical, and the so-called heterodoxy of modernity came to be opposed to the orthodoxy of tradition. Initially, however, "modernism" was a "direction", a "tendency" rather than a set of definite doctrines. It showed itself in fact at the beginning as:

> a movement which sought to remain in the Church but was still ready to accept from the modern world all that seemed refutable in the realm of thought and healthy in the line of institutions, so that Catholicism could adapt itself to an altered world and rid itself of apparently contingent and outmoded elements.
>
> (Aubert 1975: 970)

However, the ahistorical tendency in opponents of "modernism", linked to the theological agenda of the churches (i.e. the modern age also needed to be brought into line with the demands of the spirit of Christianity) effectively made this conflict one regarding truth claims, orthodoxy and legitimacy. I would identify this notion of "modernism" with a restricted view of religious history and of Christianity itself, a view which could be said to characterize much contemporary Christian resistance to change in "modern times".

Among other things these debates illustrate that the concept of "modernity" remains a privileged site, not only for the articulation of competing views about "naming the present" but of the relationship of past, present, and future, and that it is bound up, inextricably, with the contradictory cultural (including religious) legacy of European colonialism, particularly the hierarchical distinction of European-Christian from non-European cultures during the historical period of the Enlightenment. As the cultural constitution of Western societies continues to be transformed by immigration, by the globalization of technologies, economies and forms of social communication, and by religious pluralism and feminism, throwing the very concept of the "West" deeper into crisis, the prospect is opened up of new, perhaps more relevant, certainly more "hybrid" definitions of modernity, as already evident, for example in Bhabha's (1994) "postcolonial contramodernities" and Gilroy's (1993) "countercultures of modernity", bearing, as Osborne speculates, "the promise of a new historicity" (1997: 349). It is within the context of these debates and speculations that a consideration of the relationship between "psychology" and "religion" might fruitfully proceed in this ever-shifting present.

"Psychology" and "religion" in modern times

The twentieth century opened with a trust and optimism in science, reason, enlightenment and modernity. At its end we witnessed a profound under-mining of confidence in the adequacy of these means to describe and interpret human experience and reality. "Psychology" emerged in the context of modernist culture with great promise that objective knowledge could ultimately be achieved through the deployment of reason and specific scientific methods. Within recent decades, however, it has become increas-ingly clear that the empiricist foundations of "psychology" as a science are deeply flawed, and we witness psychologists reassessing their styles of theory, models of knowledge and practices in efforts to reframe and reorient their inquiries in new directions. This trajectory is paralleled in efforts to study "religion" objectively. The optimism that shaped earlier studies this century has given way to feelings of awe and dismay about the difficulty and complexity of the task (cf. O'Connor 1997). Psychologists of religion in the late twentieth century had few options but to reconsider and redefine not only their understandings of "psychology" but their understandings of "religion" as an object of inquiry. Reviewing these realities and response tendencies in the light of different understandings of modernity, I believe, not only provides a way and means to view the kinds of research that has been done in the past, but points to a new way forward.

Debates about modernity have shown that without linking discussions about rationality to a historical and social-cultural theory of modernity, "debates on reason ... tend very quickly to become a-historical and purely formal" (Tracy 1990: 69). The fact that debates in modernity rendered reason ahistorical and privileged reason in a particular way has become a problem for reason. However, from a review of philosophical activity from antiquity, it is clear that "reason" itself has a history, and that debates about human reality and the nature of human knowledge and understanding are not exactly new in the Western intellectual tradition. It is possible, however, to look at the debates and conflicts about rationality in modernist discourse in a quite different way: that is within the cultural, religious and socio-political contexts of the then "present" – within a cultural-historical framework. In fact, debates in antiquity, during the Middle Ages and Renaissance, and in the Enlightenment, as indeed in contemporary discourses, can be seen as solutions and re-solutions of problems concerning the relationships between reality and knowledge and the construction and development of models of understand-ing. In "our present", it is possible to view "psychology" and "religion" as different ways of knowing, as different lenses through which we view human experience, and different knowledges and systems of understanding, different language and symbolic systems that are created (and re-created) in what is essentially a shared human task – the construction (and reconstruction) of meanings that ground and sustain human existence, in ways that avoid absolutism on the one hand and pure relativism on the other. It is the dynamic quality and interplay between "certainty–uncertainty" in psychology's quest, and between "belief–unbelief" in the religious odyssey that I find so irresistible yet so problematic – an issue I will return to again later. Solving and re-solving these dilemmas are essentially human activities and pursuits that are played out in different ways in different cultural contexts. But, I would argue, relatively speaking they are characteristic of "modern times". Not only have they been, and are cutting-edge pursuits in all cultures (however qualitatively different, which was the point I made about modernity), but they remain as reasonably effective indices distinguishing the "old" from the "new", the innovative from the accepted, the pragmatic from the reified, abiding issues from the merely fashionable, the continuities from the discontinuities, and the "changing" from the "transcendent" in human experience and the quest for the true.

Revisiting the question: what is our present?

Try as I might, I cannot sustain for too long a pessimism about further exploring the relationship between "psychology" and "religion". In relation to this project there is, I believe, a role for further deconstructing the field's past in the various historical-cultural and personal settings in which it has emerged and in the light of the (post)modern, post-empirical genre of historical scholarship currently developing in psychology (cf. Danziger 1990; Graumann and Gergen 1996). This kind of deconstruction for me is both an informing and a confirming task, and whatever the shortcomings of researchers and their orientations (and there will always be those) I am left with a deep appreciation of past contributors and an abiding sense not only of the particularities of research and researchers that are historically, culturally and personally contingent, but of the insights and issues that transcend different psychological approaches and methods, and the different religious orientations and personal commitments of researchers. But the significance of deconstructionist activities also go beyond this. Identifying expressions of reason's history and religion's history and the shape and style of solutions and re-solutions in developing theories of knowledge and models of understanding in concrete historical-cultural contexts, point to the reconstructive challenges of "the present". "New" solutions will in turn shape and determine contemporary projects. Here I come back to the more pedestrian concomitants of the question: what is our present?

What are things like for us today? T.S. Eliot captured well a sense of "the present" when he noted in *The Waste Land* that all the great symbols of Western religious culture have become "a heap of broken images" (1969: 61). It is this sense of the breakdown and collapse of ideologies, and the decline of institutional religion and symbols that have sustained hope and given meaning, that radical deconstructionists (or "most Modern" intellectuals, as Tacey (1999) recently called them) have turned into an art form, seemingly for its own sake – looking for and finding historical prejudices, political values and out-of-date attitudes at the center of exploded myths. But over against this breakdown and pessimism, there is always the abiding movement to find and communicate beauty, transcendence and truth, and to construct meaning in human life. Parallels are also to be found in contemporary psychology and in the many overlapping conversations which seek to deconstruct Enlightenment discourse and find new ways in which a "post-empirical" or "post-positivist" science might be practiced. It is this dual movement of deconstruction and reconstruction, of disenchantment and re-enchantment, that characterizes our present in the discourses of both "psychology" and "religion". It is this inherently historical and dialectical quality that makes "the present" so attractive and so difficult for exploring the relationship between "psychology" and "religion" in different cultural and academic surrounds. It is above all the challenge to take "difference" and "authority" seriously in "psychology" and in "religion".

What constraints or oppressions bind us? In sum, perhaps "modernity" itself. The honest dismay among scholars in this field, as in others, reveals, as Tracy put it so well:

> the pathos of liberalism in our period: the forces for emancipation set loose by the Enlightenment and the great modern revolutions may end in a purely technical notion of reason from which there seems no honourable exit. No exit and no ethics. Above all, no genuine politics.
>
> (1990: 70)

That which is most opposed and feared about modernity threatens to be realized – it becomes just one more tradition. Although positivism is a spent force intellectually and in the natural sciences and most post-Kantian forms of philosophy of science (cf. Polkinghorne 1990; Faulconer and Williams 1990), culturally it is as powerful a force as ever:

> Where positivism reigns, history is emptied of real time and becomes at best a bad infinity: an infinity of more of the same. The sameness is clear: only science (understood positivistically) can count for inquiry; reason is reduced to a purely technical function; technology continues with neither direction nor hope as its genuine liberating possibilities are mixed, without reflection into a dominating and levelling power over all.
>
> (Tracy 1990: 70)

This is surely true of the forceful affirmation of religious orthodoxies and the resurgence of fundamentalist religions and attitudes in their most aggressive forms – only "religion" understood positivistically can account for truth. In the light of the discussion of "modernity" in this paper, I would argue that the reification of particular lenses, concepts, processes, methods and technologies in studies involving "psychology" and "religion" threaten a similar fate. For the modern positivist, there is no meaning in history and time and personal experience; there is no reasonable way to discuss or study how people deal with doubt in their own lives, with challenges to faith, cherished truths, religious orthodoxy and meaning; or life on the margins of religions, institutions and denominations; or their ways of solving and re-solving issues of belief and unbelief; or their calls to happiness and to justice in the world – all of which seem especially interesting issues for a contemporary "psychology of religion" in a time of cultural flux.

Elsewhere I have argued that development in this field has occurred only when researchers have gone beyond narrow conceptualizations and the utilization of restrictive methods and technologies (O'Connor 1983). This brings me back to my preoccupations with the interplay between theory and method and a few salutary recent reminders. Addressing the challenges to empiricist foundations within psychology in the broader context of cultural change, Gergen (1996) recently reiterated the observation that theories were not derived from facts but rather the reverse: that is, that data cannot, and do not, determine theoretical positions – the scientist approaches the world with a theoretical lens or lenses already in place. In his revisionist interpretation of psychology's history, Danziger (1990, 1996) challenged the accepted view that the methods and techniques of psychology are instrumentally related to theory as means to ends, contending on the contrary that "what could be done in actual practice of psychological investigation often decided what could and what could not be discussed" (1996: 17). The relationships between psychological theory and psychological practice are neither simple nor obvious, and, in "the present", considerations must be opened on the foundational problems of psychology itself – on alternative theories of knowledge, on the role of practice and the manner in which psychology constructs its own discourses.

How do we move from here? This will be determined, as the thrust of my paper suggests, by psychologists working at the issues in different psychological and religious contexts and cultures. However, while acknowledging that psychological and religious pluralism will shape the particularities of research projects, I believe that certain intellectual alliances evident in Europe, North America and Australasia offer a new hope for reason – a reason related to the human, social and cultural realities of "modern times". Among these I highlight, from the perspective of the Antipodes, developments in theoretical and historical psychology (Danziger 1990, 1996; Graumann and Gergen 1996), hermeneutics (Ricoeur 1981; Wachterhauser 1986; Messer *et al.* 1988; Terwee 1989), cultural psychology (Stigler *et al.* 1990; Shweder 1991; Voestermans 1992, 1995), narrative psychology (Hermans and Kempen 1993; Polkinghorne 1988; Sarbin 1986; Spence 1982); studies of metaphor (Leary 1990; Olds 1992; Sternberg 1990); revisions of pragmatism (Rorty 1979, 1982; Prado 1987); evolving social constructionist approaches (Danziger 1990, 1996; Gergen 1992, 1996; Harré 1986; Shotter 1993); and a consideration of the embodiment of knowledges and the ethics and politics of difference in feminist studies (Gatens 1991, 1996; Grosz 1987, 1994). Over against the challenges to empiricist epistemology and the deconstruction of Enlightenment discourse which they have in common, these approaches and emphases converge around a number of issues important for a contemporary psychology of religion. Of these I highlight the following: the systematic reexamination of theories of human nature, epistemology and the presuppositions and prejudices underlying distinctions and dichotomies (e.g. mind/body, reason/passion, nature/culture, subject/object) found in models of knowledge; the role of lay epistemics in the creation of meaning in everyday life, meaning that is intersubjective, dialogical and interactive; the relationships between scientific and lay epistemologies and discourses in the development of new models of understanding; the relationships between experience and language, and between time and change and the location of human understanding and change in concrete and embodied experience and the local/cultural settings and contexts of life and academic activity; constructed and contingent notion of self, subjectivity and community; the interactive nature of causality and interpretation; the interplay between author (or text) and reader; and the constructive, narrative and political nature of discourse. Emphases underlying these notions point to the fact that writing, speaking and thinking about alternative ways of understanding human being, about issues such as cultural, religious and gender differences and socio-political life generally *"are* themselves forms of political struggle" (Gatens 1991: 136).

With these approaches in mind, together with the ground I have covered in this paper, I come back to the relationship between "psychology" and "religion". I do this now specifically in relation to my earlier proposal about the utility of taking as points of departure the dynamic interplay between "certainty–uncertainty" in psychology's history and between "belief–unbelief" in the domain of religion in rethinking and reframing these relationships within "the psychology of religion".

The "certainty–uncertainty" dynamic in psychology's discourses

The history of psychology is replete with discussions and conceptualizations of psychology as a science. Earlier in my work in this area I summarized these as a series of polarized, most often conflicting claims of psychology's "true" purposes and objectives (e.g. that its object is to build abstract concepts and theories which at the same time should be applicable to the concrete; that its scientific objective is explanation – description; that its empirical object of investigation is external behavior – inner consciousness, etc.; O'Connor 1983). Initially I found this type of dialectical polarity modeling useful, not so much as a means to focus on the specific truth claims of psychologists with respect to psychology's objectives or findings as a science or, for that matter, for valorizing one polar position over another, but rather as a way of conceptualizing the interrelatedness of these activities and as a way of gaining a handle on the psychologist's stance – the manner in which psychologists as scientists position themselves in relation to their theories and methods and their ways of framing and discussing their research in public forums. Increasingly now, issues of voice and the discursive practices of psychologists preoccupy me particularly in relation to what I perceive to be important underlying issues of authority and the scientific and rhetorical means whereby psychologists and their texts achieve authority, the genres of voice that develop and the relationship between authors and readers that are discernible and reinforced. It is these kinds of issues and dynamics that I both retain and capture in the "certainty–uncertainty" dynamic, for it suggests something of the ongoing tension and dilemma in which research psychologists find themselves in relation to their science and their subjects in (post)modern discourse. Tracking of the textual traditions and rhetorical modalities in contemporary discourse styles, especially reflected in the move from traditional, author-centered modes of authority to those incorporating the voices of agents other than the author, and the move from impersonal, monological modes to more dialogical and poly-vocal modes of discourse, is a creative response not only to understanding "the present" within the context of the human sciences (as for example others have done in philosophy, feminist and cultural studies), but the challenge of different and expanding modes of expression and the potential reworking of the relationship between function, audience and politics in the construction of possible futures for the psychology of religion in the various cultural-historical and personal contexts in which it is currently inscribed. Implied in this approach are challenges to human sciences like psychology to reach audiences outside the academy, and the ways in which these various modes of voice favor or fashion forms of relationship. As Gergen (1992, 1996) emphasizes, in selecting a genre one simultaneously invites a particular form of cultural life. It seems important, therefore, in the psychology of religion to place not only the content of various works but the forms of writing themselves under evaluative scrutiny.

Religion and the "belief–unbelief" dynamic

Within modernist discourse, religion was conceptualized and discussed in dichotomous terms (e.g. inner–outer, personal–social, normative–pathological). Tendencies in research favored studies on inner religious experience or observable public manifestations of religious behavior. Similarly, developmental approaches favored normative stances in relation to religion, whereas clinical orientations more often focused on religious pathology and the ways in which psychopathology was linked to certain personality variables and dispositions. While this type of dichotomizing reflected the limits of "a positive psychology of religion" (e.g. the ahistoricizing and decontextualizing of religion, the valorizing of particular approaches along with certain constructs, the emphasis on the authority of the psychologist of religion), I found the identification of polar alternatives instructive in conceptualizing the dimensions of religion, for developing a perspective on the psychologist's stance to religion, to preferred theoretical and methodological positions and to their subjects, and the manner in which these were related to or shaped by specific cultural, contextual and historical issues (cf. O'Connor 1983). Again increasingly, the discursive practices of psychologists about religion preoccupy me especially in relation to the central issues of religious authority and legitimacy, and the relationships between researchers and subjects. Again, it is these kinds of issues and dynamics that I both retain and extend in the "belief–unbelief" dynamic, for it captures both the present and ongoing tension and dilemma in which research psychologists find themselves, not only in relation to the religious orientations and faith dilemmas of their subjects, but to their own. This stance implies, on the one hand, a more expansive and dynamic understanding of religion and of its intrinsic embeddedness and meaning in ordinary human life (e.g. conflicts between autonomy and dependency), and on the other, the religious orientation and conflicts about authority of researchers themselves.

With respect to the first of these issues, my current thinking is informed by Vergote's (1994, 1996) explorations of the asymmetry and conflict between belief and unbelief in monotheistic religious traditions. Although the dynamic might be present in different forms and expressions in non-monotheistic religions, by its very nature and structure in the context of the monotheistic traditions (i.e. in the context of a relationship directed towards God), religion confronts people with the alternatives of belief or unbelief. In terms of the current relevance of this emphasis, Vergote highlights the fact that "the ideological pluralism and the critical mind set typifying contemporary Western civilization open up an area of individual liberty in which this alternative, far more than in the past, becomes an existential issue" (1996: 207). Increasingly, psychological clarification can be sought on the manner in which people confront the joys, pains, disappointments and the cares of daily living, and the choices through which faith is either affirmed and substantiated, fades and dies away, or is held in a living dynamic tension. In sifting out specific variables and moments from these complex and dynamic processes, psychology can "understand such confrontations and the way they function, as well as the ways in which people seek to solve them" (Vergote 1996: 208). The reflexive import of this contemporary objective in so far as it implicates the experience and religious stance of the researcher, although inherent in Vergote's position, needs to be drawn out further. While until quite recently very little research has been conducted into the conflict between belief and unbelief in the lives of subjects (cf. Corveleyn and Hutsebaut 1994), even less has discussion and consideration been opened up on the stance and condition of the researcher and the manner in which the "belief–unbelief" dynamic impacts on research and professional choices of one kind or another. In addition to understanding better the relationships between researchers and subjects and of evolving discursive styles, this kind of approach may well permit a rapprochement between empirical, developmental, clinical and social psychological approaches in the psychology of religion, as it already appears to be doing in the exploration of narrative and hermeneutical approaches in North American (cf. Capps 1999), European (cf. Ganzevoort 1994; Day 1994; Belzen 1997), and Anglo-Australasian (cf. Hutch 1999; O'Connor 1999) traditions respectively, and the opening up of the research projects and the discourses of psychologists of religion to a very different form of scrutiny and interaction.

What I have attempted to do in opening up a consideration of "modernity" and of the utility of "certainty–uncertainty" and "belief–unbelief" dynamics for "psychology" and "religion" respectively, is to posit a space that is not dominated by classic monological structures, and to speculate on approaches to research and to discourse construction that are dialogical and related differently to psychological and religious authority. The discourses of "psychology" and "religion" are part of a network of discourses that have shaped, and are shaping our cultures. This network is implicated in the construal of human subjectivity and the structuring of the beliefs, values and behaviors of the individuals and groups upon which society and civilization in large part depends – as such, they are hardly "matters of indifference in understanding what is happening in our world" (May 1993: 56).

References

Aubert, R. (1975) "Modernism", in K. Rahner (ed.), *Encyclopedia of Theology. A Concise Sacramentum Mundi*, London: Burns and Oates.

Belzen, J.A. (ed.) (1997) *Hermeneutical Approaches in Psychology of Religion*, Amsterdam/Atlanta: Rodopi.

Bhabha, H.K. (1994) *The Location of Culture*, London, New York: Routledge.

Capps, D. (1999) "Melancholy and motherhate: the parabolic faultline in Erikson's *Young Man Luther*", in J.A. Belzen and J. Corveleyn (eds), *Crossing Boundaries in the Psychology of Religion: Case Studies in Cross-National and Cross-Denominational Context*, Abo: Abo Akademi University.

Corveleyn, J. and Hutsebaut, D. (eds) (1994) *Belief and Unbelief. Psychological Perspectives*, Amsterdam/Atlanta: Rodopi.

Danziger, K. (1990) *Constructing the Subject. Historical Origins of Psychological Research*, Cambridge: Cambridge University Press.

—— (1996) "The practice of psychological discourse", in C.F. Graumann and K.J. Gergen (eds), *Historical Dimensions of Psychological Discourse*, 17–35, Cambridge: Cambridge University Press.

Day, J.M. (1994) "Moral development, belief and unbelief: young adult accounts of religion in the process of moral growth", in J. Corveleyn and D. Hutsebaut (eds), *Belief and Unbelief. Psychological Perspectives*, Amsterdam/Atlanta, GA: Rodopi.

Eliot, T.S. (1969) *The Complete Poems and Plays of T.S. Eliot*, London: Faber & Faber.

Faulconer, J.E. and Williams, R.N. (eds) (1990) *Reconsidering Psychology: Perspectives from Continental Philosophy*, Pittsburg, Pennsylvania: Duquesne University Press.

Foucault, M. (1988) "Truth, power, self: an interview with Michel Foucault", in L. Martin, H. Gutman and P. Hutton (eds), *Technologies of the Self*, Amherst: University of Massachusetts Press.

Ganzevoort, R.R. (1994) "Crisis experiences and the development of belief and unbelief", in J. Corveleyn and D. Hutsebaut (eds), *Belief and Unbelief. Psychological Perspectives*, Amsterdam/Atlanta: Rodopi.

Gatens, M. (1991) *Feminism and Philosophy: Perspectives on Difference and Equality*, Cambridge: Polity Press.

—— (1996) *Imaginary Bodies. Ethics, Power and Corporeality*, London, New York: Routledge.

Gergen, K.J. (1992) "Towards a postmodern psychology", in S. Kvale (ed.), *Psychology and Postmodernism*, London, Newbury Park, New Delhi: Sage.

—— (1996) "Psychological discourse in historical context: an introduction", in C.F. Graumann and K.J. Gergen (eds), *Historical Dimensions of Psychological Discourse*, Cambridge: Cambridge University Press.

Gilroy, P. (1993) *The Black Atlantic: Modernity and Double Consciousness*, London and New York: Verso.

Graumann, C.F. and Gergen, K.J. (eds) (1996) *Historical Dimensions of Psychological Discourse*, Cambridge: Cambridge University Press.

Grosz, E. (1987) "Notes towards a corporeal feminism", *Australian Feminist Studies* 5: 1–17.

—— (1994) *Volatile Bodies. Towards a Corporeal Feminism*, Sydney: Allen & Unwin.

Habermas, J. (1987) *The Philosophical Discourses of Modernity*, trans. F. Lawrence, Cambridge, MA: MIT Press.

Harré, R. (ed.) (1986) *The Social Construction of Emotions*, Oxford: Blackwell.

Hermans, H.J.M. and Kempen, H.J.G. (1993) *The Dialogical Self: Meaning as Movement*, San Diego, California: Academic Press.

Hutch, R.A. (1982) "Are psychological studies of religion on the right track?" *Religion* 12: 277–99.

—— (1999) "Depersonalisation and the magic of deifying the body: clinical notes on a political hostage", in J.A. Belzen and J. Corveleyn (eds) *Crossing Boundaries in the Psychology of Religion: Case Studies in Cross-National and Cross-Denominational Context*, Abo: Abo Akademi University.

Leary, D.E. (1990) *Metaphors in the History of Psychology*, Cambridge: Cambridge University Press.

Luhmann, N. (1998) *Observations on Modernity*, Stanford, CA: Stanford University Press.

May, T. (1993) *Between Genealogy and Epistemology*, University Park, Pennsylvania: Pennsylvania State University Press.

Messer, S.B., Sass, L.A., and Woolfolk, R.L. (eds) (1988) *Hermeneutics and Psychological Theory: Interpretive Perspectives on Personality, Psychotherapy, and Psychopathology*, New Brunswick: Rutgers University Press.

Norris, C. (1995) "Modernism", in T. Honderlich (ed.), *The Oxford Companion to Philosophy*, p. 583, Oxford, New York: Oxford University Press.

O'Connor, K.V. (1983) "The structure of religion: a repertory grid approach", unpublished PhD thesis, School of Psychology, University of New South Wales, Australia.

—— (1997) "Reconsidering the psychology of religion. Hermeneutical approaches in the contexts of research and debate", in J.A. Belzen (ed.), *Hermeneutical Approaches in Psychology of Religion*, Amsterdam/Atlanta: Rodopi.

—— (1999) "Partners in dialogue: issues in hermeneutic reconstruction in psychotherapy with the religious professional", in J.A. Belzen and J. Corveleyn (eds), *Crossing Boundaries in the Psychology of Religion: Case Studies in Cross-National and Cross-Denominational Context*, Abo: Abo Akademi University.

Olds, L.E. (1992) *Metaphors of Interrelatedness: Towards a Systems Theory of Psychology*, Albany: State University of New York Press.

Osborne, P. (1997) "Modernity", in M. Payne (ed.), *A Dictionary of Culture and Critical Theory*, Oxford: Blackwell.

Pius X (1907) *Pascendi Dominici Pregis*, Encyclical of Pope Pius X on the Doctrines of the Modernists, Rome, 8 September 1907, published in English in *The Tablet* 110 (28 September 1907): 510–15 and in C. Carlen (1981) *The Papal Encyclicals 1903–1939*, New York: McGrath.

Polkinghorne, D.P. (1988) *Narrative Knowing and the Human Sciences*, Albany: State University of New York Press.

—— (1990) "Psychology after philosophy", in J.E. Faulconer and R.N. Williams (eds), *Reconsidering Psychology: Perspectives from Continental Philosophy*, pp. 92–115, Pittsburgh, Pennsylvania: Duquesne University Press.

Prado, C.G. (1987) *The Limits of Pragmatism*, New York: Humanities Press.

Ricoeur, P. (1981) *Hermeneutics and the Human Sciences*, ed. and trans. J.B. Thompson, Cambridge: Cambridge University Press; Paris: Editions de la Maison des Sciences de l'homme.

Rorty, R. (1979) *Philosophy and the Mirror of Nature*, Oxford: Blackwell.

—— (1982) *Consequences of Pragmatism: Essays 1972–1980*, Minneapolis: University of Minnesota Press.

Sarbin, T.R. (1986) *Narrative Psychology*, New York: Praeger.

Shotter, J. (1993) *Conversational Realities*, London: Sage.

Shweder, R.A. (1991) *Thinking Through Cultures: Expeditions in Cultural Psychology*, Cambridge: Harvard University Press.

Spence, D.P. (1982) *Narrative Truth and Historical Truth: Meaning and Interpretation in Psychoanalysis*, New York: W.W. Norton.

Sternberg, R.J. (1990) *Metaphors of Mind,* Cambridge: Cambridge University Press.

Stigler, J.W., Shweder, R.A., and Herdt, G. (1990) *Cultural Psychology*, Cambridge: Cambridge University Press.

Tacey, D. (1999) "Re-enchantment", in *The Religion Report*, Australia: ABC Radio National, 11 August.

Teigas, D. (1997) "Jurgen Habermas", in M. Payne (ed.), *A Dictionary of Cultural and Critical Theory*, Oxford: Blackwell.

Terwee, S.S. (1989) *Hermeneutics in Psychology and Psychoanalysis*, Amsterdam: Centrale Drukkerij Universiteit van Amsterdam.

Tracy, D. (1990) "On naming the present", special issue of *Concilium*, pp. 66–85, London: SCM Press; Philadelphia: Trinity Press International.

Vergote, A. (1994) "Epilogue", in J. Corveleyn and D. Hutsebaut (eds), *Belief and Unbelief. Psychological Perspectives*, Amsterdam/Atlanta: Rodopi.

—— (1996) *Religion, Belief and Unbelief. A Psychological Study*, Leuven: Leuven University Press; Amsterdam/Atlanta: Rodopi.

Voestermans, P. (1992) "Psychological practice as a cultural phenomenon", *New Ideas in Psychology* 10: 331–46.

—— (1995) "Cultural psychology of the body", in I. Lubek, R. van Hezewijk, G. Peterson and C.W. Tolman (eds), *Trends and Issues in Theoretical Psychology*, New York: Springer.

Wachterhauser, B.R. (ed.) (1986) *Hermeneutics and Modern Philosophy*, Albany: State University of New York Press.

Wittgenstein, L. (1958) *Philosophical Investigations*, 3rd edn, trans. G.E.M. Anscombe, New York: Macmillan.

—— (1969) *On Certainty*, ed. G.E.M. Anscombe and G.H. Von Wright, trans. D. Paul and G.E.M. Anscombe, New York: Harper & Row.

6 Mapping religion psychologically

Information theory as a corrective to modernism

Volney P. Gay

The Mercator projection map of the world published by Flemish instrument maker Gerhardus Mercator (1512–1594) represents the meridians of longitude by equally spaced parallel lines and gradually spaces out latitude lines toward the polar regions to exaggerate degrees of latitude in exactly the same proportion as degrees of longitude. This enormously simplifies the job of charting a course (the course of a ship on a constant compass bearing always appears as a straight line).[1]

Let us return to the common man and to his religion – the only religion which ought to bear that name. The first thing we think of is the well-known saying of one of our great poets and thinkers concerning the relation of religion to art and science: "He who possesses science and art also has religion; but he who possesses neither, let him have religion."
(Sigmund Freud, *Civilization and Its Discontents*, 1930: 74)[2]

Reason, with a capital R, does not exist in the singular, as given or available to any particular person ... but must be conceived of as an interpersonal process in which anyone's contribution is tested and corrected by others.
(Hayek 1948: 15)

These three citations exemplify my claims: (1) that to map religion using principles of psychology may be a good thing to do, but it is always distorting; (2) that Freud's rejection of religion is a modernist mapping of religion based, primarily, upon his idealization of reason; and (3) we might correct for this bias by taking a larger view of what constitutes reasoning. (Of course, we will, thereby, introduce another bias.) To work towards that larger view I employ a contemporary epistemology derived from information theory. In a surprising way, information theory provides ways to assess the value of religious discourse and practices without reducing them to mere errors. By maintaining an information-rich form of transmission, especially through metaphor and narrative, religious practices offer increased access to reasoning in the way that Hayek uses that term. Information theory is a corrective for modernism to the degree it helps us uncover the inevitable distortions that modernists impose upon the phenomenon we call religion.

Freud cites Goethe's poem about religion because he wishes to use Goethe's authority to demonstrate that art and science can replace religion. This is modernist, as I use the term. It views the modern age, roughly from the Enlightenment on, as superior to previous ages which, lacking science, could not forsake religion. With the rise of scientific method, modern persons could leave religion behind. When intellectuals, like Dostoevsky, did not, Freud found it bitterly disappointing.[3] To replace religion, Freud champions science and the quiet voice of reason.

I cite Hayek's comments about reason because he emphasizes the inter-personal sources of reasoning. This helps correct the distortions imposed by Freud's map of the mind, a map that locates reason primarily *within* the self. Freud denigrated Dostoevsky and celebrated Leonardo and Goethe because the latter confronted and then rejected their religious heritages. Celebrating Amenophis IV (Akhenaton), the pharaoh who introduced monotheism to Egypt, Freud cites approvingly James Breasted's famous comment that this remarkable man was "the first individual in human history."[4] The young pharaoh merits this grand title because he opposed polytheism, a tradition that had existed for thousands of years. Accompanying Freud's idealization of great individuals is the idealization of reason as a process internal to these heroic thinkers. To counter both types of error, Hayek hearkens back to Adam Smith and others who argued against this heroic concept of intellectual leadership. Because the sum of the gifts, insight, and knowledge of a group is always larger than that of any person, Hayek champions an open market for ideas. This open market means that we should expand the amount of information available to us, not restrict it. Using similar criteria, I suggest that we should evaluate religious discourse and practices in terms of their capacities to expand the amount of information available to their practitioners.

Hayek's confederates are De Tocqueville, David Hume, Adam Smith, Edmund Burke, Lord Acton, and others who defend the idea of individual-ism against hierarchical rulers. This is not the individualism of Descartes, who claimed that perfection typically derives from the handiwork and mind of a single creator (Hayek 1948: 9–11). Given this philosophic anthropology, Hayek opposes rationalism that claims especially brilliant persons can deduce the rules of society. In sharp contrast to this form of heroic individualism Hayek cites what he feels are economic and psychological facts. Because millions of persons make thousands of decisions daily, no single mind, much less verbal model of these interactions, can capture them accurately. Human beings are inherently limited, self-centered, and non-rational. Their moral lives, especially, are not the products of conscious deliberation. Human beings, therefore, will not comport or bend themselves to "reasoning" as outlined in any fully articulated treatise. The rationalist tradition, exemplified by Descartes and Soviet collectivism, disdains social institutions that have merely evolved (Hayek 1948: 8). Accordingly, Descartes and Soviet planners assert that reason "with a capital R, is always fully and equally available to all humans and that everything which man achieves is the direct result of, and therefore subject to, the control of individual reason" (1948: 8).

On the limits of mapping, three dimensions into two

The title of this book project, *Mapping Religion and Psychology*, is clever because it denotes two tasks for the academic study of religion. The first is to choose how we will conceive of our subject matter, religion. The second is to choose methods and techniques with which to investigate it. Using the concept of map, we can distinguish different schools of religious studies. One school asserts that religion is a complex but ultimately understandable human behavior. Mapping religion is thus a process of normal science, which is the pursuit of increasingly adequate models which simplify a phenomenon. Just as modern geneticists wish to map the human genome, religionists wish to map the range of human behaviors called religious.[5]

As noted above, technical problems of portraying a three-dimensional globe on to a two-dimensional map always emerge.[6] To ameliorate these problems various strategies have been offered. Each costs something: for example, the Mercator projection distorts the size of the northern and southern poles. Another map, the Peter's projection, counteracts these distortions: one square inch on its surface always equals a fixed number of square miles on the earth. This means that Greenland no longer looks larger than all of North America, as it does in the Mercator projection. As the salespeople say, "the Peter's map leads us to a new view of the world" and can help teach geography. The Peter's projection may teach geography, but not without introducing its own distortions. Mariners, for example, would find it useless, since they could not plot a straight course on it.

While we grant that cartographic distortions are inevitable, they can be minimized and, with enough goodwill and computational power, overcome. Eventually we will enjoy three-dimensional maps – or globes – on hand-held computers that will model, as exactly as we wish, any given area of the earth. Similar engineering puzzles, like establishing longitude, require massive efforts, but they are, in principle, solvable.

Mapping, in the sense of cartography, naturally aligns itself with computer-aided design. Hence, members of the Geographical Information Systems (GIS) task force see themselves as integrating knowledge from many disciplines.[7] Accurate mapping permits them to lay each map (say, of a city's housing) over another (say, the city's power grid) and match each location exactly with all the other maps. Because the objects they map are governed by natural laws and natural processes, discourses used by different groups of scientists to describe them, are, in principle, commensurate with one another.[8]

Opposed to mapping religion are members of another school of scholars who assert that religion is a response to transcendental realities, sometimes called God or Destiny or the Way. We might sum up these various names under the rubric "the sacred." Because religion is a *response* to the sacred, religion is not reducible to merely human behaviors. To focus only upon the human side of the exchange is analogous to hearing only half of a conversation and from that half attempting to understand the entire exchange. A complete map requires access to all relevant data. If, from the beginning we assume that half of the data is unavailable, then we cannot make an adequate map. Of course, for many religious persons, saying that the sacred is half of the dialogue, or half of the relationship, is itself simplistic. Because they believe that the sacred names the center, the ground, and the ultimate source of everything, including human being, ignoring the ontological reality of the sacred makes all maps of it inaccurate. This leaves open the question of whether or not different religious discourses used by different groups are, in principle, commensurate with one another.

While I recognize this defense of religious language, I do not pursue it in this paper. Instead, I pursue the implications of mapping for the problem of reductionism.

Religion, redundancy, reductionism: mapping the spectrum

To the degree that we can map religion using scientific psychology, we exclude talk about God as wholly other and we presume that the term "religion" designates a redundant structure.[9] By redundant I mean that either its causes, meanings, structures, or appearances can be simplified: religious artifacts are *not* their own best interpretation or explanation. Using this concept we can imagine a spectrum that stretches from absolute reductionism to the absolute rejection of the reductionistic enterprise.

The following lists some types of reduction. (I affix some great names relevant to religion to enliven the debate.)

A *Religion is a pernicious distortion of hidden realities*: religious artifacts, like ritual and myth, can and ought to be replaced with insights from the natural, social, or logical sciences. Religion hides, obscures, and retards. Mapping religion is a form of philosophical anthropology: we delineate the unconscious, latent, or disguised forms of subordination that are its roots. Once we have mapped these roots, and unmasked the charades they engender, religion will disappear, its opiate effects diminishing to nothing. (Karl Marx, Sigmund Freud – sometimes.)

B *Religion is nothing but archaic thought*: myth and ritual are primitive expressions of ideas better formulated using more advanced concepts. Religious ideas are proto-philosophy and proto-science. They will be

replaced fully by advances in all these disciplines. Mapping religion is a
form of translation and purification of gold: we seek ways to transform
archaic ideas, grounded in ill-expressed forms, into more rigorous and
exact expressions. (James George Frazier, Friedrich Nietzsche, Ludwig
Wittgenstein.)

C   *Religion is provisional and metaphoric*: myth and ritual may be genuine
containers of human understanding, but they are provisional. Their
truth is locked within layers of metaphors and narrations that must be
dissected. Mapping religion is a form of recovery or mining: we target
and then investigate those metaphors that seem most promising. Using
proper hermeneutic methods, we uncover their deeper meanings. When
advanced persons carry out these dissections, religious discourse and
religious practices will yield up their truths, with some poetry left over.
(Aristotle, Max Weber.)

D   *Religion is functional behavior that persists as long as it works*: myths,
rituals, and other religious artifacts are genuine expressions of human
knowledge because they cement fundamental relationships which would
otherwise collapse. Mapping religion is a form of anthropological and
sociological inquiry: we ask how non-rational beliefs and behaviors
undergird a given social structure. While social scientists can answer
these questions and name these various functions, they cannot obviate
religious institutions. Even the most exacting maps of religion, validated
by appropriate scientific methods, cannot replace religious discourse and
behavior. The sociology of religion is not an adequate substitute for
religion. (Emile Durkheim, most British social anthropologists, Freud –
sometimes.)

E   *Religion contains and conveys symbolic knowledge*: no fully reduced
formulas can replace religious artifacts. Mapping religion is a form of
literary criticism: we recognize, appreciate, and acknowledge the metaphorical richness of religious discourse. Because religious-poetic language captures an ancient form of wisdom, we cannot translate it into
modern forms without losing essential attributes. Because its wisdom is
pertinent to us in the same ways as it was to those of the past, religious
discourse cannot be replaced with modern equivalents. (Carl Jung,
Mircea Eliade, Claude Lévi-Strauss, Daniel Sperber.)

F   *Religion is what it is and nothing else*: the goals of simplification,
explanation, and mapping bespeak a reductionistic temper and are
wrongheaded. Mapping religion is an erroneous dream of philosophers
drunk on the narcissistic worship of self-consciousness and individualistic reason. Religion is an irreducible human experience, like art or music.
It is patterned but is not the product of deliberate, self-conscious
thought. Because religion is patterned, looking backwards we can find
in religious expressions beliefs and actions that resemble behaviors
typical of neurotic anxieties, for example. However, matching patterns
against patterns is not mapping, nor is it puzzle-solving. (Paul Ricoeur.)

If we accept T.S. Kuhn's notion that scientific advance requires puzzle-solving, then scientific advance in religious studies will occur by working on problems that we can reduce to puzzles, for only the latter yield to definitive solutions.[10] Can we locate logical or factual errors in mapping religion? We can, I suggest, only if we affirm some version of definitions (1) to (4), above. For each requires us to shift from using the concept of map metaphorically to using the concept map literally. This shift marks progress from a hermeneutic stance to a scientific one. For example, Charles Darwin concludes *The Origin of Species* by claiming that his book lets naturalists shift from metaphorical reasoning about species to scientific reasoning about species: "The terms used by naturalists, of affinity, relationship, community of type, paternity, morphology, adaptive characters, rudimentary and aborted organs, etc., will cease to be metaphorical, and will have a plain signification."[11]

To map religion scientifically, as Darwin mapped the transformation of species scientifically, we must assume that religion is similar to other evolved behaviors, such as language. While intricate, language is not in principle immune to complete and full reduction. In this vein, we recall that Claude Lévi-Strauss aligned his new science of mythology with linguistics.[12] Sharing this reductive idea but extending it, Charles Lumsden and E.O. Wilson (1981) compared Lévi-Straussian structuralism and psychoanalysis to ordinary science:

> Structuralists and psychoanalysts are scientists endeavoring to approximate what we call the epigenetic rule of reification and symbolization. Nevertheless, it would be a mistake to regard structuralism and psychoanalysis as independent theories or even facets of a true theory in the ordinary sense employed in the natural sciences. They are simply descriptions, however deeply they cut. They do not formulate principles from a postulational-deductive framework. *They have failed to suggest axioms that can be mapped onto the theoretical structure of other disciplines.*
>
> (354, emphasis mine)

Lumsden and Wilson mean that discourse (formulated as axioms) from one scientific domain should be translatable into discourse from other scientific domains. This is a standard concept of mapping as reductionism: truths generated in one science may not contradict truths generated in another. It presupposes that there is a single language into which all other scientific languages (or discourses) are translatable. Because mathematical propositions have no metaphorical richness, they are ideal expressions for a reductive science. Hence, Lumsden and Wilson attempted to map social science discourse on to a grid of mathematical formulas.

Information theory and the flow

In favor of the Freudian critique of religion is its modernist stringency: by comparing folk religion against normative, rational behavior Freud and others detected numerous instances of magical thought. The uncanny parallels Freud adduced between neurosis and some forms of religion are indisputable. Against the traditional Freudian critique and similar modernist critiques are (1) the ubiquity of religion in all cultures, at all times (which argues against it being analogous to a disease); (2) the equally numerous instances of religion correlated with human health; and (3) the subtle ties that link certain kinds of faith to important human virtues, such as joy and optimism. One of these ties may be that by remaining embedded in narrative, myth, metaphor and the like, religious discourses maintain richness and therefore the flow of information is less impeded.

I take the concept of flow from F. Dretske and J. Barwise (1986, 1988).[13] Keith Devlin (1991: 14–16), following Barwise, describes the following types of information available from a tree stump:

1   age of the tree when felled;
2   its species;
3   general characteristics;
4   the probable climate in which the tree grew;
5   insects and animals habitually near it, etc.

We may agree with item (1), that counting tree rings tells us the tree's age when it was felled (if we agree with the generalization "one ring equals one year."). But are items (2)–(5) information deduced by observing the flow of information from this tree? Yes, because having observed similar tree stumps and acquired knowledge about this kind of tree, we can find in this trunk evidence for each of these claims.

To clarify his idea, Dretske compares his notion of information to that offered in Shannon and Weaver's (1949) classic paper on information theory. In Shannon and Weaver's terms, digital coding means one measures or samples the original object (such as a sound wave) and assigns a discrete number to that sample, leaving no intermediate steps. To increase verisimilitude one must increase sampling rates. If the rate is too low, listeners detect discrepancies between recorded music, for example, and the richness of a live performance. Hence, audiophiles judged early digital reproductions as wretched because they did not achieve sampling rates high enough to capture the warmth of long-playing records which were produced using "analog" devices (e.g., piano, microphone, tube amplifier, speakers). The poverty of digital sampling is even more obvious in visual reproductions, like low-level computer scans of color photographs. One can see the "dots" which, as pixels, make up the digitization of an original whole.[14]

In Shannon and Weaver's paper, digital information is quantified in terms of the number of binary digits required to codify the data in question. For example, if we need to transmit only one of two possible signals, say either on or off, we need transmit only one "binary digit." If we wish to transmit extremely rich data, like the exact coloring of a Van Gogh painting, we require millions of binary picture elements (pixels) to designate accurately each of the possible color tones for each of the thousands of colored areas of the canvas.

Dretske revises this definition of "digitization." He uses this term to denote all processes in which we isolate relevant data from an original whole. He compares two instances of communication. One is the sentence "The cup has coffee in it" and the second is a photograph of the same cup of coffee: "The picture tells you that there is some coffee in the cup by telling you, roughly, how much coffee is in the cup, the shape, size, and color of the cup, and so on" (Dretske 1981: 137). The photograph conveys the sentence's precise, digitized meaning, "the most specific piece of information" (137), *plus* additional information encoded in the picture itself, in analog form.[15]

> When a signal carries the information that s is F in analog form, the signal always carries more specific, more determinate, information about s than that it is F. Every signal carries information in both analog and digital form.
>
> (137)

In other words, compared to sentences about a particular scene, pictures are wholes. Pictures and other graphical representations typically convey both digitized information, e.g., "This is a car," and rich, additional information in analog form, e.g., "Look how the setting sun makes this new Taurus look gorgeous!" One can examine photographs in minute detail and with sufficient expertise derive enormous amounts of additional information from them. For example, US reconnaissance specialists performed brilliant interpretative work upon the analog images of launchers, tents, and missile trailers from satellite and aerial photographs of Cuba. Their ability to extract this rich flow of data enabled President Kennedy to confront Soviet authorities in October 1962.[16]

Dretske says that in extracting information from these analog sources the expert digitizes the flow by abstracting from it specific bits of data: "Digital conversion is a process in which irrelevant pieces of information are pruned away and discarded. Until information has been lost, or discarded, an information-processing system has failed to treat *different* things as essentially the *same*" (141, emphasis in original). This means that once we treat subsequent items as redundant we can ignore them or denote them merely as repetitions. Indeed, we count it an advance when we can substitute numbers for real-world events, since this makes the entire process subject to quantification. Quantification merits its supreme place in the sciences because it is the least analogical form of communication, the most succinct, and most translatable.[17]

Another example of digitizing – in the sense of filtering – is the guessing game "Twenty Questions." In this game one person thinks of a thing – say, Napoleon – and the other tries to discover it by asking questions that permit yes or no answers. "Is it alive?" for example, rules out many things by presuming the distinction "living or dead." This question effectively divides up everything in binary form and thus reduces the range of possible answers. "Is it human?" and "Is it male?" carry out further reductions. Using the largest possible categories, the questioner seeks to narrow the search. By using binary sets, the questioner halves the size of the population of potential objects on each round. A perfectly constructed set of twenty questions could, therefore, designate 2^{20} objects: that is, more than a million discrete entities.

Like the psychologist J.J. Gibson (1979) Dretske argues that the flow of information streaming from objects is always richer than the information passed through the sensory, registration, mnemonic, and cognitive devices that, operating together, constitute experience in higher animals. At each stage in the sensation to cognition sequence, higher-level systems filter out data identified as noise or as redundant. Hence, at each higher stage, digitization reduces the quantity of information: "the relation between sensory processes and cognitive processes is like the relation between the preliminary analog representation and the subsequent digital representation" (143). In making this comparison Dretske exemplifies his point: he claims to find similarities between digital computer processes and mental processes. Dretske's model of cognitive processing – in which he compares analog speedometers to digital speedometers – ignores irrelevant differences between mechanical devices and the mind and emphasizes their logical similarity to one another. This is ordinary, digitizing rationality: obvious differences between speedometers and the mind are ignored for the sake of intelligibility. The mind digitizes the flow of information just as the digital speed gauge digitizes the analog flow streaming into it from the car's wheels; the mind processes data as the digital computer processes instructions. (That minds have no moving parts is irrelevant, as is the fact that minds are not made of silicon.)

Clinicians recognize a similar form of reasoning in paranoid patients. Like someone playing a life and death game of "Twenty Questions," paranoid persons ask binary questions such as "Friend or foe?" Not accidentally, this is also the question sentries ask when they confront strangers. Once a state of war exists, common sense dictates that all new data be scrutinized and categorized according to severity of threat. Under wartime conditions partial similarities between two entities, an enemy and a stranger, are often sufficient to deduce identity: all strangers are enemies. This is digitizing in Dretske's sense because complex and subtle differences are reduced to a simple binary set: friend or foe. Given this binary template, the range of the sentry's possible actions shrinks to a binary set: attack now or wait and be prepared to attack later.

Because the principal factor uniting members with one another is personal honor – which is based on love of self and hatred of the other – actors in paranoid systems may adopt the terminology of non-paranoid systems, but these are parodies. For example, in *The Godfather*, Michael, the son of a Mafia chief, wishes to kill a police captain complicit in an attack on Michael's father. Killing a police captain seems imprudent to his buddies, and they admonish him to not confuse revenge with "business."

Sonny: You're taking this very personal. Tom, this is business and this man is taking it very very personal.

Michael: Where does it say you can't kill a cop?

Hagen: Come on, Mickey ...

Michael: Tom, wait a minute. I'm talking about a cop that's mixed up in drugs. I'm talking about ah ... ah ... a dishonest cop ... a crooked cop who got mixed up in the racket and got what was coming to him. That's a terrific story. And we have newspaper people on the pay roll, don't we, Tom? [Hagen nods in the affirmative.] And they might like a story like that.

Hagen: They might, they just might ...

Michael: It's not personal, Sonny. It's strictly business.[18]

Since their business is a criminal enterprise, it is almost charming to hear Michael moralize about a bad cop. Michael is confusing hatred with business, and thus Sonny is correct. However, since the Mafia relies upon blood codes Michael must murder the police captain because that is an essential part of the family business.

In non-criminal businesses, competition, price movements, and price communication increase information to both customers and sellers. Hence, maximizing the freedom of information maximizes economic efficiency. Indeed, this is a definition of capitalism. Increasing economic efficiency increases prosperity. However, prosperity brings vast social changes and immense social pressures. As Marx put it, nothing in world history can withstand the pressures of a full, capitalist event except a deliberate, hierarchical Plan. As he says, in *Capital*:

> The life-process of society, which is based on the process of material production, does not strip off its mystical veil until it is treated as production by freely associated men, and is consciously regulated by them in accordance with a settled plan.[19]

Persons who hold a fixed tradition – or the settled Plan – as sacred find information dangerous: it must be controlled by hierarchical authorities.[20] Using Dretske's terms, these authorities must digitize all relevant sources and impose on them a fixed, narrowed reading. Terms that are critical to these discourses, such as "Christ's nature" in the Middle Ages, or "pornography" in contemporary America, and "truth" in most cultures, cannot be reduced to fixed, narrowed criteria. This means that hierarchical authorities must impose an order upon them, or tolerate the hubbub of democratic processes and free-for-alls. Authoritarian systems (such as racist regimes in the fifteenth century and criminal governments in the twentieth century) must attack new sources of information and new interpretations of the tradition.

To outsiders not caught up in the anxiety and tunnel vision of those who benefit from the system, the latter's reasoning always appears paranoid. Because they depend upon subordination and terror, as portrayed in *The Godfather*, these potentates cannot employ the information that flows towards them and with which they could improve the fit between their environments and themselves. In these contexts, the political is always personal, and this is just wrong enough to produce numerous disasters. (Clinicians will recognize Borderline Personalities who must attack anything that sounds like criticism and, consequently, cannot learn from their mistakes.)

Digitizing forms, digitizing religion

By digitizing – that is, extracting specific patterns from wholes – science becomes possible. To find and isolate patterns one must disregard superficial differences and expose underlying sameness. We saw this in Claude Lévi-Strauss's admonitions to make the study of mythology scientific: he promised to find what is the same amid thousands of different myths collected from different ages and different cultures.

If obeyed, this admonition to digitize a whole means the ruination of art. For example, in *The Accidental Tourist* (1985), Anne Tyler describes Malcolm, a middle-aged man surveying his life after his wife has left him:

> Now was his chance to reorganize, he told himself. He was struck by an incongruous little jolt of interest. The fact was that running a house required some sort of system, and Sarah had never understood that. She was the sort of woman who stored her flatware intermingled. She thought nothing of running a dishwasher with only a handful of forks stacked inside. Malcolm found that distressing.[21]

In sixty-seven words, Tyler portrays a man who is angry, denies his grief, and uses an obsessional defense to obscure the precise details of his loss. By recalling petty differences with Sarah, he tries to supplant her. The "little jolt" of interest signifies a momentary lifting of his depressed mood. Malcolm keeps disorganizing feelings at bay by organizing trivialities. This crushing loss is "his chance" to reorganize his life.

My interpretation of Tyler's sixty-seven words does not replace them. I cannot further reduce this passage; I cannot digitize it without destroying its artistic merits. For example, Tyler's comments about flatware suggest keen observations of men in kitchens. It ushers us to the next paragraph in which we learn that Malcolm keeps his dirty dishes soaking in chlorine bleach for days at a time. Reflecting upon this peculiar system, Malcolm suddenly feels as if Sarah were watching him: "he sensed that if he slid his eyes just slightly to the left, he would find her, arms folded across her chest, her head tipped and her full, curved lips meditatively pursed" (9). I find this beautiful. It evokes memories of yearning that verge on hallucination and ends with the haunting image of a woman with full, curved lips observing me. This rhythmic passage advances from Malcolm's impulse to move his eyes "just slightly," which is a tiny gesture, to the large gestures of Sarah's arms folded across her chest, to a smaller gesture, her head tilted, to a delicate gesture of a smile, and then to the minute feature of these full lips, that curve in a special way. If we could delete any words from this passage and not harm it, we should count ourselves the equal of the author.

We might agree that works of art cannot bear digitization without being destroyed, and so we defend them against the machinery of reductionism: "As we have seen, if a phrase is played twice, the effect is not like that of the repetition of an architectural motif on a façade, each playing has a different weight."[22] We cannot relinquish any of the many dozen "Louie" refrains from the Kingsmen's song, "Louie, Louie." Like other modernists, Freud ceded this point when he declared that science, combined with art, was sufficient for thinking persons. To defend the redundancy of religion we need to show that, sometimes, religion makes digitization less likely.

A benign response to a child's worry quiets the child's demand for digit-ized answers expressed in concrete-operational terms. While parents may invoke religious imagery, religion is not required. Love is. A friend tells me about his aged grandfather, who was quite ill, putting him to bed one night. The old man peered down at the boy, falling asleep, and said, "How curious, just as my life is ending, your life is beginning." This shows unusual grace. Rather than rage about dying, the old man blesses his grandson's future. He lightens the boy's fears by linking the symmetry of waking and sleeping to the symmetry of life and death. It also echoes the psalmist, "You sweep men away in the sleep of death; they are like the new grass of the morning" (Psalm 90: 5).[23]

Could my friend's grandfather have said this wonderful thing as a mod-ernist, devoted to science and art, and dismissive of religion? Of course. Would religious instruction, say in a synagogue or temple, have made his empathy more likely? In the language of this paper, can religion expand the amount of information available to us? These are empirical questions, subject to empirical investigation. One hint appears in Karl Barth's reflections on a passage from Romans, "If God is for us, who is against us?" (Romans 8: 31–2). Barth says these "words mean that the realm of contrasts lies behind us, and that the duality in which we stand, which conditions everything we see, and which renders the world's darkness to God and God darkness to the world, has been overcome."[24] The realm of contrasts and dualities is the realm of digitized rationality.

Barth's commentary on Romans is 537 pages. Surely, this is redundant. Why, indeed, are there four Christian gospels? Either these are wildly exaggerated and redundant communications or they are not. On the principle of charity, we suppose that they are more than mindless repetitions.[25] What is this more? Perhaps part of it is the urge to resist the digitization of all experience and to seek our beginning. Without digitization no science is possible, but immersed in it we cannot find our way out.

Notes

1   Trager 1995, revised slightly.
2   The poem is by Goethe.
3   Thus, Freud says, "Dostoevsky threw away the chance of becoming a teacher and liberator of humanity and made himself one with their gaolers" (1928: 177) by venerating the Tsars and the God of the Christians.
4   Freud, S. (1939: 21). The citation is from Breasted (1906: 356).
5   See Venter *et al.* 1998.
6   In making a cylindrical projection, the cartographer regards the surface of the map as a cylinder that encircles the globe, touching it at the equator. The parallels of latitude extend outward from the globe, parallel to the equator. The resulting map represents the world's surface as a rectangle. Although the shapes of areas on the cylindrical projection are increasingly distorted toward the poles, the size relationship of areas on the map is equivalent to the size relationship of areas on the globe. The Mercator projection is related to the cylindrical projection, with certain modifications. It portrays equatorial regions accurately but greatly distorts areas in the high latitudes. Directions are represented faithfully, and this is valuable in navigation. There are several other projection techniques as well.

(*Encarta* 1996–7)

7   Hence, a common sentiment is the following:

The great appeal of GIS stems from their ability to integrate great quantities of information about the environment and to provide a powerful repertoire of analytical tools to explore this data. The example above displayed only a few map layers pertaining to urban transportation planning. The layers included would be very different if the application involved modeling the habitat of an endangered species or the environmental consequences of leakage from a hazardous materials site.
(http://www.utexas.edu/depts/grg/gcraft/notes/intro/intro_f.html)

8   See University of Wisconsin 1999.
9   Gay 1978.
10 The standard citations for science as puzzle solving are Kuhn's two essays, *The Structure of Scientific Revolutions* (1962) and *The Essential Tension* (1977).
11 Darwin 1859 (gopher://gopher.vt.edu:10010/02/69/2).
12 Linguistics could only begin to evolve as a science after this contradiction had been overcome. Ancient philosophers reasoned about language the way we do about mythology. On the one hand, they did notice that in a given language certain sequences of sounds were associated with definite meanings, and they earnestly aimed at discovering a reason for the linkage

between those sounds and that meaning. Their attempt, however, was thwarted from the very beginning by the fact that the same sounds were equally present in other languages although the meaning they conveyed was entirely different. The contradiction was surmounted only by the discovery that it is the combination of sounds, not the sounds themselves, which provides the significant data.

(Lévi-Strauss 1963: 208)

13 J. Barwise (1986), "Information and circumstance," *Notre Dame Journal of Formal Logic*, 27: 324–38. Reprinted in J. Barwise (1988), *The Situation in Logic*. CSLI Lecture Notes 17. Both texts are cited in Keith Devlin (1991), *Logic and Information*, Cambridge: Cambridge University Press.

14 Hence, film (a device) differs fundamentally from digitally scanned images:

Effective film resolution: Theoretically, microfilm is capable of storing resolutions of 1,000 lppm [line-pairs per millimeter], but this theoretical limit is actually never achieved because even the best microfilm cameras operating under ideal conditions are limited to about 200 lppm. And, due to variations in lighting, exposure control, lens quality, focus, development chemistry, camera adjustment, vibration, and other variables in a production environment, high-quality 35mm 12X film is usually imaged at an effective resolution of about 120–150 lppm (the RLG standard identifies any resolution above 120 lppm, at a 12X reduction, as being excellent). This effective film resolution equates to a digital binary scanning resolution of approximately 700–900 dpi. It will be a few years before cost-effective digital image systems capable of handling this level of resolution are available on a production basis. Film is resolution-indifferent: A single frame of film can store an image at the maximum possible resolution for the film/camera combination being used. Film does not exact a premium for maximizing resolution. On the other hand, the cost of storing high-resolution digital images on any medium except film increases linearly as the resolution increases. This occurs in the digital image because with higher resolution more data points are required to accurately preserve the fidelity of the image. More data points demand more memory for storage. Film, on the other hand, is resolution-indifferent.

(http://palimpsest.stanford.edu/byauth/willis/hybrid/issues.html)

15 Michael Polyani made this point repeatedly in his essays on epistemology when he used the notion of mapping to explicate his concept of "tacit knowledge." For example, see *Personal Knowledge* (1958), pp. 4, 21, 81–3, 87–94, 117. For a brilliant expansion of these concepts see Edward R. Tufte's three recent books: *The Visual Display of Quantitative Information* (1983), *Envisioning Information*, (1990), *Visual Explanations: Images and Quantities, Evidence, and Narrative* (1997).

16 Brugioni 1996.

17 Hence, sociobiologists dream of discovering the epigenetic rules that, they assume, shape all human actions and interactions: "The number of molecules in each cubic centimeter of air exceeds the entire population of human beings on earth by a factor of billions, yet physical theory can describe them with ease" (Lumsden and Wilson 1981: 345).

18 *The Godfather* 1972: 55 (http://www.screentalk.org/galleryG.htm#Godfather, The).

19 Lichtman 1977a: 65, quoting Marx, *Capital* (New York: Modern Library, 1906: 92).

20 The utopian vision of Marxism, its sense of an open future, subject to conscious and deliberate control, is one of active, deliberate construction: "to be human is to be required, by the very absence of a fixed, instinctual disposition, to create one's own nature" (Lichtman 1977b: 38).
21 Tyler 1985: 8.
22 Rosen 1971: 75.
23 1 Corinthians 15: 51, "Listen, I tell you a mystery: We will not all sleep, but we will all be changed." (All verses from NIV.)
24 Barth 1933: 326.
25 Davidson 1986.

References

Barth, Karl (1933) *The Epistle to the Romans*, trans. E.C. Hoskyns. London: Oxford University Press.

Barwise, J. (1986) "Information and circumstance," *Notre Dame Journal of Formal Logic*, 27: 324–38.

Breasted, J.H. (1906) *A History of Egypt*. Chicago: University of Chicago Press.

Brugioni, Dino A. (1996) "The art and science of photo-reconnaissance," *Scientific American*, March: 78–85.

Darwin, Charles (1859) *The Origin of Species by Means of Natural Selection*. Sixth edn (1920) New York: Appleton (gopher://gopher.vt.edu:10010/02/69/2).

Davidson, Donald (1986) "A coherence theory of truth and knowledge," *Truth and Interpretation: Perspectives on the Philosophy of Donald Davidson*, Ernest LePore (ed.), Oxford: Blackwell, 307–19.

Devlin, Keith (1991) *Logic and Information*. Cambridge: Cambridge University Press.

Dretske, F. (1981) *Knowledge and the Flow of Information*. Montgomery, VT: Bradford Books.

Encarta 98 Desk Encyclopedia (1996–7) Microsoft Corporation.

Freud, S. (1928) "Dostoevsky and parricide," *The Standard Edition of the Complete Psychological Works of Sigmund Freud*, vol. 21. London: Hogarth Press and the Institute for Psycho-Analysis, 175–96.

—— (1930) "Civilization and its discontents," *The Standard Edition of the Complete Psychological Works of Sigmund Freud*, vol. 21. London: Hogarth Press and the Institute for Psycho-Analysis, 59.

—— (1939) "Moses and monotheism," *The Standard Edition of the Complete Psychological Works of Sigmund Freud*, vol. 23. London: Hogarth Press and the Institute for Psycho-Analysis, 3.

Gay, Volney P. (1978) "Reductionism and redundancy in the analysis of religious forms," *Zygon*, 13(2): 169–83.

Geographic Information Systems as an Integrating Technology (http://www.utexas.edu/depts/grg/gcraft/notes/intro/intro_f.html).

Gibson, J.J. (1979) *The Ecological Approach to Visual Perception*. Boston: Houghton-Mifflin.

Hayek, F.A. (1948) *Individualism and Economic Order*. Chicago: University of Chicago Press.

Kuhn, Thomas S. (1962) *The Structure of Scientific Revolutions*. Chicago: University of Chicago Press.

—— (1977) *The Essential Tension*. Chicago: University of Chicago Press.

Lévi-Strauss, Claude (1963) "The structural study of myth," in C. Lévi-Strauss, *Structural Anthropology*. New York: Basic Books, 202–12.

Lichtman, Richard (1977a) "Marx and Freud. Part 2: Antagonistic themes," *Socialist Revolution*, 7(3): 59–84.

—— (1977b) "Marx and Freud. Part 3: Marx's theory of human nature," *Socialist Revolution*, 7(6): 37–78.

Lumsden, Charles J. and Wilson, E.O. (1981) *Genes, Mind, and Culture: The Coevolutionary Process*. Cambridge, MA: Harvard University.

Polyani, Michael (1958) *Personal Knowledge*. Chicago: University of Chicago Press.

Puzo, Mario and Coppola, Francis Ford (1972) *The Godfather* (http://www.screentalk.org/galleryG.htm#Godfather, The).

Rosen, Charles (1971) *The Classical Style: Haydn, Mozart, Beethoven*. New York: Norton.

Shannon, C.E. and Weaver, W. (1949) *The Mathematical Theory of Communication*. Urbana: University of Illinois Press.

Trager, James (1995) *The People's Chronology*. New York: Henry Holt.

Tufte, Edward R. (1983) *The Visual Display of Quantitative Information*. Cheshire, CN: Graphics Press.

—— (1990) *Envisioning Information*, Cheshire, CN: Graphics Press.

—— (1997) *Visual Explanations: Images and Quantities, Evidence, and Narrative*. Cheshire, CN: Graphics Press.

Tyler, Anne (1985) *The Accidental Tourist*. New York: Berkley.

University of Wisconsin (1999) "The history of cartography project". Department of Geography (http://feature.geography.wisc.edu/).

Venter, Craig J., Adams, M.D., Sutton, G.R., Kerlavage, A.R., Smith, H.O. and Hunkapiller, M. (1998) "Shotgun sequencing of the human genome," *Science*, 280(5369): 1540–2.

7 Post-structuralism and the psychology of religion

The challenge of critical psychology

Jeremy R. Carrette

> Psychology will be saved only by a return to hell.
>
> (Foucault 1957: 158)

Michel Foucault's reflection in 1957 that psychology would only be saved by "a return to hell" was not some theological statement (far from it) but a recognition of the problematic foundations of psychological knowledge. According to Foucault, psychology was a "fatal impasse" of nineteenth-century thought, a thought grounded on "negative" constructions and "an analysis of duplications" (Foucault 1957: 158; 1962: 73; 1965: 448). There was in effect a "contradiction" in building the psychological "truth" of health in illness (Foucault 1957: 153). Foucault's challenge to psychology was supported by the work of other French historians of science such as Georges Canguilhem, who asked the fundamental question: "What is psychology?" Canguilhem in his own work exposed the fear of psychology to explore the nature of its enterprise by raising the question of the history of the discipline. But, for Canguilhem, after recognizing the historical problems of psychology to find a secure object of knowledge, the question "What is psychology?" became "What do psychologists hope to achieve, doing what they do?" (Canguilhem [1956] 1980: 49). It is this radical scrutiny of the foundations of psychological knowledge that forms the basis of engagement between what has been called "post-structuralism" and the psychology of religion. In this essay I want to show how post-structuralist ideas have been used to open up the problems of foundation in the psychology of religion and show how future work in the field must deal with a disciplinary amnesia about the historical and social conditions of the subject.[1] What I am seeking to show is that the future of the discipline is to be found in the past – in the return to hell.

Post-structuralism and critical psychology

Post-structuralism, as the name suggests, arose out of the intellectual movement of structuralism in 1960s France. Structuralism can be seen as a set of ideas that sought to identify a given number of structures or patterns within such things as language, knowledge and myth. This structuralist method was exemplified most clearly in the work of Ferdinand de Saussure in the field of linguistics, Claude Lévi-Strauss in the field of anthropology and Roland Barthes in the fields of semiotics and literary criticism. Post-structuralism, as John Sturrock indicates, did not so much kill off structuralism as extend and redirect structuralist thinking (Sturrock 1993: 137). The broad scope of post-structuralist thinking questioned the idea of a given structure and critically explored the sense in which something is either continually "deferred" in a chain of arbitrary linguistic signs or "constructed" through social and historical processes. These post-structuralist ideas were most classically represented in the work of Jacques Derrida (Deconstruction) and Michel Foucault (History of Ideas), although it is also related to the work of Jacques Lacan, Julia Kristeva and Louis Althusser (see Derrida 1967, 1972; Foucault 1966, 1969). What broadly emerged from such work was a recognition of how discourses and knowledges are shaped by hidden political assumptions and social structures.

It is important to recognize that the work of post-structuralism is often equated with the term "postmodernism," although these two areas should be kept distinct. (As we shall see, many psychologists have subsumed the critical ideas emerging from post-structuralism within postmodernism and have failed to make clear distinctions between these terms.) Postmodernism is more adequately employed to refer to the work of Jean-François Lyotard and Jean Baudrillard, who can be seen to comment on the social conditions of "postmodernity," or the social conditions of late capitalism, and whose ideas have been taken up to support a more undisciplined relativism. The terms and definitions of the debate are, however, often obscured and reflect to some extent a shorthand way of capturing the wider intellectual and social developments rather than adequately representing any specific thinker (it is thus a way of condemning or celebrating a particular set of ideas without dealing with the specific details of a thinker).[2] However, what I am concerned with in this essay is to show how the ideas of post-structuralism became integrated into psychology and how the field of the psychology of religion has started to respond to – and needs to explore further – such critical ideas.

Interest in post-structuralist ideas in psychology emerged after the mid-1970s, following the challenge, particularly in the field of social psychology, to the claims of positivistic psychology (what I shall call, following Shweder (1990: 4), "general psychology"). This challenge to "general psychology" was first seen in the work of social constructivists such John Shotter (1975), Rom Harré (1979) and Kenneth Gergen (1973). This group of psychologists questioned the "objective basis" of laboratory-experimental methods in psychology and opened up a whole series of conceptual problems between psychology and sociology (see Henking in this collection). As Gergen powerfully argued in a later overview of the situation:

> The mounting criticism of the positivist–empiricist conception of knowledge has severely damaged the traditional view that scientific theory serves to reflect or map reality in any direct or decontextualised manner. How can theoretical categories be induced or derived from observation, it is asked, if the process of identifying observational attributes itself relies on one's possessing categories? How can theoretical categories map or reflect the world if each definition used to link category and observation itself requires a definition?
>
> (Gergen 1985: 266–7)

Psychology was no longer seen to have a stable "object" to anchor its methodological assertions and re-entered a "foundational crisis." This led to a "new paradigm" school of thinking in psychology, which was further enhanced by an elaboration of the post-structuralist work of Derrida and Foucault. These shifts caused a "state of flux" in the field (Smith *et al.* 1995) and effectively led to a "changing of the subject" and to what Parker has called a "turn to discourse" (Parker 1999: 7; Shotter and Gergen 1989; Parker 1992). In this work there was a recognition of the social and political factors influencing psychological discourse. "It became more a question of thinking how different subjectivities could be constituted and how they would be differently located and locked into ideological practices" (Henriques *et al.* 1984; 96). There was, in effect, to note Smith *et al.* (1995), a "rethinking" of psychology. This "rethinking" gave birth to a diverse series of post-structuralist inspired forms of analysis, such as "discursive psychology," "discourse dynamics," "dialogical psychology," "cultural psychology" and "narratology." This diverse series of models brought together, with post-structuralist ideas, a range of critical registers, such as feminism, post-colonial theory and Marxism. What had originally been a recognition of the social processes in the construction of psychological knowledge was now an amalgamation of interlocking critical registers. This new hybrid of psychological knowledge became aptly titled "critical psychology," as distinct from "general psychology" (Fox and Prilleltensky 1997; Parker 1999).

Critical psychology takes seriously the work of post-structuralist thinkers, and the work of Michel Foucault in particular, in order to question the assumptions of psychological theory. It questioned the scientific enterprise of psychology and brought to light the hidden political and social agenda of psychological studies; it exploded the myth of neutrality in psychological testing, unearthed the limits of the laboratory, revealed the discursive conditions of psychological theory and the imperialist agendas of developmental concepts. The "subject" was transformed and a whole new literature began to document the "construction," "deconstruction" and even "reconstruction" of psychology (Danziger 1990; Parker and Shotter 1990; Bayer and Shotter 1998).

Religion and critical psychology

The engagements between post-structuralism and psychology, and the significance of work in critical psychology, have not really permeated the field of the psychology of religion. The psychology of religion has so far remained fairly insulated from the critical registers of post-structuralist theory, particularly as it has been articulated in the new area of "critical psychology." To some extent there has been resistance in the field of the psychology of religion to explore the instability of "psychology" as a discipline. This denial conveniently maintains and preserves the inter-disciplinary program, and the political ideologies it supports, by enforcing a disciplinary and political amnesia about foundational questions. There has understandably been a reluctance to question the categories and concepts that support and make possible an entire methodological framework for analyzing religion. While the psychology of religion has been able to hold the diversity of the discipline, it is wary of anything that appears to disrupt the "subject" (and, more fearfully, challenge identity, practice and careers). While many of the fears are unfounded, the reluctance to explore "critical psychology" maintains the oppressive and prejudicial models inherent within psychological theory. *What is often forgotten is that post-structuralist theory, and its disciplinary formation of critical psychology, are mechanisms and tools for identifying hidden oppressions and power structures in the practices of the discipline.* It is not a new dogma but a way to think critically about the assumptions and hidden agendas of a field of study, which is itself not immune from such criticism. This does not lead to a quagmire of relativism but the need to think ethically about an area of study. Post-structuralism, like feminist and Marxist theory before it, extends the rational platform rather than undermining it.

The psychology of religion has taken some of the critical weight of post-structuralism into account by questioning the relationship between psychology and religion. It is these foundational questions that are central to the engagement between post-structuralism and psychology. To some extent the essays in this volume dealing with "psychology *and* religion" reflect a wider cultural problematization of positivistic psychology; they question the dominant assumptions of psychology over against religion. Post-structuralist theory, with its critique of essentialist models of analysis, results in the reconfiguration of boundaries between disciplines – it recognizes the power relations of disciplinary knowledge and seeks to challenge the dominant logic. I will explore the issue of the disciplinary boundary between psychology and religion in more detail later, but what is significant at this point is to note how work in critical psychology opens a space for religious discourse in the very critique of psychology. Post-structuralism, in this sense, far from disrupting the field of the psychology of religion, re-invigorates it by opening new hermeneutical frameworks. This can be seen in Steinar Kvale's edited collection of work on "postmodern psychology" – a title incorporating post-structuralist ideas (Kvale 1992).

Kvale recognizes the dislocation of "modernist" psychology from the postmodern world and proposes a number of scenarios for the further development of psychology. He suggests that psychology will move away from an "abstracted 'psyche' " into the cultural landscape, examining specific historical and cultural situations with the help of the arts and the humanities. While doubtful whether the individualistic and rationalistic roots of psychology will be able to deal with such a radical shift, Kvale (1992: 53) indicates that one of the central aspects of this debate, along with the relation of psychology to consumer society, will be the relation of psychology to religion. Kvale highlights in passing three interrelated areas in the relation between psychology and religion that need to be reconsidered in the light of postmodernity (the social conditions of late modernity). First, consideration of how psychology "took over religion's task of providing guidelines for human life"; second, how psychology in the United States became a new religion of the self; and, third, how the religious roots of (so-called scientific) psychology need to be brought to light. In relation to this third area, he uses the doctoral work of Birnbaum to show how Watson's scientific behaviorism was "almost a literal translation of the Baptist theology that Watson studied while training for the ministry" (Kvale 1992: 54). These three areas reconfigure the psychology of religion and call for more work to unearth the political and discursive roots behind the construction of psychology and religion. (I will return to these vital questions later in the essay.)

While Kvale's suggestions have yet to be explored in detail, there are signs of a slow acknowledgement of the importance of post-structuralist ideas in the psychology of religion. The second edition of David Wulff's classic textbook, while broadly working on modernist assumptions, does include a short section detailing the "Intimations of a postmodern psychology of religion." Wulff's emphasis on the pluralistic and diverse foundations of the psychology of religion allows him to effectively incorporate the emerging fragments of post-structuralist ideas. Although brief, Wulff's section on "post-modern" ideas picks up two of the central areas of post-structuralism and the psychology of religion: first, from the work of Paul Watson, he recognizes the "ideological surround" of psychology, and, second, in a similar way to Kvale, he highlights the "commonalities between religion and psychology" (Wulff 1997: 12). What Wulff recognizes, but never fully develops, is that psychology is changing and that the psychology of religion will in turn face a new set of theoretical challenges as it engages with the issues highlighted by critical theory.

Paul Watson's essay "Apologetics and ethnocentrism: psychology and religion within an ideological surround," recognized by Wulff as important for building a postmodern psychology of religion, is significant for a number of reasons. It reveals the social and historical conditions behind psychological understanding and challenges the Enlightenment foundations of the psychology of religion ("objective reason, a value-free empiricism, and the search for universal human nature"). What Watson recognizes is how the psychology of religion is bound by "tradition-specific rationalities" and socially determined "theory laden-observations" (Watson 1993: 7). He shows how research in the psychology of religion is radically transformed when the ideology behind the hypotheses is clearly identified (Watson 1993: 8). However, what is particularly interesting about Watson's work is the fact that while he acknowledges the social constructivists, and Gergen in particular, he does not draw on post-structuralist writers such as Derrida and Foucault. He also fails to see how social constructivism (like Derrida and Foucault) is still, to some extent, grounded in Enlightenment rationality. There is indeed a challenge to certain aspects of Enlightenment thought, but social constructivism (like post-structuralism) should be seen as extending the radical critique of the Enlightenment, in a self-reflexive move, rather than rejecting rational and critical enquiry.

The lack of reference in Paul Watson's essay to key post-structuralist thinkers reveals once again how the social constructivist debate relates to wider questions in the history of science and the way post-structuralist thinking should be seen as one (albeit very significant) strand in a wider discussion of psychology. There is, as Nikolas Rose has indicated following Gaston Bachelard's work on phenomenotechnics, nothing surprising in the history of science about the nature of a constructed object (Rose 1996: 51). In this sense, historian of psychology Sonu Shamdasani is correct in recognizing how the contemporary "crisis" of psychology is "the same as the attempt at foundation itself" (Carrette 1993–4: 193). Post-structuralism, social constructivism and critical psychology are various overlapping critical frameworks through which the disciplinary amnesia of psychology has been identified. It exposes the failure of psychology to acknowledge its own history and the problems of its foundation as a scientific, as opposed to a social and philosophical, project (see Danziger 1990; Carrette 1993–4).

In this respect, the psychology of religion faces the problem of both insulating itself from and developing strategic amnesia about the subject of psychology. Post-structuralist thinkers are critical of the way the psychology of religion, and its founding figures, operate upon positivistic foundations and never question the nature of the psychological subject. This lack of self-reflexive analysis raises the question of how long the psychology of religion can ignore the implications of critical projects both within and on the boundaries of the discipline of psychology. What I am suggesting is that the emergence of critical discourses in psychology raises fundamental questions about how the psychology of religion has been constructed and offers new ways to conceive of this relationship. How does an awareness of the social and historical location of ideas change the psychology of religion? What are the implications of recognizing the discourse of psychology as a political construction of human beings? By asking these questions we are, perhaps, retrieving the forgotten memories and uncovering the (social) unconscious of a discipline by putting the "subject" on its own couch!

Critical issues for religion and psychology

If the psychology of religion is to engage with post-structuralism and critical psychology it is important to highlight in summary the key theoretical issues that reshape the discipline. We need to show how psychology is challenged through the post-structuralist critique and examine how psychological knowledge is transformed in relation to religion. In order to do this I want to present four main areas from which a post-structuralist account of the psychology of religion might begin.

Psychology and history

Post-structuralist thinkers want to highlight the historical conditions of knowledge. They seek to indicate the way that psychological concepts and ideas have emerged from within particular social contexts. This historical project, as Canguilhem pointed out, is difficult for psychologists because it threatens to expose the issue of the foundations of psychology as a discipline. As Kurt Danziger notes: "Looking at psychological categories and concepts with a historical perspective runs directly counter to one of the most deeply embedded features of modern psychology: its *ahistoricism*" (Danziger 1997: 9). Psychology, as Danziger goes on to show, does produce its own histories, but these narratives can be ahistorical in so far they assume the givenness of a particular concept or idea. They do not examine this history critically. What is required, following the work of Canguilhem and Foucault, is to produce a history of the "discursive formation" – the network of processes that brought about a particular psychological idea. It is to ask, with Foucault: what were the conditions that produced these psychological concepts? (See Foucault 1967.)

This critical endeavor challenges the assumptions that "psychological facts" exist outside of the conditions that have created them. In this sense psychological theory as much creates its objects and subjects as discovers them. Psychology sets up certain disciplinary conditions through which a particular object or subject can be defined. As Richards' (1996: 5) historical analysis of psychology indicates: "Psychology is produced by, produces, and is an instance of, its own subject matter." The human being is not a given reality but something imagined through different historical epochs. Some may accuse post-structuralists of committing a "genetic fallacy" (explaining away an object by revealing its origins) but this is a simplistic reading of very specific historical studies.[3] The historical pinpointing of psychological concepts shows that ideas serve particular social and political ideologies. In different historical periods there are different priorities and different social structures which allow different questions to be raised.

> From at least 1700 they could have run rats through mazes, circulated questionnaires, seen how many trials it took to learn word lists, or invented instruments to measure reaction times – all methods typical of

modern psychology. The reason they did not was that they were not asking these questions in the first place.

(Richards 1996: 10)

It is the need to identify the wider social processes that "produced" the questions and changed the way society conceived of itself that is important. This project becomes revealing when it is shown that psychological testing and experimentation supports certain dominant groups. It reveals how certain gendered, racial, class or sexually orientated groups are excluded (see, for example, Burman 1994). Psychologists are not so much discovering the "truth" of human beings as revealing how certain models of being human can be shaped through different experimental conditions or hypotheses which are subsequently held up as revealing the "truth." The limits of psychological theory and experimentation expose the limits and variables of psychological "truth" and the power relations hidden within such studies. It is, to give just one example, now clearly recognized that the work of Piaget examining cognitive development did not so much reveal the "truth" of children's minds as reveal how the questions and experimental tests restricted the responses of children (Donaldson 1978).

The psychology of religion, as is necessary for disciplinary identity, has produced its own histories and is continually doing so, but what post-structuralist ideas illustrate is the need for critical histories which identify the wider social, political and discursive conditions of the psychology of religion. Whose interests do the psychology of religion serve? Which social and political realities benefited from the discursive regime of the psychology of religion? *We need to identify the conditions that brought religion and psychology together, or perhaps more significantly, show how psychology separated itself out from already pre-existing models of religious introspection.* When the subject of psychology has itself been historically and critically destabilized, using the perspectives of post-structuralism, how do scholars of religion engage with the subject? How does post-structuralist theory cause us to rethink the project of the psychology of religion? These questions form the basis of future work examining the relationship between religion and psychology.

The nature of psychological discourse

The recognition of the social and historical conditions of psychological concepts is intrinsically related to the way language or discourse forms an object and creates an experience. Psychology does not suddenly invent or discover the human being out of neutral experimentation, it rather draws on pre-existing models of the human being from the wider culture and then develops a language from this basis. The language of psychology emerges from a wider cultural context and in turn shapes experience with its own framing of the human being in a new language of observation and categorization. Psychological language continually changes by creating and drawing in new registers from the cultural context. It is no surprise, in this sense, that cognitive psychology becomes dominant in an age of computer technology. The metaphorical registers of a culture are drawn into psychology. The dynamic relationship between language and psychological theory is captured by Graham Richards in his attempt to "put psychology in its place":

> Students often have great difficulty in grasping ... that nobody prior to Freud has an Oedipus complex, that nobody before Pavlov and Watson was ever "conditioned" and that nobody before c. 1914 had a high IQ ... The very act of introducing such concepts changed the situation by providing people with new terms in which to experience themselves – and only *then* can they be properly said to refer to really occurring psychological phenomena.
>
> (Richards 1996: 7)

This can be seen in the area of the psychology of religion in the way William James took the category of "mysticism" and re-worked the idea in terms of intense, ineffable experiences (Jantzen 1989). After James, mysticism was transformed into a psychological event. The significance of language in the psychology of religion is important in so far as it reveals two key issues: the way psychological language is parasitic on religious and theological traditions, and, second, the way psychological registers transform religious experience. There is also a major problem in psychological theory when ideas and concepts are reified and take on a life outside the initial observations and hypotheses. Jung's language of "archetypes" is one example of how an initial hypothesis can become a psychological fact, which in turn serves to mask the social conditions behind the oppressive models of women it generated (see Goldenberg 1979; Carrette 1994). Future work in the psychology of religion needs to examine the ways in which psychological discourse "represents" the world and "narrates" human experience.

Psychology and binary logic

Post-structuralist thinkers want to challenge the way psychology is dependent on binary logic. This challenge has principally taken place on two fronts: the challenge to the separation of the individual and the social, and, second, the challenge to the Cartesian division between body and mind (or the way the body has been marginalized). These binary divisions pervade much of the literature of psychology and in turn support oppressive social practices, particularly in terms of gender, "race" and sexual orientation. Once the body is devalued it allows those who are culturally and symbolically associated with the body (materiality) to be positioned as "other" and to be excluded from authority and value. As Jantzen (1998:66) indicates, wherever there is a binary distinction we need to ask: whose interests does such logic serve?

As a number of critical psychologists have shown, the binary opposition between the individual and social can be seen as an attempt to isolate and control the individual as a separate unit. This functional separation provided a mechanism for the control of mass societies, what Foucault called "bio-politics"; it formed part of the organization and discipline of technological societies. The individual was made a "subject" (subjectivity) and became "subject to" (authority) in the creation of a "subject" (the discipline of psychology). Psychology, supported by the economic forces of capitalism, reinforced the sense of "individualism" in Western society and obscured the sense in which the individual consciousness was part of the social con-sciousness. "Critical psychology" brings psychology back to the political realization that psychology is inseparable from the social. This is not, as Henriques *et al.* (1984: 11–25) have indicated, a matter of just following "social psychology" (which still makes a distinction between the social and individual) but the location of one within the other. It is recognizing the psychological as social. This critical position has significant implications for the study of religion, in so far as it acknowledges the relationship between different types of (social) consciousness and different religious/cultural traditions. The social and religious/cultural context is essential in under-standing the nature of human experience. Thus, for example, when we examine Maslow's (1970) "peak experiences" and religion we need to examine to what extent this type of consciousness is shaped by the politics of Western capitalism and whether it devalues the importance of community.

A more prominent debate about binary oppositions in psychology has arisen in relation to the long-running philosophical distinction between body and mind. Recent post-structuralist thinking changes this debate by locating the body and mind in specific discursive practices. It is argued that there is no neutral thing called "body" or "mind" out there, but a series of cultural registers which map the surfaces and spaces of lived and embodied minds. Bourdieu's idea of "habitus," or "the lived body," has been used to overcome the traditional dichotomy of Western thinking (Bourdieu 1977; 1990). The "mind" is always an embodied mind, in so far that minds cannot exist without bodies; and a psychology which does not locate the mind in its embodied and lived state is only ever a partial psychology. Edward Sampson (1998), one of a group of psychologists trying to re-think psychology through the body, reflects on this theme with reference to particular religious traditions. He not only draws attention to the historical division of body and mind in the Judaic-Christian tradition, but highlights contemporary religious activities which reflect the integration of body and mind in practice. Sampson is first interested in the Buddhist practices of meditation to show how the mind and body form a unity. Although such a view ignores the fact that Buddhist meditation is attempting to dissolve the illusion of personal unity/identity rather than integrate body and mind as such, he does show how bodily posture affects mental states (something which could have been developed much further in an exploration of yogic practices).[4] Sampson

(1998: 40–43) also discusses the issue of Pentecostalism and the key role of embodied religious emotion in shared community. These examples provide a key insight into how the psychology of religion has, for example, been preoccupied with such things as "altered states of consciousness" without appreciating the embodied nature of such practices. The psychology of religion, through its disciplinary amnesia, has been uncritically constrained by its adoption of binary modes of thinking and needs to find ways of thinking about religion and psychology as embodied practices.

The nature of psychological technology

Post-structuralist thinkers also want to examine the social technology of psychological ideas. They want to ask, with Canguilhem, what is being done with this psychological knowledge? How are psychological ideas implemented in terms of social structures? Such questions recognize psychology as a "technology," as an array of techniques of social inscription. As Nikolas Rose, following Foucault, points out:

> [P]sychology is intrinsically bound to "human technologies." It forms a part of the practical rationalities of assemblages that seek to act upon human beings to shape their conduct in particular directions – assemblages such as those of the legal apparatus, of schooling, of child rearing, *even of spiritual guidance.*
>
> (Rose 1996: 54, emphasis added)

Psychology, according to such a position, controls subjects in mass globalized societies. For those post-structuralist thinkers influenced by Foucault, the engagement of religious ideas with psychology is part of the adoption of a "conceptual rationale," a discourse of taxonomy and classification, by which a society can be organized. This organization of society occurs through a diffuse and heterogeneous set of practices and discourses which "psychologize" reality (Rose 1996: 59). Psychologists of religion have to be aware that to some extent they have served to provide a disciplinary apparatus for "psychologizing" religion, making religious ideas more responsive to a Western, individualistic and capitalistic regime. The use of personality tests to find prayer or spirituality "types" is but one example of the privatization and commodification of religious practices. Critical psychology is in part an attempt to examine how psychology became a "technology" for ordering religious practices in the West. The question we need to ask is: what benefits does religious discourse achieve in developing such a strategic alliance with psychology?

Rethinking the psychology of religion

In conclusion to this examination of post-structuralism and the psychology of religion, I want briefly to explore how the field of the psychology of religion can conceptually rethink its project. In this sense the critical project of post-structuralism should not be seen as the rejection of studies in psychology and religion but as the possibility of reconfiguration. In addition, my suggestions should not be seen as limiting the possibilities of engagement but as one particular step in a wider project to rethink the discipline after 130 years of foundational uncertainty and disciplinary amnesia.

Psychology and religion as models of introspection

The problematization of the foundations of psychology through post-structuralist thinking reshapes the relationship between religion and psychology, and reconfigures that relationship in terms of what Richards calls "reflexive discourse," but which I have called elsewhere "models of introspection" (Richards 1996: 13; Carrette 1993–4). Following the work of John Shotter (1975), human beings can be seen as self-defining animals and psychology can be seen to hold certain hidden images of being human. Psychology is therefore not a neutral science (presuming there can be such a thing), but a particular type of introspective discourse constructed through empirical and statistical models (see Danziger 1990). These models are always parasitic on the present cultural registers of what it is to be human. If we acknowledge that psychology is a particular type of introspective discourse it is vital to examine the underlying cultural models from which human beings are positioned. In this sense religion and psychological studies needs to reconceive itself as a critical discourse of different models of introspection. Such a focus will mean that future work in the psychology of religion will need to carry out three interrelated tasks: first, an examination of the social and historical roots of human image construction and identity; second, an exploration of the religious ideas that infiltrate into psychology; and third, a critical assessment of the models of human beings provided by psychology. Psychology and religion will perhaps in the future need to be seen as two different but related ideological frames for constructing images of the self.

Cultural psychology and religion

The psychology of religion (or "religion and psychological studies" as the field is now more carefully re-named) is uniquely placed to assess the ideological discourses of introspection by drawing on the history of different religious and cultural traditions. These discourses culturally sanction images of the human being in order to propagate and cohere the interests of a particular community. When the division between social processes and private introspection is collapsed, it is possible to re-position religion and psychology as interconnected discourses inside a framework of what Foucault (1978, 1979) called *governmentality* (see Carrette 2000: 129–41). Religion and psychology are thus seen as different types of introspective discourse that construct human images and provide models for governing the self/soul.

When religion and psychological studies are reconstructed in this way the traditional dichotomies of religion/psychology, body/mind, individual/social are suspended. The introspective discourses of religion and psychology then become reflections of the politics of "race," gender and colonial power (see Carrette and Keller 1999; Richards 1997). The future of religious and psychological studies needs therefore to be reconfigured as a critical and ethical analysis of human images in their historical and cultural context. Such a position is an attempt to understand introspection as an ideological vector of tradition, belief and practice. This requires an examination of models of introspection in other religious traditions/cultures and the building of a cultural-psychology from which to assess the political basis of human image construction. If the psychology of religion is unable to critically assess Western psychological discourse and fails to appreciate non-Western models of introspection it can only be seen as a hegemonic and imperialist reinforcement of Western ideologies of the self (King 1999: 182).

The future of the psychology of religion must be built on a cultural-psychology that recognizes diversity in human image construction and models of introspection. This also requires careful and critical assessment of whether the signifier "psychology" is useful to describe non-Western models of introspection. Is it correct to refer to "Buddhist psychology" given the very specific Western registers built into psychological discourse? To what extent do we colonize non-Western introspective discourse when we reconstruct them in terms of Western psychology? These questions provide a way to open up the field of the psychology of religion in a cross-cultural engagement which does not prioritize Western models.

Religion and the politics of psychological theory

If the wider boundaries between religion and psychology are transformed through critical perspectives, there is also a need to examine critically the specific aspects of theories and methods in the psychology of religion. The limits of this essay do not permit a more extensive study of the range of different theories, but it is important to examine the different theories in the field of the psychology of religion according to the ideological values they propagate. Religion and psychological studies needs to be aware of how its adoption of theories from "general psychology" can also be the adoption and acceptance of oppressive constructions.

In the field of developmental psychology, for example, it has now been shown how notions of development hold certain colonial and gender assumptions. This has been particularly demonstrated in Eric Burman's incisive work *Deconstructing Developmental Psychology* (1994). Following through many of the themes of critical psychology, Burman challenges the normative assumptions of developmental psychology in order to reveal the techniques of measurement and the way "the child" is constructed through social, cultural and historical processes. In her critique of Jean Piaget, for example, Burman shows how "the quintessential developing child is a boy" and "a scientist" (Burman 1994: 159; cf. Morss 1996). She also notes in passing the significant influence of liberal Protestantism on Piaget's work, something which had been explored much earlier, and in more detail, by Mary Vander Goot (Burman 1994: 159; Vander Goot 1985). Such a recognition of the religious ideas behind supposedly neutral (scientific) work reveals the importance of developing a series of religious genealogies (or critical histories) for both individual psychologists and their concepts. The proliferation of developmental theories in the psychology of religion, such as those developed from the work of Freud, Erikson and Piaget, make the task of employing the work of critical psychologist more urgent. It reflects the need throughout the discipline to re-examine concepts and theories which are so easily borrowed uncritically from psychology.

Conclusion

> "Psychology" is merely a thin skin on the surface of the ethical world in which modern man [sic] seeks his truth – and loses it.
>
> (Foucault 1962: 74)

The introduction of post-structuralist theory into the psychology of religion should not therefore be seen as some new, or even trendy, intellectual fashion, but as an essential part of any internal monitoring of a disciplinary practice, as an ethical and foundational strategy. The theoretical frameworks of post-structuralism allow the psychology of religion to re-examine its forgotten foundational assumptions and overcome oppressive and prejudicial ideas at work in the "subject." What post-structuralism and its development of critical psychology recognizes, as pointed out, is the need for psychology "to outgrow its political innocence" (Fox and Prilleltensky 1997: ix). Critical psychology is a "deconstruction" or "reconstruction," *not* a "destruction," of the discipline – it offers ways to rethink the subject politically and extend the critical apparatus to the discipline itself. The psychology of religion can no longer remain naive about the problems of its foundation and its history. The future of the psychology of religion is therefore to be found in its past – by overcoming its disciplinary amnesia and developing a "history of the present" (Foucault 1975: 31). Such a task is to recognize that the future of the psychology of religion will be found in the history of its omissions, its denials, in the forgotten and the feared, in the return to hell.

Notes

1　My idea of "disciplinary amnesia" is developed from Foucault's argument that positivistic psychology, in founding a discipline that excluded the difficult and problematic areas of human experience, fatally provided Western consciousness with the "ability to forget" (Foucault 1962: 87). I use the phrase "disciplinary amnesia" to refer to the procedure through which a discourse is able to function by suppressing issues and problems that undermine its coherence (see also Foucault 1970 for a discussion of the rules of exclusion within a discourse).

2　In this respect it is interesting to note that Foucault did not regard himself as either post-structuralist or postmodernist, and although he was labeled a structuralist (following the publication of his 1966 work *The Order of Things*) he vehemently rejected such a description of his work. It is therefore more important to examine the texts of a particular thinker rather than group them uncritically in any neat category.

3　I am grateful to Robert Segal for introducing me to the idea of a supposed "genetic fallacy" during a series of unpublished discussions between us on post-structuralism and religion. See Segal (1980) for a wider examination of Segal's work on "truth" and religious studies.

4　I am grateful to my colleague Richard King for his clarification on issues of Buddhist meditation and for his very helpful reflections on the essay.

References

Bayer, B.M. and Shotter, J. (eds) (1998) *Reconstructing the Psychological Subject: Bodies, Practices and Technologies*, London: Sage.

Bourdieu, P. (1977) *Outline of a Theory of Practice*, Cambridge: Cambridge University Press.

—— (1990) *The Logic of Practice*, Stanford, CA: Stanford University Press.

Burman, E. (1994) *Deconstructing Developmental Psychology*, London: Routledge.

Canguilhem, G. (1956) "What is psychology?" *Ideology and Consciousness* 7 (autumn 1980): 37–50.

Carrette, J.R. (1993–4) "The psychology of religion: re-examining the psychological 'subject'," *Journal of Psychology of Religion* 2–3: 171–99.

—— (1994) "The language of archetypes: a conspiracy in psychological theory," *Harvest: Journal for Jungian Studies* 40: 168–92.

—— (2000) *Foucault and Religion*, London: Routledge.

Carrette, J.R. and Keller, M. (1999) "Religions, orientation and critical theory: race, gender and sexuality at the 1998 Lambeth Conference," *Theology and Sexuality* 11: 19–41.

Danziger, K. (1990) *Constructing the Subject: Historical Origins of Psychological Research*, Cambridge: Cambridge University Press.

—— (1997) *Naming the Mind: How Psychology Found its Language*, London: Sage.

Derrida, J. (1967) *Writing and Difference*, Routledge: London (English edn 1978).

—— (1972) *The Margins of Philosophy*, Chicago: University of Chicago Press (English edn 1982).

Donaldson, M. (1978) *Children's Minds*, London: Fontana.

Foucault, M. (1957) "La recherche scientifique et la psychologie," in Daniel Defert and François Ewald (eds) *Dits et écrits*, Paris: Gallimard (new edn 1994), vol. 1, pp. 137–58.

—— (1962) *Mental Illness and Psychology*, Berkeley, CA: University of California Press (English edn 1987).

—— (1965) "Philosophie et psychologie," in Daniel Defert and François Ewald (eds) *Dits et écrits*, Paris: Gallimard (new edn 1994), vol. 1, pp. 438–48.

—— (1966) *The Order of Things*, London: Routledge (English edn 1991).

—— (1967) *Madness and Civilization*, London: Routledge (English edn 1991).

—— (1969) *The Archaeology of Knowledge*, London: Routledge (English edn 1991).

—— (1970) "The discourse on language," in *The Archaeology of Knowledge*, New York: Pantheon Books (English edn 1972), pp. 215–37.

—— (1975) *Discipline and Punish: The Birth of the Prison*, London: Penguin (English edn 1991).

—— (1978) "Governmentality," in G. Burchell, C. Gordon and P. Miller (eds), *The Foucault Effect: Studies in Governmentality*, London: Harvester Wheatsheaf, pp. (1991) 87–104.

—— (1979) "*Omnes et singulatim*: toward a criticism of 'Political Reason'," in Sterling M. McMurrin (ed.) *The Tanner Lectures on Human Values*, vol. 2, Cambridge: Cambridge University Press, (1981) pp. 223–54.

Fox, D. and Prilleltensky, I. (eds) (1997) *Critical Psychology: An Introduction*, London: Sage.

Gergen, K. (1973) "Social psychology as history," *Journal of Personality and Social Psychology* 26: 309–20.

—— (1985) "The social constructionist movement in modern psychology," *American Psychologist* 40: 266–75.

Goldenberg, N. (1979) *Changing of the Gods*, Boston: Beacon.

Harré, R. (1979) *Social Being: A Theory for Social Psychology*, Oxford: Blackwell.

Henriques, J., Hollway, W., Urwin, C., Venn, C., and Walkerdine, V. (1984) *Changing the Subject: Psychology, Social Regulation and Subjectivity*, London: Routledge.

Jantzen, G. (1989) "Mysticism and experience," *Religious Studies* 25 (September): 295–315.

—— (1998) *Becoming Divine: Towards a Feminist Philosophy of Religion*, Manchester: Manchester University Press.

King, R. (1999) *Orientalism and Religion*, London: Routledge.

Kvale, S. (ed.) (1992) *Psychology and Postmodernism*, London: Sage.

Maslow, A. (1970) *Religions, Values and Peak-Experiences*, New York: Penguin.

Morss, J.R. (1996) *Growing Critical: Alternatives to Developmental Psychology*, London: Routledge.

Parker, I. (1992) *Discourse Dynamics: Critical Analysis for Social and Individual Psychology*, London: Routledge.

—— (1999) "Critical psychology: critical links," *Annual Review of Critical Psychology*, 1 (*Foundations*): 3–18.

Parker, I. and Shotter, J. (eds) (1990) *Deconstructing Social Psychology*, London: Routledge.

Richards, G. (1996) *Putting Psychology in its Place: An Introduction from a Critical Historical Perspective*, London: Routledge.

—— (1997) "*Race*", *Racism and Psychology: Towards a Reflexive History*, Routledge: London.

Rose, N. (1996) *Inventing Our Selves: Psychology, Power, and Personhood*, Cambridge: Cambridge University Press.

Sampson, E. (1998) "Establishing embodiment in psychology," in Henderikus J. Stam (ed.), *The Body and Psychology*, London: Sage, pp. 30–53.

Segal, R. (1980) "The social sciences and the truth of religious belief," *Journal of the American Academy of Religion* 48: 403–13.

Shotter, J. (1975) *Images of Man in Psychological Research*, London: Methuen.

Shotter, J. and Gergen, K. (eds) (1989) *Texts of Identity*, London: Sage.

Shweder, R.A. (1990) "Cultural psychology – what is it?" in J. W. Stigler, R.A. Shweder and G. Herdt (eds), *Cultural Psychology: Essays on Comparative Human Development*, Cambridge: Cambridge University Press, pp. 1–43.

Smith, J., Harré, R., and Van Langenhove, L. (eds) (1995) *Rethinking Psychology*, London: Sage.

Sturrock, J. (1993) *Structuralism*, 2nd edn, London: Fontana.

Vander Goot, M. (1985) *Piaget as a Visionary Thinker*, Bristol, IN: Wyndham Hall Press.

Watson, P. (1993) "Apologetics and ethnocentrism: psychology and religion within an ideological surround," *International Journal for the Psychology of Religion* 3(1): 1–20.

Wulff, D. (1997) *Psychology of Religion. Classic and Contemporary*, New York: John Wiley & Sons.

Section 3

Psychology, religion, and gender studies

8   Analysts, critics, and inclusivists

Feminist voices in the psychology of religion

Diane Jonte-Pace

In 1992 Carol Christ warned that feminists in religious studies "will be sojourners for a long time to come" (1992: 87). Christ was correct to be concerned about the immense resistance in religious studies to feminist methods and theories, and yet, within some areas of the field, feminist scholarship has flourished. In this paper I'll consider the effects of feminist scholarship upon the psychological study of religion, arguing that feminist transformations have been enacted within one major branch of the field, while within other branches feminists continue to be sojourners, just as Christ predicted.[1]

In the psychological study of religion, as in other fields of religious studies, feminist scholars have initiated three kinds of projects (Jonte-Pace 1997b). Feminist *critics* have exposed and challenged the androcentric methods and theories previously regnant in the field (Warne 1989). Feminist *inclusivists* have proposed new methods and theories capable of interpreting and illuminating women's religious lives and experiences. And feminist *analysts* have exposed both the cultural and religious construction of gender and the gendered construction of religion and culture.

Feminist research, flourishing within the interpretive territory of the psychology of religion, is particularly prominent in relation to the work of theorists influenced by depth psychology: Freud, Jung, the object relations theorists, and the post-structuralists. Although depth psychology is certainly not the only approach to the psychological study of religion influenced by feminist theory, it illustrates clearly a set of dramatic historical shifts: psychoanalytic discourse on religion, for example, shifts from an androcentric stance in which women are virtually insignificant to a rather different stance devoted to the analysis and critique of misogyny in culture and religion. This chapter will focus on three topics particularly significant in the psychological interpretation of religion: morality, ritual, and God-imagery. Freud's study of the psychological origins of morality, Jung's study of the psychological sources of God-imagery, and object relational studies of the psychodynamics of ritual will provide the framework for our discussion; Kristeva's post-structuralist studies of these three topics – morality, God-imagery and ritual – will conclude the paper. In each case, I'll discuss both the theory of religion and the feminist responses to and extensions of the theory. Final remarks will offer speculations regarding feminist engagements with another major branch of the field: the psychology and religion movement.

The psychological origins of morality: Freud's view

Sigmund Freud is well known for his psychological analyses of the origins of religious ideas and practices and for his Enlightenment-based critique of the adverse effects of religion on psyche and culture. The foundation of his interpretation of religion and morality is his Oedipal theory of fantasies of incest and parricide accompanied by fears of castration. The young child in the throes of the Oedipus complex, he argued, expresses incestuous love for the mother and murderous hatred for the father. The father forbids the child to act on these fantasies; the male child experiences castration anxiety and abandons the Oedipal fantasies in a renunciation that Freud considered the first moral act. Castration anxiety, permanently inscribed in the psyche through the memory of the father's forbidding voice – internalized as the "superego" – sets the pattern for later moral relationships to other paternal figures including Gods and social authorities. Thus the renunciation produced by castration anxiety represents the origin of morality.

Pursuing the logic of his own argument, Freud concluded that the female equivalent to castration anxiety, penis envy, generates a weaker form of morality and a weaker connection to civilization. In a short essay called "Some psychical consequences of the anatomical distinction between the sexes," he stated,

> I cannot evade the notion (though I hesitate to give it expression) that for women the level of what is ethically normal is different from what it is in men .... Women ... show less sense of justice ... they are less ready to submit to the great exigencies of life, they are more often influenced in their judgments by feelings of affection or hostility.
>
> (1961a: 257)

Freud softened his argument with the assurance that "we shall of course willingly agree that the majority of men are also far behind the masculine ideal" (257), but the impact of his statement cannot be mitigated. Only males, within Freud's Oedipal framework, are capable of true morality: women are far less capable of the renunciations and sublimations required for the production and maintenance of culture, religion, and ethics.

Freud applied the same Oedipal paradigm to the historical and cultural origins of religion. In *Totem and Taboo* he located the origins of morality and the worship of a paternal God in the deep remorse which followed the parricidal act of a prehistoric group of young males: he speculated that a group of brothers "came together, killed and devoured their father ... [in] a memorable and criminal deed which was the beginning of so many things – of social organization, of moral restrictions and of religion" (1955: 141–2). And in *The Ego and the Id* he acknowledged explicitly the gendered nature of this narrative of the origins of belief and morality: "religion, morality, and a social sense – the chief elements in the higher side of man – were ... acquired phylogenetically out of the father-complex .... the male sex seems to have taken the lead in all these moral acquisitions" (1961b: 37).

Feminist responses to Freud

Numerous feminist critics have taken issue with Freud's theory of the gendered origins of religion and morality. Psychologist of religion David Wulff notes the deep androcentrism of the theory: "Freud's psychology of religion is ... clearly centered in masculine reactivity. It is the male's ambivalent relationship with his father, both in his own and in the race's childhood that lies at the core of religion" (1997: 285). Focusing in particular on gender and moral development, Carol Gilligan provides a classic critique of Freud's theory, questioning the notion that only men are capable of full moral development. Arguing that Freud "began with the exploration of women's experience [but] arrived at a theory that shadowed that experience" (1984: 87), Gilligan concluded that the Oedipal theory itself prevented Freud from understanding women: "Having built a theory that could not include women in its account of development, Freud can only defend his theory by showing how women fail to develop" (87). Her solution is to look elsewhere – to object relations theory, for example – for theories of female moral development. Feminist critics like Gilligan challenge Freud's moral theory for its androcentrism and phallocentrism, noting that psychoanalysis assumes male normativity and female inferiority, and that it makes the phallus crucial to cultural and moral development.

While feminist critics reject psychoanalysis for its insistence on the centrality of penis envy in female moral development, its obsession with the father–son configurations of the Oedipus complex and its exclusion of women from the work of culture, feminist analysts, many of whom were influenced by Juliet Mitchell's work *Psychoanalysis and Feminism* (1974), have asked whether Freud's account might be valuable to feminists seeking to analyze, understand and change the workings of gendered social hierarchies. Foremost among these feminist analytic theorists is Judith van Herik. Pursuing Philip Rieff's provocative insight that "Freud's misogyny is more than prejudice; it has a vital intellectual function in his system" (1979: 181), van Herik seeks to understand how "the pejorative image of woman serves as a measure of the general critical component" in Freud's theory of culture (van Herik 1982: 3). She shows that Freud associates wish fulfillment and Christian religious belief with femininity, while, by contrast, he associates the renunciation of wishes and Jewish morality with masculinity. In addition, she uncovers within his texts a notion of a "higher" form of masculinity: a post-religious, morally renunciatory, scientific rationality like the rarely achieved "masculine ideal" described above. Van Herik's project is a classic gender analysis: her interest is in the functions of the concepts of masculinity and femininity within Freud's theory of religion and culture. She also acknowledges the possibility that Freud's gendering of illusion and belief corresponds to a broad cultural pattern: she urges a serious consideration of Freud's claims "about how gender works in our moral economy and about how gender and uses of God are thereby intertwined" (200). Thus, while in Gilligan's view Freud simply failed to understand women, van Herik interpreted the same facts analytically rather than critically: rather than rejecting Freud's theory of women's inferior moral position, she examined it more closely, showing that an analysis of the masculinity of ideal morality in Freud's writings exposes the gendering of Freud's entire theory of religion and culture.

A group of scholars in "Jewish cultural studies" has produced another set of important feminist analyses of Freud in the last decade. Among these is Jay Geller, whose publications have been instrumental in demonstrating the racist cultural ideologies to which Freud's work was a response: Geller uncovers an antisemitic *Weltanschauung* within which male Jews were considered feminine or effeminate (1992a, 1992b, 1993, 1997, 1999). Geller's research provides an important context within which to understand van Herik's thesis about Freud's feminization of Christian religious belief and masculinization of Jewish morality: as a Jewish male in a misogynist and antisemitic world which feminized Jewish males, Freud turned the tables, as it were, by subtly underscoring the psychological femininity of "illusory" Christian belief, and the psychological masculinity of renunciatory Jewish morality and intellect.

Sander Gilman adds to Geller's feminist analysis of the way race and gender are intertwined in Freud's work and world. He develops a carefully textured argument claiming that Freud transmutes "the rhetoric of race into the construction of gender" (1993: 36). He shows that while Jewish males were feminized in relation to Aryan males in *fin de siècle* ideologies, Freud and his Jewish colleagues considered themselves symbolically and morally male through acculturation into the world of Western science and education. Freud felt, Gilman suggests, that "in acquiring the professional mantle of the scientist the Jew became 'masculine' ... the exclusionary category of the Jew was abrogated" (1993: 10). Gilman's work, in my view, establishes the cultural and historical context for van Herik's argument regarding the vision of science as a form of "ideal masculinity" in Freud's cultural texts. Van Herik's, Geller's and Gilman's feminist analyses of Freud point suggestively toward important insights into the unconscious and ideological deep structures of Freud's culture and our own.[2]

While the work of Gilligan exemplifies the critical project, and the works of van Herik and the Jewish cultural theorists are paradigmatic analytic projects, few inclusivists have worked with Freud's texts. Feminist inclusivists in the psychology of religion have more often turned to Jung and to the object relations theorists.

The psychological origins of God-imagery: Jung's view

Carl Gustav Jung devoted a great deal of his voluminous *oeuvre* to religion. His theories have generated an ongoing discourse about myth, religion, healing, and spirituality. Although his work is often contrasted with Freud's, the two figures share many assumptions about religion and psychology. Jung, with his "analytical psychology" and Freud with his "psychoanalysis" both developed "projection theories" in their quests for the origins of religion; both assumed that the contents of the unconscious are the primary force shaping religious ideas, images, and symbols; and both focused on religion as a primary site for the intersections of culture and psyche.

In spite of their similarities, however, there are major differences. Most significantly, Jung neither constructed an Enlightenment-based critique of religion nor proposed the abandonment of religion. Rather, he offered a diagnosis of the pathology of contemporary religion and a prognosis for its cure. Contemporary Western religion, he insisted, has lost contact with the transformative power of the unconscious and its collective, numinous, and "archetypal" components: the Christian notion of God the Father is dangerously unbalanced. He urged a substantial transformation of the Christian God image through reconnection with the archetypal feminine.

Rejecting Freud's theory of unconscious Oedipal drives and fantasies as a source of religious ideas, Jung offered his own theory of the unconscious, differentiating the "personal" from the "collective" unconscious: while the personal unconscious is the repository of individual memories, fantasies, and desires, the collective unconscious is shared by all human beings. The Jungian collective unconscious is the carrier of archetypal "forms without content," symbols *in potentia*, manifested in dreams and myths. Cross-cultural and trans-historical propensities, the archetypes produce mythic and symbolic ideas. Generated during the centuries and millennia of human history and pre-history, the archetypes continue to influence our lives and our psyches. We ignore them at our peril.

Jung devoted a great deal of attention to categorizing the archetypes, describing their manifestations, and demonstrating their relations to individual and cultural health and pathology. In Jung's archetypal theory, individuals ideally progress along a continuum toward greater "individuation" through a predictable sequence of encounters with and integrations of archetypal images (Jung 1968). First one encounters the "shadow," the darker side of the personality, often portrayed in Western religious imagery as a satanic or demonic figure. Subsequently, one encounters the "contra-sexual archetype" – the anima (the feminine, relational, "Eros" side of the male unconscious), or the animus (the masculine, rational, "Logos" side of the female unconscious). The anima appears in religious discourse as the soul, while the animus appears as a spiritual guide. The psychological process of integration with the contra-sexual archetype is often experienced, Jung thought, in dreams or fantasies of a sacred marriage or *hieros gamos*. Following the integration of anima or animus, one may encounter the archetype of the Great Mother, the Wise Old Man, the trickster, the hero, or the child. Finally, and most importantly, one confronts and, ideally, integrates the archetype of the Self which often takes the form of a deity, a four-sided "quaternity," or a "mandala." Thus the individuated human being has, in a sense, experienced God, or, to be more precise, the "God archetype."

Cultures, in Jung's view, undergo a progression similar to individuals; both individuals and cultures can fall into periods of pathology and imbalance. Jung's critique of contemporary culture and religion was based on his understanding of the archetypes, individuation, and the collective unconscious. In the post-Enlightenment period, Jung argued, Western religion has become excessively rational and masculine, losing touch with the collective unconscious in general and with the feminine archetypes in particular. While Freud was highly critical of the projection of the parental relationship on to God, he did not interrogate the gender of God: God was "an exalted father" (Freud 1957: 123). Jung, on the other hand, called for a cultural and religious rebalancing through a reincorporation of the missing archetypal and feminine elements: he was fascinated with images of female deities in religious texts, sacred iconography, fairy tales, and myths (1982). He saw Great Mother Goddesses, Divine Brides, and triads of mythic maidens, mothers and crones as components of the repressed feminine archetype. And he celebrated the mid-twentieth-century papal proclamation of the doctrine of the Assumption of the Blessed Virgin Mary as "the most important religious event since the Reformation," interpreting it as a shift toward the incorporation of the feminine archetype into the Godhead (1969: 464).

Feminist responses to Jung

Prior to the late 1980s, Jung's approach was often enlisted as a methodology compatible with feminist studies. His critique of the cultural repression of the feminine was seen as an aid in the feminist critique of culture. His interest in feminine archetypes was viewed as part of the inclusive project of feminist theory, the incorporation of women's lives into contemporary scholarship. His fascination with feminine God images was seen as a contribution to the feminist political and theological agenda. An initial enthusiasm, however, was followed by a more cautious stance as feminists began to discover problematic forms of androcentrism and misogyny within Jung's work and to express hesitation about exploiting Jungian methods in their inclusive efforts.

Jung's theory was initially acclaimed as feminist for a number of reasons. First, in its foundational principles, the theory is far from "womanless" (McIntosh 1983): feminists embraced Jung's unprecedented attention to female images and symbols. Second, Jung challenged stereotyped understandings of gender with his notion of the anima and animus. Third, his critique of culture and religion as excessively masculine resonated with feminist critiques of patriarchal culture and male God-imagery. In a classic statement of this Jungian, feminist, inclusivist position, Joan Chamberlain Engelsman wrote:

> if the feminine is not restored to its archetypal place in Western religion, the results might be catastrophic. Although the repression of the feminine dimension of the divine creates especially poignant problems for women, its restoration may be necessary for the psychic health of all people.
>
> (Engelsman 1979: 41)

Numerous Jungian feminists (Goldenberg 1979; Wehr 1987; Hall 1980; Ulanov 1971, 1981) pursued this inclusive project in what might be considered a first phase of feminist engagement with Jung's psychology of religion.

A second wave of feminists, however, has reconsidered this stance. Devoting attention to female symbols and images, they suggest – even female God-images – may appear "inclusivist," but may not, in fact, enact a feminist move, since female imagery can convey sexist, dualistic, or misogynist perspectives. They point out the presence of subtle forms of androcentrism in Jungian thought: the notion of the archetypal feminine is rife with assumptions about female inferiority. They note as well that in Jung's work the subject is typically male: the integration of the contents of the male unconscious provides the essential paradigm for individuation. Naomi Goldenberg, whose own intellectual trajectory in the psychology of religion illustrates this shift from inclusivity to critique, points out that although Jung valued the feminine, he did not value women. Jung wanted woman "to stay in the sphere of … 'Eros.' Once she moved into a 'Logos' arena she was not only at a great disadvantage, but extremely annoying as well" (Goldenberg 1977: 57–8). And she argues that Jung's archetypal theory contributes to a massive cultural pathology: a valuing of eternal, transcendent, disembodied, archetypal "truths," and a devaluation of embodiment, life, physicality, and women (Goldenberg 1990).

The Jungian interpretation of the source of the image of God in the collective unconscious, and the Jungian solution to the problem of the "repressed feminine" in the God image, thus is no longer widely embraced by feminists. While initial feminist responses to Jung's psychology of religion saw Jungian thought as "inclusive" in uncovering the repressed feminine in Western God-imagery, subsequent readings have generated important inist "critiques." Many feminist theorists now argue that a Jungian model God – even if it represents a "coincidence of opposites" incorporating feminine and masculine, material and spiritual – cannot transcend its foundations in androcentrism, gender essentialism, and ideologies of female inferiority.

Psychological origins of eucharistic ritual: the object relational view

Object relations theory brings a new perspective to the psychology of religion. With roots in psychoanalysis, object relations theory shares many of the assumptions and methods of classical Freudian theory. It differs from psychoanalysis, however, in several ways: it devotes attention to the pre-Oedipal period of human development, the period of mother–infant relationship in the earliest months and years of life, and, rather than emphasizing drives and the need for their renunciation, it focuses on the interrelatedness of human beings and the significance of "objects" (people and internal images of those people) in human development.

Freud hesitated to speculate about the psychodynamics of the pre-Oedipal period, arguing that it was like the impenetrable "Minoan–Mycenean civilization behind the civilization of Greece ... grey with age and shadowy and almost impossible to revivify" (1961c: 226). Instead, as we've seen, he emphasized the Oedipal relationship or "father-relation" as the source of psychological, cultural, and religious structures. Object relations theorists and "self psychologists" (Winnicott 1971; Klein 1975; Fairbairn 1955; Mahler 1968; Guntrip 1961; Kohut 1966, 1971, 1977), however, found the pre-Oedipal period less obscure than Freud had suggested. Rather, they argued, it is accessible to analytic recovery, and it is crucial in the development of a sense of self, a sense of the other, a capacity for ethics and morality. Some object relations theorists have extended this approach into studies of the pre-Oedipal sources and effects of theological ideas, mystical experiences, and religious practices. Prominent in this literature is the theme of ritual: a number of studies have focused on the Eucharistic ritual in Christianity.

Feminist responses to object relations theory

Among the object relations theorists the "inclusive" and the "analytic" projects of feminism are most prominent. The earliest feminists were inclusivists; later projects have been analytic. Some of the early object relations theorists (Mahler, Klein) were women. Many of these theorists held explicitly feminist views, having developed their ideas in reaction against Freud (Mitchell 1982). Nor are contemporary object relations theorists androcentric: they are as attentive to female psychological development as to male, and they emphasize the significance of the early relationship to the mother in shaping cultural and religious experience. While Freud emphasized the judging father as the source of God, morality, and ritual, the object relations theorists found a mother, often loving and benevolent, behind religious ideas and practices.

The inclusive object relational approach typically assumes that religion is valuable, adaptive, and benign, and that a loving relationship with a good or "good enough" mother (Winnicott 1971) provides the psychological foundations of faith, mysticism, ritual, and God representations. This perspective (Ross and Ross 1983; Lutzsky 1989, 1991; Raab 1997; Jones 1991, 1996; McDargh 1983; Rizzuto 1979) avoids the anti-religious animus of orthodox psychoanalysis: it assumes that religion is good and mothers are "good enough."

The analytic approach, on the other hand, assumes that religion some-times functions as a carrier for psychological and cultural fears of destruc-tive and vengeful women, and that the psychological source of these fears and fantasies lies in anxiety over the relation with the mother. Scholars in this tradition (Beers 1992; Goldenberg 1990; Capps 1997 and this volume), often drawing on Kleinian notions of the infant's "splitting" of the image of the mother, have examined religious asceticism, sacrificial ritual, and melancholic religious experiences as manifestations of fear of the mother, anxiety about the maternal body, or discomfort around issues of separation and individuation. The analytic approach thus suggests that neither mothers nor religions are unambiguously good or "good enough."[3]

The radical difference between the inclusive and analytic perspectives on religion can be thrown into relief by an examination of three studies focusing on ritual in the Christian Eucharist. One study focuses on loving mothers and positive forms of religion; one on terrifying maternal objects and religious pathologies; and the third on the potential for transformation in the symbolism of the Mass through a female priesthood.

Mary Ellen Ross and Cheryl Lynn Ross, drawing upon Winnicott's notion of "transitional space" (1971) and anthropologist Victor Turner's theory of the ritual process (1969), have developed a theory of the Eucharist as an expression of themes involving nurturance, unification, and ludic liminality. They emphasize the playful, creative dimensions of ritual, suggesting that the Winnicottian "transitional space," the "potential space" between baby and mother, provides the psychological locus for the kind of experience offered by participation in the Eucharist. Arguing that many aspects of ritual can be "comprehended within a psychoanalytic interpretation if such interpretation is extended to include the pre-Oedipal period of life" they show that the characteristics of the Mass "flow from what is essentially an experience of God as mother" (1983: 27, 39).

If Ross and Ross expose the pre-Oedipal themes of nourishment and unification, William Beers, in a second study, offers a very different analysis. Emphasizing the "sacrificial" nature of Eucharistic ritual, Beers draws upon Nancy Jay's (1992) sociological analysis of sacrifice as a practice which serves to maintain patrilineal social structures. Beers suggests that the sacrificial ritual of the Eucharist functions both socially and psychologically to affirm male power and control over women. Sacrifice is performed primarily by men; it maintains patrilineal kinship structures and symbolically denies the value of maternal descent. Psychologically, Beers argues, sacrifice expresses male narcissistic anxiety originating in the earliest phases of mother–son interaction. Mothers treat sons as "others" or "objects" while they treat daughters as extensions of themselves. As a result, male infants experience the "omnipotent maternal self" as "other." They simultaneously desire and dread a merger with the mother; they develop rigid ego boundaries to differentiate themselves from the mother; and they are likely to feel anxiety or rage later in life when boundaries are threatened. Sacrifice, in Beers' Kohutian analysis, provides a socially structured context in which archaic male rage and anxiety can be expressed in controlled performances of ritualized bloodshed, and in which male power and control over women is symbolically affirmed: "the complex ritual violence performed by men is an ancient way for men to identify with each other as men and to separate from women" (1992: 144). The Christian Eucharistic sacrifice, in Beers' reading, functions psychologically and socially in the same way.

In a third study of the Eucharist, Kelley Raab finds feminist object relations theory useful in examining gender reversal in the role of the officiating priest. "In the case of the Eucharist," she argues, "we have a 'gender masquerade' or 'gender reversal' taking place in which men appropriate women's functions while prohibiting them from performing those functions" (Raab 1997: 79). She situates this gender reversal within the context of men's unconscious identification with women, suggesting that men feel envy toward women's capacity for pregnancy, childbirth, and lactation, and that infants fear maternal functions. She concludes that "envy and fear of maternal capacities ... provide primordial motivations for men's co-optation of female functions in the Eucharist and other blood sacrificial rituals" (1997: 82). Raab proceeds to develop an argument supportive of the ordination of women as priests. When women function as priests officiating at the Eucharistic sacrifice, she argues, they perform a radically transformative function for religion and for culture, deconstructing social structures and altering the symbolism of the liturgy. When women are celebrants, "pre-Oedipal themes, through a process of symbolic association, become more prominent" (87). Female priests "reestablish female genealogical structures through the mother and give back to women their reproductive powers" (88).

These diverse analyses thus illustrate clearly the major feminist approaches to the psychology of religion found in object relations theory: Ross and Ross enact the affirmative, inclusive project, uncovering benign maternal foundations for benign religious experience. Beers, in contrast, pursues the analytic project through the exposure of terrifying maternal imagery beneath matriphobic religious experience. Raab's project is simultaneously analytic and inclusive. Like Beers, she assumes an ambivalent relationship to the mother, especially for males, interpreting male envy of maternal functions as a source of rituals of gender reversal. And she speculates, developing an inclusive argument, that a female priesthood would transform both psyche and culture. Object relations theory has thus proven itself particularly valuable for feminist scholars pursuing inclusive and analytic research in the psychology of religion. It will continue to provide rich terrain for such projects.

Ethics, ritual, and God-image re-examined: a Kristevan approach

In the 1970s, 1980s, and 1990s a group of new methodologies which can broadly be described as "post-structuralist" began to influence intellectual discourse in the West. Rejecting claims to universal truths, the discourse of post-structuralism maintains a hermeneutic suspicious of "meta-narratives" or "master narratives" (Lyotard 1984). It throws into question the notion of scholarly objectivity, the ideology of progress, and the search for origins. It is critical and self-reflexive even about its own intellectual and analytic claims. Emphasizing the effects of power on knowledge (Foucault 1970, 1978), it foregrounds the significance of language in shaping thought, gender, and culture. This approach embodies a radical challenge to the foundational assumptions of scholarship in the twentieth century. It has been particularly fruitful for feminist theory.

In the last two decades post-structuralist feminist discourse has begun to influence religious studies, first through developments in theology (Davaney 1987; Chopp 1989, 1993; Kearns 1993; Welch 1990), and more recently through developments in the psychological study of religion. Post-structuralist feminist psychological study of religion draws primarily, although not exclusively, upon the work of "French feminist" psychoanalyst Julia Kristeva (Crownfield 1992; Reineke 1997; Jonte-Pace 1997a, 1999; Poxon *et al.* forthcoming).

Without attempting to construct a systematic or comprehensive psychology of religion, Kristeva often addresses the same themes addressed by others in the depth psychological traditions: morality, ritual, and God-imagery. Her texts integrate post-structuralist perspectives with psychoanalytic and feminist methods. She develops an approach differing in subtle ways from the "origin theories" of Freud, Jung, and the object relations theorists. She is less interested in psychological origins than in the functions and effects of religion on psyche and society. When Kristeva does seek the origins of religious ideas and practices in psychological experiences, she acknowledges the embeddedness of the psychological experiences themselves in language and "the symbolic" – i.e., the territory of culture: there is no reductionistic, absolute, psychological origin in Kristeva's analyses.

Kristeva's work contains both "inclusive" and "analytic" projects. Her 1982 volume *Powers of Horror* undertakes an analysis of the maternal mytheme underlying the sense of the sacred and informing the structure of religious ritual. In an analysis similar to Beers' discovery of misogyny underlying the Eucharist, she argues that ritual represses a primal abhorrence of the mother: examining the confrontation with the maternal, the "coming face to face with the unnamable" (1982: 58), she discovers the "abject" in religious rituals of defilement and purification and in notions of sin and the sacred. "The function of these religious rituals," she argues, "is to ward off the subject's fear of his very own identity sinking irretrievably into the mother ... risking the loss not of a part (castration) but of the totality of his living being" (1982: 64). Kristeva discovers a terrifying matriphobia underlying certain ritual practices; she demonstrates as well the reappearance of the abject in contemporary social practices promoting misogyny, xenophobia, and antisemitism.

In other work, Kristeva turns from ritual to God-imagery, exhibiting a more positive evaluation of religion and its effects. *In the Beginning was Love: Psychoanalysis and Faith* (1987) echoes in some respects the inclusive feminist project within object relations theory. Like the object relations theorists, Kristeva seeks the raw material of both religious faith and psychoanalytic healing in the earliest human experiences of love "close to the maternal container" (1987: 26). She underscores, however, the fact that this "originary" maternal love is always already in language, that language and culture precede us (1987: 60). Similarly, she finds a maternal core within the imagery of "God the Father," but notes the transformation of this maternal core into the paternal symbolism of Christianity (24). In "Stabat mater" (1986a), in an interpretation with some similarities to Jung's archetypal analysis of the God-image, she examines the efficacy of the symbolism of the Virgin Mary in providing a unified vision of meaning, ethics, and aesthetics for Christianity. She examines as well the effects of the loss of Marian symbolism in the contemporary world. Fully aware of the problematic dimensions of this endeavor for feminism, she acknowledges the splitting or division of the figure of woman in Marian doctrine. Yet, unlike Jung, she does not mount an indictment of Christian God-imagery: rather, she enacts a subtle analysis of the psychological and cultural significance of these images. Thus she explores both the psychological sources and effects of the imagery of "God the Father"; she acknowledges a maternal core underlying the paternal God-image; and she untangles the meanings for men and women in the paradox of Mary's virginal maternity.

In *Strangers to Ourselves* (1991) Kristeva extends her inquiry into the territory of ethics and morality, inquiring into the internal sense of otherness underlying human ethics and relationality. If the self is born in the duality of the maternal–infant dyad, then the self is inevitably divided: we are all "strangers to ourselves." The patriarchal order of society enacts a double alienation upon women: women live in "eternal exile" (1977: 7–8). An acknowledgment of the sense of internal estrangement makes possible a transcendence of the estrangement we feel in the encounter with the external other. Kristeva finds psychoanalysis invaluable – even salvific – in the ethical project of encountering the internal Otherness of the self: through psychoanalysis new possibilities unfold for the recognition of the "other-ness" of both the self and the other (1991).

Kristeva's writings not only illustrate the vibrant presence of analytic and inclusive feminist projects in the psychology of religion, but they also illustrate clearly the impact of post-structuralist thinking on the study of religion. In Kristeva's work on religion, the subject is as likely to be female as male – an inclusive concern – while, at the same time, the very notion of the subject is thrown into question. The gendering of epistemological and cultural categories is explicitly investigated – an analytic concern – while the construction of gender is questioned. The significance of the mother, both as feared object and as loved object, is foregrounded – a concern of both the inclusive and the analytic feminists – while the devaluation of the mother is continually interrogated and the cultural and religious construction of the notion of motherhood is brought to the surface. Religious ideas and practices are examined for their psychological sources and effects on women and men, culture and psyche – an inclusive concern – while the search for origins is thrown into question. And the feminist project itself is brought under a critical gaze: in her well-known essay "Women's time," Kristeva raises questions about the tendency of feminism to make universal claims to truth and knowledge and to frame itself as an unassailable ideology with "religious dimensions" (1986b). Kristeva asks new kinds of questions – questions shaped by post-structuralism as well as by feminism and psychoanalysis – about the paradoxes of gender, culture, religion, and the unconscious in the understanding of morality, ritual, and God-image.[4]

Sojourners still? The psychology and religion movement

In recent decades, then, feminist ideas and methods have flourished within the psychological study of religion. Feminist critics, feminist inclusivists, and feminist analysts have expanded dramatically our understandings of the psychological sources and effects of morality, God-imagery, and ritual. Can the same be said of approaches such as the "psychology and religion movement" that do not draw upon these interpretive methods and assumptions?

The "psychology and religion movement" (Homans 1987, 1995; Henking 1993 and this volume) emphasizes the historical and cultural connections between psychology and religion. It is a diachronic endeavor: it assumes that religion and psychology are part of a complex and changing cultural scenario. It incorporates biographical and cultural studies, often focusing on religious traditions – or the loss of those traditions – in the lives of formative psychologists. And it examines secularization in relation to the rise of psychology and the decline of the centrality of religion within modern Western culture. Feminist thought has had relatively little impact on this branch of the field.[5]

Yet the possibilities for feminist inquiry in this branch of the field are manifold. Feminist inquiries might begin with "critical" investigations of the "womanlessness" or androcentrism of the current scholarship. Subsequently, we might initiate "inclusive" inquiries into the religious backgrounds of important female thinkers in the history of psychology. If, as cultural theorist Peter Homans suggests (1989, 1995), many early psychologists developed their theories as replacements for the religious world views they had lost or abandoned, feminist inclusivists might investigate the religious backgrounds of Melanie Klein, Lou Andreas-Salomé, Sabina Spielrein, or other women involved in the early phases of the development of psychological ideas. On the other hand, feminist analysts might utilize some of Freud's or Kristeva's writings as starting points for inquiries into the study of psychology, religion, and modernity, pursuing, for example, Kristeva's own suggestive remarks about contemporary culture in *New Maladies of the Soul* (1995). Similarly, the literature in Jewish cultural studies on Freud's response to the gendering of race and religion in *fin de siècle* ideologies might be extended into further "analytic" studies on the cultural construction of heterosexuality and homosexuality (Boyarin 1994, 1997), and on the gendering of religion, secularism, antisemitism, and modernity. It is my view that the three feminist projects outlined in this chapter have had relatively little impact within this area of discourse, but that feminist research might proceed in a number of fruitful directions.[6]

Although Carol Christ accurately predicted an arduous path for feminist sojourners in religious studies, feminist theories and methods are now widely accepted within the psychology of religion. Both male and female scholars have contributed to the critical, inclusive and analytic literature, transforming the field in important ways. The relative absence of feminist research within the "psychology and religion movement," on the other hand, is both a cause for concern and an opportunity for new kinds of research. Carol Christ's words continue to be relevant to those of us interested in asking feminist questions in the context of inquiries into the intersections of psychology and religion in contemporary culture: in the territory of the "psychology and religion movement" we remain sojourners still.

Notes

1   I am grateful for research support from Santa Clara University. I am indebted to Mary Ellen Ross, Roy Steinhoff Smith, and Kelley Raab for their comments on an earlier draft of this paper. In addition, I wish to thank Randi Warne and Russell McCutcheon for their gracious support of this project.

2   See also Boyarin (1994, 1997).

3   For feminist critiques of object relations theory, see Butler (1990) and Flax (1990).

4   Although many feminists – inclusivists as well as analysts – have embraced Kristeva's projects, her views have not escaped feminist critique. See, for example, A. Jones (1984). The feminist critics of Kristeva must be taken seriously by scholars who seek to utilize her work in the psychological study of religion.

5 Bonnie Miller-McLemore argues in this volume that feminist views and approaches *have* flourished in the field of psychology and religion; I argue here that feminist work *has not* flourished within the psychology and religion movement. While we seem to disagree, our disagreement is only apparent. Miller-McLemore's focus is on "pastoral and practical theology"; mine, in this section, is on the specific historical and cultural field of the "psychology and religion movement." Our cartographies map different regions within the larger field.
6 See, for example, Jonte-Pace (forthcoming).

References

Beers, W. (1992) *Women and Sacrifice: Male Narcissism and the Psychology of Religion*, Detroit: Wayne State University Press.

Boyarin, D. (1994) "Epater l'embourgeoisement: Freud, gender, and the (de-) colonized psyche," *Diacritics* 24: 17–41.

—— (1997) *Unheroic Conduct: The Rise of Heterosexuality and the Invention of the Jewish Man*, Berkeley: University of California Press.

Butler, J. (1990) *Gender Trouble: Feminism and the Subversion of Identity*, New York: Routledge.

Capps, D. (1997) *Men, Religion, and Melancholia*, New Haven: Yale University Press.

Chopp, R. (1989) *The Power to Speak: Feminism, Language, God*, New York: Crossroad.

—— (1993) "From patriarchy into freedom: A conversation between American feminist theology and French feminism," in C.W. Kim, Susan M. St Ville, and Susan M. Simonaitis (eds), *Transfigurations: Theology and the French Feminists*, 31–48, Minneapolis: Fortress.

Christ, C. (1992) "Feminists – sojourners in the field of religious studies," in C. Kramarae and D. Spender (eds), *The Knowledge Explosion*, 82–8, New York: Teacher's College Press.

Crownfield, D. (ed.) (1992) *Body/Text in Julia Kristeva: Religion, Women, Psychoanalysis*, Albany: State University of New York Press.

Davaney, S. (1987) "Problems with feminist theory: historicity and the search for sure foundations," in P. Cooey, S. Farmer, and M. Ross (eds) *Embodied Love: Sensuality and Relationship as Feminist Values*, 79–95, San Francisco: Harper & Row.

Engelsman, J. (1979) *The Feminine Dimension of the Divine*, Philadelphia: Westminster Press.

Fairbairn, W.D.R (1955) "Observations in defence of the object relations theory of the personality," *British Journal of Medical Psychology* 28: 144–56.

Flax, J. (1990) *Thinking Fragments: Psychoanalysis, Feminism, and Postmodernism in the Contemporary West*, Berkeley: University of California Press.

Foucault, M. (1970) *The Order of Things*, New York: Random.

—— (1978) *The History of Sexuality: An Introduction, Volume I*, Robert Hurley (trans.), New York: Pantheon.

Freud, S. (1955) *Totem and Taboo*, in James Strachey (trans. and ed.), *The Standard Edition of the Complete Psychological Works of Sigmund Freud* 13: 1–161, London: Hogarth.

—— (1957) *Leonardo da Vinci and a Memory of his Childhood*, in James Strachey (trans. and ed.), *The Standard Edition of the Complete Psychological Works of Sigmund Freud* 11: 63–137, London: Hogarth.

—— (1961a) "Some psychical consequences of the anatomical distinction between the sexes," in James Strachey (trans. and ed.), *The Standard Edition of the Complete Psychological Works of Sigmund Freud* 19: 241–58, London: Hogarth.

—— (1961b) *The Ego and the Id*, in James Strachey (trans. and ed.), *The Standard Edition of the Complete Psychological Works of Sigmund Freud* 19: 3–66, London: Hogarth.

—— (1961c) "Female sexuality," in James Strachey (trans. and ed.), *The Standard Edition of the Complete Psychological Works of Sigmund Freud* 21: 225–43, London: Hogarth.

Geller, J. (1992a) "(G)nos(e)ology: The cultural construction of the other," in Howard Eilberg-Schwartz (ed.), *People of the Body: Jews and Judaism from an Embodied Perspective*, Albany: State University of New York Press.

—— (1992b) "The unmanning of the wandering Jew," *American Imago* 49: 227–62.

—— (1993) "A paleontological view of Freud's study of religion: Unearthing the *Leitfossil* circumcision," *Modern Judaism* 13: 49–70.

—— (1997) "Identifying 'Someone who is himself one of them': recent studies of Freud's Jewish identity," *Religious Studies Review* 23: 323–32.

—— (1999) "The godfather of psychoanalysis: circumcision, antisemitism, homosexuality, and Freud's 'Fighting Jew,' " *Journal of the American Academy of Religion* 67: 355–86.

Gilligan, C. (1984) "The conquistador and the dark continent: reflections on the psychology of love," *Daedalus* 3: 75–95.

Gilman, S. (1993) *Freud, Race, and Gender*, Baltimore: Johns Hopkins University Press

Goldenberg, N. (1977) "Jung after feminism," in Rita Gross (ed.), *Beyond Androcentrism: New Essays on Women and Religion*, 53–66, Missoula MT: Scholars Press.

—— (1979) *Changing of the Gods: Feminism and the End of Traditional Religions*, Boston: Beacon.

—— (1990) *Returning Words to Flesh: Feminism, Psychoanalysis and the Resurrection of the Body*, Boston: Beacon.

Guntrip, H. (1961) *Personality and Human Interaction*, London: Hogarth.

Hall, N. (1980) *The Moon and the Virgin: Reflections on the Archetypal Feminine*, New York: Harper.

Henking, S. (1993) "Placing the social sciences: Cases at the intersection of the histories of disciplines and religions," *Religious Studies Review* 19: 116–26.

Homans, P. (1987) "The psychology and religion movement," in M. Eliade (ed.), *Encyclopedia of Religion* 12: 66–74.

—— (1989) *The Ability to Mourn: Disillusionment and the Social Origins of Psychoanalysis*, Chicago: University of Chicago Press.

—— (1995) *Jung in Context*, 2nd edn, Chicago: University of Chicago Press.

Jacobs, J. (1997) "Freud as other: anti-semitism and the development of psychoanalysis," in J. Jacobs and D. Capps (eds.), *Religion, Society, and Psychoanalysis: Readings in Contemporary Theory*, 28–41, Boulder: Westview Press.

Jay, N. (1992) *Throughout Your Generations Forever: Sacrifice, Religion, and Paternity*, Chicago: University of Chicago Press.

Jones, A. (1984) "Julia Kristeva on femininity: The limits of a semiotic politics," *Feminist Review* 18: 56–73.

Jones, J. (1991) *Contemporary Psychoanalysis and Religion: Transference and Transcendence*, New Haven: Yale University Press.

―― (1996) *Religion and Psychology in Transition: Psychoanalysis, Feminism, and Theology*, New Haven: Yale University Press.

Jonte-Pace, D. (1997a) "Julia Kristeva and the psychoanalytic study of religion: Rethinking Freud's cultural texts," in J. Jacobs and D. Capps (eds.), *Religion, Society, and Psychoanalysis: Readings in Contemporary Theory*, 240–68, Boulder: Westview Press.

―― (1997b) "New directions in feminist psychology of religion: An introduction," *Journal of Feminist Studies in Religion* 13: 63–74.

―― (1999) " 'Legitimation of hatred or inversion into love': Religion in Kristeva's re-reading of Freud," *Research in the Social Scientific Study of Religion* 10: 17–35.

―― (forthcoming) *Speaking the Unspeakable: Religion, Misogyny, and the Uncanny Mother in Freud's Cultural Texts*, Berkeley: University of California Press.

Jung, C. (1968) *Archetypes of the Collective Unconscious*, in H. Read, M. Fordham and G. Adler (eds.), R. Hull (trans.), *The Collected Works of C.G. Jung* 9: 1, Princeton: Princeton University Press.

―― (1969) "Answer to Job," in H. Read, M. Fordham and G. Adler (eds.), R. Hull (trans.), *The Collected Works of C.G. Jung* 11, Princeton: Princeton University Press.

―― (1982) *Aspects of the Feminine* (selections from H. Read, M. Fordham and G. Adler (eds.), R. Hull (trans.), *Selections from the Collected Works of C.G. Jung* 6, 7, 9, 10, 17, Princeton: Princeton University Press.

Kearns, C. (1993) "Kristeva and feminist theology," in C. Kim, S. St Ville and S. Simonaitis (eds), *Transfigurations: Theology and the French Feminists*, 49–80, Minneapolis: Fortress Press.

Klein, M. (1975) *The Psychoanalysis of Children*, New York: Delacorte Press.

Kohut, H. (1966) "Forms and transformations of narcissism," *Journal of the American Psychiatric Association* 14: 243–72.

―― (1971) *The Analysis of the Self*, New York: International Universities Press.

―― (1977) *The Restoration of the Self*, New York: International Universities Press.

Kristeva, J. (1977) *Polylogue*, Paris: Seuil.

―― (1982) *Powers of Horror: An Essay on Abjection*, L. Roudiez (trans.), New York: Columbia University Press.

―― (1986a) "Stabat mater," in T. Moi (ed.), L. Roudiez (trans.), *The Kristeva Reader*, 160–86, New York: Columbia University Press.

―― (1986b) "Women's time," in T. Moi (ed.), A. Jardine and H. Blake (trans.), *The Kristeva Reader*, 188–213, New York: Columbia University Press.

―― (1987) *In the Beginning was Love: Psychoanalysis and Faith*, A. Goldhammer (trans.), New York: Columbia University Press.

―― (1991) *Strangers to Ourselves*, L. Roudiez (trans.), New York: Columbia University Press.

―― (1995) *New Maladies of the Soul*, New York: Columbia University Press.

Lutzky, H. (1989) "Reparation and tikkun: A comparison of the Kleinian and Kabbalistic concepts," *International Review of Psychoanalysis* 16: 449–58.

―― (1991) "The sacred and the maternal object: An application of Fairbairn's theory to religion," in H. Siegalis, L. Barbanel, and I. Hirsch (eds), *Psychoanalytic Reflections on Current Issues*, 25–44, New York: New York University Press.

Lyotard, J. (1984) *The Postmodern Condition*, G. Bennington and B. Massum (trans.), Minneapolis: University of Minnesota Press.

McDargh, J. (1983) *Psychoanalytic Object Relations Theory and the Study of Religion: On Faith and the Imaging of God*, Lanham: University Press of America.

McIntosh, P. (1983) "Interactive phases of curricular revision: A feminist perspective" (Working Paper 124), Wellesley: Wellesley College.

Mahler, M. (1968) *On Human Symbiosis and the Vicissitudes of Individuation*, New York: International Universities Press.

Mitchell, J. (1974) *Psychoanalysis and Feminism,* New York: Random.

—— (1982) "Introduction 1," in J. Mitchell and J. Rose (eds.), *Jacques Lacan and the école freudienne*, New York: Norton.

Poxon, J., O'Grady, K., and Morny, J. (eds) (forthcoming) *Religion in French Feminist Thought: Critical Perspectives*, London: Routledge.

Raab, K. (1997) "Nancy Jay and a feminist psychology of sacrifice," *Journal of Feminist Studies in Religion* 13: 75–89.

Reineke, M. (1997) *Sacrificed Lives: Kristeva on Women and Violence*, Bloomington: Indiana University Press.

Rieff, P. (1979) *Freud: The Mind of a Moralist*, Chicago: University of Chicago Press.

Rizzuto, A. (1979) *The Birth of the Living God: A Psychoanalytic Study*, Chicago: University of Chicago Press.

Roith, E. (1987) *The Riddle of Freud: Jewish Influences on his Theory of Female Sexuality*, London: Tavistock.

Ross, M. and Ross, C. (1983) "Mothers, infants, and the psychoanalytic study of ritual," *Signs* 9: 21–39.

Turner, V. (1969) *The Ritual Process*, Chicago: Aldine Press.

Ulanov, A. (1971) *The Feminine in Jungian Psychology and in Christian Theology*, Evanston: Northwestern University Press.

—— (1981) *Receiving Woman: Studies in the Psychology and Theology of the Feminine*, Philadelphia: Westminster Press.

van Herik, J. (1982) *Freud on Femininity and Faith*, Berkeley: University of California Press.

Warne, R. (1989) "Toward a brave new paradigm: The impact of women's studies in religious studies," *Religious Studies and Theology* 9: 35–46.

Wehr, D. (1987) *Jung and Feminism: Liberating Archetypes*, Boston: Beacon.

Welch, S. (1990) *A Feminist Ethic of Risk*, Minneapolis: Fortress.

Winnicott, D.W. (1971) *Playing and Reality*, New York: International Universities Press.

Wulff, D. (1997) *Psychology of Religion*, 2nd edn, New York: Wiley.

Wyschogrod, E., Crownfield, D., and Rasche, C. (eds) (1989) *Lacan and Theological Discourse*, Albany: State University of New York Press.

9　Male melancholia

Guilt, separation, and repressed rage

Donald Capps

The driving concerns which fuel the interdisciplinary field of religion and psychological studies can be framed in diverse ways and from multiple perspectives. One such driving force in years past has been the field's interest in individual and corporate pathology. Indeed, it was a "clinical book," namely Erik H. Erikson's *Young Man Luther* (1962), which sparked my own interest in the field. In the past three decades, attention to gender has been a dominant (if not the dominant) driving force in the field. Harnessing the contemporary interest in gender issues and the field's historic attention to pathology, I offer a discussion of "male melancholia," a subject that permeates *Young Man Luther*. By focusing on a "localized" aspect of current religion, psychology, and gender studies, I hope to encourage those in the field to keep religion and psychological studies grounded in the everyday struggles of human life.

My discussion builds upon the argument of my recent book, *Men, Religion and Melancholia* (Capps 1997). I argued there that separation from mother is both the primary cause of male melancholia and men's development of a religious orientation to life. I used Freud's essays on "Mourning and melancholia" (Freud 1917/1957), where he discusses melancholia in terms of the internalization of, and ambivalence toward, the "lost object," and "The 'uncanny'" (1919/1955), which describes the uncanny (the "unheimlich") as the defamiliarizing of the familiar, and comments on his male patients' identification of the uncanny with mother's body (his original "home" from which he is now estranged). Putting these two essays together, I contended that the mother is the "lost object," defamiliarized while internalized, and is ambivalently longed for and rejected. Because she is now internalized, hatred toward her is self-directed, accounting for the excessive self-reproaches that characterize the melancholiac.

I then argued that a boy roughly 3 years of age, the typical age of maternal separation, becomes religious for essentially two reasons. One is that he hopes to win back the mother who loved him without condition, this time meeting her conditions by means of exemplary behavior. (This accounts for the fact that men tend more than women to view religion in terms of moral behavior.) The other is that he seeks in religion compensations and consolations for what he lost in the real-world of mother–son relationships. As the former reflects the desire to regain the mother's love, while the latter reflects resignation to the loss, these two reasons for being religious are themselves reflective of male ambivalence, and are evident in conflicts among men about whether religion is a moral or mystical matter. Thus, ambivalence toward the mother gets itself projected on to religion itself, which is then ambivalently related to. (In contrast, most women seem more "at home" with religion, viewing it as generally supportive and not inherently the object of a certain mistrust.)

In the book, I explored how William James, Rudolf Otto, C.G. Jung, and Erik H. Erikson, each in his own way, was unusually sensitive to one or more "maternal" aspects of religion, and that their psychology of religion texts are personally revealing of their efforts to find compensations and consolations in religion for their own melancholia, which had roots in the emotional loss of their mothers in early childhood. The questions that *Men, Religion, and Melancholia* left unexplored were whether Freud himself could be viewed as melancholic and whether his writings on religion are reflective of this; whether women may also suffer from melancholy (even though, historically, men have been identified with melancholia while women have been viewed as hysterical; and, in my forthcoming book on Jesus, I contrast women agoraphobics with male melancholiacs; Capps 2000); and whether the analysis has relevance for contemporary men who are not among the intellectual elite (as were the four men discussed in the book). While I am quite certain that all three questions may be answered affirmatively, I will address only the latter question here, as the first question is necessarily complex and deserving of much fuller treatment, and the second has been addressed by Julia Kristeva, who suggests a different etiology for female melancholia than that proposed in my book on men (Kristeva 1989).

To explore the third question, which has its own complexities, I will focus on three contemporary texts, Frank Pittman's *Man Enough* (1993), William Pollack's *Real Boys* (1998), and James E. Dittes' *Driven By Hope* (1996). In discussing these three books, I will be noting their allusions to maternal separation among young boys, and will use these and other discussions of the mother and son relationship in support of my own melancholia thesis, especially the melancholia–religion connection.

Mother as object of guilt

Frank Pittman's *Man Enough* centers primarily on men's relations with other men, with particular attention to father–son relationships and the importance of father–surrogacy among young males whose relations with their own fathers were negligible or non-existent; which, according to Pittman, comprises the overwhelming majority of boys in our society. There is, however, a chapter on "Mother love" (following a chapter on "Father hunger"), in which Pittman argues that the son never forgets that he owes his life to his mother, not only its procreation but also its early maintenance, and that he therefore owes her a debt that he cannot conceivably repay, but which she may call in at any time (145). He also notes that the strongest emotional pull on the male psyche is maternally induced guilt, which tends to pull the boy or adult male back to his mother, thus reversing the separation that she herself fostered (148). He adds that depressed mothers are the hardest for a son to leave, as he desperately tries to make her happy, and may throw everything else in his life overboard in the effort, ultimately hopeless, to cheer her up (151–2). Men know that the only way to confirm the self-confidence that their mothers nurtured in them is to cut the cord of dependency they have on their mothers, but sometimes mother will not let him go, while other times he cannot make himself go, with most men experiencing both (152–3). Leaving is easier if he can perform a "great deed" in her behalf, such as going to war (fighting for her and his motherland), succeeding in life, bringing home a fine daughter-in-law (who does the things for her that he is not disposed to do himself), or providing grandchildren. A sign of a man's maturity is the realization that there is nothing he can do to repay her (which, not incidentally, sounds much like theological language associated with Christ's atonement for our sins). Then, Pittman suggests, he won't have to run away from her, or feel guilty, or try to please her completely. He can be nice to her and allow her a place in his life (157).

Pittman also discusses what he calls "the war against mothers" and the specific issue of "mother bashing," suggesting that while patriarchy is the larger horizon against which these issues must be viewed, the more immediate cause is the perceived power of the mother over the son, as "she is always inside him ready to keep him from doing anything she wouldn't want him to do" (159). He also notes that "mother bashing" may originate from his fear of her, especially if our mothers "have no life except us. We are able to forgive our mothers anything except loving us more than they love themselves" (161). While he does not say that this is a prescription for melancholia, he does discuss male depression, though not in the chapter on mother love but in a chapter on how men may become part of "the quiet, accepting company of men." While acknowledging that male depression may have various causes, including "chronic pain or daily alcohol use, or because of a devastating loss, or because of an inherited tendency toward it," the "most likely cause of a man's depression is his failure to be the man he thinks he should be, a situation that leaves him beating up on himself and distrusting the love" he receives from his wife or other female and male companions (218–19).

Especially noteworthy in this list of causes of male depression is that it may be precipitated by a profound loss and a perceived personal failure leading to self-recrimination and doubting the love he has been accorded. This combination of causes is reminiscent of the original loss of mother (which was perhaps all the more devastating for its seeming naturalness and typicality), which leads to male melancholia. The separation is perceived as due to the failure to behave as mother expected or demanded; the mother's unconditional love has become conditional (i.e. must now be earned, not assumed), and the lost object – the mother who loved him unconditionally – is internalized, becoming the object of his self-hate. In Freud's language, he engages in excessive self-reproachings, whose very exaggeratedness reveals that these have an object besides himself. In Pittman's more colorful language, he "beats up on himself," its excessiveness due to the fact that he cannot also accuse his mother of bad faith.

Freud, of course, viewed religion as fundamentally associated with guilt, and his interpretations of religion as resulting from guilt following efforts to triumph over the father are well known. I will not go into these arguments here. I would, however, take note of his earliest writing on religion, "Obsessive actions and religious practices" (1907/1957), as it helps to explain the relationship between religion and *mother* guilt. Anticipating the argument that obsessive actions and religious ceremonials are not compara ble because the former is private, having meanings known only to the one who engages in them, whereas the latter is public, having communally shared meanings (an argument that Erik H. Erikson in fact makes in *Toys and Reasons*; Erikson 1977: 78) Freud counters that they have a common psychodynamic basis in the fact that both are *protective measures*, i.e., undertaken because their *omission* would produce guilt. It is not merely, or even primarily, that these behaviors are intended to atone for past wrongdo- ings, but that one wishes thereby to avoid the guilt that would ensue from not carrying these actions out. It may also be noted that Freud's description of the melancholiac in "Mourning and melancholia" as engaging in excessive self-reproachings has a direct parallel in his description of "the protestations of pious people that they know that at heart they are miserable sinners" (123). I suggest, therefore, that the "mother guilt" identified by Pittman emerges in the early separation between mother and son, and creates in the son a determination to live up to her (real or perceived) expectations of him, thus justifying the sacrifices (real or perceived) she made in his behalf when he was dependent upon her. If Freud centers in his later writings on religion on crimes against the father, his discussion of anxiety concerning the failure to do what is required in his earlier writing applies more directly to mother guilt. This, as Pittman's own analysis of male depression suggests, is a prescription for a more chronic state of male melancholia.

The trauma of separation

While Pittman assumes the necessity of separation from the mother (a section of his chapter on mother love is titled "Cutting the cord"), William Pollack in *Real Boys* challenges the commonly held assumption that mothers must foster a separation between themselves and their sons. He notes that the boy's need to separate from his mother is a strongly held cultural value, based on fear of his being "too attached" to his mother and thus unable to develop his masculinity (a homophobia subtext is apparent here), and on the assumption that a boy cannot attach to his father *unless* he separates from his mother (which disregards Freud's view that the boy's original attraction to his father is, indeed, a homosexual one; Lane 1999). Pollack wonders: What would happen to girls if they were assumed to need to separate emotionally from their mothers? Would we not assume that this would likely be traumatic for them? And would we not want to be very certain that such separation was necessary, and that she could in fact "survive" this separation emotionally? With boys, however, we assume that it must happen and that boys should be able to handle the separation without its becoming traumatic. Only the "pampered" boy will be unable to separate naturally and easily. (Pittman calls these "homeboys" who "don't know how to be man enough to make it in the real world" [153].)

A related issue is that boys are assumed to require more severe parental restraint than girls, and that their bodies can "take" more punishment than girls' bodies. Moreover, the physical punishment will toughen him up, and thus make him capable of withstanding physical hardships later in life. Pollack notes that girls are more likely to experience sexual abuse, while boys are more subject to physical abuse. In effect, adults break a girl's spirit through sexual molestation, while they propose to toughen a boy's spirit by assaulting his body with belts, two-by-fours, etc. Given the boy's dependency on his mother, physical punishment inflicted by her is the prototypical event that creates a separation between them, one that cannot be entirely healed by acts of contrition and forgiveness. The ambivalent feelings toward mother found in male melancholia reveal the bitterness and anger that accompany the longing for restoration between them.

Pollack suggests that males experience three separations, all of them traumatic (meaning that they leave painful residues and have various future consequences): separation from mother and the maternal environment at age 6; separation from the parental environment in adolescence, as a boy is expected to develop an identity and establish his independence; and separation when parents divorce. I would modify and expand this list, in part because such modifications and expansions fit the theory of male melancholia more adequately, but also because the original separation from mother casts a very long shadow over the span of life, encompassing adulthood as well.

1   Separation from mother beginning at age 3 and leading to the perception that he did something to cause or precipitate the separation (i.e., it was not a "natural" part of his individuation). Thus, he begins to develop a false conscience, one that is at least partially distortive of reality.

2   Separation in adolescence, reminiscent of the first separation, now taking the form of overt behavior reflecting the original ambivalence toward mother (which, earlier, was internalized and expressed itself as *self*-hatred). That repressed feelings are now being expressed toward mother is reflected in the fact that his rejective attitude and behavior toward her is disproportionate to her current provocations. His awareness of this fact often precipitates further feelings of self-hatred.

3   Separation from family of origin at time of marriage, reactivating guilt feelings associated with original separation from mother. Because his spouse tends to remain in more regular contact with her family, often through the mother–daughter relationship itself, he feels a greater sense of being without a family, an "orphan," as it were. If the marriage produces children, and his wife serves as "gatekeeper" to the children (a common complaint of young husbands; Vickers and Thomas 1996), he feels further isolated and alone, which, of course, adds fuel to the fire of a preexisting melancholic temperament. The home that he thought was his becomes, as had the home of his childhood, an alien, uncanny place, a place where he is decidedly not "at home." (He may claim a certain part of the home, the basement or garage, as his domain, or insist that a particular chair belongs solely to him.)

4   Separation from mother on the occasion of her death, which also reactivates ambivalent feelings toward her, in addition to accumulated guilt if he has failed to live up to her (real or perceived) expectations of him, or if he has neglected her (not "been nice to her"), or both. He may feel more free and independent as a result of her death, but also uneasy about his longings for her, his nostalgia for what might have been (had they remained "lovers"), for what unfulfilled promises there were in their relationship.

5   If he divorces, his emotionality (or seeming lack thereof) is reminiscent of his emotionality in the original separation trauma. The two experiences are, in fact, remarkably similar, for in both cases – and unlike mourning the loss of a deceased person – the "lost object," as Freud notes, is still in the neighborhood. In this sense, divorce sheds important light on the earlier separation, and should help to disabuse us from the assumption that the original separation is experienced by the boy as natural.

One could add additional separations, particularly from one's work due to job loss or retirement, as these relate to aspirations originally associated with his mother's (real or perceived) expectations for him; and his anticipated death, which may be accompanied by premonitions of meeting his mother in the after-life, or even of being summoned by her. If, as Pittman suggests, the son never forgets that he owes his life to his mother, then, as Freud also notes, she is "the silent goddess of Death," the Mother Earth who takes him into her arms at the end of life, effectively ending the old man's yearning "after the love of woman as once he had it from his mother" (Freud 1913/1958: 301). If one or another of these separations causes older boys or men to develop clinical depression, we should not assume from this that the others are free of a more chronic (perhaps low-grade melancholia) owing to their having to become inured to separations at various life intervals reminiscent of the earliest one.

Pollack has an agenda, which is to rescue contemporary boys from the "code of honor" that gained widespread sociocultural support in the late nineteenth century, and he has written a book primarily intended for concerned mothers. I have focused here on the theme of separation from mother as it relates directly to my earlier argument regarding male melancholia. The "code of honor" is also, however, relevant to my argument that one form religion takes among males is the determination to be "good" (or "moral") so that one may win back or continue to merit mother's love. (In this regard, men tend to be less "forgiving" than women of other men for acting dishonorably; witness, for example, the greater support that President Clinton received from women than men during the impeachment trials in spite of the fact that he was guilty of sexual harassment in the office place.) In the following discussion of religion, however, I will focus more on the other aspect of religion that separation from mother induces, i.e., its compensatory or consoling role.

Longing for more

In *Men on Midlife* (1996), Joanne F. Vickers and Barbara L. Thomas report conversations with several men who fit the description of "incurably religious." While many women might offer the same self-description, it seems especially congruent with James E. Dittes' view of men – ancient and contemporary – in *Driven By Hope* (1996). He argues against the common view that men are "less religious" than women (supported by statistics indicating there are some ten million fewer men than women in the US who belong to religious organizations), noting that it all depends on what one means by religious. In his view, men are inherently religious because

> Men are expectant. Men live a life that feels chronically destined, ever on the verge … intended for something that is never quite arrived at, an unending not-yet, the perpetual pilgrimage of almost … In religious terms, men are afflicted with hope. Hope means living a life that awaits, longingly, a fulfillment that must come from beyond the everyday domain, since it doesn't seem to come within that domain.
>
> (Dittes 1996: 4)

He suggests that this "affliction" derives from a profound sense of incompleteness:

> The Bible tells it clearly, from the beginning: paradise wanting. Adam looked around Eden and asked, *Is that all there is?* The sorrow of incompleteness is man's from the outset – part of creation, not a symptom of sin or fall ... This sorrow of incompleteness, life chronically destined, is what is offered to men as the avenue to wholeness and holiness.
>
> (ibid.: 4)

(It is worth noting here that Dittes' portrayal of Adam is closer to Heinz Kohut's "tragic man" than the "guilty man" Kohut attributes to Freud [Kohut 1977: 206–7; Kohut 1985: 37–45].)

Throughout the book, Dittes focuses on men's questing nature, their discomfort with what there is, and their desire to experience more. There are echoes here of William James' view of religious experience as the feeling of connection with the "more," which is then identified and described in the "over-beliefs" of religious traditions (James 1902/1982: 510–14). James, however, was notoriously uninterested in questions regarding the origins of things, including religion, and did not, therefore, ask the kinds of questions that Freud posed of religion. Dittes is not as uninterested in these questions (even though his book focuses on men's aspirations toward the future), as he discusses the effects of separation from mother on the young boy, noting, for example, that a boy knows that if he is to grow up male, he

> recognizes early on that to achieve this he must not honor and strengthen but disrupt the bonds between himself and his primary care- and life-giver. There may or may not be a father readily at hand to become the model for maleness, but the young boy does recognize that his mother is not the right model and he must distance himself from her, sometimes rejecting her clumsily, sometimes striking out with exaggerated independence, sometimes more smoothly and happily.
>
> (24)

He adds: "It is not too strong to say that the young boy is forced to choose between maleness and connectedness with life" (24). The ultimate consequence of this disconnection is "the haunting feeling that something essential is missing, that being male costs a connectedness with life" (25).

Interestingly enough, Dittes takes Freud to task for failing to recognize that, in the story of Oedipus, the tragedy is not precipitated by Oedipus' aggressive attitude toward and competition with his father, but by his father's response to the oracle that Oedipus would be his murderer of taking "the preemptive precaution of ordering the newborn abandoned on a mountainside" (34). One is therefore somewhat surprised that Dittes does not attribute any comparable volition to the mother in his portrayal of the separation of mother and son. He attributes the separation entirely to the boy's realization that he must "disrupt the bonds" between himself and his mother, to "distance himself from her," to "choose between maleness and connectedness with life." Thus, unlike Pollack, and perhaps more like Pittman, he emphasizes the boy's own actions in the severance of the bond and says nothing about her own role in the separation. Pollack, writing primarily for mothers, emphasizes that mothers do play an active role in the separation, but with the best of intentions (i.e., she wants her son to develop independence and masculinity, and may also believe that no real relationship with his father will occur unless and until he separates from her). Pollack wants mothers to understand that they hinder neither his development of independence and masculinity nor his chances for a real relationship with his father by forgoing their own efforts at separation.

The question Pollack fails to address is whether mothers play a role in the separation that is somewhat less noble. Psychoanalysis prompts us to probe more deeply for less altruistic motivations for parental actions, and D.W. Winnicott has been perhaps the most willing to do such probing regarding mothers' behavior. He paints a more realistic, less idealistic, picture of the mother's motivations toward her son, one that has bearing on what men seek from religion but, in our highly Christianized culture, rarely find. In his article, "Hate in the countertransference" (Winnicott 1993: 15–24), Winnicott makes the startling and certainly provocative observation that the mother not only loves but also

> hates her infant from the word go. I believe Freud thought it possible that a mother may in certain circumstances have only love for her boy baby; but we may doubt this. We know about a mother's love and we appreciate its reality and power. [But] let me give some of the reasons why a mother hates her baby, even a boy.
>
> (22)

Eighteen reasons follow, two of which are especially relevant to our discussion of melancholia. The first is that "if she fails him at the start, she knows he will pay her out for ever." The second is that "at first he does not know at all what she does or what she sacrifices for him. Especially he cannot allow for her hate" (22). Winnicott's conviction that the mother hates as well as loves her infant is arguably the basis for his well-known "good enough mother" concept, which is not so much about one's best efforts, even if they fall somewhat short of the ideal, being good enough, but more about the fact that a mother who hates her infant may be "good enough" in spite of this; indeed, her infant's survival depends on *her* ability to survive his own hatred toward her (Winnicott 1991: 86–94), which his "Hate in the countertransference" article suggests is mutual.

If the first of these two reasons suggests that her hatred grows out of her perception that he will make her pay, eventually, for her (real or perceived) failures with him, the second suggests that his own idealized self-perception requires that he believe she has only love for him. Thus, men have as much to gain from *rejecting* Winnicott's view that their mothers also hated them as do women (with their concerns about "mother bashing"), a fact borne out by evidence (e.g., developmental theories formulated by men) that "mother bashing" by men is usually veiled, even from themselves. Pittman notes that since the 1960s mothers have mostly been blamed by their sons for the sons' failures in later life because "they loved their boys too much," i.e., their love was "toxic and crippling" (Pittman 1993: 158). The thought does not occur to men that their mothers may actually have resented, even hated, their little boys because they anticipated that, when grown, their sons would one day attribute their own (real or perceived) failures in life to their mothers' (real or perceived) failures in raising them properly.

On the other hand, this may paint an unnecessarily dark and sinister picture of mothers' hatred as a factor in the separation between mothers and sons. While endorsing Winnicott's view that mothers are ambivalent toward their children, and accepting that there is indeed an element of hatred in this ambivalence (not merely the coldness and distance of which earlier theorists of the 1950s accused them; Pittman 1993: 158), Rozsika Parker contends in *Mother Love/Mother Hate* (1995) that Winnicott vacillates between a cynical and a sentimentalized view of mothers, and this leads him to miss

> the creative role of the mother's hatred in the development of maternal thinking ... The singing of sadistic lullabies illustrates not only a way of safely containing hatred, but also how the unbearable coexistence of love and hate for the baby continually pushes a mother into the creative act of seeking reparatory solutions.
>
> (63)

Thus, when the baby projects his own hate on to the mother, "where it meets her own infantile hatred mobilized by adult frustrated needs and desires both to satisfy and be satisfied," at such times

> a mother's love may be overwhelmed by persecutory anxiety, promoting an impulse to attack the persecuting baby, and stymying the reparatory process. It is at this point that, instead of acting on the impulse, the majority of mothers try to help by singing, rocking, soothing or feeding. The painful conflict of love and hate itself provokes the desire to know and answer the baby's needs.
>
> (63)

The question this raises, however, is whether the same "reparatory solutions" seem as urgent or necessary when the separation process itself is underway and the same societal sanctions against parental cruelty are relaxed precisely in order to foster the desired separation.

What bearing has this discussion of maternal ambivalence on men's religious affliction? Simply this: if I am right that boys become religious as a consequence of their separation from their mothers, we would expect that they would develop into the questers for something more than their everyday domain affords them, precisely as Dittes suggests. Their religion then is indeed born of sorrow, and of the sense that something is missing. There is, however, another dimension to male melancholia, which is the rage he feels for having been abandoned – cruelly, in his view, because the "lost object" is not dead, but remains a haunting presence in his life. This abandonment leads to the internalization of the lost mother, and from there to self-hatred. If religion is to serve as compensation and consolation for the loss which he has experienced – if it is to be truly reparative – it needs to do more than assuage his longings and yearnings. It needs to enable him to project his internalized self-hatred beyond the everyday domain in the form of an ambivalent mother, against whom he is given license to hurl the kinds of curses and invectives that primitive religions manifest but Christianity (in its opposition to "mother bashing") disallows. Put another way, we have nothing comparable to the Hindu goddess Kali – that bloodthirsty goddess who hates her children – in the Christianized West, only a highly idealized Virgin Mother who is without sin and harbors no evil thoughts (Kristeva 1987a: 42–3; 1987b: 234–63). There is not even a heavenly equivalent to the enigmatic singer Peggy Lee, with whom many American men associate the phrase "Is that all there is?", whose Mona Lisa smile communicated that yes, indeed, this is all you will get and maybe you need to be grateful for what you have. If men cannot have a hateful mother in the divine pantheon, is it too much to ask for a withholding one?[1]

There are, of course, consequences here for women as well, as I hardly need to point out. As Freud notes in "Mourning and melancholia" one way that melancholia comes to an end is when a man, typically in a manic act, "triumphs" over the internalized lost object. As he also notes in "The theme of the three caskets," a man's beloved is often chosen "after the mother's pattern" (Freud 1913/1958: 301). To what extent is the battered woman the victim of the convergence of these two phenomena (which seems to have been the deeper psychological meaning of the O.J. Simpson trial)? The unsuspecting wife may not realize until it is too late that he means to settle a score against the internalized lost object. If Rozsika Parker finds that singing "sadistic lullabies" enables the mother to resist the impulse to attack her persecuting baby, would some Christian equivalent to the goddess Kali enable men to engage in relatively harmless "mother bashing" so that they may exorcise their own self-hatred and view their beloved with eyes of unalloyed longing?

Perhaps, in the final analysis, Dittes' view of men as inherently religious and the popular conception that they are less religious than women are reconcilable: They *are* religious – separation from their mothers makes them so – but the religion to which they are most likely to turn offers half a loaf.

It soothes their melancholy longing, but turns a deaf ear to their melancholy rage. Is half a loaf better than none? This very question recalls the original trauma of separation. It should not therefore surprise us if there are men who answer it with a sad but honorable no.

Note

1   Freud recounts his own dream of the withholding mother in *The Interpretation of Dreams* (1900/1953: 204–8). Titled "The dream of the three fates," it was most certainly an inspiration for his later essay, "The theme of the three caskets," cited elsewhere in this paper. I have had a similar dream which could be cited in support of my argument here (i.e., the association of male melancholia and religion), but I will not recount it here. Suffice it to say that male melancholia may be more manifest in dream than waking life, as befits the fact that it involves an internalized mother, who may differ significantly from the mother of the son's subsequent life experiences. This also constitutes a response to men who assert that the argument presented in this paper does not apply to them because their adult relations with their mothers have been emotionally healthy ones. I do not dispute these assertions, but neither do they have direct bearing on my argument.

References

Capps, D. (1997) *Men, Religion, and Melancholia*, New Haven: Yale University Press.
—— (2000) *Jesus: A Psychological Biography*, Saint Louis: Chalice Press.
Dittes, J.E. (1996) *Driven By Hope: Men and Meaning*, Louisville: Westminster John Knox.
Erikson, E. (1962) *Young Man Luther*, New York: W.W. Norton.
—— (1977) *Toys and Reasons: Stages in the Ritualization of Experience*, New York: W.W. Norton.
Freud, S. (1900/1953) *The Interpretation of Dreams*, in J. Strachey (ed.), *The Standard Edition of the Complete Psychological Works of Sigmund Freud*, vols 4–5, London: The Hogarth Press.
—— (1907/1957) "Obsessive actions and religious practices," in J. Strachey (ed.), *The Standard Edition of the Complete Psychological Works of Sigmund Freud*, vol. 9, London: The Hogarth Press, pp. 115–27.
—— (1913/1958) "The theme of the three caskets," in J. Strachey (ed.), *The Standard Edition of the Complete Psychological Works of Sigmund Freud*, vol. 12, London: The Hogarth Press, pp. 289–301.
—— (1917/1957) "Mourning and melancholia," in J. Strachey (ed.), *The Standard Edition of the Complete Psychological Works of Sigmund Freud*, vol. 14, London: The Hogarth Press, pp. 239–57.
—— (1919/1955) "The 'uncanny'," in J. Strachey (ed.), *The Standard Edition of the Complete Psychological Works of Sigmund Freud*, vol. 17, London: The Hogarth Press, pp. 217–52.
James, W. (1902/1982) *The Varieties of Religious Experience*, New York: Penguin Books.
Kohut, H. (1977) *The Restoration of the Self*, New York: International Universities Press.

—— (1985) "On courage," in H. Kohut, *Self Psychology and the Humanities: Reflections on a New Psychoanalytic Approach*, C. Strozier (ed.), New York: W.W. Norton, pp. 5–50.

Kristeva, J. (1987a) *In the Beginning Was Love: Psychoanalysis and Faith*, A. Goldhammer (trans.), New York: Columbia University Press.

—— (1987b) *Tales of Love*, L.S. Roudiez (trans.), New York: Columbia University Press.

—— (1989) *Black Sun: Depression and Melancholia*, L.S. Roudiez (trans.), New York: Columbia University Press.

Lane, C. (1999) *The Burdens of Intimacy: Psychoanalysis and Victorian Masculinity*, Chicago: University of Chicago Press.

Parker, R. (1995) *Mother Love/Mother Hate: The Power of Maternal Ambivalence*, New York: Basic Books.

Pittman, F. (1993) *Man Enough: Fathers, Sons, and the Search for Masculinity*, New York: Perigree Books.

Pollack, W. (1998) *Real Boys: Rescuing Our Sons from the Myths of Boyhood*, New York: Random House.

Vickers, J.F. and Thomas, B.L. (1996) *Men on Midlife*, Freedom, CA: The Crossing Press.

Winnicott, D.W. (1991) "The use of an object and relating through identifications," in *Playing and Reality*, London and New York: Tavistock/Routledge, pp. 86–94.

—— (1993) "Hate in the countertransference," in D. Goldman (ed.), *In One's Bones: The Clinical Genius of Winnicott*, Northvale, NJ: Jason Aronson, pp. 15–24.

Part II

Religion in dialogue with psychology

Section 1

Theology and psychology in the West

10 The past and possible future of religion and psychological studies

Don Browning

The best way to understand the purposes and methods of an academic discipline is to identify the basic questions animating its various inquiries and then delve into the historical context that gave rise to these questions. In this essay, I plan to direct my review of the field of religion and psychological studies with these two issues in mind.

From the early 1950s to the mid-1970s, the field of religion and psychological studies was born and institutionalized. Scholars variously called this emerging field "religion and personality," "theology and personality," or "psychiatry and religion."[1] It had precursors in various clinical and experimental psychologies of religion and the interaction of psychology and theology during the early days of the religious education movement. But the field of religion and psychological studies was quite different from these earlier disciplines.

It is useful to identify the shared characteristics of the different programs in religion and psychological studies. They were for the most part established in university-related divinity schools, located within the wider field of graduate theological studies, critical or at least apologetic rather than narrowly confessional, ecumenical in outlook, and to varying degrees had both practical and theoretical interests. The latter emphasis was seen in their concern with the theory and practice of care, counseling, and spiritual growth in both churches and public ministries in hospitals, prisons, colleges, and universities. These shared characteristics speak volumes about both the basic questions driving these programs and the larger historical forces that brought them into existence.

At the broadest level, these programs were struggling to sort out the relative truth, cultural meaningfulness, and social usefulness of classic Jewish and Christian interpretations of human existence in relation to claims advanced by the newer social science disciplines – especially twentieth-century psychology, psychiatry, psychoanalysis, and various psychotherapies. The claims of the new psychotherapies were of particular interest since they were concerned with healing the psyche and therefore overlapped with endeavors once performed almost exclusively by religion.

This central question raised a wide range of comparative and critical issues that were largely philosophical and ethical in character, although seldom recognized as such. One frequently heard questions such as: What is the nature of human fulfillment? What is human brokenness: is it primarily sin, neurosis, psychosis, or anxiety? What is the relation of health to more encompassing understandings of the goals of life such as redemption, salvation, sanctification, or happiness, as the Greeks believed? What is the relation of therapeutic acceptance or empathy to theological ideas of love, forgiveness, and grace? The issue of grief was frequently investigated, in part as an issue in therapeutic and pastoral practice, but also as a window into human nature and a corrective to some overly individualistic theological anthropologies. Investigations were mounted into the nature of religious experience – in the context of conversion, mysticism, or ritual performance.

A typology of studies

These various questions (and there were many more) gave rise to an uneasy combination of different inquiries in *pastoral psychology*, the *dialogue between theology and psychology*, the *psychology of religion*, and various *cultural studies*. From one perspective, they all reflected one grand religio-cultural inquiry into the central question I mentioned above – how to make sense out of the older classical theological and philosophical understandings of the nature and goals of human life in light of competitive perspectives from the social sciences. This concern could be seen in Seward Hiltner's doctoral dissertation, written at the Divinity School of the University of Chicago directly before he founded there the field of Religion and Personality in the early 1950s. It was a comparative analysis of the respective theories of ethics and anthropology in representative theologians and psychologists, with special attention given to Paul Tillich and Erich Fromm (Hiltner 1952). Tillich obviously represented the older, classic theological and philosophical views and Fromm the newer social sciences, in this case a provocative synthesis of psychoanalysis and Marxism.

Such inquiries reflected the university setting of the various religion and psychological studies programs. Universities are by nature multi-disciplinary. The various human sciences, as is well known, tend to compete and set out their claims partially in opposition to one another. Theological seminaries are more isolated from the conflict of the various disciplines. Specialized institutes of psychoanalysis, Adlerian psychology, or Jungian analysis are more isolated as well. Hence, they too are less likely to ask the comparative and critical questions about the strength and limits of competing perspectives. But universities, especially universities with strong traditions in the humanities, are likely to ask such questions. It is precisely out of this environment that the field of religion and psychological studies was born.

Observers of both the classical views and the modern social science views saw a variety of points of contact between the two perspectives. Sometimes they saw near identities – points at which the new sciences and the classical models seemed to say the same things. Sometimes they saw points of nonidentity or conflict. And at times – and this was most frequently the case – they saw *analogies*. But then they had to puzzle over the question of which term was dominant in the analogy (cf. Tracy 1983: 63). To put it far too simplistically, was psychology true because it was like religion or was religion true because it reflected the truths of psychology? Or were both somehow in tune with underlying structures deeper than either?

This fundamental question – the relation of the classical to the new social sciences perspectives on the human – is simultaneously comparative, philosophical, and ethical. If the question is pursued in an open way, it must be in some sense critical as well. This means it should also be self-critical, permitting the overturning or at least the revision of preferred beginning points. It should be noted, however, that the field of religion and psychological studies did not always exercise the self-critical moment as seriously as genuine university studies are required to do.

This basic question motivating the field gave rise to a variety of more specific enterprises. Certainly, there was concern with *pastoral psychology* – how religious professionals involved in care could be informed in their practice by both theology and the psychological disciplines. Since it is a challenge to do both a foundational *and* a practical inquiry within the same study, early pastoral psychology studies were often short on theory and long on concerns with the technology and delivery of care. But careful study of the dissertations and books written in the university-related programs would reveal, I suspect, that the foundational and critical issues were never completely ignored.

There were, as well, a variety of studies that were indeed more foundational inquiries – expressions of what I will call the *dialogue between theology and psychology*. Increasingly, this dialogue spread to include the social sciences in general. The writings of Paul Tillich, especially his many occasional essays and his *The Courage To Be* (1952), as well as those of Reinhold Niebuhr, especially his *Self and the Dramas of History* (1955), were basic discussions of this issue and reflected the conversations developing in religion and psychological studies programs. Studies by David Roberts (1953), Daniel Day Williams (1961), Albert Outler (1954), and later by Thomas Oden (1966), Peter Homans (1970), and others represented inquiries that directly confronted the comparative and critical questions. My *Religious Thought and the Modern Psychologies: A Critical Conversation in the Theology of Culture* (Browning 1987) was an effort to carry forward this line of inquiry. Needless to say, many of these studies were indirectly exercises in theological or religious ethics, since it is impossible to ask the question of the goals of life without discussing in some way the norms of human action.

Then there were studies that were more directly *psychology of religion* inquiries. Actually, the psychology of religion was not an important part of most of these programs, with the exception of those influenced by the theological personalism surrounding the School of Theology at Boston University.[2] This was due to the general decline of psychology of religion during that period, its failure to escape the philosophical positivism of early psychoanalysis and academic psychology, and therefore the skepticism it provoked in neo-orthodox theology, the reigning theological paradigm of much of that era. Nonetheless, several important studies in the psychology of mysticism, conversion, and ritual did emerge during this period (e.g., Brown 1981; Engler 1983; Ross 1983; Rambo 1993; Schneider 1993; Parsons 1999). Donald Capps of Princeton Theological Seminary made outstanding contributions to the psychology of religion that gained international visibility (see, e.g., Capps 1997). James Fowler's work on faith development must be seen as a contribution to the psychology of religion (Fowler 1981). Volney Gay of Vanderbilt University put forth a wide range of highly nuanced studies that belong to this genre (Gay 1984, 1989, 1992).

Finally, there was a group of studies, especially at Chicago, that were *cultural studies* into the religious, ethical, or cultural horizons of the modern social and psychological disciplines. Max Weber on the rise of the Protestant ethic and Philip Rieff's discussions of its replacement by a new therapeutic ethic were often the inspiration of these studies (Rieff 1966). Investigations into the American tradition of mind cure (Fuller 1982), the unconscious in America (Fuller 1986), images of death in psychology and theology (Bregman 1992; Miller-McLemore 1988), the nature of conscience in theology and the social sciences (Sherman 1989), Freud's conflicts over his Jewish heritage in his later writings, Jung's conflicts over his Protestant heritage (Homans 1978), and other such inquiries became prominent during the 1980s (e.g., Browning 1975 and 1987).

At first glance, these four sets of enterprises look wildly divergent. The very fact that all four of them were being pursued within a single field (at least that was the case at Chicago) might seem to be evidence enough that the field was unstable, poorly conceived, and drifting. If one looked only at the surface, this charge might seem true. If, however, one searched for the underlying questions that motivated these different inquiries and the deep methodologies that were implicit within them, one could argue that the field of religion and psychological studies was on to an important insight, crucial to the well-being of both theological studies and the social sciences. That has to do with its implicit growing recognition of the *hermeneutic* character of both the classic theological and philosophical traditions of the West *as well as* the twentieth-century social and psychological disciplines.

The thesis

This leads me to the central hypothesis of this paper. The field of religion and psychological studies can only maintain its identity and fulfill its potential by recognizing itself as an exercise in what Paul Ricoeur calls "critical hermeneutics" (Ricoeur 1981: 87). Furthermore, all efforts to heal the tensions between these four different emphases by moving exclusively toward one or the other will end in greatly reducing the field's vitality. More specifically, to reduce religion and psychological studies to pastoral psychology, the abstract dialogue between theology and psychology, the psychology of religion, or cultural studies will end in collapsing the field into some adjacent discipline – applied theology, psychology, sociology, or history. In the process, the basic question driving the field of religion and psychological studies will be lost. Lost too will be a disciplined approach to much of the cultural, social, and practical work over which this field has presided.

The meaning of critical hermeneutics

The word "hermeneutics," as is well known, refers to the theory of interpretation – primarily the interpretation of texts. The preoccupation with hermeneutics emerged in the writings of Schleiermacher, Dilthey, Husserl, Weber, and Heidegger in response to the growing hegemony in European universities of naturalistic and positivistic perspectives in the human sciences. These thinkers feared that naturalism and positivism would alienate modern consciousness from history, tradition, and the very religious and philosophical classics that had gradually transformed humans from primitive hunters to civilized creatures capable of law, the arts, literature, and the axial religions.

Gadamer's *Truth and Method* (1982) was a profound continuation of hermeneutical philosophy. It was a critique of the modern human sciences and their shallow empiricism. It gained a wide reading and began actually to influence selected modern psychological, sociological, and legal traditions. It also helped reconceive the nature of theology. Gadamer showed the alienating effects of an overdetermined employment of "method" in the human sciences. By method, he meant empiricism – the belief that knowledge is acquired through emptying the self of all presuppositions and both observing and manipulating sense data with the mind as a blank slate. This epistemological stance disconnects humans from the wisdom of tradition and makes them forgetful of what has in fact shaped them. According to Gadamer, the knowledge that constitutes genuine understanding does not proceed through a simple-minded objectivism; it proceeds through "conversation" and "dialogue." And like all good conversation, progress toward understanding entails a play between questions and answers. The great classics of the past – the texts and monuments we return to time and again to interpret and to assimilate – have shaped our history and our personal experience. They have become, in fact, part of our "effective history," influencing our images of life, our views of human nature, and our visions of the good life in ways we do not fully comprehend (Gadamer 1982: 267–74). Understanding is having a dialogue or conversation with the classics that have already shaped us – a conversation with that which is already part of us, no matter how distorted or fragmented they have become (Gadamer 1982: 330–41).

What is Gadamer's message to the human sciences, including psychology, psychoanalysis, and the various psychotherapies? It is simply this: they too have their "effective histories." They too unconsciously draw on the classics of the past – sometimes Christian, sometimes Jewish, sometimes Greek (Platonic, Aristotelian, stoic), and sometimes interesting combinations of these and others. Or, to say it more accurately, the researchers who toil in these social science disciplines have their effective histories. Their research would be enriched, more on course, less biased, and less culturally alienating, if they did not retreat into a false objectivism but acknowledged the role of their own presuppositions (their own "prejudices" in the sense of "pre-judgments") and the important role they play in the dialogue leading to understanding (Gadamer 1982: 238). Understanding is a "fusion of horizons" between present contexts and questions *and* the dominant ideals of our traditions (Gadamer 1982: 273ff.). Gadamer claimed to be uncovering an ontology of understanding fundamental to all the human sciences.

Seen from this perspective, the central question of the religion and psychological studies field – how can we *understand* the somewhat competing claims of the classic religious and philosophical images of the human in relation to the emerging psychological and social sciences? – makes a great deal of sense. Rightly understood, it was a genuinely hermeneutic question. Why? Because we soon learned that there were elements of the tradition – the classics – in and around the conceptuality of the modern perspectives, proving that they too had their effective histories (Bulkley 1994; Barnard 1997). Freud struggled against his Jewishness, but, as Philip Rieff taught us, in the end, he still had the mind of a "moralist" (Rieff 1979: 300–28). Carl Rogers was conflicted: he was Greek in his eudaemonistic image of human fulfillment, but classically Protestant, maybe even Lutheran, in his understanding of the role of unconditioned love in overcoming brokenness (Oden 1966; Browning 1966). Deep metaphors abound in the modern social sciences, orienting them to various traditional world views in ways that they seldom fully understand.[3]

The restoration of "method"

But I do not want to be misunderstood. I am not arguing that Gadamer's understanding of hermeneutics is sufficient to undergird a discipline such as religion and psychological studies. Nor am I saying that it can completely account for the deep methodological intuitions that linked the diverse enterprises that characterized its activity during the decades of the 1970s and 1980s. Gadamer gives us only part of what is needed. Gadamer is weak on a positive understanding of science and failed to understand the role of critique in appropriating tradition. Paul Ricoeur can help with both of these issues.

In *Hermeneutics and the Human Sciences* (1981) and other writings, Ricoeur chides Gadamer for the title of his great book; rather than *Truth and Method*, Ricoeur believes it should have been called *Truth or Method* (Ricoeur 1981: 131). In the end, Gadamer pits science's drive to be "objective" *against* hermeneutic subject–object engagement; Gadamer seems to believe that it must be necessarily one *or* the other. Ricoeur believes that such a dichotomy need not be the case. There is a place for what Ricoeur calls "distanciation" in hermeneutic dialogue and understanding. Ricoeur substitutes the word distanciation for the more positivistic idea of objectivity. Objectivity suggests the need to detach the researcher completely from the tradition that formed him or her. Ricoeur sees such objectivity as both impossible and alienating – even culturally nihilistic, since it seems to put the formative power of the past on hold. In taking the strictly objective stance, the human sciences actually can function to dismantle tradition, its wisdom, and the classics that have formed it.

I see this happening in the area of my recent research on family.[4] Many social scientists believe they can study families as if they were interacting collections of people in time and space – indeed, as though the institution of family had no history, no accomplishments, no classic moments that need to be understood in relation to present questions. In studying the family "objectively," they unwittingly undermine this history and its normative achievements and contribute to our failure either to understand the past or adequately reconstruct it for a more useable future.

So, for Ricoeur, distanciation – yes; but complete objectivity – no. What does distanciation contribute, especially when seen as a sub-moment of dialogue and understanding? It provides "explanation." Human sciences rightly should be interested in the psychological, social, economic, and even biological factors that shape human life. But explanation should always be seen as a sub-moment of the understanding and reconstruction of meaning. Meaning comes in the form of a story or narrative that orients us toward the past and present yet also provides expectations for the future (Ricoeur 1981: 274–96). Causal factors shape the narrative but never completely determine it. Therefore, all human sciences should see themselves as involved in the rhythms of "understanding–explanation–understanding" where understanding principally functions to interpret the narrative level of meaning.

Distanciation also contributes to the critique of tradition. Ricoeur agrees with Habermas: Gadamer failed to understand the importance of the critique of tradition and how even the classics that open vast areas of truth can also function to harm and oppress (Ricoeur 1981: 78–87). The capacity for distanciation is grounded in the human capacity to reflect – the self's capacity to look back on and gain some distance from the very biological, material, historical, and cultural forces that have shaped it. Our capacity for reflection and distanciation makes it possible for us to isolate the core of our own classic traditions and then criticize distortions in light of its more fundamental themes. This same capacity, Ricoeur believes, makes it possible for humans to apply a kind of deontological test to the criticism of our inherited narrative traditions (Ricoeur 1987: 11–15 and 1992: 204–18). This test is close to the universalization requirements of Kant's categorical imperative. It asks, can the moral truths of our narrative traditions be universalized? But even then, since Ricoeur was primarily applying this to the Western classic traditions, the deontological test was not so much Kantian as the employment of a mixed-deontological reading of a principle internal to both Judaism and Christianity, i.e., the golden rule. But Ricoeur understands the golden rule to mean this: do *good* unto others as you would have them to do *good* unto you (Ricoeur 1992: 219–27). It is beyond the scope of this paper to unpack this formulation of the deontological test. It must suffice to point out that it combines the human quest for the good (teleology) – with all its passional and affective qualities – with a superordinate concern for its generalizability. This is a formulation quite useable for those of us working with the psychological disciplines with their concern for the affective levels of life. With this complex principle, Ricoeur incorporates within his hermeneutics a concern with critique typical of Habermas and the entire Frankfurt School, hence the appropriateness of calling his view a critical hermeneutics.

Religion and psychological studies as critical hermeneutics

An implicit critical hermeneutics was embedded in the multiple inquiries of the field of religion and psychological studies. Through most of its history, the discipline did not have the conceptual tools to clarify its own intuitions. In its early days, at least at Chicago, process philosophy tried to provide an integrating model for religion and psychological studies. Indeed, this philosophy did have an appreciation for the inheritances of the past, for the fullness of human action, for the limitations of positivistic science, and the need for multiple interpretive perspectives on human action. But it is my conviction that critical hermeneutics, not necessarily at the exclusion of insights from process thought, is the more useful for capturing the subtle interactions between tradition and modernity occurring in the tension between religious and philosophical classics *and* the contemporary human sciences.

How can we reconceptualize and reposition some of the standard pursuits of religion and psychological studies with the model of critical hermeneutics in mind? What do pastoral psychology, the dialogue between theology and psychology, the psychology of religion, and cultural studies look like when seen through the prism of this perspective on human understanding? I will try to answer these questions in a way that will be suggestive for the future.

In order to address the place of pastoral psychology and care, I need to say one more thing about Gadamer's view of hermeneutics as a dialogue moving toward understanding. It is easy to forget that Gadamer characterizes understanding as a *practical* enterprise. In fact, Aristotle's view of practical reason served as a model for Gadamer's theory of understanding. Here are Gadamer's words on this important matter:

> We, too, determined that application is neither a subsequent nor a merely occasional part of the phenomenon of understanding, but codetermines it as a whole from the beginning. Here too application was not the relating of some pre-given universal to the particular situation. The interpreter dealing with a traditional text seeks to apply it to himself ... In order to understand that, he must not seek to disregard himself and his particular hermeneutical situation. He must relate the text to his situation, if he wants to understand at all.
>
> (Gadamer 1982: 289)

If the understanding process is basically practical in nature, then it should not be an embarrassment for the field of religion and psychological studies to pursue questions of actual practice that are also informed by the Christian classics. Practices, even practices of care, will always be informed by some normative horizon. This is true for so-called secular practices of care just as it is for those that are explicitly religious. It is relatively easy to unpack the moral and quasi-religious deep metaphors of most of the dominant modern psychotherapeutic models, as I tried to show in *Religious Thought and the Modern Psychologies* (1987). Others have extended my argument, applying it to new areas of contemporary psychology (Jones and Butman 1991). Hence, the task is not to avoid the study of allegedly secular and explicitly religious systems of care because they are practical; the task is to search out, find, critique, and then try to ground adequately their assumed normative horizons. Hence, if studies in pastoral counseling and care are genuine exercises in critical hermeneutics, they can be thoroughly respectable, even within the context of university-related programs of religion and psychological studies.

What about the more abstract dialogue between theology and the psychological and social sciences? For some practitioners of religion and psychological studies, this area of inquiry is an embarrassment, just as are studies in what is commonly called pastoral care. Although abstract – and therefore not practical, with all the existing overtones that the practical cannot be rigorous – this dialogue was thought by many to be secretly confessional and automatically prejudiced in the favor of arbitrary theological beginning points.

But there are several problems with this skeptical attitude. First, hermeneutic theory points out that all reflection begins with confession, since all reflection – even the most critical and distanciated – belongs to an effective history. On this score, theological reflection is no different than other kinds; in fact, theologians may have the advantage of being more explicit, honest, and open about their beginning points, their prejudices, and their prejudgments. So the dialogue between theology and the social sciences should be seen as basically no different than any other critical hermeneutical exercise in self-understanding and self-clarification. Having been influenced by classic theological traditions and having been confronted with the emerging modern disciplines, how does the reflecting self clarify the tensions between them?

We should have learned by now that this is not just a simple comparison of faith and reason, theology and science, apples and oranges, i.e., things that cannot really be compared. Hermeneutically oriented philosophy of science associated with the names of Thomas Kuhn, Richard Bernstein, and Ricoeur himself should have made it clear enough that all of the social sciences, and perhaps even the physical sciences, have their socially and culturally embedded features (Kuhn 1970; Bernstein 1983). By the same token, theologies, as well as the philosophies often informing them, have their empirical assumptions about the "is-ness" of human nature. Hence, there are good reasons to pursue the hermeneutic dialogue between them, especially if the dialogue is critical.

How about the psychology of religion? What sense can we make of its task from the perspective of a critical hermeneutics? Even within the limits of critical hermeneutics, there is much to be learned from the psychological study of religion. But when so conceived, psychology of religion inevitably becomes a much more relative and modest endeavor. All pretenses to absolute objectivity must be renounced. Psychology is not an objective discipline that boldly uncovers the psychological infrastructures and projections of religious beliefs, symbols, and rituals. The "gotcha" mentality often surrounding early psychoanalytic studies that painted religious ideation as this or that repressed unconscious wish needing to be exposed must, at all costs, be avoided. Ricoeur's own hermeneutic interpretation of Freud that demonstrates how the "archeology" of unconscious desires can be dialectically reconstructed by the teleology of its various cultural objects shows us both the value and limitation of the psychology of religion (Ricoeur 1970: 459–93). Anna Marie Rizzuto developed much the same insight in her *Birth of the Living God* (1979). In addition, I have always read Erik Erikson's subtle psychoanalytic analysis of how the doctrine of justification reawakened Luther's earliest sense of agency and trust as precisely an illustration of Ricoeur's dialectic between archeology and teleology in healthy religious symbols (Erikson 1962: 201–22).

At most, the psychology of religion is an act of distanciation. As is the case with all acts of distanciation, it will carry with it in subdued form an effective history that will influence the scholarly task itself. Understanding the situated character of the psychology of religion, as Peter Homans has done in his subtle synthesis of Kohut's psychology of the self and sociological theory, is an important contribution to a better situated and more modest psychology of religion (Homans 1989). In this way, psychology of religion can make its own unique contribution to an understanding of both the hermeneutic situation of the inherited religious *and* modern social science views of the human.

Finally, how should we regard the cultural studies pursued within the context of religion and psychological studies? The critical hermeneutical character of these studies should now be obvious. Many of these studies uncovered the submerged religious and ethical horizons of the so-called modern human sciences, whether it be the Protestant ethic, some implicit dualism, a romantic harmonistic view of life as was often found in the humanistic psychologies, or some surprising Greek eudaemonism that seemed to pop up in the later writings of Heinz Kohut on the nature of "tragic man" (Kohut 1984: 207–8). These studies were simply showing the submerged effective history of these psychologies and the struggles of their originators to come to terms with these histories. Once again, cultural studies must renounce another kind of "gotcha" academic politics. It is not enough to say, "You said you were scientific, but you were really Protestant, Greek, or a crypto-nostalgic Jew, therefore you have been discredited." Possibly – just possibly – a Protestant, Greek, or Jewish world view has more moral and metaphysical validity than an ice-cold positivism. Cultural studies must take on the critical task of evaluating openly and convincingly the cultural visions they uncover. This is not a simple task. It inevitably brings cultural studies to the edge of philosophical or theological ethics and even to the outer borders of the philosophy of religion.

The real vision of religion and psychological studies

The academic field of religion and psychological studies was difficult to discipline and to communicate to other fields because it assigned itself an ambitious task. For that matter, it was a task quite similar to that of other so-called dialogical fields, whether they be called "ethics and society," "religion and literature," or "religion and the arts."[5] It is ironic that at the very moment that all of those fields are now under pressure and about to be absorbed once again into more traditional fields, there exists a philosophical framework such as critical hermeneutics that could give coherent order to their various pursuits.

What religion and psychological studies was really about can be illustrated by recalling Richard Cabot's vision for a new academic discipline at Harvard. Ian Evison perceptively tells the story in his doctoral dissertation titled *Pragmatism and Idealism in the Professions* (1995). Richard Cabot was part of the elite Cabot family of Boston. He went to Harvard, studied pragmatism with William James, but decided that to really live out the implications of this philosophy, he should enter a practical discipline such as medicine. After distinguishing himself in various fields of medicine, helping to found the field of medical social work, and also helping to conceive the field of specialized pastoral care and counseling, he returned to teach philosophy – mainly ethics – at Harvard University.

There, with Alfred North Whitehead and Ralph Barton Perry as his colleagues, he proposed a startling idea, but one that in spite of his prestige he could not sell to his academic colleagues. This idea was to found a new interdisciplinary department – one that combined theology, philosophy of religion, ethics, the social sciences, and social work. This would be a single, integrated program that would plumb the depths of a critical theory of human action – one informed by religion – but also one that would address contemporary social and cultural problems and practices.

He was convinced that social work and social action needed grounding in moral philosophy. He was aware that it also needed the tools of social and psychological description, i.e., the explanatory moments provided by the distanciated observations of those disciplines. He knew that moral philosophy could never easily disconnect itself from a religious horizon, or what some philosophers call "background beliefs," that ground and orient ethical inquiry. Hence, Cabot had the audacity to propose that these various tasks be held together in one field. He believed that philosophical pragmatism could hold these diverse inquiries together. It probably could have, if rightly interpreted. The affinities between philosophical pragmatism and critical hermeneutics is an issue that has been investigated by Richard Bernstein (1983: 6, 178). In the end, I find them compatible and mutually enriching. But that is a discussion for another time. The point is, intellectual resources for undergirding such a venture do exist.

Cabot's vision was put forward at a time when the modern beast of academic specialization began walking boldly through the halls of academia. Academic progress, it bellowed, could only be made if questions were narrowed and more controlled inquiries were championed. There was truth in this claim; it was, in effect, a case for the role of distanciated inquiry in the pursuit of explanations. The problem with this strategy, however, was that no discipline was given the task of assembling the discrete inquiries into an intelligible practical whole. Religion and psychological studies as a vague exercise in critical hermeneutics was an effort to do just that. It had continuities with the academic vision of Richard Cabot.

Religion and psychological studies within the framework of practical theology

Having said this, it should not come as a surprise to readers who know something about the trajectory of my academic career to see me conclude with a word or two about religion and psychological studies within the larger framework of practical theology. To me, a critical practical theology and a critical hermeneutics are nearly identical. Both start their reflection out of the context of situations facing challenge, conflict, and disruption. Both first of all interpret situations from the perspective of the horizons of their effective histories even though, in a secondary way, they may also use the explanatory insights of the modern social sciences. Hence, both inquiries *must take history very seriously*. To clarify their goals in facing concrete problematics, they both return to the ideals or classics that have shaped their effective histories. This brings them to the task of the retrieval and critique of these ideals. Since practical concerns – concerns with application, as Gadamer called it – shape both inquiries from the beginning, their concluding interest in the actual task of concretely and strategically addressing situations is simply a completion of the *praxis*-oriented character of the entire understanding process. The task of practical ethical reconstruction and the task of understanding overlap.

Because I see such a close association between practical theology and critical hermeneutics, it never occurred to me that I was necessarily leaving the field of religion and psychological studies when I wrote my book called *A Fundamental Practical Theology* (1991). Instead, I saw it as an attempt to find a more comprehensive framework for holding together the various directions in which the field of religion and psychological studies had gone. By the same token, the book *From Culture Wars to Common Ground: Religion and the American Family Debate* (1997) that I wrote with Bonnie Miller-McLemore, Pamela Couture, Bernie Lyon, and Robert Franklin, exemplifies most of the methodological moves of *A Fundamental Practical Theology*. Both books are partial exercises in care, the dialogue between theology and the social sciences, the psychology of religion, and cultural studies. Both books are submitted as exercises in critical hermeneutics. But I would not want to leave the impression that every study in this general field should try to pursue the entire practical or critical hermeneutical task. Some should, but my main point is this: such frameworks are useful for helping to position the various more discrete enterprises and reminding us how they can complement one another and contribute to a larger whole.

But for those who are reluctant to incorporate the word "theology" or "practical" into their academic self-understanding, I am quite happy to settle for my central point: the field of religion and psychological studies can be best ordered if seen as an expression of critical hermeneutics.

This discipline, if it is to thrive anywhere, will probably fare best in the very context that gave it birth – the modern, university-related divinity school. It can, of course, radiate outward from there, as it has in the past. But this context, more than other academic settings, is most likely to keep alive the central question driving religion and psychological studies – the question of the comparative meaning and validity of classic religious and philosophical images of the human in relation to modern challenges from the social sciences.

Notes

1 I speak primarily of programs established at the Divinity School of the University of Chicago, Union Theological Seminary (in close association with courses at Columbia University), Candler School of Theology, Drew Divinity School, the Divinity School of Vanderbilt University, Claremont School of Theology (in association with the Claremont Graduate Schools), the Berkeley Graduate Theological Union, School of Theology at Boston University, Garrett-Evangelical Seminary connected with Northwestern University, and Iliff Seminary connected with the University of Denver. I will use the phrase "religion and psychological studies" since that was the title of the program at the University of Chicago after 1971. Before that, the phrase "religion and personality" was the title of the discipline.
2 This included the programs at the School of Theology of Boston University, Garrett-Evangelical at Northwestern, and Iliff at the University of Denver.
3 Analyzing the deep metaphors of detachment, control, joy, and care present in the modern psychologies was the objective of my *Pluralism and Personality* (1980), and *Religious Thought and the Modern Psychologies* (1987).
4 See the summary volume of the eleven-volume Religion, Culture, and Family Project financed by a generous grant from the Division of Religion of the Lilly Endowment, Inc. (Browning *et al.* 1997).
5 These are names of three other dialogical fields that were born at Chicago and flourished there for approximately three decades.

References

Barnard, B. (1997) *Exploring Unseen Worlds: William James' Philosophy of Mysticism*, Albany, NY: State University of New York Press.

Bernstein, R. (1983) *Beyond Objectivism and Relativism*, Philadelphia: University of Pennsylvania Press.

Bregman, L. (1992) *Death in the Midst of Life*, Grand Rapids, MI: Baker.

Brown, D. (1981) "Mahamudra meditation-stages and contemporary cognitive psychology," PhD dissertation, University of Chicago.

Browning, D. (1966) *Atonement and Psychotherapy*, Philadelphia: Westminster Press.

—— (1975) *Generative Man: Society and the Good Man in Philip Rieff, Norman Brown, Erich Fromm and Erik Erikson*, New York: Dell.

—— (1980) *Pluralism and Personality*, Lewisburg, PA: Bucknell University Press.

—— (1987) *Religious Thought and the Modern Psychologies*, Minneapolis: Fortress Press.

—— (1991) *A Fundamental Practical Theology*, Minneapolis: Fortress Press.

Browning, D., Miller-McLemore, B., Couture, P., Lyon, B., and Franklin, R. (1997) *From Culture Wars to Common Ground: Religion and the American Family Debate*, Louisville, KY: Westminster John Knox.

Bulkley, K. (1994) *The Wilderness of Dreams: Exploring the Religious Meanings of Dreams in Modern Western Culture*, Albany, NY: State University of New York Press.

Capps, D. (1997) *Men, Religion, and Melancholia: James, Otto, Jung, and Erikson*, New Haven, CT: Yale University Press.

Engler, J. H. (1983) "Theravada Buddhist insight meditation and an object-relational model of therapeutic-developmental change," PhD dissertation, University of Chicago.

Erikson, E. (1962) *Young Man Luther*, New York: W.W. Norton.

Evison, I. (1995) "Pragmatism and idealism in the professions: the case study of Richard Clarke Cabot, 1869–1939," PhD dissertation, University of Chicago.

Fowler, J. (1981) *Stages of Faith*, San Francisco: Harper & Row.

Fuller, R. (1982) *Mesmerism and the American Cure of Souls, 1835–1900*, Oxford: Oxford University Press.

—— (1986) *Americans and the Unconscious*, Oxford: Oxford University Press.

Gadamer, H.-G. (1982) *Truth and Method*, New York: Continuum.

Gay, V. (1984) *Reading Jung: Science, Psychology and Religion*, Chico, CA: Scholars Press.

—— (1989) *Understanding the Occult: Fragmentation and Repair of the Self*, Minneapolis: Fortress.

—— (1992) *Freud and Sublimation: Reconsiderations*, Albany, NY: State University of New York Press.

Hiltner, S. (1952) "Psychotherapy and Christian ethics: an evaluation of the ethical thought of A.E. Taylor and Paul Tillich in the light of psychotherapeutic contributions to ethics by J.C. Flugel and Erich Fromm," PhD dissertation, University of Chicago.

Homans, P. (1970) *Theology After Freud*, New York: Bobbs-Merrill.

—— (1978) *Jung in Context*, Chicago: University of Chicago Press.

—— (1989) *The Ability to Mourn: Disillusionment and the Social Origins of Psychology*, Chicago: University of Chicago Press.

Jones, S. and Butman, R. (1991) *Modern Psychotherapies: A Comprehensive Christian Appraisal*, Downers Grove, IL: Intervarsity Press.

Kohut, H. (1984) *How Does Analysis Cure?*, Chicago: University of Chicago Press.

Kuhn, T. (1970) *The Structure of Scientific Revolutions*, Chicago: University of Chicago Press.

Miller-McLemore, B. (1988) *Death, Sin, and the Moral Life*, Atlanta: Scholars Press.

Niebuhr, R. (1955) *The Self and the Dramas of History*, New York: Charles Scribner's Sons.

Oden, T. (1966) *Kerygma and Counseling*, Philadelphia: Westminster Press.

Outler, A. (1954) *Psychotherapy and the Christian Message*, New York: Harper.

Parsons, W. (1999) *The Enigma of the Oceanic Feeling*, Oxford: Oxford University Press.

Rambo, L. (1993) *Understanding Religious Conversion*, New Haven, CT: Yale University Press.

Ricoeur, P. (1970) *Freud and Philosophy*, New Haven, CT: Yale University Press.

—— (1981) *Hermeneutics and the Human Sciences*, Cambridge: Cambridge University Press.

—— (1987) "The teleological and deontological structure of action: Aristotle and/or Kant?", in A.P. Griffiths (ed.), *Contemporary French Philosophy*, Cambridge: Cambridge University Press.

—— (1992) *Oneself as Another*, Chicago: University of Chicago Press.

Rieff, P. (1966) *The Triumph of the Therapeutic*, New York: Harper Torchbooks.

—— (1979) *Freud: The Mind of a Moralist*, Chicago: University of Chicago Press.

Rizzuto, A.M. (1979) *The Birth of the Living God*, Chicago: University of Chicago Press.

Roberts, D. (1953) *Psychotherapy and the Christian View of Man*, New York: Charles Scribner's Sons.

Ross, M.E. (1983) "Object-relations theory and the psychoanalytic theory of ritual," PhD dissertation, University of Chicago.

Schneider, G. (1993) *The Way of the Cross Leads Home*, Bloomington, IN: University of Indiana Press.

Sherman, C. (1989) "Acknowledging early childhood: common grace in the moral life in the moral psychology of Reinhold Niebuhr," PhD dissertation, University of Chicago.

Tillich, P. (1952) *The Courage to Be*, New Haven: Yale University Press.

—— (1959) *Theology of Culture*, New York: Oxford University Press.

Tracy, D. (1983) "Foundations of practical theology," in D. Browning (ed.), *Practical Theology*, San Francisco: Harper & Row.

Williams, D.D. (1961) *The Minister and the Care of Souls*, New York: Harpers Brothers.

11 Shaping the future of religion and psychology

Feminist transformations in pastoral theology

Bonnie J. Miller-McLemore

In an essay earlier in this volume, Diane Jonte-Pace argues that compared to the feminist advances in the "psychology *of* religion," feminist scholarship has had relatively little impact on the "psychology *and* religion" movement. The accuracy of her claim depends on how one understands the latter. Jonte-Pace is correct only if one employs a narrow definition of psychology and religion. While she is right to acknowledge the work still to be done on the historical and cultural backgrounds of psychological theorists, I want to challenge and modify her claim that feminist scholarship has had little influence by characterizing the developments of the last two decades in pastoral and practical theology in the area of religion, psychology, and gender. An expanding body of literature in this domain should not be overlooked. This growth suggests interesting potential directions for the field's future evolution.

Defining the field

In defining the field known as religion and psychological studies, scholars immediately run into problems. One of the easiest and perhaps clearest ways to delineate the field is unidirectionally, i.e., as involving psychological attempts to understand religion. Of the various depictions, the "psychology of religion" definition is perhaps the simplest one. Given the academic climate of suspicion toward overt declarations of religious faith, it may also be the safest.

Scholars have had greater difficulty defining and defending the enterprise of "psychology and religion." The two-way interaction between psychology and theology as scholarly disciplines, therapy and pastoral intervention as practical endeavors, and psychoanalysis and religion as historical and cultural phenomena has made succinct outline of the field's agenda more complicated. It is in this second area that my interests lie – in the complex arena where secular science and faith-driven religious interpretation meet as analogous, albeit often divergent, partners in the scholarly enterprise of understanding human struggle, survival, and healing.

Scholars of psychology and religion include not only those interested in cultural and historical factors in the rise of psychology, as depicted by Jonte-Pace. From the beginning there have been others, such as Seward Hiltner and Paul Tillich, or more recently, Don Browning and Charles Gerkin, whose primary vocational identity remains theology and whose fundamental community often includes the congregation and related religious institutions. This offshoot might better be called the "psychology and *theology*" movement or, along the lines explored in the first part of the next section, psychology and theology "in dialogue." While interested in hermeneutical exploration of the foundations of psychology, these scholars see interpretation for the sheer sake of interpretation as an incomplete or arrested agenda. Instead, psychology is viewed as subordinate or propaedeutic to the aims of theological hermeneutics and religious practices. To a certain degree, psychology is employed in the service of shaping and preserving faithful, prophetic, caring religious practices and communities. The interest in psychology goes beyond psychological study of religious phenomena and cultural study of psychology to an understanding of psychology as an expansive self-contained, culture-forming discipline, with a variety of theories besides psychoanalysis, and to therapy as a learned practice in its own right.

From this perspective, psychology appears in at least two prominent ways: as a tool for the enhancement of the faithful care of others and as a cultural force that shapes moral ideals and spiritual hopes and hence requires critical evaluation. Religion is also seen differently: it is not simply an object of study but rather a body of beliefs and practices about ultimate and mystical dimensions of life to be encountered, experienced, tried, and perhaps followed. Theology is the contemplation and testing of this endeavor of religious encounter and trial.

Recent history and the future of the field

As Freud himself contended, mapping the future requires remembering the past, not so it may rule but to respect and hence to steady its load. In the past two decades, scholars in the different areas of psychology of religion and psychology and religion have drifted apart, not only as a result of increased specialization and academic secularization but also as a corollary of current controversies over the place of religious studies in a free-standing university and the emerging, although controversial, distinction between religious and theological studies. Simply stated, religious studies asserts its validity as a university discipline by establishing itself over against the supposedly faith-driven biases of theological studies. Oddly enough, this gap widened alongside postmodern disclosure of the politically motivated prejudices behind the most objective scientific claims, a contention that would seem to weaken the so-called objectivity of religious studies. Nonetheless, the division persists in spite of the questionable claim that religious studies obtains a purer, less tainted rationality than theological studies.

Heightened divergence has also been a result of difference in location. Those in psychology of religion largely teach in universities and colleges. Those in psychology and religion often teach in seminaries and divinity schools. This division reflects the uncertainties of mainline Protestantism in an increasingly diverse society as well. Mainline Protestantism no longer defines mainstream US culture or higher education as it did at the start of the twentieth century. At one time, the creation and sustenance of programs in religion and psychological studies depended in part on the financial and philosophical benevolence of religious institutions and believers. With dwindling numbers and finances, this source of support carries less weight today.

Nonetheless, the two areas of psychology of religion and psychology and religion are historically intertwined. While distance and even defensiveness characterized relationships between psychiatry and religion during the heyday of the psychology of religion in the early part of the twentieth century, by mid-century scholars and clinicians in both religion and psychology had entered into new phases of appropriation, affiliation, and critical assessment (Pattison 1978a, 1978b). Such alliances helped strengthen the position of scholarly research and fostered the creation of academic programs in religion and psychology.

The success or failure of the field today and its survival as a whole, I would argue, rest on the ability to sustain the interconnections between two otherwise largely distinct enterprises. In other words, wed initially in their attempts to make inroads into the academy, scholars in divergent branches shall sink or swim together. This strategic interdependence is particularly requisite in terms of sustaining strong doctoral programs, even if it is less pertinent for those who teach in professional schools or undergraduate programs. The associations between the areas have relevance in the latter two educational contexts as well. On college campuses, when young people arrive with particular faith experiences or alienated from specific religious communities, the connections between the scientific study of religion and theological debate can hardly be avoided. Inversely, seminaries ignore the contributions of reductionist studies of religion in the wider academy at their own intellectual risk.

I am more urgent about strategic interdependence in the context of this book, which continues a discussion begun by a panel on the future of the field at a 1997 American Academy of Religion (AAR) conference. The panel included only one person from a seminary context and his paper contained a rather pessimistic forecast about the future of pastoral theology (Evison 1997). Another panelist was quite adamant about avoiding theology, ministry, and the quagmire of a "nonreductionist approach to religion" in which religion becomes more than a mere object of study (Henking 1997).

Granted, those in the field have good reason to be both pessimistic and cautious. Pastoral theology must continue to prove itself worthy of academic attention; and faith convictions can distort research. Nevertheless, these problems need not overshadow the importance of grappling with our stark differences, curious compatibilities, and contrasting contributions to the study of religion and psychology. We continue to have a good deal to learn from each other and to offer the academy at large. The panel discussion attracted an audience that included several divinity school and seminary faculty members, even though some pastoral theologians avoid the AAR entirely, ridiculing its ivory tower pretensions and trivialities. Pastoral theologians need to become more willing to engage in the intellectual and political dealings of higher education; at the same time, the contributions of pastoral theology need to be taken more seriously by the academy.

Scholars in religion and psychological studies would do well then to resist the centrifugal pull that spins us off in increasingly different directions. We would do well to stay our immediate biases against the specialized academic study of religion as an end in itself or, inversely, our biases against the incorporation of faith claims as a further aim shaping the scholarly vocation of religious study. For a variety of reasons, feminist scholars in religion and psychology may have the resources and the motivation to bridge the gap and soothe antagonisms between various branches of the field. By articulating the fresh parameters established through feminist scholarship in pastoral theology on both national and international levels,[1] I hope to further one of the goals identified in the introduction to this volume: to challenge the segmentation currently dividing the field and to encourage awareness, communication, and even collaboration between participants in different areas. In the remainder of the chapter, I will draw on three recent research reviews of the state of feminist studies in pastoral theology and then will offer several observations about the nature of the contemporary transformations in religion, psychology, and gender and their implications for religion and psychological studies.

Developments in feminist scholarship in pastoral theology

Three essays by Kathleen Greider, Elaine Graham, and myself, each surveying the expansion of feminist theory and pastoral theology, have appeared in the last year. The fact that all three appeared in such a short span of time, with Greider's and my own in the same edited volume (Miller-McLemore and Gill-Austern 1999), and Graham's piece (1999) in an international journal but written after taking part in a panel responding to an earlier version of my essay, highlights several phenomena. Scholars have reached a place where they believe they need to take stock of progress. A substantial body of feminist scholarship has accrued. Ultimately, distinct themes have arisen that point toward a shift in prominent models of study and practice in religion and psychology in the area of pastoral theology.

My own essay, "Feminist theory in pastoral theology," was first delivered at a pre-session sponsored by the American Association of Practical Theology at the 1997 AAR and then revised for an edited book, *Feminist and Womanist Pastoral Theology* (1998b; Miller-McLemore and Gill-Austern 1999). The book itself represents an attempt to attend to broader issues in the development and the future of the field. Although many of the authors have done other research on "first-order" matters of pastoral care and "second-order" use of psychology and theology to investigate women's experiences, this book's goal is to step back and offer "third-order" reflection on the methods and substance of the field (see Jennings 1990: 862, cited by Doehring 1999: 100). More specifically, the collection articulates fresh directions resulting from the increased activity of feminist scholars:

> What does it mean that several significant edited collections in pastoral theology as well as single-authored volumes on numerous topics have appeared in the last decade, all done by feminist scholars? How will this influence pastoral ministry and care in congregations? And how will it shape theological schools and the academy of religion? Feminist work in pastoral theology is actually proceeding at a breakneck pace … Pausing to consider what all this fresh activity means for the state of pastoral theology, care, and counseling, for congregations, and for the academy is absolutely requisite.
>
> (Miller-McLemore and Gill-Austern 1999: 9–10)

The book identifies some of the major shifts in focus, subject, and method and their implications.

Until the past few years, I joined the crowd in lamenting the decline of the field and the late arrival of feminist scholarship. On both counts, I have revised my thinking. In complaints on the demise of the field, I began to notice a pattern. Many of those worrying about the future of the "movement" are among the retiring generation who participated in the early rapid growth in the 1960s and 1970s but feel uneasy or slightly displaced by new developments. Addressing the Society for Pastoral Theology in 1994, James Lapsley identifies his fear that "pluralism and its advantages of inclusiveness … comes with [the] price" of conceptual incoherence and dismissal by the wider academy (1995: 52). Liston Mills, Lapsley's close colleague, worries that next-generation pastoral theologians will misuse the increased responsibility that comes with the transition from an up-and-coming movement to an established discipline (1994).

Lapsley, Mills, and others, however, sometimes mistake change and difference for decline. The disturbing difference of the voices of women and minorities, the seemingly distracting fascination with inclusivity in the Society for Pastoral Theology, the dramatic decline in courses on counseling and the increase in courses on public policy, gender, and race, as well as spirituality, the move away from verbatims and role-play to other teaching tools, and the use of new feminist methods in research – all these changes have led to what I believe are false conclusions about the weakening of the field. The decline in the numbers of family therapy courses or even in the number of positions in the field (previously filled by white men) need not spell disaster.

In an important edited collection of international perspectives on practical theology, South African theologian Denise Ackermann and Dutch theologian Riet Bons-Storm complain that the "endless debates" at conferences about the identity of practical theology distract us from the "pressing concerns of practical theology in a world full of want" (1998: 2). There is an additional negative effect. Scholars who are anxious about their position and status in the academy "are not eager to let 'others' join them," because the "unfamiliar and the unexplored" seem to make the field even more precarious and vulnerable to dismissal and attack (3).

But are such fears genuinely warranted? Might there be a less than benevolent association between doomsday forecasts of future demise and issues of gender? Is there an unhealthy relationship between predictions of decline and the arrival of the "other" on the scene?

The tendency to emphasize the generational lag in feminist scholarship in pastoral theology also needs reconsideration. In her recent article on the impact of feminist theory on the field, Graham concludes that feminist scholarship "only made an impression in the last ten years" (1999: 185, 193). I have made similar observations a number of times over the past decade (1993: 368; 1996: 19–20; 1998b: 5–6). While perhaps an accurate claim in the early 1990s, I now believe these assessments to be dated and narrow. Patterns of feminist work need a more friendly reading, one that acknowledges the delays in scholarship caused by sexism and clericalism but also recognizes earlier contributions and applauds the progress made despite these impediments. While the 1990s do represent a distinct turning point, Graham's analysis is short-sighted with respect to prior developments and perhaps limited by her location in an English university.[2]

While I cannot judge well the evolution of feminist research in England, the so-called dearth of explicit reflection on feminism in pastoral theology in the US needs to be characterized differently. Distinct patterns of growth have occurred. Over the past three decades, feminist pastoral theology has generated a steady body of literature with three projects in mind, somewhat analogous to Jonte-Pace's identification in her chapter of moments of critique, analysis, and inclusivity in feminist scholarship: implicit critique of patriarchy; explicit critique and advocacy for women and other marginalized populations; and topical reconstruction.

The first project – implicit critique and unrest – appears in the largely unpublished but compelling activities of women in the field, perhaps best exemplified by the work of Peggy Way and Sue Cardwell. Beginning in the 1960s and 1970s, Way mentored women in the field and used public speaking engagements to disturb the status quo on such subjects as violence in the family. She contested the conventional boundaries dictated by the study of religion and demanded that theology grapple with the particularities of suffering and the ecclesial context of care (Way 1970; 1980; 1990). While most of Cardwell's publications focus on student success in theological education and ministry (e.g., 1982), her own clinical and pedagogical expertise also functioned in an exemplary way for many women. Other more recent texts focus on the experiences of women, assuming but not explicitly pursuing feminist and womanist theory and politics (Glaz and Moessner 1991; Hollies 1992; Graham and Halsey 1993). The primary agenda of this project is incorporating women's lives and voices into the traditions of practical theological reflection and practices of care.

In the first "official" book on women and pastoral care, *Women in Travail and Transition*, the critique of patriarchy, while less overt, is woven between each line. While the editors do not attempt to define feminist scholarship nor require that individual authors identify with any particular feminist agenda, the book as a whole represents a "persistent methodological shift in that all contributors take seriously women's experiences, feelings, and formulations" (Glaz and Moessner 1991: 195). It includes chapters on such concerns as care of women in situations of violence and abuse, changes in women's roles and lifestyles, women's bodily demands and needs. Emerging out of these subjects are a whole host of theological formulations to be combated: the perception of women as the source of evil or temptress; the doctrine of original sin in which sin is communicated at conception; the deification of a Protestant work ethic that negates women's labor and jeopardizes children's lives; the double standards that deny female sexuality and bodily needs; doctrines that equate love with self-sacrifice and selfless suffering with godliness; rigid images of God as solely father or male; the institutional church's promotion of white male supremacy and an unquestioning stance toward religious authority; doctrines of condemnation that foster an immobilizing guilt; and complicity in condoning male domination, female submission, and the related violence in families. In a word, "unraveling the biblical injunction to love God, self, and neighbor in such a way that is not neurotic for women is surely a [critical] theological task" (Moessner and Glaz 1991: 38).

Criticism of psychology throughout this text focuses less on particular theories or classical theorists and more on the generic absorption of psychological "truths" in society and the church. One must combat psychological doctrines of female penis envy, masochism, the assumption of female dependency, misrepresentations of women's development, and consider alternative theories that note "man's dread of women," "male fear and anxiety provoked by the mystery of motherhood," "envy of woman's essential creativity and centeredness in being," and women's experiences of connective selfhood (Moessner and Glaz 1991: 38, 48; Miller-McLemore 1991: 75-9). In general, the authors make only limited efforts to reconstruct a feminist theology and psychology. More important, perhaps, at this stage are their many pragmatic, programmatic suggestions that help clergy and counselors make a positive difference in women's lives.

The second project – explicit critique of the classic texts and theories of pastoral theology – has been more erratic but no less momentous. A constellation of articles by three different scholars, Christine Neuger, Carrie Doehring, and Nancy Ramsay, once again appear within the same year, marking an important historical moment (Doehring 1992; Neuger 1992; Ramsay 1992; see also DeMarinis 1993; Neuger 1993; Bons-Storm 1996). Ramsay and Doehring begin with concise definitions of their feminist agenda. Ramsay asserts the demand to resist and transform "sexism and patriarchy toward an inclusive human community" (1992: 245). Doehring calls for "taking on the gods of patriarchy," those beliefs and structures that create "ecclesiastical, political, economic, and personal oppression for all peoples" (1992: 24). Neuger wastes little time on definitions, quickly claiming the "world in which women live" as her fundamental starting point and then moving right into a list of condemning statistics on oppression in all the areas that Doehring names in general (Neuger 1992: 37, 39–43).

In all three essays, practical illustrations fill in the actualities and complexities of enacting this new approach of psychology and religion in the care of women. From case illustrations emerge fresh constructions of theological doctrines of God-imagery, atonement, prevenient grace, community, Christology, and ultimately human empowerment – a prevalent theme in each essay. Conventional psychology and theology are considered limited and inept: as Neuger asserts, "I can rely on no personality theory or handbook of assessment" and no "adjustment oriented theological starting place" to understand adequately the fullness of women's lives and their plight. This means that in practice at least, if not in academic theory, "psychoanalytic, object relations, cognitive-behavioral, most forms of family systems, and humanistic [psychologies] must be held suspect" before the concreteness of lived experience (1992: 49).

As in the first project, the primary goal in this body of literature remains pastoral and practical. For the most part, we find first-order language and scholarship describing practices of care. The focus in all three essays is on incorporating feminist theory into the clerical ministries of pastoral care and counseling. These and other texts in this second project suggest the importance of a hermeneutic of suspicion toward traditional scholarship and advocate active resistance to patriarchy. As in the introduction to *Through the Eyes of Women*, the overarching intent is to give "hope to women in the midst of despair" (Moessner 1996: 4; see also Neuger 1996).

The third project – topical reconstruction – moves into second-order engagement in which the disciplines of psychology and theology are applied to specific subjects. Efforts in this area involve extensive engagement with particular thematic practices or topics, placing them within a broader panorama of psychological, cultural, and theological critique and reformulation. Several book-length treatments of important themes pertaining to women but also relevant to men and the field as a whole have appeared in just the last decade – poverty (Couture 1991), self-esteem (Saussy 1991), anger (Saussy 1995), depression (Dunlap 1997), aggression (Greider 1997), violence (Cooper-White 1995), power dynamics in ministry (Doehring 1995), work and family life (Miller-McLemore 1994), loss in mid-life (Robbins 1990), and family (Browning *et al.* 1997).

These are paradigmatic texts that have not yet received adequate attention as a significant body of literature in feminist theory, religion, and psychology. While diverse in specific focus, they establish a new example of pastoral theological method in religion and psychology unified by at least five elements: a cultural-political version of the revised correlational method; critical use of psychological and cultural resources; power analysis; explicit feminist positioning; and pastoral or transformative intent.

Drawing on Tillich, Hiltner, David Tracy, and others, these scholars understand the primary method in religion and psychology as involving the critical correlation of the Christian tradition and its contemporary reinterpretations with historical and contemporary cultural understandings, including psychology. In using this approach, however, feminist scholars in religion and psychology do not ignore its limits as a product of liberal Christian theology. While feminist scholars in pastoral theology have not explicitly turned to "critical praxis" or "cultural-political" critiques of this method, such as developed by Rebecca Chopp and Mark K. Taylor, they implicitly adopt many of their recommendations in unmasking the "compliancy of Christianity with ... bourgeois existence" and speaking for the marginalized (Chopp 1987: 121; also Chopp 1989a; Taylor 1990: 26–8). In other words, the two poles of tradition and experience are radically reformulated.

This reformation results in part from the other four elements – critical use of psychological and cultural resources; power analysis; explicit feminist positioning; and pastoral or transformative intent. First, psychology, while still foundational as an important cognate discipline, is now critiqued and supplemented by other disciplines in the social sciences. Theological analysis must grapple with the ways in which human agency and social systems co-constitute one another. Second, adequate analysis and understanding require attention to the dynamics, distribution, and distortions of power. Such analysis could occur from a number of vantage points but in the case of this third project the chosen position is feminist advocacy for women and women's experience as criteria of adequacy and truth (see Ruether 1983). Finally, the intent is empowerment and transformation through concrete pastoral practices.

This typology of the three partly sequential projects in religion, psychology, and gender still focuses primarily on the heyday of the 1990s. Kathleen Greider, Gloria Johnson, and Kristen Leslie also go back to the first published article by a self-identified woman pastoral theologian (Way 1963). Then they trace a more complete trajectory of thirty years of feminist scholarship in the area of religion and psychology (Greider *et al.* 1999). In terms of sheer numbers, they compile some interesting statistics:

> From the 1960s through the late 1970s, books by women pastoral theo-logians were few in number – the majority of the literature and its im-pact is in journal articles. In the 1980s, the number of published books more than tripled. In the most recent period, 1990–97, the number of published books again nearly tripled. Women were barely represented in the academy at the beginning of the period and, for the first 17 years of the period under consideration, were rarely the authors of book-length publications. During the last 17 years, still statistically underrepresented on faculties and among professionals in ministry, women scholars have contributed [to pastoral theology, care, and counseling] 94 book-length publications.
>
> (24)

To organize the otherwise daunting task of summarizing the contribu-tions of a 34-page single-spaced bibliography, Greider, Johnson, and Leslie track the evolution of the field through seven loosely chronological themes or objectives in pastoral studies in religion, psychology, and gender: strengthening the *ekklesia*; attending to marginalized people and taboo topics; articulating female experiences; facilitating theological education; attending to the "needs of human souls searching"; countering violence against women and children; and building systems of care. Research and teaching in each of these categories has contributed significantly to a major movement in the field away from a clinical therapeutic paradigm toward the emergence of a "communal contextual paradigm" in method and practice (see Patton 1993). For example, efforts to reclaim the biblically promised community or to understand the effects of marginalization have helped to foster an effective movement "away from the tendency to see therapy as the definitive act of pastoral care toward formulating theory and practice in and responsive to corporate human experience in its variety of cultural contexts" (Greider *et al.* 1999: 22). Such documentation of the feminist contribution to this shift is invaluable since recent introductory texts written by the old guard (see Patton 1993; Gerkin 1997) acknowledge the importance of this change but tend to give feminist theory minimal credit.

Conceptual shifts in religion, psychology, and gender studies in pastoral theology

Role of psychology and therapeutic practice

Psychological theory alone is ultimately insufficient to the task of under-standing gender and religion from the perspective of pastoral theology. Recognition of psychology's limits results from a commitment to both transformative praxis and a broader philosophical hermeneutics. Pastoral method requires a movement nicely described by Neuger from "culture to story to traditions for critique and reconstruction, back to story and pastoral strategy" (1992: 48). In many cases, such as the one Pamela Couture presents of a poor single mother, caring witness comes "through a practice more like social work than psychology" (1998a: 36; see Couture 1996).

Knowledge in religion and psychology, then, is no longer defined along conventional psychological lines. Clinical assessment involves social, contextual analysis. Psychological theory, while still important, plays a less commanding role. Other humanistic and social-science disciplines that contribute to understanding the broader cultural context, such as public policy, history, and sociology, have a place. So do theological analysis and reconstruction. Doehring chooses the term "isomorphic" to describe the way in which intrapsychic, family, and larger cultural systems are nested together, giving as an example the parallel between an anorexic woman's self-distortions and the media's distortions of femininity (1992: 24). This approach challenges the privatization and personalization characteristic of many psychological readings of religious beliefs and pastoral care. It calls for a careful philosophical, moral, and theological engagement and critique of psychology as a practice and a discipline.

Second, throughout recent developments in pastoral theology, few feminist scholars aligned themselves solely with one school of psychology, although psychoanalytic feminism has influenced pastoral theology powerfully, perhaps more than other psychological theories. Emphasis on the role of a sexist social environment in shaping and distorting male and female development (Horney 1950; 1973) or on the prominent role of the mother in reproducing patterns of female fear of separation and male fear of relationship (Chodorow 1974; 1978) have proven especially useful in rethinking pastoral care of women and men. Moreover, psychoanalytic feminists provide a cultural critique of the biases of psychology and therapeutic practice (Mitchell 1974; Sturdivant 1980) – a moral critique already familiar to theologians concerned about the unreflective adoption of psychology by pastoral caregivers and the culture at large (Browning 1987).

Few pastoral theologians, however, would identify themselves solely as psychoanalytic feminists. More typically, people pick and choose from many schools of thought. At least one rationale for moving beyond psychoanalytic feminism lies in the broader moral and communal concerns of pastoral theology. Feminist theory itself warrants employment of other approaches, such as socialist feminism. Socialist feminists contend that women are also oppressed by economic inequities and patriarchal devaluing of domestic and childbearing responsibilities. Hence, a woman's status and function "in all these structures must change if she is to achieve anything approximating full liberation" (Tong 1989: 6).

Role of theology, religious symbols, and religion

In many cases, feminist pastoral theologians are more adamant than their predecessors about both the importance of theological exploration and the articulation of religious commitments. As Graham argues, "Feminist pastoral care requires more than good therapeutic technique: it necessitates a critical engagement with theological language, church structures and ministerial practice as crucial arenas of feminist protest and reform" (1999: 198). Theology is not simply "an abstract series of philosophical propositions, but a performative discipline," known more through its impact on social relations and practical strategies than through its static properties and categorizations (208). It is an active, life-shaping framework for making sense of the world. Like gender, theology is more of a verb than a noun (see Butler 1990, cited by Graham 1999: 205). Theology forms and deforms lives.

Hence, religious symbols are not merely items to be studied and described in their psychic function as transitional objects or collective archetypes; they are events to be met, embraced, or rejected individually and communally, depending on whether, in Couture's words, they "exert the power of the status quo over women and the vulnerable" or "subversively strengthen women and the vulnerable in their quest to transform the status quo" (1998b: 8).

In her recent work, Couture exemplifies a second shift in the role of theology and religion in pastoral scholarship. In two articles, she demonstrates with boldness and clarity the centrality of her own commitments (1998a; 1998b; see also Couture 1991). She begins one essay, "I am a feminist, Wesleyan, practical theologian" (1998a: 27). These are "lenses" through which she interacts with individuals, families, and society to promote love and justice in God's realm. These commitments require privileging women's experience, protecting the vulnerable, and insisting on the embeddedness of theory in practice in the creation of loving and just communities. Such a position has a precedent in the early work of Way in the 1970s. Way says her identity as a minister carries more weight in her self-definition than her actual job description as teacher or administrator. Faith, rather than scripture, tradition, or institution, grounds her ministerial authority, leading her to challenge the "masculine consciousness" that orders church and academy (Way 1970: 88).

Like Way, Couture readily acknowledges that her understanding of the scholarly vocation can spark discord with the "demands of scholarly guilds and the standards of scientific legitimacy" (1998b: 1). Yet this clash does not ultimately deter the conviction that theological scholarship in religion, psychology, and gender requires participation in personal and social transformation and not just the investigation of it. Instead, the clash gives cause for critique of the academy of religion.

For the most part, the theological convictions of pastoral theologians have remained partially hidden behind philosophical claims. Browning, for example, has seldom located his partiality for Kantian ethics or communities of moral discourse as partly shaped by a particular Protestant denominational tradition that has emphasized rational, empirical, pragmatic reflection. While Couture does not argue for Wesleyan theology as *the* most appropriate foundation for scholarship in religion and psychology, she does claim it as instrumental in her understanding of experiences of God and the evolution of her scholarship. It clearly lies behind her predilection for a social ecological focus in pastoral theology and her view that academic pursuits in religion and psychology must be guided by a desire to contribute to a better world. The more clearly we can articulate the influence of our faith assumptions on our work the better. If theological claims are to serve a practical purpose, how can one *not* claim one's faith commitments? If pastoral truth entails transformation and theological wisdom involves passionate engagement with knowledge, then how or even why would one bracket one's convictions (see Charry 1997)?

Definition of subject matter

Couture declares, "Because of my theological commitments, I have specialized not in clinical pastoral counseling but in exploring the social and cultural context in which pastoral care occurs" (1998b: 13; see Couture and Hunter 1995). This means judging the adequacy of pastoral care and, indeed, scholarship and teaching by their implications for the "treatment of the most poor and vulnerable, particularly children." Bons-Storm makes a similar declaration: her "canon" or "'measuring rod'" for effective scholarship is the following:

> Can [it] be heard as liberating, challenging and inspiring for the most vulnerable, for the children? Do our thoughts and practices bring them further along the way to a world of faith and hope where they can grow up without violence, hunger or refugee camps?
>
> (1998: 19)

Does a theology of praxis, asks Ackermann, contribute to the healing of her country and of women and children (1998: 80)? Healing, transformation, and social and individual holiness become criteria of adequate research and, in effect, define the necessary and appropriate subject matter.

As noted above, feminist scholarship in pastoral theology has sparked a shift in focus from the individual to the community, from personal distress to social injustice, from personal fulfillment to the common good, from an ontology of separative selfhood to an open web of relationality. Brita Gill-Austern talks about the importance of fostering an "ecology of care" (1995); Couture uses a similar metaphor of a multi-tiered "social ecology" that includes consideration of individuals, families and fictive kin, society, government–church relations, culture, economics, and nature. Particular individuals remain important but are now seen through the "wide-angled lens" that places them within the "nexus of a macrocosmic" system (1998b: 18; see also 1998a: 31–5).

A related and perhaps more prevalent metaphor for this shift in conceptualization of the subject of pastoral theology is that of the "living web." This image arose almost simultaneously in a number of places. Until recently, most scholars in pastoral theology looked to Anton Boisen's powerful foundational metaphor for the existential subject of pastoral theology – "*the study of living human documents rather than books*" (1950, cited by Gerkin 1984: 37). But when the "focus on care narrowly defined as counseling shifted to a focus on care understood as part of a wide cultural, social, and religious context," the "living human *web*" suggests itself as a better term for the appropriate subject of investigation, interpretation, and transformation (Miller-McLemore 1993: 367; 1996: 16). Larry Graham (1992), Gill-Austern (1995), and Couture (1996) have also employed the metaphor of web or variations, such as "matrix" or "psychosystemic view," to identify the interacting constellation of factors that foster or frustrate caregiving.

Definition of primary pastoral functions[3]

To think about pastoral theology from a feminist perspective has led to a fundamental reorientation of the core functions of pastoral care. In place of or in addition to the traditional pastoral modes — healing, sustaining, guiding, and reconciling – articulated by Hiltner (1958) and amended by William Clebsch and Charles Jaekle (1983), four practices acquire particular importance: resisting, empowering, nurturing, and liberating. Although not yet formally classified as four distinct typologies of pastoral care, these four practices have received extensive attention in many recent writings in pastoral theology. These activities are not exhaustive of new modalities sparked by feminism, but they need to be recognized and marked as prominent ways of reorganizing the functions of pastoral care.

While all or some of the four functions of resisting, empowering, nurturing, and liberating have operated during the historical periods described by Clebsch and Jaekle, they did not receive the kind of preeminence that has come recently as a result of feminist theory. For the moment, I offer rather terse definitions to give a general flavor of recent feminist-influenced trends. "Compassionate resistance" requires confrontation with evil, contesting violent, abusive behaviors that perpetuate undeserved suffering and false stereotypes that distort the realities of people's lives. Resistance includes a focused healing of wounds of abuse that have festered for generations (Ramsay 1998; see also Poling 1996). Empowerment involves fierce advocacy and tenderness on behalf of the vulnerable, giving resources and means to those previously stripped of authority and power. Nurturance is not sympathetic kindness or quiescent support but passionate, dedicated proclamation of love that makes a space for difficult change and fosters solidarity among the vulnerable. Liberation entails both escape from unjust, unwarranted affliction and release into new life and wholeness as created, redeemed, and loved people of God. Resistance, empowerment, nurturance, and liberation all entail a deconstruction of unjustly limited definitions of reality and a reconstruction of new views of the world and one's valued place within it.

Pastoral care in these modalities is not particularly "pastoral" or "nice" in the truncated ways in which "pastoral" has sometimes been defined. As Neuger demands, "Isn't my role to engage in a pastoral therapy of *mal*adjustment" rather than to encourage adjustment to a crazy, sick society (1992: 49, emphasis in text)? Pastoral care disturbs as well as comforts, provokes as well as guides. It breaks silences and calls for radical truth telling; it names shame and guilt, calls for confession, and moves vigilantly toward forgiveness and reconciliation, knowing that both are more difficult to effect than people have hoped.

Indeed, if pastoral theology keeps the term "shepherd" as a central motif (and even that becomes questionable in a world where sheep herding and shearing are no longer common experiences upon which to ground metaphor), a feminist perspective reminds us that sheep are not the warm, fuzzy, and clean creatures our Sunday School books have portrayed. Womanist pastoral theologian Marsha Foster Boyd rejects "shepherd," "servant," and "wounded healer" as distorted and deforming images. She suggests instead "empowered cojourner" as better capturing the nature of providing company and encouragement on life's pilgrimage (1997: 199–200).

Definition of audiences and publics

Paradigmatically, Graham titles her recent article, "From 'terrible silence' to 'transforming hope' " (1999), referring to Bons-Storm's book on pastoral care that protests the deadly silence surrounding women in the church and making so many subjects taboo (female body, gender roles, violence, etc.) for safety's sake (Bons-Storm 1996). Work in religion, psychology, and gender renders visible the hidden assault of patriarchy in pastoral practice. Women write "for our lives," writing not just for enlightenment, but for survival, putting into words realities that seemed unreal when hidden (Greider *et al.* 1999). Gaining a voice and "hearing into speech" bring the possibility of change.

In the move from silence to hope, feminist theologians assume a slightly different relationship than their predecessors to the three publics of society, church, and academy distinguished by David Tracy (Tracy 1981: 5; see Miller-McLemore 1999: 90). Historically, theologians addressed multiple publics. Today pastoral and practical theologians are left trying to bridge the recent divisions among these publics in terms of language, standards of truth, practices and rituals, and norms. Feminist scholars are especially dedicated to addressing all three publics. Couture takes an even stronger normative stance, arguing that "it is incumbent upon the practical theologian to write for a variety of audiences." The practical theologian must obtain the "linguistic versatility" to speak to academic peers, church leadership, and social constituencies beyond faith communities (Couture 1998a: 43).

This position is embodied pragmatically in several ways. Many feminist scholars in pastoral theology attempt to function in both academic and ecclesial capacities. Many maintain an allegiance to several different kinds of academic and clinical societies, however ambiguous and difficult. That is, they attend both the AAR and pastoral and practical theology societies as well as clinical organizations. From this, we might surmise that many women desire a more holistic approach to the study of religion. They refuse conventional definitions of disciplinary boundaries, feel less constrained by or less connected to ministry and its institutions as formally defined by men, and appreciate the freedom of thought and expression sometimes more characteristic of the academy and programs in religion and personality.

Feminist scholarship in religion and psychology has also assumed a slightly different tactic for achieving academic standing. Early forerunners in the field, with Hiltner exemplifying the pattern, strove for recognition and legitimacy within the modern university. They hoped to move closer to the center of intellectual activity, arguing for pastoral theology as a new discipline that, alongside systematics, would become a fundamental form of theology (Hiltner 1958: 15, 24–9). More recently, Browning continued down this path. In *A Fundamental Practical Theology*, he argues that the hierarchy in theological study should be turned on its head, with practical theology as foundational, not merely a "subspecialty" but the "model for theology as such" (1991: 7–8). As well received as these analyses have been, their impact on the actual organization of the academy itself is less apparent.

By contrast, as early as 1970 Way claimed her position of "historical exclusion" from the mainstream as an "unexpected source of insights" and did not seem to mind staying on the border. She refused to celebrate her appointment to a highly acclaimed divinity school out of acute awareness of the ongoing marginalization of women (1970: 77, 88). More recently, Couture observes, "When a theologian constructs her scholarship from commitments which may place her at the margins of the academy and the church," she does not fight against such marginalization. Other women such as Bons-Storm have been her "allies" in this process. Speaking from the position of "other" requires the use of "imagination to create scholarship" out of the rich potentialities of the context in which one finds oneself (Couture 1998b: 1).

Many feminist scholars acknowledge and even welcome the position of marginality. As Luce Irigaray and others contend, it is from the position of "other" or even "lack" that rich knowledge emerges (see Irigaray 1977). Chopp provides a strong theoretical argument for the value of this position:

[T]o preserve the differences [liberal theology] negates through its ordering of discourses and practices, feminism must acknowledge its own
discourse as marginal. *From the space of marginality* feminism must
declare the unthinkable in terms of the liberal strategy: the liberal assumption that the center can hold all is not a principle of inclusion but a
strategy of containment.

(1989a: 66, emphasis added)[4]

The intent, then, is not to move into the center but to transform an
ordering of academic status that rests on the oppression of certain persons
and disciplines. External standards that determine academic status and
theological standards that define the "orthodox" tradition need radical
reconception. Like Ackermann and Bons-Storm with their petition that we
cease lamenting our identity crisis as a field and get on with addressing life's
pressing needs, Chopp argues that feminist theologians ought to celebrate
our decentered context for "it is only by looking away from our ...
preservation and our own identity that we have any hope in offering the
world what it so desperately needs" (1989a: 76).

In all five of these areas – role of theology, role of psychology, definition
of subject matter, pastoral function, and public responsibilities – feminist
scholarship in religion and psychology in the area of pastoral theology has
made significant contributions in method and substance. General observations about these contributions may exaggerate their importance and
distinctiveness. But at this point in the history of the field it is best to risk
overstating the case, if only to get a fair hearing that will lead others to pay
attention to this growing body of feminist literature in pastoral theology and
to develop fresh and critical assessments of their own. Only through this
kind of ongoing dialogue and debate will the future of the study of religion
and psychology be well secured.

Notes

1   While I speak specifically from a US context, the international conversation on
    pastoral and practical theology has grown in ways not well reflected in this book.
    See, for example, D.M. Ackermann and R. Bons-Storm 1998; F. Schweitzer and
    J.A. van der Ven 1999; and *The International Journal of Practical Theology*
    website (www.deGruyter.com/journals/ijpt).
2   In an examination of the pastoral care literature in Europe and North America,
    Graham notes the deeply entrenched exclusion of women (Graham: 1989: 23–5;
    see also Graham 1998 and Pattison 1994).
3   This section appears in much the same form in Miller-McLemore 1999: 80–81.
4   For a further elaboration of the processes of containment of feminism, see
    Chopp 1989b.

References

Ackermann, D.M. (1998) " 'A voice was heard in Ramah': a feminist theology of
    praxis for healing in South Africa," in D.M. Ackermann and R. Bons-Storm

(eds), *Liberating Faith Practices: Feminist Practical Theologies in Context*, Leuven: Peeters.

Ackermann, D.M. and Bons-Storm, R. (eds) (1998) *Liberating Faith Practices: Feminist Practical Theologies in Context*, Leuven: Peeters.

Boisen, A. (1950) *The Exploration of the Inner World: A Study of Mental Disorder and Religious Experience*, Chicago: Willett, Clark.

Bons-Storm, R. (1996) *The Incredible Woman: Listening to Women's Silences in Pastoral Care and Counseling*, Nashville: Abingdon.

—— (1998) "Putting the little ones into the dialogue: a feminist practical theology," in D.M. Ackermann and R. Bons-Storm (eds) *Liberating Faith Practices: Feminist Practical Theologies in Context*, Leuven: Peeters.

Browning, D. (1987) *Religious Thought and the Modern Psychologies: A Critical Conversation in the Theology of Culture*, Philadelphia: Fortress.

—— (1991) *A Fundamental Practical Theology: Descriptive and Strategic Proposals*, Minneapolis: Fortress.

Browning, D., Miller-McLemore, B.J., Couture, P.D., Lyon, B., and Franklin, R. (1997) *From Culture Wars to Common Ground: Religion and the American Family Debate*, Louisville: Westminster John Knox.

Butler, J. (1990) *Gender Trouble: Feminism and the Subversion of Identity*, New York: Routledge.

Cardwell, S.W. (1982) "Why women fail/succeed in ministry: psychological factors," *Pastoral Psychology* 30(4); 153–62.

Charry, E.T. (1997) *By the Renewing of Your Minds: The Pastoral Function of Christian Doctrine*, New York: Oxford University Press.   .

Chodorow, N. (1974) "Family structure and feminine personality," in M. Zimbalist Rosaldo and L. Lamphere (eds), *Women, Culture, and Society*, Stanford, Calif.: Stanford University Press.

—— (1978) *The Reproduction of Mothering*, Berkeley: University of California Press.

Chopp, R.S. (1987) "Practical theology and liberation," in L.S. Mudge and J.N. Poling, *Formation and Reflection: The Promise of Practical Theology*, Philadelphia: Fortress.

—— (1989a) "When the center cannot contain the margins," in D.S. Browning, D. Polk and I.S. Evison (eds), *The Education of the Practical Theologian: Responses to Joseph Hough and John Cobb's Christian Identity and Theological Education*, Atlanta: Scholars.

—— (1989b) *The Power to Speak: Feminism, Language, God*, New York: Crossroads.

Clebsch, W. and Jaekle, C. (1983) *Pastoral Care in Historical Perspective*, 2nd edn, New York: Aronson.

Cooper-White, P. (1995) *The Cry of Tamar: Violence Against Women and the Church's Response*, Minneapolis: Fortress.

Couture, P.D. (1991). *Blessed are the Poor? Women's Poverty, Family Policy, and Practical Theology*, Nashville: Abingdon.

—— (1996) "Weaving the web: pastoral care in an individualistic society," in J. Stevenson Moessner (ed.), *Through the Eyes of Women: Insights for Pastoral Care*, Philadelphia: Westminster John Knox.

—— (1998a) "Feminist, Wesleyan, practical theology and the practice of pastoral care," in D.M. Ackermann and R. Bons-Storm (eds), *Liberating Faith Practices: Feminist Practical Theologies in Context*, Leuven: Peeters.

—— (1998b) "Feminist theological commitments: Calling for new modes of care," unpublished English version of a chapter published in Dutch in a festschrift for Riet Bons-Storm, "Vanuit een feministisch-theologisch engagement: Pleidooi voor nieuwe manieren van zorg," in *Geroepen om te spreken. Over verbeelding en creativiteit in theologie en pastoraat. Een bundel van vriendinnen, aangeboden aan Riet Bons-Storm*, Uitgeverij: Kok-Kampen.

Couture, P.D. and Hunter, R. (eds) (1995) *Pastoral Care and Social Conflict*, Nashville: Abingdon.

DeMarinis, V.M. (1993) *Critical Caring: A Feminist Model for Pastoral Psychology*, Louisville: Westminster John Knox.

Doehring, C. (1992) "Developing models of feminist pastoral counseling," *Journal of Pastoral Care* 46 (1): 23–31..

—— (1995) *Taking Care: Monitoring Power Dynamics and Relational Boundaries in Pastoral Care and Counseling*, Nashville: Abingdon.

—— (1999) "A method of feminist pastoral theology," in B. Miller-McLemore and B. Gill-Austern (eds), *Feminist and Womanist Pastoral Theology*, Nashville: Abingdon.

Dunlap, S.J. (1997) *Counseling Depressed Women*, Louisville: Westminster John Knox.

Evison, I. (1997) "The dialogue between psychology and religion: historical considerations," presentation at the American Academy of Religion, 1997.

Foster Boyd, M. "Some reflections on the pastoral care and the transformation of African American women," in E.M. Towns (ed.), *Embracing the Spirit: Womanist Perspectives on Hope, Salvation, and Transformation*, Maryknoll, N.Y.: Orbis.

Gerkin, C. (1984) *The Living Human Document: Revisioning Pastoral Counseling in a Hermeneutical Mode*, Nashville: Abingdon.

—— (1997) *An Introduction to Pastoral Care*, Nashville: Abingdon.

Gill-Austern, B. (1995) "Rediscovering hidden treasures for pastoral care," *Pastoral Psychology* 43(4): 233–53.

Glaz, M. and Moessner, J.S. (1991) "Travail as transition," in M. Glaz and J.S. Moessner (eds), *Women in Travail and Transition: A New Pastoral Care*, Minneapolis: Fortress.

Graham, E.L. (1989) "The pastoral needs of women," *Contact: The Interdisciplinary Journal of Pastoral Studies* 100: 23–5.

—— (1998) "A view from a room: feminist practical theology from academy, kitchen or sanctuary?" in M. Ackermann and R. Bons-Storm (eds), *Liberating Faith Practices: Feminist Practical Theologies in Context*, Leuven: Peeters.

—— (1999) "From 'terrible silence' to 'transforming hope': the impact of feminist theory on practical theology," *International Journal of Practical Theology* 6(2): 185–212.

Graham, E.L. and Halsey, M. (eds) (1993) *Life Cycles: Women and Pastoral Care*, Cambridge: SPKC.

Graham, L.K. (1992) *Care of Persons, Care of Worlds: A Psychosystems Approach to Pastoral Care and Counseling*, Nashville: Abingdon.

Greider, K.J. (1997) *Reckoning with Aggression: Theology, Violence, and Vitality*, Louisville: Westminster John Knox.

Greider, K.J., Johnson, G.A., and Leslie, K.J. (1999) "Three decades of women writing for our lives," in B. Miller-McLemore and B. Gill-Austern (eds), *Feminist and Womanist Pastoral Theology*, Nashville: Abingdon.

Henking, S. (1997) "Religion and the social sciences: an historical perspective," presentation at the American Academy of Religion, 1997.

Hiltner, S. (1958) *Preface to Pastoral Theology*, New York: Abingdon.

Hollies, L. (ed.) (1992) *Womanist Care: How to Tend the Souls of Women*, Joliet, Ill.: Woman to Woman Ministries Publications.

Horney, K. (1950) *Feminine Psychology*, New York: W.W. Norton.

—— (1973) *Neurosis and Human Growth*, New York: W.W. Norton.

Irigaray, L. (1977) *This Sex Which is Not One*, translated by A. Sheridan, New York: Norton.

Jennings, T.W., Jr. (1990) "Pastoral theology methodology," in R. Hunter (ed.), *Dictionary of Pastoral Care and Counseling*, Nashville: Abingdon.

Lapsley, J.N. (1995) "Remarks on a panel at the Society for Pastoral Theology: Where we have been and where we are going," *Journal of Pastoral Theology* 5: 50–55.

Miller-McLemore, B.J. (1991) "Women who work and love: caught between cultures," in M. Glaz and J.S. Moessner (eds), *Women in Travail and Transition: A New Pastoral Care*, Minneapolis: Fortress.

—— (1993) "The human web and the state of pastoral theology," *Christian Century* (April 7): 366–9.

—— (1994) *Also a Mother: Work and Family as Theological Dilemma*, Nashville: Abingdon.

—— (1996) "The living human web: pastoral theology at the turn of the century," in J. Stevenson Moessner (ed.), *Through the Eyes of Women: Insights for Pastoral Care*, Philadelphia: Westminster John Knox.

—— (1998a) "The subject and practice of pastoral theology as a practical theological discipline: pushing past the nagging identity crisis to the poetics of resistance," in D.M. Ackermann and R. Bons-Storm (eds), *Liberating Faith Practices: Feminist Practical Theologies in Context*, Leuven: Peeters.

—— (1998b) "Feminist theory in pastoral theology," *Association of Practical Theology Occasional Papers* 2: 1–11.

—— (1999) "Feminist theory in pastoral theology," in B. Miller-McLemore and B. Gill-Austern (eds), *Feminist and Womanist Pastoral Theology*, Nashville: Abingdon.

Miller-McLemore, B. and Gill-Austern, B. (eds) (1999) *Feminist and Womanist Pastoral Theology*, Nashville: Abingdon.

Mills, L. (1994) "Background and initiatives in pastoral care," unpublished panel remarks, the Society for Pastoral Theology, Denver, 17 June.

Mitchell, J. (1974) *Psychoanalysis and Feminism*, New York: Random.

Moessner, J.S. (ed.) (1996) *Through the Eyes of Women: Insights for Pastoral Care*, Philadelphia: Westminster John Knox.

Moessner, J.S. and Glaz, M. (1991) "The psychology of women and pastoral care," in M. Glaz and J.S. Moessner (eds), *Women in Travail and Transition: A New Pastoral Care*, Minneapolis: Fortress.

Neuger, C.C. (1992) "Feminist pastoral theology and pastoral counseling: a work in progress," *Journal of Pastoral Theology* 2: 35–57.

—— (1993) "A feminist perspective on pastoral counseling with women," in R.J. Wicks and R.D. Parsons (eds), *Clinical Handbook of Pastoral Counseling: vol. 2*, New York: Paulist.

—— (ed.) (1996) *The Arts of Ministry: Feminist-Womanist Approaches*, Louisville: Westminster John Knox.

Pattison, E.M. (1978a) "Psychiatry and religion circa 1978: analysis of a decade, part I," *Pastoral Psychology* 27(1): 8–25.

—— (1978b) "Psychiatry and religion circa 1978: analysis of a decade, part II," *Pastoral Psychology* 27(2): 119–41.

Pattison, S. (1994) *Pastoral Care and Liberation Theology*, Cambridge: Cambridge University Press.

Patton, J. (1993) *Pastoral Care in Context: An Introduction to Pastoral Care*, Louisville: Westminster John Knox.

Poling, J.N. (1996) *Deliver Us From Evil: Resisting Racial and Gender Oppression*, Minneapolis: Fortress.

Ramsay, N. (1992) "Feminist perspectives on pastoral care: implications for practice and theory," *Pastoral Psychology* 40(4): 245–52.

—— (1998) "Compassionate resistance: an ethic for pastoral care and counseling," *Journal of Pastoral Care* 52(3): 217–26.

Robbins, M.B. (1990) *Mid-life Women and Death of Mother: A Study of Psychohistorical and Spiritual Formation*, New York: Peter Lang.

Ruether, R.R. (1983) *Sexism and God-Talk: Toward a Feminist Theology*, Boston: Beacon.

Saussy, C. (1991) *God Images and Self-Esteem: Empowering Women in a Patriarchal Society*, Louisville: Westminster John Knox.

—— (1995) *The Gift of Anger: A Call to Faithful Action*, Louisville: Westminster John Knox.

Schweitzer, F. and van der Ven, J.A. (eds) (1999) *Practical Theology: International Perspectives*, New York: Peter Lang.

Sturdivant, S. (1980) *Therapy with Women: A Feminist Philosophy of Treatment*, New York: Springer.

Taylor, M.K. (1990) *Remembering Esperanza: A Cultural-Political Theology for North American Praxis*, Maryknoll, New York: Orbis.

Tong, R. (1989) *Feminist Thought: A Comprehensive Introduction*, Boulder and San Francisco: Westview Press.

Tracy, D. (1975) *Blessed Rage for Order: The New Pluralism in Theology*, New York: Seabury.

—— (1981) *The Analogical Imagination: Christian Theology and the Culture of Pluralism*, New York: Crossroad.

Way, P.A. (1963) "What's wrong with the church: the clergy," *Renewal* 3: 8–9.

—— (1970) "An authority of possibility for women in the church," in S.B. Doely (ed.), *Women's Liberation and the Church: The New Demand for Freedom in the Life of the Christian Church*, New York: Association Press.

—— (1980) "Pastoral excellence and pastoral theology: a slight shift of paradigm and a modest polemic," *Pastoral Psychology* 29(1): 46–57.

—— (1990) "Violence in the family: a theological perspective," Disciples Lecture, Vanderbilt University Divinity School.

12 When is religion a mental disorder?

The disease of ritual

Luis O. Gómez

In Francine Prose's novel *Household Saints*, the Santangelos are stunned when their only child, Theresa, announces that she wants to become a nun. The daughter of this Italian-American family, inspired by her namesake, Thérèse de Lisieux, the Little Flower, confidently declares that God has called her, Theresa Santangelo, to be His bride. Exasperated, her father Raphael Santangelo, a practicing Roman Catholic but also the practical neighborhood butcher, inveighs against his daughter:

> The thing about nuns is: they don't want anything. They come in for an order of veal and you don't have veal, they never blink they never miss a beat. You can practically see them thinking: It's God's will, I'll have chicken ... Nuns are sick women, Theresa. And my daughter isn't sick.
>
> (Prose 1981: 146)

This short exchange, amusing at a distance, is a mine of suggestions, some of which take us to a history that is not always humorous. It embodies a sociology of the ambivalence of Western attitudes toward the religious vocation. And it suggests a psychopathology of sainthood.

The words of an irritated Catholic parent remind us of both dimensions of Western attitudes towards sainthood; they remind us that sainthood is never "normal." Ironically, the daughter, Theresa Santangelo, is set on imitating Thérèse de Lisieux, the Little Flower, who presumably embodies the holiness of the insignificant daily act, the quotidian. Yet, in making this their goal both women set themselves apart from their families, and ultimately apart from "the quotidian" as it is conceived and experienced by other humans. Like Thérèse de Lisieux, Theresa Santangelo sets out to observe and perform the ordinary, and to do it fastidiously, with a ritualistic self-consciousness that paradoxically removes daily behavior from conventional notions of agency and self-awareness. She will iron and do the dishes with a dedication and a concentrated selflessness that strike us as somehow mindless. In short, her ordinary behavior is quite out of the ordinary.

By the time she has her first vision, Theresa Santangelo, the fictional character, with all the irony and uncertainty of the novel, already has us wondering whether she was in fact a true saint, an eccentric, or simply mentally ill. Thus, her father's voice represents the reader's voice – and, I will add, the voice of Western tradition.

However, this notion has pre-modern roots. Western views of holiness as madness belong to a larger family of cultural presuppositions that associate sainthood with mental defect – be that the defect of the fool or the breakdown of the insane.

The idea of a connection between madness and religiosity has deep roots in Western views of the inspired individual. We find literary evidence of this preconception in Plato (427?–347? BCE), who, speaking through Socrates in the *Phaedrus*, glorified divine madness (*theia mania*).[1] There he has Socrates speak of madness in a context that leaves no doubt that "mad" is meant as a term of praise. In this dialogue Socrates proposes four types of divine madness (*theia mania*): (1) erotic, that is, love as madness; (2) mantic or divinatory; (3) telestic, or ritual; and (4) poetic. In all four cases madness is a gift from divine sources, and therefore a positive force. As stated by Socrates (244D):

> "False is the tale" which says that because the lover is mad and the non-lover sane [one should prefer] the non-lover. If it were true without qualifications that madness (*mania*) is an evil, that would all be very well, but in fact, madness, provided it comes as a gift of heaven, is the channel by which we receive the greatest blessings.

According to this classical passage, the inspired madness of lovers is the beginning of self-knowledge, and the beginning of the knowledge of pure forms. Still other forms of madness provide other forms of knowledge. There is, for instance, the divine madness of the prophetess at Delphi and the priestesses at Dodona (244DE):

> Consider all the benefits which individuals and states in Greece have received from them when they were in a state of frenzy, though their usefulness in their sober senses amounts to little or nothing ... [M]adness comes from God, whereas sober sense is merely human.

I shall not attempt to discuss Plato's complex views on madness and the "sober senses" (*sōphrosynē*). Here I only wish to show the early presence of a positive view of madness as a source of knowledge and social benefit – themes that Plato also connects to the Dionysian traditions. His glorification of divine frenzy and madness is of course qualified and sanitized. But this is not the only view we have received from our past traditions. Euripides (485/480?–406 BCE), for instance, has left in his *Bacchae* one of the most forceful and troubling statements of Western ambivalence toward the irrational. He compresses into one drama all the ideological and emotional conflicts we associate with the need for genuine religious feeling and the potential destructiveness of religious enthusiasm.

The full spectrum of our cultural ambivalence was grounded and completed by Plato's older contemporary Hippocrates (c. 460–c. 377 BCE), who, in the "Divine Madness," criticized precisely the notion that the altered states of ecstatics – such as that of the priestesses of Delphi and Dodona – could be caused by divine agency. For him, the divine madness is nothing more than a natural illness, possibly a disease of the brain. Hippocrates is arguing primarily that religious madness is nothing but madness: that is, nothing but a natural disease. But it is also possible to argue that he is implying that religion is madness.

The second, stronger interpretation also has a long tradition in the West, interrupted by the Middle Ages, but revived since the Enlightenment. This stronger reading is commonly associated with what has been called the naturalistic fallacy.[2] But it is also an easy way to generate capricious *argumenta ad hominem* against religion: if it sounds like insanity, then it must be false.

Clinical models

The conception of "madness" as illness, and the extension of that category of disease to "religious madness," gained ground with modernity, and flourished in the West between the seventeenth and nineteenth centuries. Such theories usually claimed that intense or extraordinary religious behaviors are manifestations of mental illness, that religious enthusiasm or a religious commitment that are too demanding can be sure signs of pathology.

As already suggested, this assumption can be used as an easy way to attack views or customs that are not to our liking. Robert Burton's *Anatomy of Melancholy* (1989, orig. 1621) reveals its author's religious prejudices when it pronounces Puritanism, Evangelical Christianity, Judaism, and Catholicism as forms of melancholic lunacy. The Church of England, of course, does not qualify.

Nineteenth-century psychiatry retained this metaphor in a clinical diagnosis: "religious melancholy," or "psychasthenia religiosa."[3] This diagnosis was reserved for persons of excessive religiosity – the religious belief and practice of the gentleman parishioner was of course immune to such attacks. Or at least so it seemed until Freud. Freud was more ... shall we say "even-handed?" He was working under the assumption that every belief without scientific or empirical foundation was a distortion of reality, and therefore a form of neurosis, if not psychosis. Hence, in his view, all religious behavior was suspect.

A pathology of religious rituals

William James' *The Varieties of Religious Experience* (1902) is appropriately used as the milestone to mark the beginning of modern psychology of religion, bringing the young and tottering science in tandem with the beginning of the new century. However, only a few years after the publication of *The Varieties*, the first scholarly journal devoted to the psychology of religion began publication in Leipzig. The inaugural number of the *Zeitschrift für Religionspsychologie* included Freud's first formal excursion into the psychology of religion (1907). Titled, in the English *Standard Edition*, "Obsessive actions and religious practices," the article set one of the great themes of the first decades of the psychology of religion. Furthermore, the essay tied religion to "obsessional neurosis," a pathology that Freud considered one of the great challenges of theoretical psychopathology, a primary disorder that held the key to understanding the other neuroses.

In that first paper on the psychology of religion Freud identified some formal or phenomenological similarities between religious rituals and the behavior of compulsives. These were at first applied to ritual behavior, but soon Freud and his disciples would also see connections between obsessions and dogmatism (Reik 1927).

The argument of the paper is, of course, not simply a scientific hypothesis. It is a cultural critique. I cannot delve into the Reformation and the Enlightenment as preconditions for this critique. Nor will I discuss how Freud's own sociocultural setting is reflected in this short essay. But part of the paper's allure was in the way it met the expectations of certain audiences beyond Freud's Vienna – expectations that survive today in American popular idioms such as "ritualistic," "bizarre rituals," "hazing rituals," "satanic rituals," and "ritual abuse."

Only recently have we begun to hear expressions like "therapeutic rituals." But I am still waiting for someone to say "we had our Bible-reading rituals," or "I am attending a satanic service on Sunday." Be that as it may, such presuppositions were already rife in the cultural milieu of the turn-of-the-century European intelligentsia, and found the expected confirmation in the strongest formulations of Freud's thesis:

> In view of these similarities and analogies [between obsessive ceremonials and religious rituals], one might venture to regard obsessional neurosis as a pathological counterpart of the formation of a religion, and to describe *that neurosis* as an individual religiosity and religion as a universal obsessional neurosis.
>
> (Freud 1907: 126–7)

Yet in the same breath Freud qualifies (or, shall we say, "he undoes"?) his statement:

The most essential similarity would reside in the underlying renunciation of the activation of instincts that are constitutionally present; *and the chief difference would lie* in the nature of those instincts, which in the neurosis are exclusively sexual in their origin, while in religion they spring from egoistic sources.

(Freud 1907: 127, my italics)

In spite of this important qualification, Freud's essay has been traditionally interpreted as establishing "the famous conclusion that religion is a universal obsessional neurosis" (Fine 1979: 401).

The stronger formulation was preferred in part because of the Zeitgeist of early psychoanalytic thinking, but also because Freud's hesitation, in the 1907 essay and thereafter, was biased toward the stronger view. As Freud's thought matured, he became bolder in pursuing a goal that we would call today at best "deconstructionist," at worst reductionistic.

His goal I rather call the "pathological template" – the assumption that clinical explanations transfer to cultural explanations without qualifications. More specifically, one may criticize the Freudian model as an example of the dangers of subsuming all "rituals" under a single type, as if religious rituals were phenomenologically of one piece, while proposing an equally monolithic set of obsessional "ceremonials," as if all obsessive-compulsive behaviors were identical in origin and function.

The main weakness in the strong pathology model is its assumption that we can learn something about culture from pathology only if the latter is a template for the former – more specifically it presumes that religion and pathology are structurally and etiologically identical.

There is no room for more subtle interactions between culture and biology, no room for religion as a voice capable of defining, legislating, and attending to, if not shaping, pathology. There is no sense of the close historical and social parallelism between pastoral care, religious healing and the task of the clinician. And, finally, there is no sense here that pathology could be a breakdown of the same psychic mechanisms that maintain religious behavior, and not their cause.

It remains now to examine these possibilities. Within the confines of a limited essay this will only be the outline of a project. I will outline a cursory exploration of some highlights in the history of compulsive behaviors – a historical itinerary that circumvents Freud in order to consider precisely the points already mentioned as problematic.

First, we need to know the extent to which religious traditions, at least in the West, considered some aspects of obsessive behavior by addressing it as a specific pathological counterpart of healthy religious life. Second, we need to explore, at least cursorily, the connection between these judgements of pathology and specific forms of pastoral care. And, finally, we need to consider the extent to which the pathology of obsessive behaviors is a breakdown of the same psychic mechanisms that maintain some important aspects or forms of religious behavior.

In the end, I shall suggest a different way of understanding pathology as an entry way to religious behavior.

Historical note

The clinical use of the terms "obsession" and "compulsion" is younger than the use of the term "ritual" as a critical category, and only slightly older than the use of the term "ceremony" to refer to compulsive behaviors. But long before these usages appeared in medical and lay literature, various dimensions of obsessive behavior had been noted in Western medical literature.

The earliest strata of the Hippocratic corpus do not seem to recognize anything like obsessive behavior – definitely not in the works now accepted as "original."[4] However, already in the work of second-century physician Rufus of Ephesus (flourished under Trajan, 98–117) we find description of a type of melancholy characterized by doubt (Jackson 1986). Various dimensions of obsessive behavior had been observed in the medical literature since the late Hippocratic period, and in Christian religious literature as early as the fourteenth century. Graeco-Roman descriptions of melancholic doubt found their way, through Galen and the Byzantine commentators, into Islamic medicine, and from there vague notions of melancholic doubt entered into late Medieval and Renaissance medicine, where they met Medieval notions of possession. At this point it became possible to conceive of mental illness as a natural disorder or as a supernatural anomie. One could then speak of the apparent loss of control of various forms of mental illness as representing a state of being under attack, of being "obsessed," that is of being "assailed" or "besieged" by the Devil. It was the latter concept that would give us our modern terminology.

At first, the critics of demonic theories had limited scientific resources. Johann Weyer (1515–88), whose *De praestigiis daemonum* (1564) stands as a milestone in the growth of a naturalistic view of mental illness, contributed little to our understanding of specific syndromes. Similarly, the writings of Paracelsus (1493?–1541), praised for their revival of the Hippocratic critique of a divine origin for mental diseases, are best conceived as works announcing the twilight of the Middle Ages, not as pioneering works of the scientific age.

In his *The Diseases that Deprive Man of his Reason* (*Von den Krankheiten so die Vernunft berauben*, written c. 1520, published 1567), Paracelsus speaks of a type of mentally ill called the *obsessi* ("obsessed" – Paracelsus 1567).[5] This has misled some into assuming that he recognized the symptoms of obsessive-compulsive behavior, when in fact he was still using the term in its Medieval sense (feeling assailed by the Devil). Obsessions, in the sense the term acquired in the twentieth century, are not discussed at all in his work.

Rather, *obsessi* is a category of madness supplementary to the four subtypes of "true insanity" – the four having a natural explanation, whereas obsession still has a supernatural explanation in Paracelsus.

The first record of obsessions in the context of post-Renaissance medical literature is in the work of Felix Plater (1536–1614). In a brief description of pathological doubt found in his *Golden Practice of Physick* (1662), Plater focuses on the depressive features of obsessive worry and doubt. This particular approach is similar to the approach in Robert Burton's *The Anatomy of Melancholy* (1989, originally 1621) mentioned above. Burton understood religious doubt and "superstitious rituals" as symptoms of melancholy. Even at this early date religious intolerance and fanaticism, and religious rituals deemed to be "superstitious," were understood as symptoms of religious melancholy (Moore 1692). This clinical assumption may be seen as a harbinger of the notion that dogmatic rigidity or ritualism are social counterparts to obsessionality. Yet, there was in this body of literature no assumption that the very act of performing a ritual was in some way connected to the underlying psychopathology.

However, a different sort of connection between religious ritualism and pathology had been first suggested, in a different vein, long before Plater and Burton, in late Medieval religious literature. At a time that we cannot pinpoint with any certainty, Catholic confessors had noted that some persons suffered from a morbid preoccupation with sin and purity, or failed to be relieved of guilt by proper confession. These persons were considered to be suffering from "scrupulosity" (*scrupulositas*).[6] They retained the capacity to understand that their morbid doubts were not in harmony with church teachings, but they could not control these preoccupations, manifesting an extravagant piety to a degree not required by any church standard. The earliest mention of this condition that I have found is in the work of Jean C. de Gerson (1363–1429), who recognizes the well-known connection with melancholic illness. Gerson warns spiritual advisors and pastors not to confuse scrupulosity with either piety or possession (Gerson 1960, 1987).

A century after Gerson, first c. 1523, then in 1560, Ignatius of Loyola[7] referred to an unnamed spiritual advisor who confirmed his own intuition regarding scrupulosity (Loyola 1947: sections 22–6). Like Gerson, Ignatius distinguished errors of judgement, in which a person *mistakenly*, but confidently, believes he has sinned, from "scruples," which are persistent doubts regarding the possibility that one *might have sinned*. The latter are perceived as external to conscience and will, and can only be explained as Satan laying siege on the soul. They are also often accompanied by an irresistible urge to avoid or undo the putatively sinful act – hence, scruples often lead to repeated and pointless acts of confession and contrition, or to pointless rituals.

Had he known contemporary terminology, Ignatius could have said that Satan is able to carry out this deception precisely because *the content* of the obsessive thoughts and behaviors is "ego-syntonic," that is, they embody values accepted and cherished by the person suffering from scruples. The person is able to avoid complete surrender to Satan, because *the form* of the obsessions are ego-dystonic, that is, they are perceived as external to the person's own will.

Ignatius himself suffered from a broad spectrum of compulsive symptoms. It is now believed (Meissner 1992) that he suffered from both obsessive-compulsive disorder (OCD) and obsessive-compulsive personality disorder (OCPD).[8] Ignatius described some of his own obsessions and compulsions, and the strategy he followed to overcome them, in his *Life*, composed c. 1555 and published in 1560.[9] He had earlier (1522–3) referred to these same symptoms in his *Exercises*, which, I would argue, were in part structured to combat his own scrupulosity with a substitute obsessive religiosity (see Loyola 1534). Ignatius's account of his own struggles with "scruples" is arguably the earliest documented attempt to deal with obsessional and compulsive behavior "therapeutically." Perhaps following Gerson, he separated his scruples from sinful conscience. Ignatius distinguished errors of judgement, in which a person *mistakenly*, but confidently, believes he has sinned, from "scruples," which are persistent doubts regarding the possibility that one *might have sinned*.

Paradoxically, Ignatius's obsessive thoroughness provided him with the pastoral equivalent of a keen clinical eye. His spiritual exercises, designed as a cure for "disordered affect," may be regarded as the first "behavioral treatment plan" for the cure of obsessions and the earliest explicit statement of a connection between religious ritual and obsessionality. Among other things, the exercises served to desensitize the scrupulous believer. However, very much like modern techniques of exposure, these exercises were set in structured and controlled schedules, and in this manner transformed the involuntary act into a voluntary one. By dictating the scruple on a strict, voluntary schedule, they redirected obsessive thoughts and prescribed substitute rituals that displaced Ignatius's compulsive tendencies. We may say that the structure of the *Exercises* provided a paradoxical behavioral plan that "scheduled" obsessing as part of the "examination of conscience," and structured both obsessions and compulsions, as part of a program of prayer and meditation. The plan forced closure on obsessing without attempting to block it off by a direct attempt at thought suppression, and allowed for compulsivity, again in a ritually closed context, without denying those dimensions of compulsive behavior that were evidently ego-syntonic.

Ignatius's work was followed by more detailed observations in the guides of moral theologians like the Spaniard Tomás Sánchez (*Opus morale* 1614), the Englishman Jeremy Taylor (*Ductor dubitantium* 1660), and the Italian Alphonsus Liguori (1759). All three indirectly offered perceptive observations on the phenomenology of obsessional behavior in their detailed reflections on "cases of conscience."

Ignatius's strategy was in a manner of speaking the exact opposite of that followed by John Bunyan (1628–88). Ignatius scheduled the obsession, because in his case the content of the scruple was morally and theologically positive. Bunyan, whose obsessions and compulsions apparently led to blasphemy, and endless ruminations, that he perceived as "temptations," chose a different strategy to reduce his resistance to obsession. He found the answer in Reform theology and Pietism by a therapy of acceptance rather than by a behavioral schedule. For him, accepting the obsessive thought was synonymous with accepting his own inherent sinfulness. This act of acceptance brought the believer into an agreement with his Savior (God, after all, considered the blasphemous thoughts sin). Therefore, this was also an acceptance of helplessness and a surrender to God's will. In this way, Bunyan accepted somehow the fact that his sinfulness was external to him, and came to believe that his own sinfulness was a road to his own salvation (e.g., *Pilgrim's Progress* 1960: 134 ff.).

It is no accident that the Reformation, Counter-Reformation, and Enlightenment (fifteenth to eighteenth centuries) should be pivotal in the recognition of clinical obsessiveness. This is the same period that brings to maturity the Western sense of individual self and conscience (C. Taylor 1989) that gave us the birth of psychiatric observation and reflection.[10] It is also the period during which the turn inwards toward conscience and spirituality of the late Middle Ages gradually transformed into a new sense of individuality and the cultural presupposition that mental events determined human behavior. This self-awareness grew even as "spiritual" causes and meanings were gradually discredited by the birth of positive science in the Renaissance and by its arrogant self-confidence in the Enlightenment. It became more fashionable to conceive of deviant behavior as "obsession" rather than "possession." Ritualism and magical thinking, variously conceived, were under constant attack, first by those who emphasized "interior spirituality" over the "externals" of ceremony in the late Middle Ages (as in e.g., Devotio Moderna, or the *Imitation of Christ*), then in the iconoclasm of radical reformers like Calvin, and finally by the appearance of a positive science that expected all human action to be either rational and instrumental or deviant and pathological. A new concept of self and other entailed not only a new understanding of "unusual" behavior, it also made new demands on the rational will, and on the individual self as monitor and mover of its own behavior (C. Taylor 1989). Since the inward turn of the Reformation and the Counter-Reformation, the flourishing genres of biography and autobiography and self-reflective fiction documented accurately and vividly the obsessions and compulsions of literary and religious geniuses. Ignatius and Bunyan have been chosen as emblematic, but similar behaviors were depicted, for instance, in the biographic narratives and writings of Martin Luther (1483–1546), and subsequently in those of figures like Samuel Johnson (1709–84 – see Boswell 1791) and Søren Kierkegaard (1813–55).

The birth of modern psychiatry

But modernity not only strengthened Western notions of interiority and conscience, it also revived the ancient Hippocratic model – soon scruples would come under the purview of the physician as well as the confessor, so much so that already in the middle of the nineteenth century Catholic pastors were using medical categories to explain the problem of counseling scrupulous confessors (Carroll 1964; O'Flaherty 1966; Catalan 1989).

By the first decades of the nineteenth century, Jean-Etienne Dominique Esquirol (1772–1840) had formulated the first systematic description of obsessions in the medical literature (Esquirol 1838). But it would take some sixty years before obsessive syndromes would be recognized as a distinct major category of mental illness. At the turn of the last century Pierre Janet called attention to several fundamental aspects of the phenomenology of obsessions and compulsions (Janet 1889; Janet and Raymond 1903). He was the first to document amply the intrusive character of "fixed" or "assailing" mental representations. He also noted that these symptoms could be described as breakdowns of the normal mechanisms of the will – a feature that had been insinuated, theologically, by Ignatius. Janet conceptualized these breakdowns as a "weakening" of certain normal functions of the "psyche" (hence, a "psychasthenia"), with the subsequent loss of the normal capacity to follow a mental or bodily process from beginning to completion with a proper accounting in memory of completion or "perfection" (Pitman 1987a). This is a crucial point, because here we see the outline of a fundamental difference between pathological ritualization and religious ritual: the former is a failure of closure, the latter a mechanism of closure.

The foundational textbook of German nosology, Kraepelin's *Lehrbuch*, first published in 1883, preserves in its various editions a record of a great physician's process of growth. The earlier editions recognized a broad class of compulsion neuroses that developed from a more general weakness of the nerve system. Their common characteristic "consists in a forcible overpowering of the weak psychic constitution (*Persönlichkeit*) by irresistible representations, feeling, and impulses that assail it" (Kraepelin 1887: 377). This definition gave a central role to compulsivity, and also suggested a certain affinity to Janet's "impulsions."[11]

In the major revisions that led to the eighth edition, Kraepelin gave a much more prominent role to the phobias, and began to conceive of anxiety (*Angst*) as the root of compulsivity (Kraepelin 1909–15). The root of obsessionality is an underlying sense of fear, not intrusiveness or compulsive power. With this, he provided a model that reinforced Freud's understanding of obsessive-compulsive disorder.

However, we find a return to Janet in an alternative model proposed by Karl Jaspers (1946). For him, "compulsive phenomena" (*Zwangserscheinungen*) are primary, and concomitant anxiety is secondary.[12] Compulsions are also an extension of normal variations in our experience of the will:

The experience of psychic compulsion is an ultimate fact (*Tatsache*). I may feel under quite normal conditions that I am being driven, impelled or overpowered not only by outer forces and other people but by my own psychic life. We have to keep this normal phenomenon well in mind and realize that it is strangely possible for us to oppose ourselves ... Psychic compulsion is possible only where there is a *psychic life subject to a certain degree of volitional control*. Psychic events can become *compulsive events* only when they contain an experience of self-activity ... There is, therefore, no psychic compulsion where there is no volitional control and no choice, as with idiots and very young children ... *The limits of compulsion are coextensive with the limits of our will.*[13]

Will, function and meaning

Jaspers raises two important issues that may be regarded as both medical and philosophical. First, obsessive-compulsive phenomena are somehow coextensive with the range of volition or will. Second, obsessions and compulsions may be related to affect or anxious disposition, but the obsessive-compulsive event is experienced as primary. Unfortunately, his insights were not accompanied by a concrete medical or nosological strategy. On the first of Jasper's insights, the psychiatric and psychological tradition would have very little to say for another twenty years. The second of his suggestions remained ignored – Freud and Kraepelin prevailed and obsessive compulsive disorder would remain essentially an anxiety disorder in an etiological sense.

Shortly after the publication of Jaspers' *Psychopathology* clinical research began to focus almost exclusively on two sets of new models, which have proven so productive theoretically and clinically that they have eclipsed all others. I am referring, of course, to the behavioral-evolutionary and the neuro-biochemical models of obsessionality. We must now explore quickly the ways in which these models may throw light on the question that interests us: obsessionality and its possible connection to religious behaviors.

As I have mentioned, Freud and his disciples had already suggested that rituals work because they relieve anxiety (cf. Homans 1941). Freud's contemporary, Nobel Laureate Ivan P. Pavlov (1849–1936), would give obsessive-compulsive disorder theorists other good reasons to continue to believe in anxiety as the primary mechanism behind the malady (Pavlov 1941 and 1994, originally 1961). J. Wolpe's early Pavlovian work on experimentally produced neurotic reactions in cats led to the application of similar principles toward the elimination of phobic reactions in humans. In his landmark monograph *Psychotherapy by Reciprocal Inhibition* (1958) Wolpe perfected the technique that has proven most useful in the psychological treatment of obsessive-compulsive disorder: systematic desensitization.

The main etiological model behind behavioral theories of anxiety disorders is a learned-response model. It assumes an initial anxiety-provoking stimulus, and a gradual generalization. As applied today, behavioral therapy is meant to reverse this process – it presupposes an effective heightening of anxiety by exposure, and desensitization to the anxiety, followed by desensitization to the generalized stimulus.

The success of the hypothesis as a model for therapeutic intervention is undeniable. However, when applied to ritual the theoretical model is reduced to the questionable statement that ritual reduces or is induced by anxiety. One may have to turn to another way of looking at ritual from the perspective of a learning model.

From their inception, behavioral theories have been tied to animal models and subsequently to evolutionary models (so-called "ethological" models). Several hypotheses of this type have been proposed (Simon *et al.* 1988). Obsessive-compulsive related behaviors are sometimes understood as part of normal strategies for learning and unlearning fear: that is, strategies for coping with fear. But obsessive-compulsive related behaviors are also seen as a subclass of ritualized displays, sometimes as extensions of grooming behaviors. Obsessive-compulsive disorder is then seen as a breakdown of one of these coping mechanisms (e.g., Marks and Tobena 1990; Marks and Nesse 1994).

Generally, models of the first type see obsessive-compulsive disorder as a special manifestation of anxiety, and hence an exaggeration or faulty learning of normal fear behavior (Marks 1987). A displays model, on the other hand, assumes that psychopathology may be a type of "behavior out of context," a displacement behavior (Tinbergen 1949, 1952, 1974; Lorenz 1966; Holland 1974).

These models have been discussed extensively in the literature since the heyday of ethology and were formulated in several ways at a symposium organized by J. Huxley (1966). Since then, the tendency has been to assume that agonistic ritualized displays underlie human depression (Price *et al.* 1994), and that some sort of breakdown of adaptive grooming behaviors or fear-management behavior is involved in obsessive-compulsive disorder (Marks 1989; Marks and Nesse 1994).

The notion that obsessive-compulsive disorder may result from a disin-hibited philogenetically mediated grooming behavior received some support from the observation of obsessive-compulsive disorder-like behaviors in certain domestic animals (Wiepkema 1985). A particular canine acral lick, a disorder found in certain breeds of large dogs, manifests symptoms that are suggestive of obsessive-compulsive disorder (Rapoport *et al.* 1992). The animal engages in compulsive self-grooming (especially licking its paws, sometimes to the point of producing sores), and the disorder responds to drug treatments similar to those used in human obsessive-compulsive disorder (Rapoport 1991a; critical response in Insel 1991; rejoinder in Rapoport 1991b; see also Winslow and Insel 1991).

Behavioral and anatomical models lead to a crucial question: what are the cognitive dimensions of obsessive-compulsive related behaviors? Both Freud and Janet's models of obsessionality could be understood as predicting characteristic cognitive styles or cognitive deficits in obsessive-compulsive disorder (see also Shapiro 1965, 1981). But, strictly speaking, these models do not require a deficit in cognitive processing, whereas behavioral models could be construed as implying irregularities in the processing of percepts and ideational evaluations.

As mentioned above, a contemporary reading of Janet (1889) led Pitman (1982, 1987a, 1987b) to hypothesize that obsessive-compulsive disorder may be a dysfunction of informational feedback processes. Unaware of Pitman's work, Wegner (1989) carried out experimental studies on the capacity of subjects to "suppress" irrelevant or unwanted thoughts. These experiments also suggested that a failure of closure in cognition is at the root of obsessional thought patterns.

Evolutionary and learning models, however, compete with those suggested by the success of pharmacological and surgical interventions. Since the late 1950s these treatment modalities have strengthened a disease model that presumes either an insult to, or an inherited deficit in, a specific area of the brain. We cannot discuss here the history of clinical successes that led to the hypothesis. Suffice it to say that the pharmacological model most widely favored at present, the serotonergic hypothesis, suggests a location in the brain that tallies with some animal models of compulsive behavior, and with the characteristic ritualistic nature of compulsions.

Furthermore, other empirical findings converge on an apparent association of obsessive-compulsive disorder with the same locations, primarily with the basal ganglia. The hypothesis has been suggested by the results of psychosurgery, by brain imaging studies, and by case studies of damage to this area of the brain (Baxter 1990; Biver *et al.* 1995; Breiter *et al.* 1996; Insel and Winslow 1990; Insel *et al.* 1990; Irle *et al.* 1998). It has been strengthened by the close association of obsessive-compulsive disorder to Gilles de la Tourette's syndrome, Trichotillomania and Sydenham's chorea, and by family history and twin studies (Black and Noyes 1990).

A neuro-anatomic base in the ganglia is suggestive, because this center is involved not only in the regulation of movement but also in the processing and regulation of sensory information relative to motor output. Moreover, this area is connected to the brain stem only indirectly, so that its regulation of movement and the mental representation of movement is mediated by other parts of the forebrain and the cortex. Such mediation includes complex neural connections to the limbic system, which are central to the regulation of affect, and to affective judgements of both reality and volition. This strengthens the hypotheses of obsessive-compulsive disorder as a cognitive or information processing dysfunction, but it is also consistent with the serotonin hypothesis and the depressive phenomenology of obsessive-compulsive disorder. It is consistent, furthermore, with a psychodynamic emphasis on ambivalent inhibition-disinhibition, and also with the earlier notion of a "disease of the will." Finally, it is consistent with the hypothesized behavioral disregulation manifested in the compulsive caricature of ritual. Maladaptive ritualization could then be conceived as a breakdown of adaptive mechanisms of psychomotor and information processing.[14]

The biochemical and anatomical models bring us back to the crucial question of the cognitive dimensions of obsessive-compulsive related behaviors and to their possible connection to ritual behavior. As already noted, behavioral theories would suggest dysfunctions in the processing of percepts and ideational evaluations. But the neuro-anatomic hypotheses suggest that some informational feedback processes may not necessarily entail, and may not be preceded by, cognition as ideational processes.

As speculative as these nosological reflections might be, they suggest a connection not only between impulse and compulsion, but also between compulsion and will. To be compelled might not be as different from acting on one's own free will as it seems. And ordering (restraining) the will may be in a spectrum with *not* restraining it.

The question of "rituals"

I would be the last to want to suggest that all repetitive behaviors are ritualistic, or that all ritualizations are rituals, much less that such behaviors have a single origin, context, course, function, or resolution. Still, I would argue that the analogy between ritual and compulsion is a useful lead in the psychological study of ritual.

Early Western and Islamic medicine, like contemporary observation, shows that obsessive-compulsive related behaviors can occur without any connection to religious ideation or ritual. The study of religious rituals also demonstrates how different they can be from compulsive behaviors. However, Christian notions of scrupulosity suggest to me a potential connection between obsessive behaviors, religious ritual, and moral judgement; theological reflection also suggests that our moral and ritual orders, like our sense of cleanliness and order (and beauty as pulchritude) may be closely related to the mystery of human will. In all of this I see connections to the cognitive, behavioral and neural bases of will and compulsion.

This may be otherwise expressed by proposing a possible connection between order and cohesion on the one hand, and will and control on the other. The study of the obsessive behaviors thus may raise important issues regarding the will as a fulcrum for our sense of a unitary self.

In *The Principles of Psychology* William James reminds us of the central role of will and intentionality in defining the parameters of identity.

> The first point to start from in understanding voluntary action, and the possible occurrence of it with no fiat or express resolve, is the fact that consciousness is *in its very nature impulsive*. We do not have a sensation or a thought and then have to *add* something dynamic to it to get a

movement. Every pulse of feeling which we have is the correlate of some neural activity that is already on its way to instigate a movement.

(James 1902: vol. 2, 526, James' italics)

James' introspective insight helps us understand Jaspers' observations regarding the limits of the will; again in *The Principles*, James speaks of the interpenetration of the voluntary and the involuntary in a manner that comes close to Jaspers' choice of words:

Decisions with effort merge so gradually into those without it that it is not easy to say where the limit lies. Decisions without effort merge again into ideo-motor, and these into reflex acts ... Where there is effort just as where there is none, the ideas themselves which furnish the matter of deliberation are brought before the mind by the machinery of association.

(ibid.: vol. 2, 575)

The key point here is lost in James' rhetoric; for the implication is that effort and decision play a major role in defining self and concepts of the self. Only a few lines after the passage just quoted, where James discusses the theories of Lipps' *Grundtatsachen des Seelenlebens*:

Where the forces are ideas, both sets of them, strictly speaking are the seat of effort – both those which tend to explode, and those which tend to check them. We, however, call the more abundant mass of ideas *ourselves*; and, talking of its effort as *our* effort, and of that of the smaller mass of ideas as the *resistance*, we say that our effort sometimes overcomes the resistances offered by the inertias of an obstructed [will], and sometimes those presented by the impulsions of an explosive will.

Really both effort and resistance are ours, and the identification of our self with one of these factors is an illusion and a trick of speech.

(James 1883: vol. 2, 575–6)

As is often the case in *The Principles*, James expresses masterfully one of the great quandaries of psychological reflection. Here, his insights come close to those of Jaspers. Their views of the will as choice and resistance to choice suggest that however important our clinical insights and goals may be, ultimately our sense of "self" and "will" have to be constructed artificially by defining that which is in-volu-ntary, that which is resistance, as "not self," and ignoring the degree to which the incompleteness of volition and conscious life impinges on our sense of being whole, yet is an integral part of our experience of self. Conversely, we can infer that it is possible to turn certain forms of resistance into voluntary actions, and hence into self. This, I would argue, is one of the functions of ritual, and one of the functions that separate it phenomenologically from compulsion – a separation that I would argue is phenomenological and functional, but not necessarily etiological.

It has been observed that "the unity of the self is a culturally reinforced illusion" (Kluft 1993: 5). It is true that culture constructs and reinforces this unity, but it does so through an ordering of the cosmos that is, at its most primary level, based on our "daily rituals" of order and cleanliness, as well as on our belief that we have a will. The unity of self may then be a biological drive, although its construct may forever remain fluid and fragile. And it may be that the constructs and the drive can easily break down.

Without denying the significant differences that separate secular ceremonies and religious rituals from the "rituals" of obsessive-compulsive related behaviors, one can conceive of them in a spectrum of behaviors with a set of common features. Fiske and Haslam (1997) understand obsessive-compulsive disorder as "a pathology of the human disposition to perform socially meaningful rituals." Although they limit themselves to a discussion of content, their emphasis on the social context as central to even the most basic forms of ritualization is suggestive (cf. Price *et al.* 1994). Turbott (1997) attempts to reconstruct a meaning and function for psychiatric rituals that can reproduce the meaning of religious rituals and daily ritualizations.

But one does not need to see meaning as fundamental. Meaning can be conceived as an important by-product of something more fundamental – albeit a by-product that creates a reinforcement loop, confirming the truth and necessity of the ritualization. This loop binds together a social unconscious with an individual unconscious and consciousness.

To this one can add the hypothesis of a common set of locations for ritualization and obsessive-compulsive related behaviors – in culture, in self-awareness, and in the brain. Research into obsessive-compulsive related behaviors remains a part of the investigation of the events that occur in these three separate places. The three locations may never come together in a unified theory, and the most fruitful research will not be grounded in speculation, but we may eventually approach an understanding of the mechanisms that operate in these three areas of human experience.

Nevertheless, one can speculate as a way of suggesting models that need to be operationalized for empirical research. I follow Pitman in turning Janet's nineteenth-century model on its head: it is not so much that obsessionality represents a "weakening of the self," but that it represents a dysfunction of ritualization (mental and bodily): that is, of a class of behaviors that in its normal or adaptive functions plays a central role in a person's definition of selfhood. In other words, clinical obsessionality is ritualization gone awry. Behaviors of this class can be called "ritualizations," because they belong to the class of phenomena to which rituals proper also belong.

Pitman's reading of Janet suggests that defective ritualization results from breakdowns in crucial feedback loops that should be amenable to empirical biological and behavioral investigation. This notion also inverts Freud's fundamental intuition by suggesting that obsessionality is a subclass of a coping mechanism, the most adaptive dimensions of which are represented by many socially sanctioned rituals (public or private, secular or religious). Insofar as meaning is an extension of coping relevance, obsessional ruminations may in fact be meaningless, whereas rituals generally may represent one of the most basic forms of "meaning," psychological and social.

Religious behavior is not neurosis – insofar as psychodynamic theory has suggested that it is the theory displays its lack of sensitivity to the complexity of religion as social and cultural event. Yet religion, and culture generally, share with neurosis important elements: fixed and overvalued ideas, the construction of meaning by repetition and complex symbolization, among others. Such common features are still in need of explanation. And, before I conclude with a more humanistic note, I should also mention that some of these features may be amenable to empirical study, and should be studied with the tools of the empirical sciences.

Shifting to an even more speculative mode, one may say that the normal process of "repetition," of walking trodden paths, serves to organize experience (adaptive cognitive obsessiveness). We all use varying degrees of adaptive rigidity to maintain or safeguard certain self-constants. We rely on adaptive assimilations that integrate new information into established, more or less stable self-concepts.

For all my nervousness about Plato's glorification of madness, I will borrow and transform a metaphor from the *Phaedrus* to summarize the state of my thinking. One can find an apposite and suggestive answer to the question of "When are ritualistic behaviors unhealthy, and when are they healthy?" in the words Plato attributes to Socrates (*Phaedrus* 244E):

> When an ancient curse has brought severe maladies and troubles, which afflict the members of certain families, madness has appeared among them and by breaking forth into prophecy has brought relief by the appropriate means ... prayer and worship. It has discovered in rites of purification and initiation a way to make the sufferer well and to keep him well thereafter, and has provided for the man whose madness and possession were of the right type a way of escape from the evils that beset him.

This final reflection makes me wonder whether the question of Theresa Santangelo's pathology was not phrased inappropriately – a butcher's common sense notwithstanding. The first order of inquiry should not be whether a particular religious behavior is pathological, or whether religion generally is pathological, but rather what it is about religion that elicits such questions.

I will venture, by way of conclusion, a provisional answer to this difficult question. Speaking in the manner of Socrates to disagree with him, I propose that "obsessive actions and religious practices," in pushing the limits of the real and the imaginary, remind us (or "are a faint memory of") the limits of our own rationality.

Speaking in the manner of a contemporary psychologist, and keeping in view the specific focus of this essay, I will also venture to say that religious rituals and obsessive behaviors reveal the necessarily pre-rational human need to walk a trodden path, to repeat, to create predictable order for its own sake, and to formalize world and self. This need is rooted in thought processes that are so deep in us that only their breakdown reminds us of their presence, and of the fact that they antecede, if not support, our own rational existence.

Notes

1 The passage is located at 244DE, according to the classical referencing system. All quotations below are from this passage as translated in Hamilton 1973.

2 On this fallacy, see Segal 1989.

3 Compare also Griesinger's "religious melancholia" (1861: section 120). One should note that Burton does not use the words "obsession" or "compulsion."

4 Since the matter of the attribution of Hippocratic works is controversial, I have arbitrarily chosen the Loeb Classical Library edition (Hippocrates 1923) as the limit of the medical thought of Hippocrates.

5 Also see the introduction and notes to the English version: *The Diseases that Deprive Man of his Reason, Such as St Vitus' Dance, Falling Sickness, Melancholy, and Insanity, and their Correct Treatment,* in Paracelsus 1988.

6 Clinical histories sometimes manifest a certain confusion regarding the etymology of the term "scrupulosity," reflecting the word's double etymology. The word is derived from Latin *scrupulus* (diminutive of *srüpus*, "stone"). From this ancient meaning, two etymologies appear since the earliest times. As *scrüpulus* the word refers to a small, usually sharp or rough pebble that gets into one's shoe and, although small, causes great pain and vexation. Hence, a scrupulous person is someone who is vexed or anguished by something very small. As *scrupulum* or *scriptulum*, the etymology is less clear, although it may also mean a small stone, but in its use as a weight. It was one of the smallest units of weight in classical Rome (equivalent to 20 "grains"). According to this second etymology, a person who is *scrupulosus* worries about the finest distinctions of measure, price or moral value.

7 The English convention is to refer to this author as Ignatius of Loyola (sometimes preceded by the epithet "Saint"). In the body of the essay I have adopted this convention. In the bibliography, however, works published under his Spanish name appear under Loyola, Ignacio de.

8 These abbreviations are common in the psychological and psychiatric literature, but are not used in this paper, which is intended for a wider audience that includes readers outside the mental health professions.

9 Modern edition in *Obras completas* (1947: vol. 1, 118–580).

10 Possible historical connections between the modern and Reformation attitudes towards ritual and the rise of psychiatry need to be explored further. It is possible that the rejection of ritual and magic contributed to the rise of psychiatry not only by opening the way for naturalistic explanations, but also by contributing to the pathologization of religious belief.

11 The notion appears to be that of a primary or underlying disease entity consisting in an individual being forced to feel, think, or behave in a manner

contrary to that person's will. This notion has been rendered outside of the German cultural sphere with the terms "anancastic neurosis" or "anankastia," This is from Greek *ananke*, "necessity, inevitability." Ananke was the mother of Adrasteia, the distributor of rewards and punishments. The term "anankastic" is still occasionally used (outside of North America, and sometimes spelled "anancastic") for a variety of obsessive-compulsive related behaviors (e.g., Videbech 1975; Ramos Brieva 1984; Ishisaka 1992). The term is found in the ICD-10 diagnosis of "anancastic personality disorder," but "obsessive-compulsive disorder" has been adopted by the ICD-10 for the disease so named in the North American standard, the DSM-IV (American Psychiatric Association 1994 – see also 1991 and 1993 for significant variants in the diagnostic criteria).

12 Like most German nosologists since Westphal, including Freud, Jaspers uses one superordinate term to encompass both obsessions and compulsions: namely, *Zwang*, "coercion, imposition, pressure, violent force, duress" (verb, *zwängen*, "to pressure, force, impose, coerce, constrain"). Obsessions and compulsions are distinguished by prefixing the term *Zwang* to the common words for act and mental representation: *Zwangshandlung* and *Zwangsvorstellung*, that is, "compelled" or "imposed representation" and "compelled action." In this terminology, compulsion or compelling was the umbrella term; hence, obsessions were conceived as "compulsive representations."

13 Jaspers (1946: 111–12), quoted from the Hoenig and Hamilton translation (1997, vol. 1: 133–4) (with minor changes based on the 1959 German edition). Italics are Jaspers' own.

14 Unfortunately, the location of obsessive-compulsive disorder in the basal ganglia would only represent a gross anatomical location, as these ganglia are more a set of interconnected clusters than a single isolated neuronal cluster. Yaryura-Tobias and Neziroglu (1997: 264) summarize these intricate interconnections first by noting that "obsessive-compulsive disorder patients have a gamut of symptoms involving thought, perception, mood, will, and motor activity." This they characterize as a "mosaic," which "seems to emerge from an extensive cerebral territory."

References

American Psychiatric Association (1991) *DSM-IV Work in Progress (9/1/91)*, American Psychiatric Association Task Force on DSM-IV, Washington, DC: The American Psychiatric Association.

—— (1993) *DSM-IV Criteria (3/1/93)*, Washington, DC: The American Psychiatric Association.

—— (1994) *Diagnostic and Statistical Manual of Mental Disorders*, 4th edn, revised (DSM-IV), Washington, DC: American Psychiatric Association.

Baxter, L.R., Jr (1990) "Brain imaging as a tool in establishing a theory of brain pathology in obsessive compulsive disorder," *Journal of Clinical Psychiatry* 51(2), supplement: 22–5, discussion 26.

Biver, F., Goldman, S., Francois, A., De La Porte, C., Luxen, A., Gribomont, B., and Lotstra, F. (1995) "Changes in metabolism of cerebral glucose after stereotactic leukotomy for refractory obsessive-compulsive disorder: a case report," *Journal of Neurology, Neurosurgery and Psychiatry* 58(4): 502–5.

Black, D.W. and Noyes, T. (1990) "Comorbidity in obsessive-compulsive disorder," in J.D. Maser and C.R. Cloninger (eds), *Comorbidity in Anxiety and Mood Disorders*, Washington, DC: American Psychiatric Press, pp. 305–16.

Boswell, J. (1791) *The Life of Samuel Johnson, LL.D.*, London, privately printed for the Navarre Society (1924).

Breiter, H.C., Rauch, S.L., Kwong, K.K., Baker. J.R., Weisskoff, R.M., Kennedy, D.N., Kendrick, A.D., Davis, T.L., Jiang, A., Cohen, M.S., Stern, C.E., Belliveau, J.W., Baer, L., O'Sullivan, R.L., Savage, C.R., Jenike, M.A., and Rosen, B.R. (1996) "Functional magnetic resonance imaging of symptom provocation in obsessive-compulsive disorder," *Archives of General Psychiatry* 53(7): 595–606.

Bunyan, J. (1960) *The Pilgrim's Progress from this World to That Which is to Come*, ed. James Blanton Wharey, 2nd edn rev. by Roger Sharrock, Oxford: Clarendon Press (originally 1678).

Burnet, J. (ed.) (1901) "Plato, *Phaedrus*," in *Platonis opera, recognovit brevique adnotatione critica instruxit Ioannes Burnet, Tomus II*, Oxford Classical Texts, Oxford: Clarendon Press, vol. 2, pp. 223–95.

Burton, R. (1989) *The Anatomy of Melancholy, What it is, with all the Kinds, Causes, Symptoms, Prognostics, and Several Cures of it. In Three Partitions* by Democritus Junior (Robert Burton), Oxford: Clarendon Press, New York: Oxford University Press. Based on the edn of 1652; first edn 1621.

Carroll, M.G. (ed./trans.) (1964) *The Treatment of Scruples*, Cork, Netherlands: The Mercier Press.

Catalan, J.-F. (1989) "Scrupule," in M. Viller, F. Caballera *et al.* (eds), *Dictionnaire de spiritualité, ascétique et mystique: Doctrine et histoire*, Paris: Beauchesne, vol. 15, fascicules 92–4, col. 461–7.

Doctor, R.M. and Kahn, A.P. (eds) (1989) *The Encyclopedia of Phobias, Fears, and Anxieties*, New York: Facts on File.

Esquirol, J.E.D. (1838) *Des maladies mentales considerées sous les rapports medical, hygienique et medico-legal*, 2 vols, Paris: J.-B. Bailliere, vol. 1, ch. 11, "De la monomanie."

Fine, R. (1979) *A History of Psychoanalysis*, New York: Columbia University Press.

Fiske, A.P. and Haslam, N. (1997) "Is obsessive-compulsive disorder a pathology of the human disposition to perform socially meaningful rituals? Evidence of similar content," *Journal of Nervous & Mental Disease* 185(4): 211–22.

Freud, S. (1907) "Zwangshandlungen und Religionsübungen," *Zeitschrift für Religionspsychologie* 1: 4–12. Repr. in *Gesammelte Werke*, 7:129–39. Trans. into English as "Obsessive actions and religious practices," in James Strachey (ed.), *The Standard Edition of the Complete Psychological Works of Sigmund Freud*, London: Hogarth Press (1959), vol. 9, pp. 115–27. Also in *Collected Papers*, London: Hogarth Press (1955), vol. 2, pp. 25–35.

Gerson, Jean le Charlier (1960–73) *Oeuvres complètes [de] Jean Gerson*, Introd., texte et notes par Mgr [Palemon] Glorieux, 10 vols, Paris, Tournai, Rome and New York: Desclée; vol. 7, *L'oeuvre française*, especially document 306, "Contre conscience trop scrupuleuse," pp. 149–52.

—— (1987) *Opera omnia*, ed. Louis Ellies Du Pin, 5 vols, photographic reproduction, Hildesheim, Zurich and New York: Olms (originally 1706).

—— (1998) *Jean Gerson: Early Works*, trans. and introduced by Brian Patrick McGuire, preface by Bernard McGinn, New York: Paulist Press.

Griesinger, W. (1861) *Die Pathologie und Therapie der psychischen Krankheiten, für Aerzte und Studierende* 2, umgearb. und sehr verm. Aufl. Stuttgart: A. Krabbe.

Hamilton, W. (trans.) (1973) *Plato: Phaedrus, and, The Seventh and Eighth Letters*, trans. with introductions, Harmondsworth, Middlesex: Penguin.

Hippocrates (1923) *Hippocrates,* with an English trans. by W.H.S. Jones, 6 vols, London: Heinemann, New York: G.P. Putnam's Sons.

Holland, H.C. (1974) "Displacement activities as a form of abnormal behavior in animals," in H.R. Beech (ed.), *Obsessional States,* London: Methuen, pp. 161–74.

Homans, G.C. (1941) "Anxiety and ritual: the theories of Malinowski and Radcliffe-Brown," *American Anthropologist* 43: 164–72.

Huxley, J. (organizer) (1966) "A discussion on ritualization of behaviour in animals and man," *Philosophical Transactions of the Royal Society of London, Series B, Biological Sciences* 251(772): 247–56.

Insel, T.R. (1991) "Has OCD research gone to the dogs? Comments on 'Recent advances in obsessive-compulsive disorder'," *Neuropsychopharmacology* 5(1): 13–17.

Insel, T.R. and Winslow, J.T. (1990) "Neurobiology of obsessive-compulsive disorder," in M.A. Jenike, L. Baer and W.E. Minichiello (eds), *Obsessive-Compulsive Disorders: Theory and Management,* 2nd edn, Chicago: Year Book Medical Publishers, pp. 118–31.

Insel, T.R., Zohar, J., Benkelfat, C., and Murphy, D.L. (1990) "Serotonin in obsessions, compulsions, and the control of aggressive impulses," *Annals of the New York Academy of Sciences* 600: 574–85, discussion 585–6.

Irle, E., Exner, C., Thielen, K., Weniger, G. and Ruether, E. (1998) "Obsessive-compulsive disorder and ventromedial frontal lesions: clinical and neuropsychological findings," *American Journal of Psychiatry* 155(2): 255–63.

Ishisaka, Y. (1992) "Depressive anancastia in childhood and adolescence," *Japanese Journal of Child and Adolescent Psychiatry* 33(3): 193–204.

Jackson, S.W. (1986) *Melancholia and Depression. From Hippocratic Times to Modern Times,* New Haven: Yale University Press.

James, W. (1890) *The Principles of Psychology,* 2 vols, New York: H. Holt; references to reprint, New York: Dover (1950).

—— (1902) *The Varieties of Religious Experience: A Study in Human Nature, Being the Gifford Lectures on Natural Religion Delivered at Edinburgh in 1901–1902,* New York: Longmans, Green, and Co.

Janet, P. (1889) *L'automatisme psychologique: Essai de psychologie expérimentale sur les formes inférieurs de l'activité humaine,* Paris: Félix Alcan. Reprint from the 4th printing of the 1st edn, Paris: Société Pierre Janet (1973).

Janet, P. and Raymond, F. (1903) *Les obsessions et la psychasténie,* vol. 2, Paris: Félix Alcan; reprint New York: Arno (1976).

Jaspers, K. (1946) *Allgemeine Psychopathologie,* 7th edn, Berlin: Springer Verlag; 1st edn published 1923. English translation from the German 7th edn *General Psychopathology,* trans. J. Hoenig and M.W. Hamilton, Manchester: Manchester University Press; Chicago: Chicago University Press (1963, reprinted 1997).

Jowett, B. (trans.) (1908) *Dialogues of Plato,* 4 vols, New York: Charles Scribner's Sons. *Phaedrus* is in vol. I, pp. 549–57.

Kluft, R.P. (1993) "Multiple personality disorder: a contemporary perspective," *The Harvard Mental Health Letter* 10(4): 5–7.

Kraepelin, E. (1883) *Compendium der Psychiatrie: Zum Gebrauche für Studierende und Aerzte,* Leipzig: Abel.

—— (1887) *Psychiatrie: Ein kurzes Lehrbuch für Studierende und Aerzte,* 2nd edn, "zweite Gänzlich umgearbeitete Auflage," Leipzig: Verlag von Amber Abel.

—— (1909–15) *Psychiatrie: Ein Lehrbuch für Studierende und Ärzte*, 8th edn, "Achte, vollstandig umgearbeitete Auflage," 4 vols, Leipzig: J.A. Barth.

Krafft-Ebing, R. von. (1897–99) *Arbeiten aus dem gesammtgebiet der psychiatrie und neuropathologie*, Leipzig: J.A. Barth.

Liguori, A.M. de (1759) *Theologia moralis*, Venetiis (Venice): Ex Typographia Remondiniana, superiorum permissu, ac privilegio.

Lipps, T. (1883) *Grundtatsachen des Seelenlebens*, Bonn: M. Cohen.

Lorenz, K.Z. (1966) "Evolution of ritualization in the biological and cultural spheres," in J. Huxley (ed.) "A discussion on ritualization of behaviour in animals and man," *Philosophical Transactions of the Royal Society of London, Series B, Biological Sciences* 251(772): 273–84.

Loyola, Ignacio de (1534 (*versio prima*)–1541 (*autograph*)) *Ejercicios espirituales*, Spanish text, known as the *Autograph*, ed. J. Roothaan in *Monumenta historica Societatis Iesu*, Madrid/Roma: Institutum historicum Societatis Iesu (1919–20), reprinted 1952 in *Obras completas de San Ignacio de Loyola: Edición manual*, transcripción, introducciones y notas del P. Ignacio Iparraguirre, S.I., con la *Autobiografía* de San Ignacio, editada y anotada por el P. Cándido de Dalmases, S.I., Madrid: Editorial Católica, Biblioteca de Autores Cristianos.

—— (1947) *Obras completas de San Ignacio de Loyola*, Introducciones y comentarios del R.P. Victoriano Larranaga, S.I., 2 vols, Madrid: Biblioteca de Autores Cristianos. Includes *Autobiografía* or *Relato del peregrino*, vol. 1, pp. 118–280.

—— (1952) *Obras completas de San Ignacio de Loyola: Edición manual*, transcripción, introducciones y notas del P. Ignacio Iparraguirre, S.I., con la *Autobiografía* de San Ignacio, editada y anotada por el P. Cándido de Dalmases, S.I., Madrid: Editorial Católica, Biblioteca de Autores Cristianos.

Marks, I.M. (1987) *Fears, Phobias, and Rituals: Panic, Anxiety, and their Disorders*, New York: Oxford University Press.

—— (1989) "Foreword," in R.M. Doctor and A.P. Kahn (eds), *The Encyclopedia of Phobias, Fears, and Anxieties*, New York: Facts on File.

Marks, I.M. and Nesse. R.M. (1994) "Fear and fitness: an evolutionary analysis of anxiety disorders," *Ethology and Sociobiology* 15: 247–61.

Marks, I.M. and Tobena, A. (1990) "Learning and unlearning fear: a clinical and evolutionary perspective," *Neuroscience and Biobehavioral Reviews* 14: 365–84.

Martin, L.H. (1988) "Technologies of the self and self-knowledge in the Syrian Thomas tradition," in L.H. Martin, H. Gutman and P.H. Hutton (eds), *Technologies of the Self: A Seminar with Michel Foucault*, Amherst: University of Massachusetts Press, pp. 50–63.

Martin, L.H., Gutman, H., and Hutton, P.H. (eds) (1988) *Technologies of the Self: A Seminar with Michel Foucault*, Amherst: University of Massachusetts Press.

Meissner, W.W. (1992) *Ignatius of Loyola: The Psychology of a Saint*, New Haven, CT: Yale University Press.

Moore, J. (1692) *On Religious Melancholy*, London, published by Her Majesty's special command.

O'Flaherty, V.M. (1966) *How to Cure Scruples*, Milwaukee: Bruce Publishing Company.

Paracelsus, P.A. (Theophrastus Bombastus von Hoheim or Bombastus Paracelsus) (1567) *The Diseases that Deprive Man of his Reason*, in P.A. Paracelsus (1988) *Four Treatises Together with Selected Writings*, Birmingham, AL: Classics of Medicine Library, pp. 135–212 (completed c. 1520, but not published until 1567).

Pavlov, I.P. (1941) *Lectures on Conditioned Reflexes*, ed. and trans. W. Horsley Gantt and G.V. Folbort, 2 vols, New York: International Publishers.

—— (1994) *Psychopathology and Psychiatry*, trans. D. Myshne and S. Belsky, New Brunswick, NJ: Transaction Publishers (originally 1961).

Pitman, R.K. (1982) "Neurological etiology of obsessive-compulsive disorders," *American Journal of Psychiatry* 139: 139–40.

—— (1987a) "A cybernetic model of obsessive-compulsive psychopathology," *Comprehensive Psychiatry* 28: 334–43.

—— (1987b) "Pierre Janet on obsessive-compulsive disorder (1903)," *Archives of General Psychiatry* 44: 226–32.

Plater, F. (1662) *A Golden Practice of Physick By Felix Plater and Abdiah Cole*, Microfilm Series: Early English Books, 1641–1700; 1237.5 (reproduction of original in the Cambridge University Library), Ann Arbor, MI: University Microfilms International (1982).

Plato *Phaedrus* Text in J. Burnet (ed.) (1901) *Platonis opera, recognovit brevique adnotatione critica instruxit Ioannes Burnet, Tomus II*, Oxford Classical Texts, Oxford: Clarendon Press, vol. 2, pp. 223–95; trans. in B. Jowett (1908) *Dialogues of Plato*, New York: Charles Scribner's Sons, vol. I, pp. 549–57, and in W. Hamilton (1973) *Plato: Phaedrus, and, The Seventh and Eighth Letters*, Harmondsworth, Middlesex: Penguin.

Price, J., Sloman, L., Gardner, R., Gilbert, P. and Rohde, P. (1994) "The social competition hypothesis of depression," *British Journal of Psychiatry* 164 (Special Issue: Depression): 309–15.

Prose, F. (1981) *Household Saints*, New York: St Martin's Press.

Ramos Brieva, J.A. (1984) "Capacidad predictiva del mini-inventario de rasgos anancásticos de la personalidad," *Actas Luso-Españolas de Neurología y Psiquiatría y Ciencias Afines* 12(2): 135–40.

Rapoport, J.L. (1988) "The neurobiology of obsessive-compulsive disorder: clinical conference," *Journal of the American Medical Association* 260(19): 2888–90.

—— (1991a) "Recent advances in obsessive-compulsive disorder," *Neuropsychopharmacology* 5(1): 1–10.

—— (1991b) "Reply to commentaries on 'Recent advances in obsessive-compulsive disorder'," *Neuropsychopharmacology* 5(1): 21–2.

Rapoport, J.L., Ryland, D.H., and Kriete, M. (1992) "Drug treatment of canine acral lick: an animal model of obsessive-compulsive disorder," *Archives of General Psychiatry* 49: 517–21. Summarized in *The Harvard Mental Health Letter* 9(8): 7 (February 1993).

Reik, T. (1919) *Ritual: Four Psycho-Analytic Studies*, with a preface by Sigmund Freud. Eng. trans. reprinted New York: International Universities Press (1958).

—— (1927) *Dogma and Compulsion: Psychoanalytic Studies of Religion and Myths*, trans. B. Miall, New York: International Universities Press (1951).

Rieff, P. (ed.) (1963) *Freud: Therapy and Technique*, New York: Collier Books, Macmillan.

Sánchez, T. (de Córdoba, or Thomae Sanchez Cordubensis) (1614) *Opus morale in praecepta decalogi: Sive summa casuum conscientiae* ... , Coloniae Agrippinae: sumptibus Antonij Hierati. Microfiche: Zug, Switzerland: Inter Documentation Co. AG (c. 1950, no date), 14 microfiches (CA-69/1).

Segal, R.A. (1989) "The social sciences and the truth of religious belief," in *Religion and the Social Sciences: Essays on the Confrontation*, Brown Studies in Religion, no. 3, Atlanta: Scholars Press, pp. 75–86.

Shapiro, D. (1965) *Neurotic Styles*, New York: Basic Books.

—— (1981) *Autonomy and Rigid Character*, New York: Basic Books.

Simon, P., Soubrié, P., and Widlocher, D. (eds) (1988) *Selected Models of Anxiety, Depression and Psychosis*, Animal Models of Psychiatric Disorders, no. 1, Basel and New York: Karger.

Strachey, J. (ed.) (1953–) *The Standard Edition of the Complete Psychological Works of Sigmund Freud*, trans. from the German under the general editorship of James Strachey, in collaboration with Anna Freud, assisted by Alix Strachey and Alan Tyson, 24 vols, London: Hogarth Press.

Taylor, C. (1989) *Sources of the Self: The Making of the Modern Identity*, Cambridge, MA: Harvard University Press.

Taylor, J. (1660) *Ductor Dubitantium, or the Rule of Conscience in All Her General Measures, Serving as a Great Instrument for the Determination of Cases of Conscience. In Four Books*, 2 vols, London: printed by J. Flesher, for R. Royston.

Tinbergen, N. (1949) *Social Behavior in Animals*, London: Methuen.

—— (1952) "Derived activities: causation, biological significance, origin and emancipation during evolution," *Quarterly Review of Biology* 27: 1–32.

—— (1974) "Ethology and stress diseases," *Science* 185(145): 20–27.

Turbott, J. (1997) "The meaning and function of ritual in psychiatric disorder, religion and everyday behaviour," *Australian and New Zealand Journal of Psychiatry* 31(6): 835–43.

Videbech, T. (1975) "The psychopathology of anancastic endogenous depression," *Acta Psychiatrica Scandinavica* 52(5): 336–73.

Viller, M., Cavallera, F., and de Guibert, J. (eds) (1937–) *Dictionnaire de spiritualité ascetique et mystique, doctrine et histoire*, publié sous la direction de Marcel Viller, S.J., assisté de F. Cavallera et J. de Guibert, S.J., avec le concours d'un grand nombre de collaborateurs, 17 vols, Paris: G. Beauchesne et ses fils.

Wegner, D.M. (1989) *White Bears and Other Unwanted Thoughts: Suppression, Obsession and the Psychology of Mental Control*, New York: Viking.

Weyer, J. (of Brabant) (1564) *De praestigiis daemonum, et incantationibus ac veneficiis*, Basileae: per Ioannem Oporinum. Modern edn and Eng. trans. *Witches, Devils, and Doctors in the Renaissance*, trans. John Shea, foreword by John Weber, collaborators Erik Midelfort and Helen Bacon, Binghamton, NY: Medieval and Renaissance Texts and Studies (1991).

Wiepkema, P. (1985) "Abnormal behaviours in farm animals: ethological implications," *Netherlands Journal of Zoology* 35: 279–99.

Winslow, J.T. and Insel, T.R. (1991) "Neuroethological models of obsessive-compulsive disorder," in J. Zohar, T.R. Insel and S.A. Rasmussen (eds), *The Psychobiology of Obsessive-Compulsive Disorder*, New York: Springer, pp. 208–26.

Wolpe, J. (1958) *Psychotherapy by Reciprocal Inhibition*, Stanford: Stanford University Press.

Yaryura-Tobias, J.A. and Neziroglu, F.A. (1997) *Obsessive-Compulsive Disorder Spectrum: Pathogenesis, Diagnosis, and Treatment*, Washington, DC and London: American Psychiatric Press.

Section 2

Comparative studies

Psychological perspectives on
non-Western religions

13 Themes and debates in the psychology–comparativist dialogue

William B. Parsons

In the last few decades the dialogue between psychology and comparative studies has become an increasingly influential and popular enterprise. A few cursory cultural observations indicate why this might be so: the steady influx into the West of Eastern holy men and women, increasing access by scholars and laypersons to other cultures and their sacred traditions, the seeming "scientific" character of certain Eastern practices, holistic conceptions of health, the proliferation of meditational systems, and the status of various kinds of psychology as preferred modern and Western forms for promoting spirituality. Of course such a cultural topography hardly grew overnight and the generative forces behind the latter observations and related others are multiple and complex, extending well back to the beginning of the twentieth century. The history of the interaction between psychology and comparative studies is a long one with many thematic twists and methodological turns.

In the following I seek to trace the historical contours of what has become a discernible category within the broad field of religion and psychological studies: the *psychology–comparativist dialogue*. Since the latter designation, unlike the *psychology–theology dialogue* which ruled the field in the 1950s and 1960s, has only recently been formally dubbed and instantiated (see Parsons 1997, 1999), a major goal of this essay (and this section as a whole) is to provide further data for its circumscription. In order to facilitate my analysis, I divide the history of the dialogue into three stages: 1880–1944; 1944–70; 1970–2000.[1] My approach will be historical and descriptive, with an aim to show where the major thrust of the psychology–comparativist dialogue "has been" and where it appears "to be going."

I should note, however, that I do not aim at a detailed, comprehensive survey. One simply cannot do justice to the sheer number of theorists and diversity of analyses in the space of a single essay. Given this, certain limits and qualifications must apply. Commensurate with the aims of this book, and in the hopes for more comprehensive studies in the future, I offer a survey sufficient to establish a general framework for the more detailed essays in this section. In the main, I shall concentrate for the most part on Buddhism and Hinduism as treated by the founders of depth-psychology (Freud, Jung), their heirs, and the psychologies which, in a loose sense, are part of the humanistic tradition (i.e., William James and his legacy, Maslow's humanistic/transpersonal psychology and experimental studies). I rest content, then, with noting the links between a few major figures, their models of the mind and associated central issues and debates, providing as much socio-historical context as space allows. To prefigure the analysis to come, the historical drift among these theorists is from a general dearth of dialogue, orientalism and reductionism (1880–1944), to collaboration and the recognition of differences (1944–70), to the consolidation of two opposite modes of engagement (1970–2000): a leveling, Western repackaging of Eastern spirituality and a culturally sensitive, multi-disciplinary dialogue which accentuates real differences. At the end of my survey I shall return to the question of the place and role of the psychology–comparativist dialogue with regard to the future of religion and psychological studies.

1880–1944: initial forays

By the time the psychology of religion had established itself as a discipline in the late nineteenth century, interest in Eastern religions in both Europe and the United States had begun to percolate. Before 1840 the engagement with the East had been sporadic and confined to missionary activity, business enterprises, travel and trade. However, starting in 1840 a new, more profound series of exchanges took place which impacted the socio-cultural and intellectual atmosphere in dramatic and irreversible ways. Part of this was due to a new social base of immigrants who carried with them Eastern forms of worship. To wit: by the end of the century approximately one million Asians had emigrated to the United States. Places of worship were established for various forms of Buddhist, Hindu, Sikh, Confucian and Taoist beliefs. Moreover, crowned by the World's Parliament of Religions in 1893, Eastern holy men like Swami Vivekananda, Anagarika Dharmapala, Soyen Saku and Yogananda made their way westward. Their efforts secured societies and institutions for the proliferation of Vedanta, Yoga, Zen and an assortment of Eastern meditative techniques.

At the same time, on a purely academic level, one finds the establishment of chairs in oriental studies and comparative religion at prestigious universities: Ivy League schools, the University of Chicago and major institutions in Europe. A new generation of scholars (Hermann Oldenberg, Max Müller, Paul Deussen, de la Valleé Poussin, Sylvian Levi, Rhys Davids, etc.) and accessible translations (notably Müller's *Sacred Books of the East* [1875]) helped disseminate the details of Eastern traditions among the intellectual elite. Many of these scholars (e.g., Caroline Rhys Davids, Friedrich Heiler), socially significant lay sympathizers (e.g., Paul Carus, Edwin Arnold) and the above named Eastern adepts were quick to frame Hindu and Buddhist modes of introspection as commensurate with psychology and the scientific enterprise (see Tweed 1992: 104; Clarke 1997: 152). With complicity from poets, philosophers and various cultural institutions and figures (e.g., Nietzsche, Schopenhauer, Emerson and "The Dial," Henry Steel Olcott, Madame Blavatsky and the Theosophists) the cause was extended beyond intellectuals and disseminated to the common man and society at large.[2]

Given this socio-cultural atmosphere, it is easy to understand why the leading psychologists of religion of this era were careful to include Eastern traditions in their survey of religious thought and practice. However, as we shall see, the attempt at a bona fide dialogue remained problematic on a number of levels. Only a few studies had any lasting impact on the nature and direction of the relation between psychology and comparativist studies. Moreover, the psychological studies of this period are diverse, issuing from both North America and Europe and from the pens of many researchers now rarely studied. Given this, the organization of the figures and studies of this period are best centered around its three most recognizable and historically significant psychologists: William James, Sigmund Freud, and Carl Jung.

Concerning the central North American researchers of this period, namely, the Harvard-based James, his colleague G. Stanley Hall (at Clark University), their students (and here I include James Leuba and James Pratt) and the Canadian psychologist R.M. Bucke, one finds a general dearth of sustained, insightful work in the psychology–comparative dialogue. A perusal of the works of Hall (and other researchers of this time like Edwin Starbuck and George Coe), all concerned in the main with Protestant Christianity, reveal only nominal references to Eastern religions. Leuba, in his classic *Psychology of Religious Mysticism*, devotes a chapter to Patanjali's Yoga (Leuba 1926: 37–48). The treatment, however, is cursory and reductive. Leuba was heavily influenced by the French psycho-physiologist Pierre Janet and adduced Patanjali only to buttress his view that all mysticism, while potentially socially adaptive and capable of contributing to the nurturance of strong ethical ideals, could be explained solely with respect to psycho-physiological hypotheses. However, despite the fact that Leuba's researches have been largely eschewed by modern participants in the dialogue, the issue his interpretations paradigmatically represent, namely, the matter of reductionism, is one that lingers throughout all phases of the psychology–comparativist dialogue.

William James is another matter. His classic study *The Varieties of Religious Experience* incorporates Eastern mystical literature to complete one of his stated tasks, description. The treatment centered on the Buddhist stages of dhyana (meditative absorption) and Vivekananda's commentary on yogic states of realization. James adduced such descriptions to further his other two aims of providing *existential* judgments (the subconscious dynamic) and *spiritual* judgments (the pragmatic value) of religious experience (James 1936). Like Leuba, the attempt at description was cursory, even prejudicial. Certainly James was more sympathetic to the religious perspective than Leuba had been. But James's use of Western categories and preference for a

,pirituality that championed the individual and immediate experience over tradition and its accouterments tended to give *The Varieties* a Protestant bias. As the historian of religion Erwin Goodenough has noted, no Eastern adept "would have used [James's Protestant categories to outline] the subject or would feel much personal relevancy in James's brilliant description" (Wulff 1997: 499).[3]

James's work can be framed as an instance of "orientalism." Admittedly, since the pioneering work of Edward Said, the term has become somewhat problematic. In brief, Said used the term to refer to ways in which the Western imagination has utilized its own categories, narratives, and stereotypes to envision and revision the East for the purpose of domination and the maintenance of cultural and racial hegemony (Said 1979). More recently it has become linked to issues in current intellectual debates: postmodern thought, postcolonialism, multiculturalism, discourse theory.[4] James can be accused of a milder form of orientalism insofar as he distorted Eastern religious texts by revisioning them along Protestant lines. Indeed, one could say that some form of "orientalism" marks all studies of this period. To take another example, James's student James Bisset Pratt's books on the psychology of religion and the history of religions (*The Pilgrimage of Buddhism and a Buddhist Pilgrimage* (1928); *India and its Faith* (1915)) have been evaluated as instrumental in heightening awareness of Eastern religions in the West (Wulff 1997: 506). But while Pratt often engaged Eastern religions with sensitivity and empathy, his analysis, as is evinced in his treatment of the nature of Indian goddesses (e.g., Kali), also displayed orientalist tendencies. As Jeffrey Kripal notes, Pratt's analysis neglects left-handed tantra and he utilizes Christian categories to legitimate the Sakta tradition: "Ramakrishna's Kali becomes the Christian mystic's Madonna, and the left-handed practices of the Tantrikas are said to parallel the 'Christs' sect of Russian Orthodoxy" (Kripal 2000).[5]

Another associate of James, the Canadian psychiatrist Richard Maurice Bucke, spoke at length of Eastern religions. His notion of "cosmic consciousness," his descriptions of his own experiences of the same and attempt to establish a perennialism through a textual analysis of religious and unchurched mysticism have remained a part of the literature on the comparative study of mysticism to this day. Bucke's grand vision consisted of articulating the psychological and "scientific" nature of an evolutionary process he saw reaching its denouement in a utopian future: the establishment of unchurched, mystical humankind in a socialist state (Bucke 1993). Unfortunately Bucke's attempts at framing his evolutionist views through a rudimentary form of cognitive psychology were vehemently rejected even in his own day. Moreover, his simple form of perennialism proceeded without any awareness, much less justification, of the philosophical and hermeneutical problems it involved. Rather, Bucke's perennialism was completely rooted in his own personal experience. His presentation of the two Eastern mystics he thought had experiences of cosmic consciousness (Buddha and Sri

Ramakrishna) failed to take into account the complexities of their respective mystical traditions, suffering as it did from a reliance on now outdated translations and misleading secondary literature (principally the writings by Rhys Davids and Max Müller). Indeed, like the issues of reductionism and orientalism, one can unequivocally state that problems stemming from misleading translations and incomplete, biased scholarship can be found to some degree in all studies of this era.[6]

Turning to the Continent, the most historically significant studies from this period issue from the camp of the depth-psychologists Sigmund Freud and Carl Jung. As one might expect, psychoanalytic researchers interpreted the ideation and practices of Eastern religions in terms of various phases of the developmental cycle. The Chicago psychoanalyst Franz Alexander's study of Buddhist meditation is a paradigmatic example of psychoanalytic pathologizing. Focusing his analysis on the stages of meditation, Alexander describes a regressive movement which ignites stages of pathology (from depression to catatonia), culminating in the nirvanic return to intrauterine existence (Alexander 1931). This analysis was essentially that advocated by Morel in his *Essai sur l'introversion mystique* (1918). The Norwegian brothers Kristian and Harald Schjelderups, trained by the Protestant lay-analyst Oskar Pfister, advocated a variation of this theme, seeing in Ramakrishna a submissive "mother religion" and in Zen and Yoga a "self-religion" explained by a still deeper regression to infantile grandiosity (Wulff 1997: 321, 351). A more adaptive and positive view can be found in Joe Tom Sun's (pseudonym for the Chicago psychoanalyst Joseph Thompson) small essay "Psychology in Primitive Buddhism" (Sun 1924/1998). In marked contrast to Alexander, Sun's essay frames the insights of the Buddha on the nature of desire and suffering and his prescriptions for their cure as virtually equivalent to that of psychoanalysis. Sun's essay is significant for it prefigures a trend followed by the Neo-Freudians in their encounter with Eastern religions, namely, the reading of Buddhism as but a culturally variant healing enterprise commensurate with the aims and ideals of psychoanalysis (see below). It is important to note, however, that no awareness of what Edward Conze observed, namely, that Buddhism and psychoanalysis "differ profoundly in their theoretical assumptions about the structure of the mind and the purpose of human existence, and in the methods which they prescribe for the attainment of mental health," had yet reached the shores of psychoanalytic discourse (Conze 1969: 38). The attempt by psychoanalysts to conceptually manage Buddhist practices as harboring equal, different, even incompatible aims from that of psycho-analysis would not emerge until the third period (see below).

While not the first psychoanalytic study, Freud's debate with the French mystic, novelist and social critic Romain Rolland over the nature and origin of the "oceanic feeling" has become the *locus classicus* of psychoanalytic researches into mysticism and Eastern religions. Unlike the studies by Sun and Alexander, Freud's dialogue centered around Hinduism. Freud sponded to Rolland, his biographies of Ramakrishna and Vivekananda, his championing of Hindu practices (Yoga) and central tenets of the Indian worldview (e.g., Maya) as well as its primary texts (the *Bhagavad Gita* and *The Upanishads*) through a series of brief and often uneasy interpretations. Freud stressed not only the well-known "classic" (reductive/pathological) psychoanalytic understanding of mysticism (the oceanic feeling as the preservation of primary narcissism; Maya as religious rationalization of feelings of derealization) but, at times, the socially "adaptive" and therapeutic as well (mystical practices and "intuition" as a means of insight into the unconscious). Rolland countered with what can be called a "transformational" reading. Rolland asked Freud to grant his imprimatur to a "mystical psychoanalysis," which he framed as faced with the challenge of developing a theoretical basis for legitimating the transcendent claims of the mystics (see Parsons 1999).

Both Freud and Rolland's forays into the East were flawed. Neither man was equipped for serious comparativist discourse and both were orientalists: Freud's tendency was to denigrate the East; Rolland idealized and romanticized it. Moreover, the matter of the relation between conflicts (e.g., Oedipus) and "developmental lines," conceived of by many psychoanalysts as invariant and universal, and the formative power of culture, so important for anthropologists and the contemporary dialogue between psychoanalysis and comparative studies, was left dormant. Only in Freud's correspondence with the Indian psychoanalyst Girindrasekhar Bose was the latter issue explicitly entertained, albeit briefly and, by contemporary standards, in a thoroughly unsatisfactory manner (see Vaidyanathan and Kripal 1999). On the other hand, what has been conceptualized as the three models (classic, adaptive, transformational) discussed by Freud and Rolland, have proven to be central to psychoanalytic forays into the comparative study of religion and mysticism, finding expression not only in the studies of Freud's era (e.g., the "classic" and "adaptive" studies by Alexander, Sun, Morel and the Schjelderups cited above) but, as we shall see, for subsequent psychoanalytic studies up through the present (see Parsons 1999). These facts alone merit evaluating Freud's seemingly minor flirtation with comparative studies as a significant chapter in the psychology–comparativist dialogue.

Despite the plethora of studies stemming from psychoanalysis, the more determinative psychologist for the establishment of the psychology–comparativist dialogue, at least *during* this period, was Carl Jung. From his introduction to the Hindu Gods in childhood (through readings in the *Orbis Pictus*), his exposure during his teenage years to Schopenhauer and inclusion of Eastern religions in his early works (e.g., *Symbols of Transformation*) to his later collaboration with Richard Wilhelm, Heinrich Zimmer and D.T. Suzuki, subsequent writings on Taoism, Hinduism, Buddhism, his visit to India/Ceylon, and establishment of the Eranos conferences, Jung's encounter with Eastern religions and culture was impressively wide-ranging. As R.C.

Zaehner notes, Jung "has done more to interpret Eastern religion to the West than any other man" (Wulff 1997: 469).

Jung's interpretative forays into Eastern religions were less than systematic, being comprised of a series of introductions to various translations (Wilhelm, Evans-Wentz, Suzuki and others), various short essays and conversations with adepts like Shin'ichi Hisamatsu (see below). Jung found in the ideation and practices of Eastern religions but instances of the tenets grounding his archetypical psychology. Thus Taoist thought as found in the *I Ching* and *The Secret of the Golden Flower* enabled Jung to elaborate on his notion of synchronicity, his theory of the opposites and the notion of the psyche as a self-balancing system. Yoga becomes a therapeutic system (the task of introversion and attempt at liberation from the bondage of opposites), the concept of Atman-Brahman corresponding to the Jungian understanding of the Self. Tantra, interpreted symbolically, denotes various phases of individuation. Similarly, the journey into the Bardo as depicted in *The Tibetan Book of the Dead* is a symbolic one revealing the encounter with the unconscious and its archetypical contents. Again, the Zen Koan is but a dramatic way to break into the contents of the collective unconscious while mandalas become archetypical expressions of the self and markers of wholeness.[7] Jung found such archetypical expressions, because they were universal, in his Western patients, as well as in his own self-analysis, most notably in his childhood dream of the subterranean phallus (later interpreted as the same archetypical force behind that of the Hindu symbol of the lingam) and in the later emergence in his life of mandala symbolism (see Jung 1963).

Jung's forays have been found to be problematic on several levels. Most obviously, he was a reductionist. Jung was clearly not an expert in comparative thought, lacked knowledge of relevant primary languages, and much of what he says reflects not primary text or practice but an unnuanced application of archetypical theory. Perhaps as good an example of this as any is Jung's inability to address two central and interrelated issues found most clearly in Vedanta and Buddhism: the notion of a formless self and the possibility of complete freedom from suffering. Jung could not logically conceive of a self without an object ("pure consciousness") nor could he easily admit that freedom from all suffering was a fact capable of realization (see Clarke 1994; Coward 1985; Meckel and Moore 1992). Jung has further been accused of a selective and misleading reading of Eastern texts and as distorting the cakra system and kundalini Yoga (Coward 1985; Bishop 1984/1992); as unaware of the diversity of meditational practices (Bishop 1984/1992); as relying on a misleading understanding of Vedanta; as working with bad translations; as essentially "orientalist" (see Clarke 1994).[8]

At the same time, it should be noted that Jung is still a major force in the psychology–comparativist dialogue. Jung has influenced generations of comparativists (e.g., R.C. Zaehner, Rudolph Otto, Mircea Eliade, D.T. Suzuki, Wendy Doniger, Luis Gómez, Joseph Campbell, etc.) and his holistic manner of viewing the psyche has direct continuities with humanistic and transpersonal psychologies, both of which are indebted to Eastern modes of thought (Clarke 1994: 183ff.). Further, many have come to defend Jung and Jungian approaches. For example, in pointing out the role Jung played in helping to initiate historical advancements in the encounter with Asian traditions, Luis Gómez argues that in appropriating Yoga Jung turned it into an adjunct of his own analytic theory. But paradoxically, in so doing, he empowered Yoga in the West by giving it psychological prestige (Gómez 1995). J.J. Clarke notes that Jung prefigured later comparativist trends by framing Buddhism as a method of self-healing and individuation – a interpretation that went against the grain of the prevalent view of his time that read Buddhism as essentially nilihistic. Clarke goes on to note that while Jung's forays into Taoism, Buddhism and Hinduism are flawed, he should be applauded for engaging in an unusual and courageous dialogical mode of discourse. In the Europe of his day there was an intellectual atmosphere of scientism and positivism which was allied with an aggressive Eurocentrism. But Jung did not accord Western culture superiority in the dialogue, nor was his project that of a syncretist or universalist in the manner of a Radhikrishnan. Rather, he accorded to the East an equal and complementary status. Jung was a "pluralist" (in that he recognized the validity of multiple religious perspectives) and, to a point, a cultural relativist (because he refused to say Europe was superior and that Christianity was the only true and valid perspective) (see Clarke 1994: 143–92).

Looking back over this period, then, one can say that given the state of comparative studies and the attendant cultural surround at the beginning of the century, the initial encounter between psychology and comparative studies reveals about what one would expect. The relationship was marred by mediocre translations, misleading and incomplete secondary scholarship, reductionism and orientalism. Indeed, in light of the rudimentary state of comparativist studies and virtual absence of any extended, bona fide debate with Eastern adepts, it is questionable whether one can speak of a "dialogue" at all. Certainly the conversation was a one-way street, with psychological models of various sorts, all framed as empirical, scientific (and thus unable to reflect on the ways their models embodied Western values, assumptions and prescriptions) ruling the day. The implications of such colonialist and orientalist interpretative forays seemed lost on the few Eastern adepts that did shop their wares westwards. On the contrary, they were all too happy to further their missionary aspirations by framing Eastern religious convictions and practices as commensurate with the scientific enterprise. Yet despite this irony, a foothold was established – one that would lead to a progressive series of exchanges in the years ahead.

1944–70: expansion and collaboration

The atmosphere surrounding the Second World War did not bode well for progress in the psychology–comparativist dialogue. As Tweed and Prothero point out, this was a time of quiescence and exclusion for Asian religions. Indeed, Asian religions in general were seen with suspicion if not contempt. In the United States the Asian Exclusion Act of 1924 (which was not fully rescinded until 1965) had already reduced immigration from Asian countries to a trickle. Chinese, Japanese and Indian populations leveled off or fell and interest in Buddhism and Hinduism declined (see Tweed and Prothero 1999: 159ff.). However, after the war was over a new era of revitalization began, spearheaded by a new wave of Asian immigration (particularly during the 1960s) and the rise of significant cultural movements. The latter was instigated in particular by the Beat and Hippie generations, who engaged in existential experiments signaling the creation of new social forms and values: the turn to altered states, neo-transcendentalism and the promotion of spontaneity, inwardness, immediate, ecstatic "experience" and liminal modes of being. This fresh air enhanced the cultural appeal of a new cadre of Eastern gurus and teachers. Eastern adepts like D.T. Suzuki (Rinzai) and Shunryu Suzuki Roshi (Soto) gathered around them notable groups of Western followers (e.g., Allen Ginsberg, Jack Kerouac, Gary Snyder, Alan Watts, Richard Baker, Timothy Leary, Aldous Huxley). The latter, in turn, helped establish a series of centers and retreats (e.g., the San Francisco Zen Center; Esalen). And while Zen was clearly the Asian tradition of choice, the Western imagination was similarly captured by other figures championing introspective techniques (e.g., Swami Akhilananda, Sri Aurobindo Ghose, Maharishi Mahesh Yogi [and the establishment of Transcendental Meditation], A.C. Bhakytivedanta Swami Prabhupada [and the founding of Hare Krishna]) as well as those Asian religious figures who exploded on to the international socio-political scene (Gandhi, the Dalai Lama). Faced with increasing pluralism and the cultural appeal of a plethora of Asian intellectuals many of the most highly esteemed Western-based comparativists and theologians (e.g., Paul Tillich, Mircea Eliade, R.C. Zaehner) began a new round of scholarly engagement with the East. In all this one finds a strenuous effort to create a common ground (exemplified in the popularity of concepts like "ultimate concern," "the primordial," "the perennial philosophy," etc.) upon which religions could meet and dialogue.[9] Certainly this was the case with respect to the major developments in the psychology–comparativist dialogue, where one can well say that the defining characteristic was that of collaboration. And, as one might expect with collaborative enterprises populated by such diverse participants, there was an undeniable tension, for alongside the search for common ground and the desire to minimize differences lay the equally powerful reality of real, perhaps unbridgeable differences.

The dominant trends in depth-psychological engagements with the East are illustrative of this tension. For example, soon after the death of its founder, classical psychoanalysis came to be reformulated by a new generation of theorists (e.g., Melanie Klein, Anna Freud, Heinz Hartmann, Erik Erikson). Pre-Oedipal and Kleinian theories were manifest in the significant studies on Hinduism of this era by G.M. Carstairs (Carstairs 1957) and Philip Spratt (Spratt 1966) who argued, among other things, for the preponderance of the mother in Hindu tenets and myths and in the Indian developmental schema. But it was the formulation of the central concepts of ego psychology (alloplastic adaptation, regression in service of ego, epigenesis) which led to the most far-reaching ways of legitimating the deeper recesses of religious subjectivity. Displacing the more pejorative psychoanalytic studies of the previous era (e.g., Freud's *The Future of an Illusion*), studies of this "adaptive" school of psychoanalysis made their presence felt, as is so paradigmatically illustrated in the most highly touted psychoanalytic study of its time, Erikson's *Young Man Luther*.

Commensurate with the cultural appeal of Zen, this new development was most pronounced with respect to psychoanalytic interpretations of Buddhism. An extended dialogue between the Neo-Freudians, representatives of Eastern traditions and hybrid psychologies like Morita therapy (promoted by influential Japanese theorists like Akahisa Kondo and Takeo Doi) took place.[10] In many ways Karen Horney exemplified this trend. One finds in works like *Our Inner Conflicts* and *Final Lectures*, most notably in Horney's concept of "wholeheartedness" (a psychological state described as being fully present, wholly absorbed, wholly attentive and thus wholly absent [i.e., operating with all of one's faculties yet entirely oblivious of oneself] in any engaged action) a noble attempt to integrate psychoanalysis with Zen and Morita therapy.

Herbert Fingarette's *The Self in Transformation* adopted a similar approach. Fingarette utilized ego psychology and a series of clinical vignettes to argue that the terminology of Zen (selflessness, emptiness) was not, as many had assumed, indicative of pessimism and escapism but rather a culturally specific use of therapeutic terms which, when properly translated, had analogs in the psychoanalytic tradition. Thus the nature of the self "lost" through Zen was really the "transference self." In its stead was built a cohesive self that integrated infantile residue and promoted freedom and individuality (see Fingarette 1965).

But most paradigmatic in this respect is the collaboration between Erich Fromm, D.T. Suzuki and Richard De Martino in the classic *Zen Buddhism and Psychoanalysis*, a work which, as Anthony Molino has noted, "superseded, in impact and importance" all other psychoanalytic forays into the East of this era (Molino 1998: vii). Like Horney, Fromm met Suzuki in the 1950s and developed an interest in Zen. And like Jung, Fromm saw man as going through a spiritual crisis which could be alleviated by the dialogue between psychoanalysis and Buddhism. Fromm observed that while the methods of Zen and psychoanalysis differed, their healing aims could be made to tally if one reformulated Freud's psychoanalytic motto ("where Id was there Ego shall be") around a humanistic framework. Freud's motto indicated that he wanted to make only a localized aspect of the unconscious conscious – that dealing with childhood trauma, the instinctual life and symptom formation. However, if one enlarged that purview to include the *full* recovery of the unconscious, one would achieve a psychological aim broadly commensurate with Zen, Suzuki's notion of the "art of living" and the ethical aims of the spiritual, humanistic orientation which grounded it (see Fromm 1960). At the same time, Fromm could not bring himself to address the radical claims of formlessness, as is evident in his interpretation of satori as

> a repetition of the preintellectual, immediate grasp of the child, but on a new level, that of the full development of man's reason, objectivity, individuality. While the child's experience, that of immediacy and one-ness, lies before the experience of alienation and the subject-object split, the enlightenment experience lies after it.
>
> (Molino 1998: 65)

Finally, Fromm was adamant that just as Zen could help psychoanalysis extend its therapeutic reach, so too could psychoanalysis help the Zen master and his student by offering a more sophisticated and precise map of pathology. Such a map could be used to distinguish between true enlighten-ment and a "false" one based on psychotic or hysterical phenomena or on self-induced, illusory states of trance.

Jung's influence during this period also continued to gain ground. In this regard one cannot overestimate the significance of his collaborations with comparativists, the establishment of the Eranos conferences, and the contributions of the seminal Jungian researcher Erich Neumann (Neumann 1955). In particular, one can point to the continued use of Jung in the works of the preeminent comparativist of his time, Mircea Eliade, and in Joseph Campbell's enormously popular attempt to create a form of Jungian psychology for use in the comparative study of mythology (see Eliade 1960; Campbell 1962).

For our purposes, however, it is Jung's dialogue with the Zen philosopher Shin'ichi Hisamatsu that affords the closest parallel to the above cited developments in psychoanalysis. It took place in Jung's home on 16 May 1958, just two years before his death. Unfortunately, no tape recording of the conversation exists, only shorthand notes by Aniela Jaffé (Jung's secretary), which were later translated into Japanese and English. In the published account of this conversation the transcript of notes was followed by a brief commentary by Hisamatsu, a discussion by several scholars (Koji Sato, Hitoshi Kataoka, Richard De Martino, Masao Abe, Hayao Kawai), and then a much later reflection by Abe (see Meckel and Moore 1992: 101ff.; Molino 1998: 37ff.). The salient points in the discussion and subsequent reflections are as follows. First, one gets the impression that Jung was uneasy, being drilled by Hisamatsu on the two aspects of his theory that Zen disputes: the impossibility of the existence of an utterly formless self, and the inability to be totally liberated from suffering. Jung's uneasiness seems confirmed by an unusual self-contradiction in which he first states that total liberation from suffering is not possible or desirable (the standard Jungian line) and then, under probing from Hisamatsu, reverses himself. Subsequently, Jung refused to grant permission for the conversation to be published on the grounds that cultural differences and language barriers prohibited a fair and equal exchange of ideas (a refusal Muramoto links to Jung's wish to hide the fact that he had contradicted himself [see Molino 1998: 48]).

For his part, Hisamatsu insisted that the experience of the formless self eradicated suffering once and for all. He saw his conversation with Jung as revealing three essential points: (1) the concept of the "unconscious" in Jung is entirely different from that of "no-mind" in Zen; (2) the "true self" of Zen is not the same as and not adequately captured by Jung's metapsychological concept of the Self; and that (3) insofar as Jung seemed to indicate that freedom from the vicissitudes of the collective unconscious (and hence freedom from suffering) is theoretically possible, that a real bridge between Jungian psychology and Zen could be built. At the same time Hisamatsu observed, as we noted above, that Jung contradicted himself with regard to this point for he had, early on in the conversation, stressed that suffering could not be eliminated, nor should it be (see Meckel and Moore 1992: 116ff.). The subsequent dialogue between Sato, Kataoka, De Martino, Abe and Kawai on the Jung–Hisamatsu conversation confirmed that these three points were the defining ones of the dialogue. Abe's later essay reiterated this but added, and here he echoed Fromm, that psychology could help Zen insofar as the latter "tends on the whole to neglect psychological problems that occur sometimes in the process of Zen practice, in particular the delusory apparitions known as makyo" (Meckel and Moore 1992: 139). In other words, another way in which Western psychology differed from Zen was the advances it had made with respect to mapping the realm of the pathological.

The above documents the first extended dialogue between originative psychologists and honored representatives of Eastern religious traditions. Their search for common ground led to shifts in positions from both camps. With respect to psychoanalysis, exposure to Suzuki and Zen helped the Neo-Freudians enlarge their conceptions of health and forms of subjectivity, thus expanding the "adaptive" metapsychological purview of psychoanalysis. Similarly, while Jung, like Fromm, could not allow himself to grant legitimacy to claims of formlessness, he seems to depart from his stated convictions when he states that freedom from the collective unconscious is possible. In response, Zen was seen as benefiting from its exposure to psychology. As both Fromm and Abe note, psychology can help the Zen master (and student) become more aware of the role played by the unconscious in the journey inwards.

At the same time, one sees an awareness among the above participants that despite common ground and a bona fide attempt to engage in dialogue, depth-psychology and Zen also mapped radically different realms of subjectivity. Moreover, if in an unsophisticated and undeveloped way, the question of the impact of culture on the different healing enterprises and the problems it could pose for any true dialogue was broached.[11] The latter observations, then, illustrate the tension of which we spoke earlier. The search for common ground and dialogue gave rise to the dawning realization that substantial differences between Eastern and Western healing enterprises remained.

Another, later trend of this era dealt with this tension in a different way. This trend is characterized by the attempt to level differences altogether and is best evinced by the human potential movement and its utilization of experimental studies to harness the wisdom of Eastern meditative practices.

To elaborate: the decade of the 1960s saw the growing popularity of experimental studies of meditation. As ably catalogued by Murphy (1993), Murphy and Donovan (1997) and Wulff (1997), the latter concentrated mainly on Zen and Yoga in an attempt to ascertain whether such disciplines had discernible physiological effects (respiration, heart rate, blood pressure, skin resistance, cerebral activity, etc.) or could effect personality changes (concerning levels of anxiety, depression, neurosis, self-esteem). Such studies stemmed from the researches in the 1930s by Koovor Behanan, a Yale graduate student invested in studying Yoga, who conducted researches on himself (he found increased oxygen consumption, endurance and emotional stability) and later, guided by Swami Kuvalayananda, an adept who had established a center outside Bombay which became central to experimental studies of Yoga up through the 1960s, several Indian gurus as well (see Behanan 1937). His researches were furthered by Therese Brosse, who concluded that yogis had voluntary control over autonomous physiological functions (Brosse 1946), important studies in the 1950s by Bagchi and Wenger, who measured respiration, skin temperature, breathing and EEG rates (Bagchi and Wenger 1957), and several studies of Yoga and Zen analyzing the relation of alpha and beta waves during meditation. The latter are important, for they suggested that Zen leads to heightened awareness of the outer world during meditation while Yoga leads to inner absorption and exclusion of the outer world – differences which dovetail with the aims of their respective techniques (see Das and Gastaut 1957; Anand *et al.* 1961; Kasamatsu and Hirai 1966).[12] Their results were added to by the work of Arthur Deikman, who postulated that the major mechanism triggered by meditation was deautomatization. Deautomatization reversed the habitual "automatisms" of physiological and mental processing and led to those typical characteristics found in meditative states: unity, noesis, intense realness, sensory translation and ineffability (Deikman 1966/1980).

These studies were utilized by figures and psychologies belonging to the human potential movement in the United States during the 1950s and 1960s. This movement, which incorporated leading psychologists (e.g., Abraham Maslow, Fritz Perls, Carl Rodgers, Rollo May, Gordon Allport) and created new forms of healing techniques and institutions, was born in the context of significant cultural changes: those that attacked reigning forms of Christian heteronomy, impacted traditional conceptions of government, politics, work, gender, equality, race, and sexual relations, saw the rise of neo-transcendentalism and social experiments, gave impetus to studies by Timothy Leary, Stanislav Grof, and Walter Pahnke on altered states and mind-expanding drugs (LSD, psyilocybin, mescalin) and led to a gravitation towards "Eastern" values like receptivity, spontaneity, non-interference, nowness, and the promotion of personal experience. Developments in humanistic psychology, evinced in the psychologies of Allport and Maslow, continued to stress empirical scientific research and a view of religion as an enabler of social adaptation and container for issues concerning self-actualization. In this sense it is correct to see the approaches and sympathies of humanistic psychology in historical continuity with the earlier researches of James, Jung and Bucke.

Of the above, the contributions of the founder of humanistic psychology, Abraham Maslow, was the most pivotal. Over against classical psychoanalysis and behaviorism, Maslow spoke about the possibility of freedom from childhood determinism, the advocacy of conscious choice, and the development of higher states of consciousness. Over and above basic physiological (food, water, sleep), safety (protection, security, order), belongingness (home, family, friends), and self-esteem needs, Maslow pointed to needs for self-actualization. Actualized people (and here Maslow included D.T. Suzuki) were on their way to having a greater acceptance of reality, deeper relationships, philosophical humor, moral elevation, "B-cognition and B-values" (wholeness, justice, beauty, simplicity, etc.), and "peak-experiences." The latter, a designation for experiences of joy, completeness and unity, became crucial for Maslow's engagement with religion. Distinguishing between the "legalists" (the curators of a bureaucratic understanding of religion) and the "mystics" (who grasped its liminal essence), Maslow declared that mystical experiences, including Eastern notions like nirvana (now understood as instances of peak-experiences), were the common core uniting all religions. Such states, which had been previously phrased in churched discourse, were in fact of a naturalistic order and could be examined by a new understanding of "science" as being ruled by a wider, humanistic paradigm. This conception of human beings as "peakers" became the foundation of a new mode of social relations and planning Maslow termed "Eupsychian." Maslow thus advocated a naturalistic, unchurched religion which was commensurate with the scientific enterprise and around which a new social whole integrating the East and the West could be built (see Maslow 1964; 1971).

Maslow's widespread popularity, the advocacy of experimental studies and the focus on a perennialism based on self-actualization and peak-experiences had a dramatic impact on the psychology–comparativist dialogue. By divorcing meditational techniques from their worldviews and then leveling differences through the "scientific" notion of an unchurched perennialism based on peak-experiences, Maslow and the human potential movement lent an aura of legitimacy to self-actualization and its accouterments in Western culture. It popularized Eastern techniques, making them widely accessible and user-friendly for the Western consumer. Further help along these lines was to come, notably in the form of Maharishi Mahesh Yogi's packaging of transcendental meditation as a "science" of creative intelligence, the plethora of experimental studies it gave rise to, and the mutation of humanistic psychology into transpersonal psychology.

1970–2000: the leveling of differences and the flowering of dialogue

Certain socio-cultural and intellectual developments have fueled the shape of the contemporary period. A major factor has been the emergence of a new cadre of participants who were socialized into the plethora of alternate, legitimate religious worldviews offered by the emerging pluralistic society of the 1960s. In adhering to Eastern religions, their pilgrimages, retreats (often in other lands) and meditational practices, they became the equivalent of "cultural insiders," having first-hand experiential knowledge of the differing realms of subjectivity mapped by a variety of global healing enterprises. For the first time there appeared a statistically significant rise of not simply Western students but Western teachers of Hinduism and Buddhism. Another significant cultural factor emerged from continued waves of immigration, educational exchange and the participation of natives from the East in Western psychotherapeutic enterprises both as analysands and analysts – a reversal that has heightened awareness of cultural issues and their impact on differing healing enterprises. Alongside these socio-cultural factors, one finds the continued growth of departments of comparative studies, related cultural studies, significant improvements in translations and increased scholarly specialization. With respect to the current status of the psychology–comparativist dialogue, these developments have served to accentuate and solidify the trends of the previous period. Indeed, the contemporary period exhibits in full bloom two opposing modes of dialogue: a culturally significant movement which consists of a wholesale Western repackaging of Eastern traditions and a renewed appreciation of differences and the attempt to navigate them through interdisciplinary dialogue.

Perhaps the most characteristic mark of this period, the veritable explosion of experimental studies of Eastern religious techniques, emerged from those baby boomers who came of age in the 1960s. These studies ranged from those championing cognitive, neuro-physiological and bi-hemispheric perspectives to empirical research into the effect of drugs, altered states and psycho-physiological analyses of near-death experiences (see Woods 1980; Tart 1975; Grof 1975; Zaleski 1987). Of particular import are the studies focusing on transcendental meditation (or TM). Starting in 1970, with the doctoral dissertation of the meditator and TM advocate Keith Wallace (and, subsequently, by his colleagues at Harvard and at Maharishi Mahesh International University), over a thousand studies of TM have been undertaken to demonstrate its physiological and behavioral effects. The evidence suggests that TM leads to lower heart rates, reduced blood pressure, reduction in oxygen consumption, respiration, and muscle tension. The evidence also indicated improvements in responses to stress and favorable behavioral changes (e.g., heightened perception, deautomatization, concentration, empathy, memory). Wallace, David Orme-Johnson and Herbert Benson postulated the existence of a fourth state of consciousness, the hypometabolic waking state, which was physiologically distinct from normal waking, sleep, deep sleep. Medical programs linked to Harvard (under the direction of Benson) and the University of Massachusetts Medical Center (MBSR: Mindfulness-Based Stress Reduction, under the direction of Jon Kabat Zinn) initiated programs which utilized meditation and synthesized TM, Vipassana meditation, Hatha Yoga, and Zen to treat disease, hypertension, stress, anxiety, cancer, chronic pain, and heart disease.[13]

As in the case of humanistic psychology, such studies have been utilized by transpersonal psychology. Maslow defined the latter as that successor to humanistic psychology designed to analyze higher states of awareness: unitive consciousness, bliss, awe, wonder, self-actualization, ecstasy, oneness. The reigning psychological model became the "spectrum of consciousness," best articulated in the works of Ken Wilber. The latter assumes the "perennial psychology" i.e., the "universal view as to the nature of human consciousness which expresses the very same insights as the perennial philosophy but in more decidedly psychological language" (Wilber 1975: 105). This view of consciousness and therapy is a highly eclectic one, drawing from the map of consciousness found in Western psychotherapies and the world's mystical traditions (with an emphasis on Eastern mysticism). The human personality is seen as a multi-leveled manifestation of a single consciousness, ranging from "the Supreme identity of cosmic consciousness" through multiple layers down to "egoic consciousness." Each "level" of mind, be it the "shadow level," "existential level" or "cosmic consciousness," has a corresponding therapeutic technique through which it can be accessed, worked through and developed.

Many questions remain about this form of the psychology–comparativist dialogue. With the caveat that there does exist some variation among transpersonal theorists, it is nevertheless fair to characterize the general thrust of such models as representing a technological, therapeutic-access view of Eastern religions which comes with the cultural baggage of unexamined Western values: an overly simple and idealized developmental schema, an unjustified perennialism that waters down significant differences between religions, and the promotion of a psychology which functions as an unchurched, naturalistic way of organizing and expressing one's religious proclivities (see Parsons 2000). Indeed, here we have an instance of the blurring of boundaries between a bona fide psychology–comparativist dialogue and that related Western cultural hybrid known as "psychology *as* religion" (see the articles by Barnard and Bregman in this volume).

Insofar as Jung has been appropriated by the transpersonalist agenda one could mount a similar critique. Certainly Jung, like James, stressed the value of an unchurched, psychological mode of expressing and monitoring one's religious proclivities. From this perspective Jung is a major intellectual source and contributor to the formation of the "psychological perennialism" which has come to animate much of that mystical element which defines the New Age movement (see Parsons 2000). At the same time, some comparativists and psychologists are embarking on a new, critical form of dialogue with respect to Jung and the East – one that suggests a more "dialogical" Jung at work. For example, one sees the contemporary upsurge in scholarly specialization resulting in numerous studies exposing, critiquing and then utilizing a qualified Jungian approach with respect to a broad number of comparative topics: Tantric conceptions of the alaya-vijnana and the "middle way" (Moacanin 1986); practices of the pure land nien-fo and the Zen ox-herding pictures (Miyuki 1992; Speigelman and Miyuki 1985); Buddhist notions of the Dakini (Katz 1992) and the Bodhisattva (Thomas 1992); master/disciple vs. analyst/analysand relationships (Kasulis 1992); comparisons between Jung and pivotal Indian concepts like kundalini, karma, and prana (see Coward 1985). Similarly, one now finds instances of Hindu adepts who have become Jungian analysts or who have attempted to create developmental maps synthesizing Jung's analytic psychology and those extant in Eastern traditions (e.g., Speigelman and Vasavada, 1987; Ajaya 1983; Singh 1986).

At the other end of the spectrum, this period has seen a marked development in the interdisciplinary sophistication and nuance of psychoanalytic studies of Buddhism and Hinduism. Part of the reason for these advances lies in the development of psychoanalytic metapsychology. Alongside the continued reductive focus of the "classic" school of psychoanalytic theorizing about Eastern traditions (see Masson 1980; Sil 1991), one finds developments of the "adaptive" approach in the form of object-relations theory and Kohut's Self psychology (notably evident in the works of Sudhir Kakar). Similarly, along the lines advocated by Romain Rolland, one finds in psychoanalytic metapsychology the development of "transformational" theory (e.g., Lacan's notion of the "Real," Wilfred Bion's concept of "O," Heinz Kohut's postulation of the existence of "cosmic narcissism") – one which grants metapsychological legitimacy to the religious claim of accessing a transcendent realm beyond the reaches of developmental determinism (see Parsons 1999).

These advances have also accrued in part as a result of the social base articulated above. One now finds researchers familiar with the subjective states cultivated by both meditation and psychoanalysis (e.g., Jack Engler, Mark Epstein, Jeff Rubin). Psychoanalysts with Eastern analysands (e.g., Alan Roland), those native to the East who have subsequently become analysts (e.g., Sudhir Kakar) and culture theorists who utilize psychology (e.g., Richard Shweder [1991], Gananath Obeyesekere [1990], Stanley Kurtz [1992]) have garnered insights contributing to the demand that psychoanalysts analyzing the East must become culturally sensitive and conversant with relevant anthropological perspectives. No longer are Buddhist and Hindu categories of self, development and maturity unreflectively reduced to the implicit value orientations underlying psychological categories. A respect for the interdisciplinary hurdles which must be navigated to insure a bona fide, non-reductionistic dialogue between equal and different ways of configuring self, development and maturity has begun to emerge.

One can point to a number of such studies which exemplify the creative and dialogical upsurge which has come to define the new breed of psychoanalytic forays into Eastern religions. A case in point is Sudhir Kakar's construction of a theoretical basis for adjudicating between psychoanalytic universalism and cultural relativity, so well evinced in his reconfiguring of Erikson's life cycle theory and attempts to legitimate the culturally different views of self, gender and reality which ground the varying practices and aims of Eastern and Western forms of therapy (see Kakar 1981, 1982, 1991). Alan Roland's attempt to mediate between the Western notion of the "individual" and the Eastern focus on the we-self and spiritual self also belongs here (Roland 1988), as does Stanley Kurtz's carefully documented distinction between Western "separation-individuation" and Eastern "separation-integration" lines of development (Kurtz 1992). In his study of Ramakrishna, Jeffrey Kripal has broken new ground through his insightful and nuanced use of Obeyesekere's distinction between "private" and "public" symbols, Ricoeur's dialectical interplay between arche and telos, Lacan's mystical, "transformational" category of "the Real," and Kripal's original cross-cultural category of "the erotic," which seeks to ground mystical desire in both psychoanalytic libido theory and the ontological claims of the Hindu Tantric tradition (see Kripal 1995; Vaidyanathan and Kripal 1999). Turning to Buddhism, a study of pivotal importance is Jack Engler's attempt to configure the relation between Western "conventional" lines of development, which have as their aim the development of a "cohesive" self, and Eastern "contemplative" lines of development, which seek to show the illusory nature of being a separate "self": one has to *be* somebody before one can *be* nobody (Engler 1983). So too can one include Jeff Rubin's careful consideration of culture studies in his attempt to steer a middle path between "Orientocentrism" (defined in terms of privileging

Asian thought and practices to the neglect of Western psychological perspectives) and "Eurocentrism" (Rubin 1996).[14] These studies indicate that psychoanalytic contributions to the psychology–comparativist dialogue have come to champion not only psychoanalytic reductionism and universalism but a sophisticated, interdisciplinary agenda mindful of real differences as well.

Conclusion: on the psychology–comparativist dialogue

In the 1950s and 1960s religion and psychological studies was dominated by the dialogue between theology and psychology. New ways of legitimating theological discourse in the face of modernity and secularization became of paramount importance. Religious intellectuals of this period, notably Paul Tillich, Reinhold Niebuhr and Martin Buber, began to incorporate a number of psychological theories into their theological agendas, focusing especially on psychoanalytic, Jungian and existentialist thought. Utilizing dialogical principles like Tillich's "correlational method," which sought to frame the "answers" of theological discourse in the language of the "questions" posed by the culturally pervasive introspective psychologies, theologians were able to add sophistication to religious concepts like transcendence, faith, morality, heteronomy, despair, sin, guilt, and redemption without falling prey to unwarranted reductionism. Tillich's effort in his classic *The Courage to Be* to articulate a specifically Protestant form of religious subjectivity is a case in point. Tillich showed how psychoanalytic views of neuroses and existential understandings of despair and anxiety could be utilized and transcended by a form of pastoral psychology which mediated (Protestant) theological understandings of faith and courage.

To the extent that one identifies the field of religion and psychological studies with the prestige, popularity and pervasiveness of the psychology–theology dialogue, the perception that the field is "in decline" is understandable. Protestant intellectuals like Tillich no longer command the pages of *Time* magazine; pluralism is here to stay and the era of unambiguous Protestant cultural and intellectual hegemony is over. At the same time, in the last twenty years the appearance of significant works in the post-Tillichian Protestant era (e.g., Don Browning's use of a "revised" critical correlational approach and articulation of a new basis for practical theology [Browning 1987]; W.W. Meissner's attempt to adjudicate between theology and psychoanalysis [Meissner 1984]; James Fowler's postulation of "stages of faith" [Fowler 1981]; Bonnie Miller-McLemore's efforts on behalf of a feminist pastoral theology), as well as the development of studies in pastoral care from Jewish, Catholic and African-American perspectives (see Smith and Barnes 1997; Kepnes 1990; McCarthy 1990) have insured the maintenance of the psychology–theology dialogue. More to the point, other "dialogues" and approaches have grown alongside the psychology–theology dialogue. To borrow a metaphor from Peter Homans (Homans 1989), the multiple dialogues and approaches constituting religion and psychological studies have been on the "stage" since the turn of the twentieth century. On occasion the cultural spotlight has focused on one dialogue (as with the psychology–theology dialogue) to the extent that the others have become but minor figures lurking in the shadows. But now the cultural forces have caused the spotlight to shift yet again. The needs of an increasingly pluralistic and post-modern cultural atmosphere have brought to maturity one such dialogue: the psychology–comparativist dialogue. In this essay we have tried to show the vicissitudes of that dialogue in the hands of a few central theorists. Given that the future holds in store the kinds of cultural consequences that have come to be associated with ongoing global shrinkage, one can unequivocally state that the continued interest in and further development of this form of dialogue is insured.

Notes

1 I depart only slightly from the historical divisions favored by Beit-Hallahmi (1974) and Homans (1987) in their survey of the field of religion and psychological studies. My rationale for doing so lies in my wish to accentuate the major theorists of each period: Jung in the first period, the psychologies associated with the human potential movement in the second, and the tremendous rise of experimental studies and culturally sensitive psychoanalytic studies in the third. Jung's final major contribution to the interpretation of Eastern texts was published in 1944. The starting date for the second period (1970) is less defensible (but neither is it arbitrary). I choose 1970 in part because it marks the beginning of the explosion of experimental studies of TM and in part because it lies near the mutation of humanistic psychology into transpersonal psychology.

2 I have compiled this sketch from a number of sources: Tweed (1992), Clarke (1994, 1997); Parsons (1999); Fields (1992); Versluis (1993); Schwab (1984); Tweed and Prothero (1999); Kitagawa (1959).

3 At the same time, Goodenough's observation must be qualified in light of the insights of those investigating the impact of colonialism (see Sharf 1995). As noted in our analysis during the period 1944–70, James had a direct influence on the understanding of Zen as advocated by both Hisamatsu and Suzuki – a fact that had enormous ramifications for the psychology–comparativist dialogue.

4 Here I follow J.J. Clarke's treatment of the term as it has impacted Western psychological scholarship aimed at investigating the Orient. See Clarke 1994: 9ff.; 1997: 3ff.

5 Pratt's books are still respected as useful introductions to Eastern religions. However, unlike his mentor James, Pratt's major psychological and philosophical analyses have fallen by the wayside.

6 However, it should be noted that James and Bucke continue to play an important role in the psychology–comparativist dialogue. Both have been embraced by humanistic and transpersonal psychologists as prefiguring their attempt to legitimate the existence of a generically religious and "higher" nature to human beings. James has figured prominently in recent debates in the comparative study of mysticism and the establishment of the R.M. Bucke Society has played no small role in facilitating psychological scholarship aimed at investigating contemporary researches in the psychological study of comparative mysticism.

7 An excellent collection of Jung's writings on the East can be found in Meckel and Moore (1992).

8 Jung relied on the translations of Wilhelm, Max Müller and Evans-Wentz. Thomas Cleary, commenting on Jung's use of the translation of *The Secret of the Golden Flower*, says that the text was "a garbled translation of a truncated version of a corrupted recension of the original work" (Clarke 1994: 170). As for his orientalism, Jung regularly used phrases such as "the mysterious Orient" and the "dreamlike world of India"; depicted the East as introverted, passive, and gentle and the West as extroverted, active, materialistic (see Clarke 1994).

9 Again, I have compiled this sketch from a number of sources: Tweed (1992), Clarke (1994, 1997); Parsons (1999); Fields (1992); Versluis (1993); Schwab (1984); Tweed and Prothero (1999).

10 For representative studies see Molino (1998), Part One.

11 It is important to note that despite the awareness that metapsychological, philosophical and cultural differences between Zen and depth-psychology existed, Western psychological concepts appear to have influenced the cross-cultural dialogue in subtle ways. This avenue of thought is most forcefully promoted by Robert Sharf, who pursues the issue of the extent to which Suzuki and Hisamatsu represented an already Westernized understanding of Buddhism and Zen. As Sharf notes, Suzuki's Zen was a "therapeutized" one which betrayed Western influences long before he met Fromm. Sharf convincingly shows that Suzuki was influenced by many socio-cultural and intellectual forces, central to which were the "New Buddhism," the figure of Paul Carus, and Kitaro Nishida and the "Kyoto school." Nishida championed the notion of "direct experience" as the core of Zen. His influence on Suzuki and Hisamatsu contributed to the framing of Zen to Western psychotherapists as composed primarily of an unmediated and direct personal experience. That Westerners found this view congenial is no accident. It fit well with the views on religious experience as propagated by scholars like Schleiermacher, James, and Otto. And, ironically enough, the works of James were a factor in leading Nishida to frame Zen in terms of direct, unmediated experience (see Sharf 1995). However, in taking Sharf's observations into account one must be careful not to posit an idealized, authoritative form of "Zen" or "Buddhism" existing outside the context of a particular time and place. Certainly one could claim that despite colonial, Western influences, Suzuki and Hisamatsu were representatives of a Zen which would, along with other forces, help to construct an American form of Buddhism.

12 A comprehensive summary and analysis of experimental studies of meditation can be found in Murphy and Donovan (1997).

13 For an overview of these studies see Murphy (1993) and Murphy and Donovan (1997). These studies were not without their problems (Wulff 1997: 185ff.) while others warned of the negative effects of meditation (depersonalization, derealization, dissociative trance states, uprushes of bad memories, anger, insomnia [Murphy and Donovan 1997: 1–44]).

14 For comprehensive surveys of the various contemporary psychoanalytic strategies for analyzing Buddhism and Hinduism, see Molino (1998); Parsons (1999); Vaidyanathan and Kripal (1999).

References

Ajaya, S. *Psychotherapy East and West: A Unifying Paradigm*. Honesdale, Penn.: The Himalayan International Institute, 1983.

Alexander, F. "Buddhistic training as an artificial catatonia," *Psychoanalytic Review*, vol. 18(2), 1931: 129–41.

Anand, B.K., China, G.S., and Singh, B. "Some aspects of electroencephalographic studies in yogis," *Electroencephalography and Clinical Neurophysiology*, vol. 13, 1961: 452–56.

Bagchi, B.K. and Wenger, M.A. "Electrophysiological correlates of some yogic exercises," *Electroencephalography and Clinical Neurophysiology*, vol. 7, supplement, 1957: 132–49.

Behanan, K.T. *Yoga: A Scientific Evaluation*. New York: Macmillan, 1937.

Beit-Hallahmi, B. "Psychology of religion 1880–1930: the rise and fall of a psychological movement," *Journal of the History of Behavioral Sciences*, vol. 10, 1974: 84–90.

Bishop, P. "Jung, Eastern religion and the language of imagination," in D. Meckel and R. Moore (eds), *Self and Liberation: The Jung/Buddhism Dialogue*. New York: Paulist Press, 1992: 166–81.

Brosse, T. "A psycho-physiological study of Yoga," *Main Currents in Modern Thought*, vol. 4, 1946: 77–84.

Browning, D. *Religious Thought and the Modern Psychologies*. Philadelphia: Fortress Press, 1987.

Bucke, R.M. *Cosmic Consciousness*. New York: Citadel, 1993.

Campbell, J. *The Masks of God: Oriental Mythology*. New York: Viking Books, 1962.

Carstairs, G.M. *The Twice-Born: A Study of a Community of High Caste Hindus*. Bloomington: Indiana University Press, 1957.

Clarke, J.J. *Jung and Eastern Thought*. London: Routledge, 1994.

—— *Oriental Enlightenment*. London: Routledge, 1997.

Conze, E. *Buddhist Meditation*. New York: Harper & Row, 1969.

Coward, H. *Jung and Eastern Thought*. Albany: State University of New York Press, 1985.

Das, N.N. and Gastaut, H. "Variations de l'activité électrique du cerveau, du coeur et des muscles squelettiques au cours de la méditation et de l'extase yogique," *Electroencephalography and Clinical Neurophysiology*, vol. 6, supplement, 1957: 211–19.

Deikman, A. "Deautomatization and the mystic experience," in *Understanding Mysticism*, edited by Richard Woods. Garden City: Image Books, 1980: 240–60.

Eliade, M. *Myths, Dreams and Mysteries*. New York: Harper & Row, 1960.

Engler, J. "Vicissitudes of the self according to psychoanalysis and Buddhism: a spectrum model of object relations development," *Psychoanalysis and Contemporary Thought*, vol. 6(1), 1983: 29–73.

Fields, R. *How the Swans Came to the Lake*. Boston: Shambhala, 1992.

Fingarette, H. *The Self in Transformation*. New York: Harper & Row, 1965.

Fowler, J. *Stages of Faith*. San Francisco: Harper & Row, 1981.

Fromm, E. *Zen Buddhism and Psychoanalysis*, D.T. Suzuki and Richard De Martino (eds). New York: Harper & Row, 1960.

Gómez, L. "Oriental wisdom and the cure of souls: Jung and the Indian East," in D. Lopez Jr (ed.), *Curators of the Buddha: The Study of Buddhism under Colonialism*. Chicago: University of Chicago Press, 1995: 197–250.

Grof, S. *Realms of the Human Unconscious: Observations from LSD Research*. New York: Viking, 1975.

Homans, P. "The psychology and religion movement," in M. Eliade (ed.), *The Encyclopedia of Religions*. New York: Macmillan, 1987, 12: 66–74.

—— *The Ability to Mourn*. Chicago: University of Chicago Press, 1989.

James, W. *The Varieties of Religious Experience*. New York: The Modern Library, 1936.

Jung, C. *Memories, Dreams, Reflections*. New York: Vintage, 1963.

—— *Psychology and the East*. Princeton: Princeton University Press, 1978.

Kakar, S. *The Inner World: A Psycho-Analytic Study of Childhood and Society in India*. Delhi: Oxford University Press, 1981.

—— *Shamans, Mystics and Doctors: A Psychological Inquiry into India and its Healing Traditions*. New York: Alfred A. Knopf, 1982.

—— *The Analyst and the Mystic*. Chicago: University of Chicago Press, 1991.

Kasamatsu, A. and Hirai, T. "An electroencephalographic study on the Zen meditation ('Zazen')," *Folio Psychiatrica Neurologica Japonica*, vol. 20, 1966: 315–36.

Kasulis, T. "Zen Buddhism, Freud, and Jung," in D. Meckel and R. Moore (eds), *Self and Liberation: The Jung/Buddhism Dialogue*. New York: Paulist Press, 1992: 143–66.

Katz, N. "Dakini and Anima – on Tantric deities and Jungian archetypes," in D. Meckel and R. Moore (eds), *Self and Liberation: The Jung/Buddhism Dialogue*. New York: Paulist Press, 1992: 302–30.

Kepnes, S. "The Jewish response to psychiatry: contributions to a public philosophy for psychiatry," in D. Browning, T. Jobe, L. Evison (eds), *Religious and Ethical Factors in Psychiatric Practice*. Chicago: Nelson-Hall, 1990: 67–88.

Kitagawa, J.M. "The history of religions in America," in M. Eliade and J.M. Kitagawa (eds), *The History of Religions: Essays in Methodology*. Chicago: University of Chicago Press, 1959: 1–30.

Kripal, J. *Kali's Child: The Mystical and the Erotic in the Life and Teachings of Ramakrishna*. Chicago: University of Chicago Press, 1995.

—— "Hinduism and psychoanalysis: thinking through each other," in T.G. Vaidyanathan and Jeffery J. Kripal (eds), *Vishnu on Freud's Desk: A Reader in Psychoanalysis and Hinduism*. New Delhi: Oxford University Press, 1999.

—— "Kali in the psychoanalytic tradition: or why the Tantrika is a hero," unpublished manuscript 2000.

Kurtz, S. *All the Mothers are One*. New York: Columbia University Press, 1992.

Leuba, J. *The Psychology of Religious Mysticism*. New York: Harcourt and Brace, 1926.

McCarthy, M. "A Roman Catholic perspective on psychiatry and religion," in D. Browning, T. Jobe and I. Evison (eds), *Religious and Ethical Factors in Psychiatric Practice*. Chicago: Nelson-Hall, 1990: 41–67.

Maslow, A. *Religion, Values and Peak-Experiences*. Columbus: Ohio State University Press, 1964.

—— *The Farther Reaches of Human Nature*. New York: Viking, 1971.

Masson, J. *The Oceanic Feeling: The Origin of the Religious Sentiment in Ancient India*. Dordrecht: D. Reidel, 1980.

Meckel, D. and Moore, R. (eds) *Self and Liberation: The Jung/Buddhism Dialogue*. New York: Paulist Press, 1992.

Meissner, W.W. *Psychoanalysis and Religious Experience*. New Haven: Yale University Press, 1984.

Miyuki, M. "Self-realization in the ten oxherding pictures," in D. Meckel and R. Moore (eds), *Self and Liberation: The Jung/Buddhism Dialogue*. New York: Paulist Press, 1992: 181–206.

Moacanin, R. *Jung's Psychology and Tibetan Buddhism: Western and Eastern Paths to the Heart*. London: Wisdom, 1986.

Molino, A. (ed.) *The Couch and the Tree: Dialogues in Psychoanalysis and Buddhism*. New York: North Point Press, 1998.

Morel, F. *Essai sur l'introversion mystique*. Geneva: Kundig, 1918.

Murphy, M. *The Future of the Body*. New York: Jeremy P. Tarcher, 1993.

Murphy, M. and Donovan, S. *The Physical and Psychological Effects of Meditation: A Review of Contemporary Research with a Comprehensive Bibliography 1931–1996*. Sausalito: Institute of Noetic Sciences, 1997.

Neumann, E. *The Great Mother: An Analysis of the Archetype*, trans. R. Manheim. New York: Pantheon, 1955.

Obeyesekere, G. *The Work of Culture*. Chicago: University of Chicago Press, 1990.

Parsons, William B. "Psychoanalysis and mysticism: the case of Ramakrishna," *Religious Studies Review*, vol. 23(4), 1997: 355–60.

—— *The Enigma of the Oceanic Feeling*. New York: Oxford University Press, 1999.

—— "Psychologia perennis: historical developments in unchurched mysticism," in E. Wolfson and J. Kripal (eds), *The Unknown Remembered Gate: Religious Experience and Hermeneutical Reflection*. New York: Seven Bridges Press/Chatham House, 2000.

Pratt, J.B. *India and Its Faiths*. New York: Macmillan, 1915.

—— *The Pilgrimage of Buddhism and a Buddhist Pilgrimage*. New York: Macmillan, 1928.

Roland, A. *The Search of Self in India and Japan*. Princeton: Princeton University Press, 1988.

Rubin, J. *Psychotherapy and Buddhism*. New York: Plenum, 1996.

Said, E. *Orientalism*. New York: Vintage, 1979.

Schwab, R. *The Oriental Renaissance: Europe's Rediscovery of India and the East, 1680–1880*, trans. Gene Patterson-Black and Victor Reinking. New York: Columbia University Press, 1984.

Sharf, R. "The Zen of Japanese nationalism," in D. Lopez Jr (ed.), *Curators of the Buddha: The Study of Buddhism under Colonialism*. Chicago: University of Chicago Press, 1995: 107–61.

Shweder, R. *Thinking Through Cultures: Expeditions in Cultural Psychology*. Cambridge: Harvard University Press, 1991.

Sil, N. *Ramakrishna Paramahamsa: A Psychological Profile*. Leiden: E.J. Brill, 1991.

Singh, S.P. *Sri Aurobindo and Jung*. Aligarh: Madhucchandas Publications, 1986.

Smith, A. and Barnes, G.B. *Navigating the Deep River: Spirituality in African American Families*. Cleveland, Ohio: United Church Press, 1997.

Spiegelman, J. and Miyuki, M. *Buddhism and Jungian Psychology*. Phoenix: Falcon Press, 1985.

Spiegelman, J. and Vasavada, A. *Hinduism and Jungian Psychology*. Phoenix: Falcon Press, 1987.

Spratt, P. *Hindu Culture and Personality: A Psychoanalytic Study*. Bombay: Manaktalas, 1966.

Sun, J.T. "Psychology in primitive Buddhism," in A. Molino (ed.), *The Couch and the Tree: Dialogues in Psychoanalysis and Buddhism.* New York: North Point Press, 1998: 3–12.

Tart, C. (ed.) *Transpersonal Psychologies.* New York: Harper & Row, 1975.

Thomas, J. "The Bodhisattva as metaphor to Jung's concept of self," in D. Meckel and R. Moore (eds), *Self and Liberation: The Jung/Buddhism Dialogue.* New York: Paulist Press, 1992: 206–32.

Tweed, T. *The American Encounter with Buddhism, 1844–1912: Victorian Culture and the Limits of Dissent.* Bloomington: Indiana University Press, 1992.

Tweed, T. and Prothero, S. *Asian Religions in America.* New York: Oxford University Press, 1999.

Vaidyanathan, T. and Kripal, J. (eds) *Vishnu on Freud's Desk: A Reader in Psychoanalysis and Hinduism.* Delhi: Oxford University Press, 1999.

Versluis, A. *American Transcendentalism and Asian Religions.* New York: Oxford University Press, 1993.

Wilber, K. "Psychologia perennis: the spectrum of consciousness," *Journal of Transpersonal Psychology*, vol. 7, 1975: 105–30.

Woods, R. (ed.) *Understanding Mysticism.* Garden City: Image Books, 1980.

Wulff, D. *Psychology of Religion: Classic and Contemporary.* New York: Wiley, 1997.

Zaleski, C. *Otherworld Journeys.* New York: Oxford University Press, 1987.

14 Re-membering a presence of mythological proportions

Psychoanalysis and Hinduism

Jeffrey J. Kripal

> *devāstaṃ parāduryo'nyatrātmano devānveda.* May the gods abandon him who
> thinks the gods dwell anywhere other than in the self.
>
> (*Bṛhadāraṇyaka Upaniṣad* 2.4.6)

> *garbhe chilām joge chilām.* When I was in the womb, I was in mystical union.
>
> (Ramakrishna Paramahamsa in *Kathāmṛta* 1.173)

The anthropologist and social scientist Stanley Kurtz has noted that Hindu
society now stands "second to none as a generative locus of scholarship in
the field of psychological anthropology" (Kurtz 1992: 30). The same could
be said about Hinduism's role in the historical genesis, development, and
present conceptual status of the comparative study of religion. From the
time of the Sanskritist and comparativist Max Müller and his *Sacred Books
of the East* project (1875), which in some sense simultaneously founded the
discipline and defined its Asian focus, through the early researches of Mircea
Eliade on Indian yoga, whose Tantric structures secretly informed much of
his later pioneering work in the discipline (Kripal 1999), down to the oeuvres
of any number of accomplished contemporary historians of religions, no
complex of religious traditions has generated so much comparative
scholarship as what is now called "Hinduism."

Certainly this Hindocentric tendency can be partly explained as a function of colonialism and the long shadows it has cast over both modern
Indian and Western constructions of Hinduism and the Western enterprise
of making sense of religion, two civilizational projects which have deeply
informed one another within these same colonial and now postcolonial
spaces. It also, no doubt, has something to do with the general orientalist
structure that came to define India as the archetypal religious land of
wonder and wisdom against the West's more prosaic and pragmatic
worldview. Developed from ancient tropes dating as far back as Alexander's
campaign into northwestern India (327–325 BCE) and early Christian
Gnosticism (c. 200 CE) (Halbfass 1988: 2–23) – contrary to what is often
implied, "orientalism" did not originate with European colonialism – the
structure was revitalized in the modern period by European and American

Romantic, Transcendentalist, and Theosophical writers to idealize India, employed by British colonialists to legitimate their imperialism (with a masculine, rational West civilizing a feminine, superstitious East), and later mimetically reversed by such Indian reformers as Swami Vivekananda and Sarvepalli Radhakrishnan to establish a national religious consciousness for India over against the West's materialistic, and now spiritually deadening, civilization (King 1999: 135–42; cf. Halbfass 1988 and Schwab 1984).

No doubt because of the creative conflicts inherent in such sociohistorical origins, the psychoanalytic literature on Hinduism, not unlike its religious subject matter, is vast and powerfully diverse in its perspectives – "thousand-headed," we might say, borrowing a Hindu mythical-methodological metaphor from Brooks (Brooks 1994) – and speaks in no simple monolithic voice. My own choice of organizing the literature flows out of what I perceive to be the main lines of development within this hermeneutical tradition. With deep roots in Western thought, the tradition has followed linguistic and conceptual patterns well represented in Western thinking on religion, particularly those of the mythical, the mystical, and the political. Although each becomes problematic when applied to Indic materials,[1] each has played a major role in the psychoanalytic study of Hinduism. Here I will treat the first two, the mythical and the mystical,[2] each of which I will approach as an act of "re-membering," which I am defining as *a religious form of human creativity encompassing both intellectual-emotional recall in the coded rhetoric of social narrative (the mythical) and physical re-embodiment in the psycho-physiological experiences of ecstasy, trance, and possession (the mystical)*. So construed, both the mythical and the mystical entail the recollection of profound conceptual, emotional, and physical experiences from early childhood and the attempted integration of these experiences in the social and personal presents. Religiously speaking, both are also essentially artistic attempts to re-member, that is, make whole, the primordial human experience of the body understood here in both a social (the body politic) and a personal psycho-physiological sense (the body self). Finally, I will conclude such reflections with some self-reflexive musings on the ontological, psychodynamic, political and potentially mystical dimensions of a "transformative psychoanalysis" (Parsons 1999), approached here as itself a kind of cross-cultural, dialogic re-membering that can liberate, enlighten and heal.

The mythical: narrating the presence

No category has received and continues to receive more attention in psychoanalytic studies of Hinduism than that of myth, a Western term of Greek origin (*muthos*) now central to the academic study of religion. One traditional Indic classification scheme divides Hinduism into three broad mythical strands: the Śaiva, Vaiṣṇava, and Śākta traditions, or, more generally speaking, those traditions dedicated to the worship of Śiva, Viṣṇu, and the Goddess (or Śakti, literally "Power"), respectively. Each of these deities has received what Doniger has aptly called a "deep academic devotion" (1985: vii), although the goddess-centered traditions have received the proverbial lion's share (perhaps an appropriate metaphor here, since the lion is one of the goddess's traditional mounts). I will be restricting myself here to the Śaiva and Śākta traditions, which are historically, mythically, and sexually related (the goddess being the consort of Śiva).[3]

Whatever the mythological focus, however, the basic theoretical model has remained relatively consistent, as most psychoanalytic thinkers have approached their academic *iṣṭa-devatā*s ("chosen deities") with the same general purpose, namely, to reveal "the social and psychological roots of Hinduism's kaleidoscopic yet somehow unified system of deity multiplication" (Kurtz 1992: 20). The unity of that system, according to psychoanalytic Indology, lies not in the abstract ontological heights of an Advaitic absolute (as some popular neo-Vedantic interpretations would argue) but in the intimate and emotionally powerful contexts of childhood, the Indian family, and the broader Hindu society. The psychological and mythological unity of the gods and goddesses (and of those who worship them), in other words, is grounded in a shared sociological reality and a common developmental structure.

Sudhir Kakar and a consensual model of Indian male[4] psychosocial development

Psychoanalytic constructions of this shared developmental structure developed gradually throughout the twentieth century, especially in the pioneering work of Girindrisekhar Bose and in the later studies of G.M. Carstairs and Philip Spratt. But no one has been more influential in this matter than Sudhir Kakar. Indeed, I think that it can be said without too much exaggeration that there are two kinds of texts in the twentieth-century study of Hinduism: those written before Kakar's *The Inner World* (1978/1981), and those written after it. The book is so important because it is here that Kakar sets out a developmental model that would come to define – either positively or negatively – virtually every study that followed. Not that everything Kakar argued was entirely new. The emotionally rich, indulgent nature of Indian mothering, the relaxed nature of toilet training and the traumatic abruptness of weaning, the absolute centrality of the mother, a passive oedipal resolution and a subsequent submission to male authority in society, the narcissistic tendencies of the Indian male psyche, the rich cross-sexual fluidity of Indian male identity – all this, and much more, had been treated at some length by Bose, Das, Carstairs and Spratt before him, often with a considerable array of textual and ethnographic evidence. But whereas Carstairs' Kleinian speculations sometimes appear forced or Spratt's more classical psychoanalytic method often seems heavy-handed, Kakar's reflections are inevitably nuanced in their sociological understanding, careful in their conclusions, and artful in their literary presentation. It is as if all that had preceded Kakar matured and came to a new focus in his work.

In Kakar's model (which has become a consensus), the Indian male child experiences infancy as a prolonged, emotionally intense, and deeply intimate bonding with a mother, who, simultaneously deprived by the Indian family structure of sufficient sexual access to her husband and raised immeasurably in family-status by the birth of a male child (her "savior," in effect [Kakar 1981: 29, 88]), pours her sexually toned affections (and her aggressive, destructive impulses born of the culture's misogyny [Kakar 1981: 89]) on to her infant son, overwhelming him with intense experiences of love, merger, and the fear of emotional-sexual engulfment. The son eventually learns to "split" this ambiguity into two Kleinian images – the "good mother," who is idealized as "totally good" (Kakar 1981: 83), and the "bad mother," who is imagined in myth and dream as an orally and sexually voracious figure determined to deny individuation to the son. These two internalizations of the mother are now said to exist side by side, without contradiction, in the primary-process thinking of the young child (Kakar 1981: 108). According to Kakar, it is this "maternal-feminine" complex that functions as the "hegemonic narrative" of Hindu culture (Kakar 1989) and defines the Hindu male psyche as suggestively androgynous and unusually in touch with the maternal wellsprings of imagination, fantasy, and creativity; the result is a psyche more balanced and "more human" (Kakar 1981: 109).[5]

At the age of 4 or 5, however, the male child is rather suddenly removed from the external maternal-feminine presence and is introduced into the male, patriarchal world of the father and society, an event Kakar calls, playing off the brahmanic notion of the "twice-born," the "second birth." Kakar does not hesitate to use the word "traumatic" to describe this sudden existential change, arguing that such trauma sets the Hindu male up for "regression to an earlier 'happier' era and a tendency to consolidate one's identification with the mother in order to compensate for her loss" (Kakar 1981: 130). Very much related to this second birth is Kakar's notion of the Indian oedipal complex and its "passive" resolution via the male child's renunciation of his sexuality *vis-à-vis* his mother and his absolute submission to the elder males of the family, the "psychosocial diffusion" of the extended family having rendered the father a distant figure (Kakar 1981: 134). Psychosocially speaking, the result is twofold: a hierarchical pattern of homosocial submission to male authority in society and a relatively weak, undifferentiated superego, the structures of caste and patriarchy functioning as a kind of "communal conscience" (Kakar 1981: 135).

Kakar is certainly not alone here. Bose had emphasized early on the feminine qualities of the Indian male psyche and its culturally specific oedipal resolution (Bose 1956/1998). Carstairs and Spratt had also argued something similar before Kakar, as would Obeyesekere, Roland, and – perhaps most famously – A.K. Ramanujan after him. There are dissenting voices, however, foremost among them Robert P. Goldman, who turns to the epics to argue for a more classical (if displaced) oedipal structure (Goldman 1978), and Stanley Kurtz, who develops his own ingenious developmental model out the conviction that the consensual model inappropriately assumes a Western-style individualism and that Indian child-rearing patterns, rooted in the extended family and the practice of shared mothering, produce a much more shared sense of self (cf. Roland 1988), which in turn produces on a cultural level the traditional Hindu motifs of unity in philosophical ontology (e.g., "The self is *brahman*") and myth (e.g., "All the Mothers [goddesses] are one") (Kurtz 1992). Kurtz's model, which seems especially promising, is nevertheless relatively recent, and there is little question that it is within the consensual developmental model advanced most convincingly by Kakar that most studies of Hindu mythology and mysticism have developed over the last quarter of a century. Within either model, however, the presence of the gods and goddesses, whether told in the sacred stories or psycho-physiologically experienced in the body through ecstasy and trance, are read as re-memberings, attempted resolutions, and powerful transforma-tions of the love, conflicts, and overwhelming emotions of the very earliest years of the life cycle of the Hindu male and their impact on the vagaries of psychosocial identity.

What distinguishes these re-membrances, be they mythical or mystical, is how far they go back in the developmental process. Here we can do no better than cite Erikson's beautiful description of those three psychological objects awakening "dim nostalgias" in the human being who peers into the proverbial glass darkly: (1) the "pure self itself, the unborn core of creation," which he describes, drawing on Angelus Silesius, as "the – as it were, preparental – center where God is pure nothing: *ein lauter Nichts*"; (2) the "simple and fervent wish for a hallucinatory sense of unity with a maternal matrix," which supplies the psyche with a rich fund of unconditional acceptance, approval, and provision; and finally, (3) the "paternal voice of guiding conscience," which pushes one to act in the world but in the process "puts an end to the simple paradise of childhood" and exposes the psyche to the torments of guilt, wrath, and sin (Erikson 1958: 264). Whereas the Western monotheistic traditions stressed and therefore developed the third paternal object, it is the first two – the self and the mother – that came to the fore in Hinduism.

Psycho-indological meditations – still very much through that glass darkly – on three important Hindu deities (Śiva, the Devī, and Gaṇeśa) and three forms of mysticism follow in an attempt to glimpse something of these same three, dare we say universal, psycho-religious objects.

Śiva the erotic ascetic

As the god of the iconic phallus (*liṅga*), it is perhaps not too surprising that Śiva (Figure 14.1) was the first Hindu deity to receive a book-long study by a major Western scholar conversant in psychoanalytic methods, i.e., Wendy Doniger O'Flaherty's magisterial *Asceticism and Eroticism in the Mythology of Śiva* (O'Flaherty 1973/1981). Writing well before Kakar's *The Inner World*, O'Flaherty does not frame her central questions in any consensual developmental schema. Indeed, her questions are of a different order and not technically psychoanalytic, framed as they are within the structuralist methods of Claude Lévi-Strauss. In her own terms, O'Flaherty is after the meaning of what she calls "the central paradox of Śaiva mythology," namely, the fact that "the great ascetic is the god of the phallus (the *liṅga*)" (O'Flaherty 1981: 4), a fact most potently expressed in the subtitle of the book's second and more well-known title (*Śiva: The Erotic Ascetic*, 1981).

O'Flaherty explores this central paradox through elaborate explorations of Śiva's ascetic and sexual exploits as they are lovingly and often humorously told in the multiple and bewilderingly diverse variants of the Sanskrit

Figure 14.1 Śiva

Purāṇas. In one important cycle Śiva is both the creator of Kāma (the god of sexual desire) and the god who vaporizes Kama with his third eye (Kāma had tried to disturb Śiva's meditation). In another, when Śiva dances naked and ithyphallic before the wives of the Pine Forest sages, the sages angrily curse his *liṅga* and it falls to the ground. But a terrible conflagration ensues, neither the gods Brahmā nor Viṣṇu can find the top or bottom of the phallus, and peace is restored only when the sages and their wives agree to worship it. In still another, a male demon takes the form of Śiva's wife to slay him with a *vagina dentata* (Śiva sees the ruse and impales him with his *liṅga*). And so on and so on, through myth after myth, variant after variant. By examining *in toto* all of these literally hundreds of cycles of myths dealing with ascetic practice and the sexual joys of the householder life (the renouncer and the householder being the two primary socio-religious categories of Hindu society), O'Flaherty is finally able to see the total mythic corpus as a temporally immense, pendulum-like process that, forever alternating between the extremes of asceticism and eroticism, swings out myth after myth in an attempt (never completely successful) to resolve artistically on a divine level what can never truly be resolved within the actual practices and realities of Hindu social life: that is, the permanent reconciliation of the ascetic renouncer and the erotic householder. In the end, "[t]he conflict is resolved not into a static icon but rather into the constant motion of the pendulum, whose animating force is the eternal paradox of the myths" (O'Flaherty 1981: 318).

So where is Freud? Given Lévi-Strauss's reported assumptions concerning the unconscious and its relationship to myth and dream as collective projections (O'Flaherty 1981: 14), the master structuralist and the master analyst are comfortable, if not always perfect, methodological partners. And this is, of course, a book about Śiva's sexuality. Consequently, Freud's psychoanalysis lies just below the surface of O'Flaherty's prose as a kind of barely latent subtext, guiding, if never quite determining, her questions, and her choice of texts. Like some powerful dream-figure, even when the Master is not explicitly evoked, he is there, sitting towards the front or the top of what O'Flaherty (now Doniger) has long called her "tool-box," that is, her multidisciplinary approach to myth. The facts that Doniger has been at the forefront of both the Western study of Hindu mythology and the comparative study of religion for the last quarter of a century and that her writings have always been imbued with an existentially profound and rhetorically playful psychoanalytic spirit[6] make *The Erotic Ascetic*, her first monograph, a true watershed or turning-point in the psychoanalytically informed study of Hinduism. No one before her had so artfully embedded psychoanalysis within the larger and richer context of a comparative understanding of religion, defined by an interdisciplinary array of methods and an openness to both the particularities of indigenous meaning and the possibilities of mythically expressed universal human truths.

Kakar would give a different, but by no means contradictory, answer to the paradox of Śiva's *liṅga* in his *The Inner World*, where he interpreted Śiva's popular cult as a religious response to the narcissistic wound or trauma of being permanently separated from the maternal presence. For Kakar, the worship of Śiva's *liṅga* represents two particularly prevalent defense mechanisms against such a traumatic separation: the fantasy of the grandiose self (now more or less identified with the penis), and what Kakar calls "a self-sufficient bisexuality in service of narcissism" (Kakar 1981: 159). The latter, according to Kakar, is expressed in the uniquely Indian image of the *liṅga-yoni*, the "penis" (*liṅga*) *inside* the "vagina" (*yoni*): "The solution to the threat [to self-esteem] is a symbolic withdrawal of the overcathected penis into oneself, into an internal organ, the vagina, where the phallus (and the ego) is safe and beyond harm" (Kakar 1981: 158). Hence Kakar comes to his own answer to Doniger's question about the paradox of the ascetic phallus:

> Psychologically, the liṅga does not have an erotic connotation, if by eroticism one means the direction of sexuality towards the world of "objects," the desire for others. In other words, the liṅga is not a symbol of object libido but of narcissistic libido, of sexual investment in the self. Thus, although sexuality is the essence of the symbol, the liṅga is both "chaste" and "erotic" at the same time.
>
> (Kakar 1981: 160; cf. Spratt 1966: 1, 11, ch. 5)

Kālī: or why the Tāntrika is a hero

But it has not been Śiva but Śiva's spouse, the goddess or Devī, particularly in her role as Kālī (Figure 14.2), who has received the most psychoanalytic devotion. It is not difficult to see why. She wears a garland of (always male) heads tied together by the hair and a skirt of human arms, her breasts and hips are usually full and shapely, her hair is wild and unkempt, and her tongue is extended in an expression of cannibalistic fury, emotional rage, and sexual arousal. Whereas her two right arms promise boons and freedom from fear, her two left arms promise and indeed deliver death – the top holds a sacrificial sword, the bottom a (male) decapitated head. Kālī stands on the prone body of her husband, Śiva, who is said to be, alternately, asleep, a corpse, or engaged in reversed sexual intercourse (*viparītarati*) with her. And yet, she is "Kālī-Mā," "Kālī the Mother" who protects and nourishes her children. The Kleinian possibilities seem almost ridiculously obvious here, for Kālī appears as the unconscious made conscious, the latent rendered manifest, almost *too* manifest.

The psychoanalytic literature on Kālī is especially rich with meditations on her. The result has been some striking insights into the pre-oedipal origins of many features of India's innumerable goddess traditions,

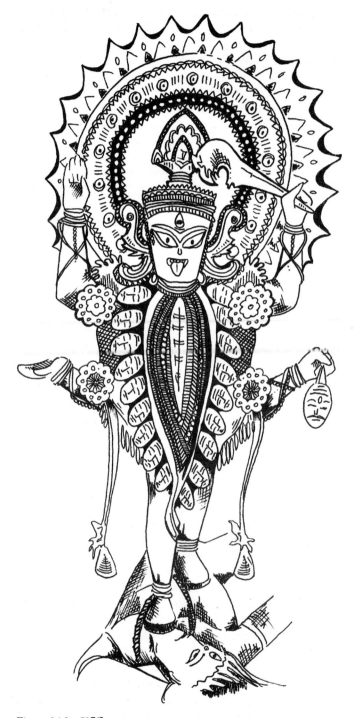

Figure 14.2   Kālī

particularly their emphasis on the emotional-devotional states of the infant or child, their often stated goal of mystically merging with the mother, and their bewildering symbolic complex of beheading, motherliness, sexuality, grace, and violence. One way to approach all of this is to ask the questions: Why is the male Tāntrika, who sexually engages Kālī, either imaginally or through a female ritual partner, described as a "hero" (*vīra*)? What is so special about mystical heteroeroticism?

The history of psychoanalytic speculation on Kālī, when taken as a whole, approaches such a question developmentally: that is, through speculations on the Indian male child and his psychological experience of the mother in fantasy and "real" life. The Schjelderup brothers' early German study *Über drei Haupttypen* (1932), for example, drew on eighteen case studies of glossolalia to categorize the religious personality, well before Erikson, into three basic types (*Grundtypen*) along a developmental perspective – the oedipal, the pre-oedipal, and the narcissistic – each of which they then demonstrated again with an historical case-study (of Martin Luther, Ramakrishna, and Bodhidharma, respectively). For the Schjelderups, Ramakrishna and Kālī were powerful examples of that "mother-religion" that is free from the emotions of guilt and sin (prominent in a later oedipal stage of conflict and most developed in the Western monotheistic "father-religions"), emphasizing instead the bliss of physical intimacy and security and a "tendency towards mystical unity with the Divinity" (Schjelderup and Schjelderup 1932: 58). A helpful start, but not much help with our question.

Girindrasekhar Bose, often cited as the father of psychoanalysis in India, was much closer to the mark. Drawing on his own clinical practice and reading of Freud, with whom he corresponded, Bose suggested that the maternal deity of Hinduism can be traced back to the culturally specific characteristics of the oedipal resolution in India (Bose and Freud 1997: 17). According to Bose, Indian child-rearing practices encourage the male child to identify with the actions and ultimately the egos of both parents, making it possible "for the child to appreciate the threefold relationship of child–mother–father from three different angles" (Bose 1956: 28). This in turn tends to produce a male psyche especially attuned to both its masculine and feminine natures and, more specifically, to the "desire to be female" that Bose found to be so prominent in Indian men. Such a desire, according to Bose, "is more easily unearthed in Indian male patients than in European" (Bose and Freud 1997: 17). Still, it is by no means absent in European males. For example, in "Case 334," that of a religiously inclined, young, unmarried European male displaying a flight from "normal sexual love," the desire to be a woman, and efforts to combine sexuality and religious experience (even as he desires an "unrestricted sexual life"), Bose suggests that such patterns can produce a marked homoerotic spirituality (Bose 1956: 38), an astute observation that would be repeated, qualified and developed many times throughout the history of the discipline (Caldwell

1999; Carstairs 1957; Goldman 1993; Kakar 1981, 1989; Kripal 1995; Obeyesekere 1984; Sarkar 1943).

Although other essays appeared occasionally, both skeptical of psycho-analysis (Boaz 1944) and (too) convinced (Chaudhuri 1956), further sophistication would have to wait for G.M. Carstairs' *The Twice-Born* (1957) and Philip Spratt's *Hindu Culture and Personality* (1966). For Carstairs, Kālī functions as one of those defining Kleinian "nuclear phantasies" that form the modal Indian personality. Her contradictions flow from the experiences of Indian childhood, which begins as "an abundantly rewarding experience" (Carstairs 1957: 170) but changes dramatically with weaning and the child's separation from the mother. Such a late reversal shatters the child's confidence and leads to the Kālī phantasy: "In his phantasy she becomes someone terrible, revengeful, bloodthirsty and *demanding* in the same limitless way as the formerly imperious child" (Carstairs 1957: 172). Such a figure can become a mother "only when one has surrendered one's manhood and become a helpless infant once again" (Carstairs 1957: 172), hence the prominence of symbolic castration, that is, decapitation of male animals associated with sexuality (the goat or the bull) in her cult. Spratt, who read the Indian psyche as structured along pre-oedipal (in terms of a "mother fixation") and narcissistic lines, came to a virtually identical conclusion, emphasizing the goddess's decapitating/castrating role in returning the male devotee to an identification with the mother and, further back, to a mystical *regressus ad uterum*. In Kleinian terms, Kālī is both "a mother who by denying the breast arouses destructive fantasies in the infant" and the womb to which the devotee seeks to return (Spratt 1966: 229). A rather astonishing display of ethnographic and textual evidence linking the goddess and self-mutilation appear in his work, leaving even the most skeptical reader wondering if he is not correct in his general assessment.

Kakar's own reading is less speculative and more careful but quite similar in its developmental approach to the goddess: "the rapture of recognizing (and being recognized by) the mother's affirming presence together with the ambivalent anguish in response to her individuality-destroying embrace are the complementary affects evoked and condensed in the worship of Kālī" (Kakar 1981: 173). Or more generally with respect to the goddess: "In psycho-sexual terms, to identify with one's mother means to sacrifice one's masculinity to her in order to escape sexual excitation and the threat it poses to the boy's fragile ego" (Kakar 1981: 102).

It is in such a matured consensus, I think, that we can at least begin to place, understand, and appreciate the striking prominence of decapitation, the fear of semen loss, transvestism, and homoeroticism in the worship of the mother-goddess (see, for example, Caldwell 1999; Kakar 1981: 102–3; Kripal 1995; Spratt 1966: 67, 77–80, 229–48, ch. 8). The Tāntrika's heroism, in other words, lies in his courageous refusal to renounce his adult heteroeroticism before the mother and her individuality-denying, if sexually blissful and loving, presence. In this, it seems, he almost stands alone. Indeed, comparatively speaking, it is astonishing just how rare heteroeroticism is in the history of male erotic mysticism, especially in the West where the doctrinal necessity of a single male divinity renders a homoerotic structure almost predictable in Christian bridal mysticism (with the male "marrying" Christ in a mystico-erotic encounter), medieval Kabbalah (Wolfson 1994), or antique Judaism (Eilberg-Schwartz 1994). It is as if society "captures" heteroeroti-cism for biological reproduction and the maintenance of public social structures and will allow only socially liminal sexualities to "escape" into the realms of mysticism and ecstasy. And even the Indic Tantric traditions, which may on first glance seem to be an important exception to this general rule, are considered "heroic" precisely because they preserve, at great psychologi-cal threat, Indian forms of heteroeroticism, and even then they are consid-ered to be radically heterodox, esoteric traditions that go directly against the more public, orthodox concerns of the culture – once again, it is a mystical heteroeroticism "that does not fit," hence the Tantric "hero."[7]

Gaṇeśa the beheaded son

The endearingly comic, pot-bellied, elephant-headed son of Śiva and the Devī, Gaṇeśa (Figure 14.3), has also received significant psychoanalytic attention. Goldman (1978), Leach (1962), Ramanujan (1983), Spratt (1966), O'Flaherty (1976), and Kakar (1981, 1989) all have noted the rather obvious oedipal themes evident in his mythology, but it was Paul Courtright who gathered all of this material (and much more) together to produce a full-length monograph on the god, his *Gaṇeśa: Lord of Obstacles* (1985). Like O'Flaherty's earlier work on Śiva, Courtright insisted on methodological eclecticism to capture the many truths (social, psychological, ritual, etiological and political) of the different layers of myth and successfully embedded his psychoanalytic method within a beautifully written analysis of the primary Sanskrit texts, adding in this case discussions of the myths' contemporary ritual and political uses.

Although, much like Gaṇeśa's delicious sweets, psychoanalytic insights pile up quickly throughout the book, it is in Courtright's discussion of "Father, mother, son, and brother" (Courtright 1985: 103–29) that psychoanalysis as an explicit method comes powerfully to the fore. It is of some interpretive significance, Courtright points out, that Gaṇeśa is born without his father's consent outside the normal sexual channels, is violently beheaded by his father (who doesn't recognize him) for preventing the latter's access to his wife, is given an elephant's head (with a broken tusk and a long compensatory, if flaccid, trunk) when his mother intervenes on his behalf, surrenders his mother and submits to his father, is commonly understood to be a life-long celibate, is famous for his insatiable appetite for sweets, and is iconically represented as an ambiguously gendered child who never grows into adulthood. "One need not be an ideological Freudian," Courtright

Figure 14.3   Gaṇeśa

writes, "to see the fruitfulness of raising psychoanalytic questions about a myth that involves such a violent and complex account of father/son relations" (Courtright 1985: 103).

For Courtright, such myths evoke "a process similar to the developmental one that Hindu males experience around the age of four to five years" (Courtright 1985: 108), a clear and unambiguous reference to Kakar, whom he generously quotes. Specifically, Kakar had suggested that Ganeśa myths portray an oedipal resolution in which the boy-Ganeśa realizes that "the only way to propitiate the mother's demands and once again make her nurturing and protective is to repudiate the cause of the disturbance in their mutuality: his maleness" (Kakar 1981: 101). Here we see this pattern worked out in the castration themes of beheading and tusk-breaking, in Ganeśa's never quite satisfied oral fixation on sweets in compensation for a renounced adult genital satisfaction, in his life-long celibacy, and in a plump, cute, childlike body without clear gender. Ganeśa thus "wins by losing" (Courtright 1985: 120), and his story is "in part, the story of maternal attachment, loss, and indirect but incomplete compensation" (Courtright 1985: 114). Ganeśa, Courtright concludes, "is the mythical expression of the male wish for maternal intimacy denied in real life in the course of growing up, a fantasy in which the defeats the son must suffer at the hands of the father are compensated indirectly by an orally erotic celibate proximity to the mother" (Courtright 1985: 114). As such, the general problems that the Ganeśa myths address – individual psychosexual development and what Courtright calls "the brute facts of human connections at the most intimate of associations" (Courtright 1985: 104) – are universal, even if their resolutions are quite specific to traditional Hindu society. Here the psychoanalytic hermeneutic is at its best, straining for comparative, universal insights into human nature, but always through the delightful thicket of mythological, anthropological, and ethnological specificity.

The mystical: embodying the presence

Psychoanalytically speaking, the Hindu mystical search for ontological nonduality or devotional oneness with a maternal deity manifests rather clear developmental patterns and two distinct psychological objects, what Erikson calls the "unborn self" and the "maternal matrix," although, as we will see, the paternal presence of the oedipal object also often shows itself. The secret (*mustikon*) of the mystical is here *the family*, and the mystical process reveals itself as an attempt to "undo the process of ego development" (Kakar 1981: 21) in order to realize and restore in the present the ontological bliss (*ananda*) of one's psychic, sexual and physiological origins. Without denying the orientalist/colonial histories and potentials of a term like "mysticism" (King 1999), then, it is nevertheless important to keep in mind that the Hindu "mysticism" of which the Indo-psychoanalytic tradition speaks, far from being a Romantic projection or colonial trope with no representational force in Indian civilization, is in fact radically grounded in (if never fully encompassed by) the material, culturally conditioned realities of Indian psychosocial development[8] and the physiological givenness of the human body. Moreover, to the extent that all human beings mature within such developmental systems and possess a genetically determined body, we can indeed thus speak of a psychoanalytically informed "comparative mysticism," as long as we do so self-reflexively.

The mystical as the self and the mother

The "self" (*ātman*), of course, is one of the most common religious categories within the Hindu traditions, dating back to the oldest *Upaniṣad*s (c. 600–300 BCE) and their famous identification of this *ātman* with the cosmic substratum (*brahman*). Here too psychoanalytic interpreters have not been silent. Carstairs, for example, has written of the ascetic's "release from separate self-hood" as a "return to the dark mindless 'togetherness' of prenatal existence" (Carstairs 1957: 174). Spratt has examined this same phenomenon in terms of "projective introversion" (Spratt 1966: ch. 2) and a return to the mystical womb (Spratt 1966: 79, 94–103, 194). More recently, Collins (1991) and Collins and Desai (1998) have given us two rich and creative essays on the topic, largely in terms of Kohut's self psychology. In the latter study, the authors demonstrate how the *Upaniṣad*s delivered a new approach to the problem of achieving a "cohesive self." Whereas the earlier Vedic texts dealt with this problem in terms of the primordial sacrifice (that is, self-fragmentation) of the Cosmic Man and subsequent efforts to restore his lost wholeness, the Upanisadic formula for cohesion (*ātman=brahman*) located the self's ultimate sources of nurturance, mirroring, and idealization (its "selfobjects") entirely within the self. Other writers have invoked Kohut's notion of a "cosmic narcissism which has transcended the bounds of the individual" (Kohut 1978: 455) in order to posit a psychological state that is genetically predetermined by the mother–child relation but which nevertheless goes far beyond the simple preservation of pre-oedipal unity to achieve a "continual communion with a contentless and supraordinate Self" (Parsons 1999: 164). Here indeed the psychoanalyst begins to resemble an Upanisadic sage.

But perhaps the easiest and most dramatic way to demonstrate the manner in which psychoanalysis might approach such a self-mysticism is to examine a contemporary case-study.

Consider, for example, the following case as reported by Jeffrey Rubin. A 12-year-old boy loses his father to death. At 16 he suddenly becomes deeply religious and spends hours at the local temple weeping for God. At 17 he becomes terrified of death, loses all interest in life, neglects his schoolwork, and then runs away after leaving the following note: "I have started from this place in search of my Father in accordance with His command." He hardly sleeps or eats and stops speaking for four years. He stops bathing, and this despite the fact that his back becomes covered with insect-bite sores, which he ignores. When family members later find him, he ignores them with an equal indifference. "In his subsequent long life," Rubin comments, "he never worked at a job, never married, never developed normal relationships" (Rubin 1996: 48). None of this would be significant for our present purposes if it were not for the fact that this is none other than Venkatarem Iyer, better known as Ramana Maharshi, by all accounts one of the greatest modern mystics India has produced. Rubin tells his story to call into question the common assumption that spiritual attainment presupposes an absence of psychopathology. I would go further and suggest that mystical accomplishment usually *requires* psychopathology, even if the former cannot and should not be reduced to the latter. What we have here, I think, is a "trigger" phenomenon (the image implies an explosion), or, if you prefer a different metaphor, a kind of traumatic "door" into the deepest (and one of the most beautiful) developmental levels of the psychic house.

Now there are, of course, clear paternal patterns here – foremost among them the boy's heart-rending search for his lost father – but the actual content of Maharshi's religious teachings spoke almost solely of Erikson's pure "unborn self," framed here in the categories of Advaita Vedānta as the *ātman*, unborn, eternal, bodiless, blissful, always and already here, before and beyond all religious striving – that which simply *is*. Could have the young Venkatarem realized in his person such an ontological vision without the benefit of his long adolescent trauma? I doubt it very much. Can such a gnosis be reduced to this same trauma? Again, I doubt it very much.

Further along the developmental line, pre-oedipal and maternal patterns have been demonstrated in the lives of three Bengali mystics, Sri Ramakrishna (Kakar 1991; Kripal 1995), Swami Vivekananda (Kakar 1981), and Aurobindo Ghose (Nandy 1983). Nandy, for example, demonstrates how Aurobindo's later mysticism was tied into both his early childhood experiences of an enthusiastically Westernizing anglicized father and an emotionally absent, clinically insane mother and the colonial structures of his consciousness, which "split" the self into two, virtually irreconcilable "Western"/rational and "Eastern"/spiritual halves. In such a family context, Nandy writes, "young Aurobindo showed signs of mutism and interpersonal withdrawal, which his admirers were to later read as an early sign of spirituality" (Nandy 1983: 88).

At 7, young Aurobindo's parents took the boy and his brothers to London and left them there with an English family where Aurobindo, protected from any Indian influence, received the finest of Western classical educations. When he returned to India fourteen years later, he found that his father had died and that his mother had become insane. Here in his motherland, however, a fourteen-year depression lifted, he began to have mystical experiences (of a second divine body and of the mother-goddess Kālī), and he was drawn into the nationalist movement, which he saw, according to Nandy, as a way "to drive out the English language, Krishnadhan's [his father] beloved English, from India and install his *mother*-tongue at its place" (Nandy 1983: 92; his italics). "I know my country as Mother," Aurobindo wrote (quoted in Nandy 1983: 92). The oedipal (and orientalist) structure of both the mystic's nationalism and his mysticism was set – the Western Father had to be defeated for the sake of the Indian Mother.

In 1901 Aurobindo married a young Mrinalini Devi but only to ignore and ultimately leave her for the life of renunciation. Put in jail for a year, including a stint in solitary confinement, for his terrorist activities, Aurobindo had more mystical experiences that led him to abandon his political activities for a more religious lifestyle. Thus in 1910 he moved to Pondicherry and became a renouncer, where, four years later, he met a Frenchwoman by the name of Mira Paula Richard. Significantly, Aurobindo called her Śri Mā, that is, "the Mother." By 1926 he had accepted Richard as his Tantric *śakti* (power-consort) and withdrew into solitude. Henceforth, the Mother took control of the ashram, Aurobindo's image, and the future. Aurobindo had his mother back, this time on a cosmic level:

> For him, the freed East had at last met the non-oppressive West sym-
> bolized by the Mother ... The West once separated him from nearness,
> love and nurture. Now a part of the West had returned to put him in
> touch with them. "There is one force only," he declared, "the Mother's
> force – or, if you like to put it that way, the Mother is Sri Aurobindo's
> Force" ... Gradually, discovering the East in oneself by losing oneself in
> the East-in-the-West became a transcendent goal and a practical possi-
> bility. The last stage of perfection became complete surrender – "when
> you are completely identified with the Divine Mother and feel yourself
> to be no longer another and separate being, instrument, servant or
> worker but truly a child and eternal portion of her consciousness and
> force."
>
> (Nandy 1983: 95–6)

"Perhaps," Nandy concludes in his unique way of synthesizing the psychological and the political, "Aurobindo did after all find a protection
against failures of intimacy and nurture, against meaningless silence and
emptiness, and against the innermost separations and disjunctions the West
had induced in him" (Nandy 1983: 96).

Re-membering to forget: the mystical as possession

Not all forms of mystical experience in Hinduism, however, invoke the pure
self or the mystical mother. There are other presences in the psyche, and
hence other types of religious experience, of which possession and trance are
perhaps the most important. Mystical insight, sexuality, and possession have
a remarkably long history together in India. For example, in perhaps the
oldest and most venerated of the *Upaniṣad*s, the *Bṛhadāranyaka Upaniṣad*,

the wife of a sage is said to be possessed by a Gandharva (a heavenly spirit often associated with uninhibited sexuality), who grants her ontological gnosis about the meaning of *brahman* (3.7). The literature on possession in contemporary psychological studies of Hinduism is equally suggestive, even if it comes to some very different conclusions regarding the meaning of such possessions. It is here, I think, that what Richard Castillo calls a "paradigm shift" may be in the making, not just for psychiatry but for the study of Hindu mysticism as well. It is here also, I think, that psychoanalysis begins to take on a definite, if hardly acknowledged, ethical function. Here, in other words, we slip into the political.

Interpreters of Hindu mysticism often fail to note that many of the psychological states they study can best be classed, not as ethically innocent "altered states of consciousness," but as possession or trance states symptomatic of dark and disturbing, if also potentially healing, truths. This hermeneutic was developed quite early in the Freeds' famous study of Daya, the village woman who lost two friends to a sexualized death (one was forced to commit suicide for having sex with an older man, the other was raped and killed by her father for having sex with her teacher) and later became possessed (and sexually frozen) by a "spirit" in her marriage bed (Freed and Freed 1964). The same model was suggested again with Masson's important "The Psychology of the Ascetic" (1976) and was made most famous by Gananath Obeyesekere's analyses of tongue-piercing, hook-swinging, matted-haired ecstatics in his now classic *Medusa's Hair* (1981), which functioned as a kind of astonishing "warm-up" to his massive *The Cult of the Goddess Pattini* (1984) and his later theoretical statement *The Work of Culture* (1990). Here possession and trance are seen as culturally constructed forms of hysteria (often oedipally structured) with both regressive and progressive features. Hence Abdin, who relives and works through his father's physical abuse by pulling the cart of the "father" god of Kataragama in a state of trance. In so doing, he moves away from domination by the archaic motivations of childhood and into the progressive direction of reflexivity, meaning, and healing (Obeyesekere 1981).

The explanatory power of this possession-model has hardly subsided, as can be seen in the more recent works of Richard Castillo (1994a, 1994b), Elizabeth Fuller Collins (1997) and Sarah Caldwell (1999). Castillo's two essays on "Spirit possession in south Asia" are an especially fruitful entry into this discourse. Here Castillo critiques the accepted psychoanalytic (oedipal) explanation for possession (as a defense against fantasied incestuous wishes) and opts for the more humane (and, I would add, more ethical) dissociation model of Breur and later Janet and Prince. This model sees possession as the result of *real* physical and/or sexual abuse, posits independent secondary forms of consciousness, claims that direct communication can occur (e.g., in possession), and acknowledges that trance can sometimes serve adaptive purposes (Castillo 1994a: 9–10). Along the way, Castillo also effectively challenges the reigning neurobiological model of psychiatry (which sees psychiatric disorders as objective diseases of the brain) through a sensitivity to what he calls the "anthropology of experience," that is, the culturally specific ways and symbolic idioms in which psychological disorders are expressed within a particular cultural *habitus* (Castillo 1994a: 3). Trance here is a culturally coded attempt to survive:

> An example of this mechanism would be a case of repeated childhood physical and sexual abuse. When the child is under attack, he or she narrowly focuses attention away from the event and thus enters a spontaneous self-induced trance which allows the child to psychologically escape from this intolerable situation. If this situation occurs often enough the child may develop an alternate personality whose job is to take the place of the child's ordinary personality during episodes of abuse. The child's primary personality will become unconscious while the alternate is "out" and will have amnesia for the period of abuse.
>
> (Castillo 1994a: 5)

Such a "presence," moreover, can return repeatedly later in life in contexts that remind the person of the original abuse (Castillo 1994a: 6), hence the commonality of Multiple Personality Disorder (MPD) in North America and Dissociative Trance Disorder (DTD) in South Asia.

Now up to 97 per cent of reported cases of MPD in North America are connected to childhood abuse, physical and/or sexual (Castillo 1994a. 12). The social structure of Indian culture, with females on the bottom of power and open to all sorts of dramatic abuse (from abortion and infanticide to bride-burning and forced suicide), and the overwhelming prominence of females among recipients of possession make it extremely likely that we are dealing with the same traumotogenetic factors here (Castillo 1994b: 152–4). And this, of course, is where a psychological theory becomes a hidden form of cultural criticism. The fact that the symptoms are effectively coded or hidden within a religious idiom makes it difficult indeed to uncover the real roots of the suffering (Castillo 1994b: 156); nor does the usual mode of "healing," with the "ghost" stripped away through exorcisms (often of a violent kind) (Castillo 1994b: 157), offer much hope for psychic integration or, more radically, a correction of what amounts to a socio-cultural gender crisis. It is important, however, to note that such a hermeneutic is no more forgiving of Western culture than it is of South Asia; in both, childhood physical and sexual abuse, especially of females, appears to be astonishingly common.

Conclusion: hermeneutics as re-membering

Finally, perhaps it is not inappropriate in this context – which is, after all, dedicated to what Parsons has aptly called an emerging "transformational" school of psychoanalysis that emphasizes self-reflexivity, a dialogic approach to the religions, and an openness to ontological possibility (Parsons 1999) – to end with a series of reflections on the question of ontology and some thoughts on the social positions of the Indologist.

I have always felt and still feel that the ontological question (and with it the issue of reductionism) is the most basic. In terms of our discussion here, it is important to note that the mythical and the mystical cannot easily be read as "only" psychological manifestations of early family life without seriously distorting the material. With regard to mystical forms of religious experience, their physiological intensity and transformative effects on the personality often overflow and explode any such simple reduction. As for the mystical's maternal dimension, why read these re-membrances of the earliest moments of human life in any but the most profound and poignant of terms? Why not read the archaic as "primordial" instead of as "infantile"? "If this is partial regression," Erikson writes, "it is a regression which, in retracing firmly established pathways, returns to the present amplified and clarified" (Erikson 1958: 264). Along similar lines, I simply do not see how anyone could seriously argue that he or she knows, without a shadow of a doubt, what human sexuality *is* and that the Tāntrika is wrong to see and feel in it a presence of mythological proportions. After all, referring to sexual forces as "libidinal," as the psychoanalyst might, instead of as manifestations of a divine *Śakti* (the term again carries maternal and erotic connotations), as the Tāntrika certainly would, is simply to exchange one unknown for another. It proves nothing except one's own ontological assumptions.

In terms of the scholar's social position, I can certainly understand why South Asian theorists turn to psychoanalysis to understand (and heal) their own postcolonial Indian identities. Kakar (1981: 12–14, 182–8), Obeyesekere (1984: xv–xvii), and Nandy (1983) have all spoken eloquently to this issue. I cannot and will not speak for them, but I can and must ask questions of my Western colleagues. Why do we do what we do? What are we looking for? Confessionally speaking, I have often marveled at the strangeness, even weirdness, of my own life – a Nebraska boy spending much of his life studying Hindu goddesses and saints is a bit unusual, to say the least. Do we sometimes turn to the Other for compensatory or balancing reasons, to complete or make whole a humanity that is only half developed in our own culture (Kakar 1981)? And do the long years of "academic devotion" required to produce a major monograph on a specific Hindu motif or deity sometimes indicate the presence of psycho-religious needs – oedipal, pre-oedipal, or narcissistic – on our part? More radically, is there something genuinely "religious" about the understanding that emerges from these years of intellectual and imaginative *sādhana*? Can we speak of a certain "hermeneutical union" between the interpreter and the interpreted, at least in particular cases, as when we meet Eliade practicing Tantric yoga (Kripal 1999), Collins training to master hypnotic trance (1997), or Caldwell (1999) relating her own mystico-hermeneutical experiences of Bhagavati-Kālī and reflecting on their salience in light of her own past experiences of sexual and physical abuse? Doniger has written of scholars of mythology who end up living out the myths they so passionately study (1988); can we also speak of scholars of mysticism who embody or re-member the states they so faithfully study?

I think so. If both mythology and mysticism are culturally specific forms of re-membering, so too is hermeneutics; the fact that we re-member within our own distinctly intellectual and sociological contexts renders it no less meaningful. It is only differently so. There is little doubt, for example, that much of modern scholarship on Hindu goddesses, at least that inspired by historical-critical or anthropological methods, has been informed by the political and social agendas of feminist thought (Hawley and Wulff 1996; Hiltebeitel and Erndl 2000), which seems especially sensitive to the psychoanalytic themes of pre-oedipal ideation and the maternal presence. Nor, I think, are such quests restricted to women. Western monotheistic religions, with their consortless father-gods and oedipally based son-sacrifices (Delaney 1998), their banishment of the sexual from the sacred (a logical corollary of a consortless god), and their relatively late oedipal structures, are also quite inadequate to address Western males whose psychological structures are set up along pre-oedipal or narcissistic – that is, more mystical – lines. Hinduism, on the other hand, is fantastically rich here, for developmental reasons I have examined above. Despite all their famous critics, then, the Western and Indian orientalists were not wrong to see in Hinduism something especially "mystical" and powerfully "feminine" (read "maternal"), even if they missed the developmental and sociological reasons for these justly famous cultural traits and their colonializing contemporaries used their ideas for their own oppressive purposes (with a masculine and rational West civilizing an effeminate and dreamily mystical East). The political abuse of an idea does not render it a bad idea, just a badly used idea.

This comparative enterprise is also, I believe, a uniquely modern or postmodern form of "liberation" (a modern *mokṣa*, if you will), for it reveals, as few other quests can, the ultimately illusory, constructed nature of one's own cultural world, one's own *saṃsāra*. To study "other people's myths" (Doniger 1988) or "other people's mysticisms," then, is not just to understand better one's own – it is to be jarred loose from *all* myths and *all* mysticisms in order to recognize, however dimly, a shared humanity telling and embodying stories of mothers, fathers, and their children, and the mysteriously sexualized *Grund* in which they have always lived, moved, and had their being. It is thus to "live ironically," as Rolland would say, paradoxically recognizing the ephemeral nature of one's own constructed identity but choosing nevertheless to play it out passionately as a unique aspect of the impersonal "Ocean" of being (Parsons 1999: 98–9).

Psychoanalysis, I would argue, is a particularly apt methodological path to adopt for such dialogical, comparative, and even mystical purposes. It shares in both the diurnal (secondary-process) realms of Western critical theory and the nocturnal (primary-process) modes of intuition, dream, ecstasy, and sexuality and so seems particularly appropriate for rationally exploring the emotional, mythical, and mystical dimensions of human religiosity. Its balanced insistence on developmental universals and cultural particularities makes it a uniquely comparative instrument (*pace* its often grossly uninformed critics, psychoanalysis has done a remarkable job in adjusting or "refashioning" itself to Indian culture). Moreover, its insistent refusal to look away from the subterranean and forbidden zones of the human psyche and body, its ritualized calling forth of these zones in the therapeutic context and in the visionary realm of dream, its implicit ethical thrust, and its awareness of the distorting dynamics of transference and countertransference all make it an invaluable, if always imperfect, instrument of understanding oneself and the Other. Admittedly, at the moment there are great obstacles to such a knowledge, for in the present climate of cultural and ethical relativism, anti-orientalism, radical anti-representationalism ("whereby everyone is involved in constructing imaginary conceptions of 'the Orient' that have no identifiable referent in extra-linguistic reality" [King 1999: 94–5]), and the consequent demonization of normative knowledge itself as inherently "colonial" or "imperialistic" – in effect, the Foucauldian reduction of "truth" to "power" – the psychoanalytically inclined hermeneut or comparativist who *knows* across cultures and times and grounds that knowledge in the material (and very messy) specificities of the human body and its familial socialization cannot be forgiven. He or she must remain, for the time being at least, a genuine scandal, if an exceptionally compelling one.

Notes

I would like to thank Daniel Meckel, William Parsons, Diane Jonte-Pace, and Sudhir Kakar for reading this essay and offering me their individual comments and suggestions, and Dee Drisko for penning the three images of Śiva, Kālī and Gaṇeśa.

1 See especially King 1999 for an eloquent and bracing Foucauldian genealogy of both "mysticism" and "Hinduism."

2 The political will have to wait for a future essay. Two issues would especially concern me in such a piece: (1) the psychological natures of colonialism and postcolonialism (so eloquently analyzed in the work of Ashis Nandy); and (2) the ethics of a kind of cross-cultural scholarship, such as psychoanalysis, that inevitably ends up deconstructing traditional belief-systems and values. I have explored the latter issue with reference to my own work elsewhere (Kripal 1998, forthcoming).

3 For psychoanalytic discussions of Vaiṣṇavism, see Carstairs 1957; Doniger 1993; Goldman 1978; Hawley 1983: 288–307; Kakar 1978: 111, 141–53; Masson 1974, 1975; Obeyesekere 1984; Roy 1972; Sarkar 1943; Spratt 1966: ch. 14.

4 My discussion, like most of the literature, is restricted to male psychosocial development. For discussions of female psychological development, see Caldwell 1999; Kakar 1981; and Roy 1972.

5 Kakar, however, is quite aware of the "dark side" of such a psyche:

Of course, in its defensive aspect, the maternal-feminine identification of men may serve to keep the sexes apart and may even contribute to discrimination against women. A precarious sense of masculine identity can lead to a rigid, all-or-nothing demarcation of sex roles; this kind of rigid differentiation is a means of building outer bulwarks against feared inner proclivities.

(Kakar 1981: 109–10)

Kakar also interprets such cultural processes as the fear of female sexuality, menstruation taboos, *vagina dentata* legends, and problems with sexual impotence within this same model (Kakar 1981: 92–5, 98).

6   Of particular note in this context are O'Flaherty 1980, 1984, 1985 and Doniger 1999.

7   It should be noted that Kālī is not the only Hindu goddess to receive psychoanalytic attention. Carmel Berkson, for example, has recently studied the goddess Durgā through her arch-nemesis, the anthropomorphic buffalo-demon Mahisa who managed to steal control of the cosmos from the gods until he was ultimately decapitated by the goddess (Berkson 1995). Berkson argues, well within the psychoanalytic hermeneutical tradition, that this myth is a story about the development of the male ego in India and its desperate (and ultimately unsuccessful) attempt to win its independence from its own loving and terrible mother, who finally decapitates the son, thereby symbolically castrating him and ending his heroic quest for individuality and a separate existence apart from her. The goddess may be different here (Durgā instead of Kālī), but the conclusions are remarkably the same, lending more power to an already strong consensus.

8   Such developmental patterns, of course, can be radically altered by colonial processes. Consider, for example, the studies of Ashis Nandy on the divided colonial self (Nandy 1983).

References

Berkson, Carmel (1995) *The Divine and Demoniac: Mahisa's Heroic Struggle with Durga*, Delhi: Oxford University Press.

Boaz, G.D. (1944) "The terrible mother," *Journal of the Madras University* 16/1: 62–74.

Bose, Girindrisekhar (1956/1998) "The genesis and adjustment of the Oedipus wish," *Correspondence Regarding Psychoanalysis* 10; reprinted in T.G. Vaidyanathan and J.J. Kripal (eds), *Vishnu on Freud's Desk: A Reader in Psychoanalysis and Hinduism*, Delhi: Oxford University Press.

Bose, G. and Freud, S. (1997) *The Beginnings of Psychoanalysis in India*, Bose–Freud correspondence, Calcutta: Indian Psycho-Analytical Society.

Brooks, Douglas (1994) "The thousand-headed person: Hinduism and the study of religion," *Journal of the American Academy of Religion* 62/4: 1111–26.

Caldwell, Sarah (1999) *Oh Terrifying Mother: Sexuality, Violence and Worship of the Goddess Kālī*, Delhi: Oxford University Press.

Carstairs, G.M. (1957) *The Twice-Born: A Study of a Community of High Caste Hindus*, Bloomington: Indiana University Press.

Castillo, Richard J. (1994a) "Spirit possession in South Asia, dissociation or hysteria? Part 1: Theoretical background," *Culture, Medicine and Psychiatry* 18: 1–21.

—— (1994b) "Spirit possession in South Asia, dissociation or hysteria? Part 2: Case histories," *Culture, Medicine and Psychiatry* 18: 141–62.

Chaudhuri, Arun Kumar Ray (1956) "A psycho-analytic study of the Hindu mother goddess (Kālī) concept," *American Imago* 13/2: 123–48.

Collins, Alfred (1991) "From Brahma to a blade of grass: toward an Indian self psychology," *Journal of Indian Philosophy* 19: 143–89.

Collins, Alfred, and Desai, P. (1998) "Selfhood in Indian context: a psychoanalytic perspective," in T.G. Vaidyanathan and J.J. Kripal (eds), *Vishnu on Freud's Desk: A Reader in Psychoanalysis and Hinduism*, Delhi: Oxford University Press.

Collins, Elizabeth Fuller (1997) *Pierced by Murugan's Lance: Ritual, Power, and Moral Redemption among Malaysian Hindus*, Dekalb: Northern Illinois Press.

Courtright, Paul B. (1985) *Gaṇeśa: Lord of Obstacles, Lord of Beginnings*, New York: Oxford University Press.

Delaney (1998) *Abraham on Trial: The Social Legacy of Biblical Myth*, Princeton: Princeton University Press.

Doniger, Wendy (1985) "Foreword," to P.B. Courtright, *Gaṇeśa: Lord of Obstacles, Lord of Beginnings*, New York: Oxford University Press.

—— (1988) *Other People's Myths: The Cave of Echoes*, New York: Macmillan.

—— (1993) "When the lingam is just a good cigar: psychoanalysis and Hindu sexual fantasies," in L. Bryce Boyer, Ruth M. Boyer and Stephen M. Sonneneberg (eds) *The Psychoanalytic Study of Society, Volume 18: Essays in Honor of Alan Dundes*, The Analytic Press; reprinted in T.G. Vaidyanathan and J.J. Kripal (eds), *Vishnu on Freud's Desk: A Reader in Psychoanalysis and Hinduism*, Delhi: Oxford University Press.

—— (1999) *Splitting the Difference: Gender and Myth in Ancient Greece and India*, Chicago: University of Chicago Press.

Eilberg-Schwartz, Howard (1994) *God's Phallus: and Other Problems for Men and Monotheism*, Boston: Beacon.

Erikson, E.H. (1958) *Young Man Luther*, New York: Norton.

Freed, R.S. and Freed, S.A. (1964) "Spirit possession as illness in a north Indian village," *Ethnology* 3/2: 152–71.

Goldman, Robert P. (1978) "Fathers, sons and gurus: Oedipal conflict in the Sanskrit epics," *Journal of Indian Philosophy* 6: 352–96.

—— (1993) "Transsexualism, gender, and anxiety in traditional India," *Journal of the American Oriental Society* 113/3: 374–401.

Halbfass, Wilhelm (1988) *India and Europe: An Essay in Understanding*, Albany: SUNY.

Hawley, John Stratton (1983) *Krishna, The Butter Thief*, Princeton: Princeton University Press.

Hawley, J.S. and Wulff, Donna Marie (1996) *Devī: Goddesses of India*, Berkeley: University of California Press.

Hiltebeitel, A. and Erndl, K.M. (eds) (2000) *Writing Goddesses. Is the (Indian) Goddess a Feminist?*, Sheffield and New York: Sheffield Academy Press and New York University Press.

Kakar, Sudhir (1978/1981) *The Inner World: A Psycho-Analytic Study of Childhood and Society in India*, Delhi: Oxford University Press, 2nd edn.

—— (1989) "The maternal-feminine in Indian psychoanalysis," *International Review of Psycho-analysis* 16: 355–62.

—— (1991) *The Analyst and the Mystic: Psychoanalytic Reflections on Religion and Mysticism*, Chicago: University of Chicago Press.

King, Richard (1999) *Orientalism and Religion: Postcolonial Theory, India and "The Mystic East,"* London: Routledge.

Kohut, Heinz (1978) *The Search for the Self: Selected Writings of Heinz Kohut, 1950–1978,* edited by Paul Ornstein, 2 vols, New York: International Universities Press.

Kripal, Jeffrey J. (1995/1998) *Kālī's Child: The Mystical and the Erotic in the Life and Teachings of Ramakrishna,* Chicago: University of Chicago Press.

—— (1998) "Preface to the second edition: 'Pale plausibilities,' " in J. Kripal, *Kālī's Child: The Mystical and the Erotic in the Life and Teachings of Ramakrishna,* Chicago: University of Chicago Press.

—— (1999) "The visitation of the stranger: on some mystical dimensions of the history of religions," *Cross Currents* 49/3: 367–86.

—— (forthcoming) "Teaching the Hindu Tantra with Freud: transgression as critical theory and mystical technique," in Diane Jonte-Pace (ed.) *Teaching Freud in Religious Studies,* New York: Oxford University Press.

Kurtz, Stanley N. (1992) *All the Mothers Are One: Hindu India and the Cultural Reshaping of Psychoanalysis,* New York: Columbia University Press.

Leach, Edmund R. (1962) "Pulleyar and the Lord Buddha: aspects of religious syncretism in Ceylon," *Psychoanalysis and the Psycho-analytic Review* 49: 80–102.

Masson, J.M. (1974) "The childhood of Kṛṣṇa: some psychoanalytic observations," *Journal of the American Oriental Society* 94: 454–9.

—— (1975) "Fratricide and the monkeys: psychoanalytic observations on an episode in the Vālmīkirāmāyaṇam," *Journal of the American Oriental Society* 95: 672–8.

—— (1976) "The psychology of the ascetic," *Journal of Asian Studies* 35. 611–23.

Nandy, Ashis (1983) *The Intimate Enemy: Loss and Recovery of Self Under Colonialism,* Delhi: Oxford University Press.

Obeyesekere, Gananath (1981) *Medusa's Hair: An Essay on Personal Symbols and Religious Experience,* Chicago: University of Chicago Press.

—— (1984) *The Cult of the Goddess Pattini,* Chicago: University of Chicago Press.

—— (1990) *The Work of Culture: Symbolic Transformations in Psychoanalysis and Anthropology,* Chicago: University of Chicago Press.

O'Flaherty, Wendy Doniger (1973/1981) *Śiva: The Erotic Ascetic,* Oxford: Oxford University Press.

—— (1976) *The Origins of Evil in Hindu Mythology,* Berkeley: University of California Press.

—— (1980) *Women, Androgynes, and Other Mythical Beasts,* Chicago: University of Chicago Press.

—— (1984) *Dreams, Illusions, and Other Realities,* Chicago: University of Chicago Press.

—— (1985) *Tales of Sex and Violence: Folklore, Sacrifice, and Danger in the Jaiminīya Brāhmaṇa,* Chicago: University of Chicago Press.

Parsons, William B. (1999) *The Enigma of the Oceanic Feeling: Towards a Revisioning of the Psychoanalytic Theory of Mysticism,* New York: Oxford University Press.

Ramanujan, A.K. (1983) "The Indian Oedipus," in Lowell Edmunds and Alan Dundes (eds) *Oedipus: A Folklore Casebook,* Garland Publishing; reprinted in T.G. Vaidyanathan and J.J. Kripal (eds), *Vishnu on Freud's Desk: A Reader in Psychoanalysis and Hinduism,* Delhi: Oxford University Press.

Roland, Alan (1988) *In Search of Self in India and Japan,* Princeton: Princeton University Press.

—— (1996) *Cultural Pluralism and Psychoanalysis*, Princeton: Princeton University Press.

Roy, Manisha (1972/1975) *Bengali Women*, Chicago: University of Chicago Press.

Rubin, J.B. (1996) *Psychotherapy and Buddhism: Toward an Integration*, New York: Plenum.

Sarkar, Sarasi Lal (1943) "A study of the psychology of sexual abstinence from the dreams of an ascetic," *International Journal of Psycho-analysis* 24: 170–75.

Schjelderup, H. and Schjelderup, K. (1932) *Über drei Haupttypen der religiosen Erlebnisformen und ihre psychologische Grundlage*, Berlin: de Gruyter.

Schwab, Raymond (1984/1950) *The Oriental Renaissance: Europe's Rediscovery of India and the East, 1680–1880*, New York: Columbia University Press.

Spratt, Philip (1966) *Hindu Culture and Personality: A Psychoanalytic Study*, Bombay: Manaktalas.

Vaidyanathan, T.G. and Kripal, Jeffrey J. (eds) (1998) *Vishnu on Freud's Desk: A Reader in Psychoanalysis and Hinduism*, Delhi: Oxford University Press.

Wolfson, Elliot (1994) *Through a Speculum that Shines: Vision and Imagination in Medieval Jewish Mysticism*, Princeton: Princeton University Press.

15 Experimental studies of meditation and consciousness

Jonathan Shear

I

The meditation procedures best known in the West in general derive from Buddhism and Hinduism. Roughly put, these procedures in general are supposed, among other things, to allow the meditator's mental activity to diminish and cease altogether in an empirically qualityless state variously referred to as "pure consciousness," "pure voidness," "pure silence," etc. As this takes place, the meditator's body is said to gain an unusually deep state of rest, with decreased metabolic activity and decreased and even completely suspended respiration. This psychophysical state is then supposed to promote physical health, mental acuity, equanimity, and overall "self-actualization." Finally, "higher states of consciousness," and even all sorts of extraordinary insights and abilities, are said to be further effects. Enough research on many of these variables has now been completed and published to have become the subject of meta-analyses, and to provide an answer to the question of whether meditation can in fact produce significant empirical results.

The term "meditation" has two usual meanings; the first signifies thinking deeply about things; the second refers to mental procedures intended to modify the functioning of consciousness itself. That is, the immediate concern of the first sort of "meditation" is the cognitive contents of awareness, that of the second is *awareness or consciousness itself*. Our concern here is "meditation" in the latter sense, of procedures for the development of consciousness, rather than in the first sense of "thinking deeply." This is a relatively new scientific topic, largely stimulated by growing Western curiosity about claims made in Eastern religious traditions about the existence of systematic procedures to refine and develop consciousness itself. Over the last thirty years this has become a lively field of research, with thousands of studies completed and presented at scientific conferences, and over a thousand published in a variety of scientific journals.

The religious traditions of the world make many claims about meditation and its effects. These include claims of unusual experiences, states of consciousness, psychological growth, and types of knowledge about the world. Many of these claims are so widespread that they are tantamount to central theses of the so-called "perennial philosophy." All of them, furthermore, are mind-related, and some, if true, would require theories of mainstream psychology to be reevaluated. In this chapter we will outline some of these traditional claims, and examine implications of already conducted experimental studies for psychology and religion. We will also discuss briefly implications of further, not-yet-conducted research, both for religious claims and for our scientific understanding of human nature.

We should note first, however, that the research results on meditation are hardly monolithic. The thousands of studies examine all sorts of different procedures. Some are purely mental, others use sensory modalities; some are intensely concentrative, others are very relaxed; some are traditional, others are recent clinical constructions. Thus there is no reason to expect that such different procedures should all produce the same effects on any given measure. In addition, the studies often use different experimental protocols. As a result, they often seem to give contradictory results, and it is often difficult to make significant generalizations about them. In recent years, however, formal meta-analytic protocols to deal with these combinatorial problems have been developed, and meta-analysis has become a standard scientific tool. A number of meta-analyses of meditation studies have now been completed and published, and several of them will prove very useful for our discussion.

II

Let us begin with the basic question of whether anything at all is produced by meditation other than what can be expected from merely sitting and resting with eyes closed. A review conducted by Holmes and published in 1984 in the journal *American Psychologist* (Holmes 1984) concluded that no significant difference in effects from eyes-closed rest were to be found. A subsequent review by Dillbeck and Orme-Johnson, published three years later in the same journal, however, came to a different conclusion. This time the authors conducted a formal meta-analysis. They separated out the results for different techniques and focused on the TM technique, since "the large majority of studies on this topic use this technique and," as we noted above, "because discrimination can only be obscured by mixing studies of meditation techniques that may be quite different in methods and effects." Asking whether "meditation produces a state of relaxation that is physiologically different from eyes-closed rest," they computed basal skin resistance, spontaneous skin resistance responses, respiration rate, heart rate, and plasma lactate levels – all measures of physiological relaxation. Using the data from the 31 studies located through computer searches that gave sufficient data to compute effect sizes for any of these variables, the authors found that the TM technique was associated with significantly larger effect size than eyes-closed rest for the variables of basal skin resistance, respiration rate, and plasma lactate, but not for heart rate and spontaneous skin resistance (Dillbeck and Orme-Johnson 1987: 879).

These results indicate that at least some techniques produce some effects of the sort indicated by the traditional literature. Even if we confine ourselves to the parameter of "rest," however, we find the traditional literature going quite beyond the above sorts of results. As Gharma C.C. Chang, for example, from the traditions of Zen and Tibetan Buddhism, puts it

> In the higher states of meditation, the circulation of the blood is slowed down almost to cessation, perceptible breathing ceases, and the yogi experiences some degree of illumination, or "brightness," together with the thoughtfree state of mind. Then not only does a change of consciousness occur, but also a change in the physiological functioning of the body. In the body of a fully enlightened being, the breathing, the pulse, the circulatory and nerve systems are quite different from those of ordinary men. Much evidence in support of this fact is available from Hindu, Tibetan, and Chinese sources.
>
> (Chang 1959: 234)

In the meta-analysis cited above, however, no significant reduction of heart rate (presumably a central factor for circulation to be "slowed down almost to cessation") was noted; nor was there indication that "perceptible breathing ceases." We should note, though, that Chang qualified his claim by referring to "higher states of meditation," and the bulk of meditation studies, including the meta-analysis described above, do not focus on particularly experienced, much less "advanced" meditators. Nevertheless, some studies do specifically examine more advanced meditators, and also, perhaps surprisingly, provide evidence for cessation of perceptible breathing.

Traditionally, the deepest states of meditation, where all thought and other determinate contents awareness have stopped, have been intimately associated with the (temporary) cessation of all respiratory activity. As Chang puts it

> Another major characteristic of *Samadhi* [the completely settled, empty state of mind, "pure consciousness"] is the stoppage of breath. Without a complete cessation of breathing, the progressive thought-flow will never stop its perpetual motion. A number of different names have been used to designate *Samadhi*, one of them being "stoppage of breath" (Chinese *chi shih*).
>
> (Chang 1959: 204)

And as Maharishi Mahesh Yogi, who brought the TM technique out from India, put it, to create transcendental ["pure"] consciousness the brain must ... be held ... in a state of suspension ... For this to be possible the breath must be held in a state of neither breathing out nor breathing in. The breath must be between flowing and not flowing, and must be suspended there.

(Maharishi 1984: 296)

It is clear, of course, that both the subjective and the objective states referred to in such traditional claims are highly unusual. Indeed, the state of pure consciousness, consciousness completely devoid of empirical phenomenal qualities (thoughts, sensations, spatio-temporal manifold, etc.) is so unusual that philosophers often hold it to be an impossibility, and writers on mysticism often refer to it as "the central mystical experience." Complete, non-pathological cession of respiration obviously is also a very unusual phenomenon. Yet traditional texts insist that both the experience and the physiological state not only are possible, but occur together. There is now some experimental evidence supporting these claims.

This evidence is found most clearly in a series of studies of advanced TM meditators, beginning with Hebert (1977), extended by Farrow and Hebert (1982), and followed by Badawi *et al.* (1984). In one of Farrow and Hebert's studies, for example, a pneumotachygraph was used to measure respiration, and 11 experimental subjects were asked to press a button when they emerged from pure consciousness episodes in meditation. The subjects pressed buttons 84 times, and of the 84 button pushes, 36 occurred within ten seconds of the end of one of the 57 breath suspension episodes recorded by the pneumotachygraph. The authors note that "The probability that 36 or more of 84 randomly distributed event marks would occur within 10 seconds of the offset of a breath suspension episode is $p < 10^{10}$" (Farrow and Hebert 1982: 141).[1]

In their later study, Badawi *et al.* again observed extremely high correlation between pure consciousness experiences and 57 breath suspension episodes in the 18 subjects studied; they also noted increased EEG coherence during these periods, consistent with various earlier studies (Badawi *et al.* 1984).

Furthermore, while Dillbeck and Orme-Johnson's meta-analysis did not show significant decrease in heart rate in TM versus sitting quietly with eyes closed, other studies on both TM and other procedures often have shown this result. As Murphy and Donovan put it in their review of contemporary research on meditation,

Many contemporary studies have indicated that the heart rate usually slows in quiet meditation and quickens during active disciplines or moments of ecstasy, as we would expect from contemplative writings ...

Most studies of Transcendental Meditation (TM), Zen Buddhist sitting, Herbert Benson's "Relaxation Response," and other calming forms of meditation indicate that meditating subjects generally experience a lowering of the heart rate.

(Murphy and Donovan 1997: 45)

As Dillbeck and Orme-Johnson point out, however, meditation is often "a dynamic process," and different experiences, with significantly different physiological correlates, can occur in a single session. Thus, they conclude, "the most useful research strategy may not be to average over whole meditations, but to examine the correlates of particular experiences, such as the 'pure consciousness' " experience where, as traditional texts would lead us to expect, "studies have found more extreme reductions in somatic arousal" (Dillbeck and Orme-Johnson 1987: 881).

If averaging measures obtained over entire meditation sessions has its limitations, meta-analysis, which "averages" variables over *collections* of studies of meditation sessions, clearly has limitations, too. It has the considerable advantage, of course, of reducing statistical noise and displaying real effects that would otherwise be obscured. But it is dependent on the number of studies it integrates, and in the field of meditation only a very few procedures have been widely studied. By far the most widely researched traditional procedure is the TM (Transcendental Meditation) technique as taught by Maharishi Mahesh Yogi, with approximately six hundred studies published,[2] The Relaxation Response method put together by Benson has also been widely studied. Thus the meta-analyses often allow specific conclusions to be drawn about these two procedures. But, the small number of studies of most of the other procedures (whether traditional from Yoga, Zen, Theravada, Tibetan Buddhism, etc., or contemporary, such as Carrington's "clinical standard meditation") usually requires that they be grouped together, for statistical power in the meta-analyses. This limits the conclusions we can draw about the less widely studied procedures. But our concern here is with meditation research in general, rather than particular procedures, and this limitation will not prevent us from making some useful general observations.

Consider, for example, the traditional claim of significant reduction of metabolic activity, including temporary cessation of respiration. As Murphy and Donovan report, more than forty studies of a variety of meditation techniques have found reduction of oxygen consumption, carbon dioxide elimination, and respiration rate during meditation (Murphy and Donovan 1997: 69). These general results are consistent with the in-depth meta-analysis on TM, and in the direction of the studies of advanced TM meditators showing respiratory suspension (with no significant reduction of oxygen or increase of CO_2 in the blood) as correlates of reports of pure consciousness experiences.[3] These results suggest that the wider claims of respiratory cessation as correlate of pure consciousness experience found in the traditional literature of other procedures as well, must be based in fact. For it would strain credulity to think that so many different procedures, from different traditions, with different metaphysical beliefs, and from different cultures, would come to correlate a given, highly unusual physiological state (respiratory suspension) with reports of a given, equally unusual experiential state (pure consciousness), except on the basis of actual observation. How efficient any particular procedure might be at producing these unusual states is of course a question requiring further research.

III

The research we have been discussing thus supports the traditional accounts of correlations between specific physiological parameters and reports of pure consciousness experiences. It also has implications for how we should understand the reports themselves. The defining characteristic of the experience, as reported, is the complete absence of empirical content, including even the spatio-temporal manifold that our experiences normally are always embedded in. For the experience is completely unimaginable, since anything one can imagine is irrelevant to it. This experience, of course, is very problematic, and contemporary thinkers often argue as a result that there cannot be any such experience for reports to refer to. Two types of argument are worth noting here, one phenomenological, the other hermeneutical.

Our ordinary experience always has some kind of phenomenological content, such as thoughts, images, sensations, perceptions, etc. This fact has led to the claim that consciousness *always* has to have such content (i.e., "be intentional"), or, put linguistically, that *by definition* it has to be *of* something. Such claims of course are simply generalizations from our ordinary experience, and there is *in principle* no reason to think they have to hold for all possible conscious states. Indeed, to the extent that these claims are empirical, they must be *in principle* empirically falsifiable – and the experiences in question appear to be precisely the ones that could falsify them. Thus these phenomenological sorts of rejection cannot be expected to have much force for anyone who has had and remembers (what they take to be) the experiences in question.

The hermeneutical arguments are more substantial. It is clear that our experiences usually have various culturally conditioned components, and that many of these components are culture-specific. Hermeneutical thinkers extend this observation to argue that all of our experiences are *constructed* from culture-dependent and culture-specific components (words, symbols, expectations, images, etc.). Thus, they argue, no experiences in general, and therefore no "pure consciousness" experiences in particular, can be the same across different cultures. But it is easy to see that however true it might be for experiences in general, the hermeneutical argument misses the mark completely with regard to the pure consciousness experience. For the identifying characteristic of this experience is the absence of all empirical content, including in particular all the kinds of content (words, symbols, etc.) hermeneutical thinkers are concerned with. Indeed, meditation traditions as diverse as Yoga, Taoism, Zen, and Medieval Catholicism emphasize the need to "strip the mind of" and "forget" all such content in order to gain this experience.[4] In short any reasonable candidate for a pure consciousness experience clearly lies completely outside the domain of applicability of these hermeneutical arguments.[5]

Such arguments readily overturn the standard objections to the idea of even talking about a pure consciousness experience. But overturning objections is a far cry from producing evidence that such talk is actually significant. The research we have been discussing, however, provides us with this kind of evidence, for it allows us to take seriously the widely reported correlation between reports of pure consciousness and observations of respiratory suspension. And this correlation in turn strongly suggests that the reports describe the natural, culture-invariant subjective response to the correlated physiological state. The alternative would be to hold that unspecified factors in very different cultures somehow serendipitously conspire to produce (1) the same reports, (2) the same physiology, and (3) the correlation between the two, and also (4) that the experiences produced are differentiated in some unexplained, and indeed unspecifiable, way. In short, the research supports the conclusion that diverse meditation practices, developed in different contexts (and for a variety of purposes) must at least at times be capable of producing the widely described empirically contentless experience described, as so many different traditions insist.

How this experience ought to be *interpreted* is, of course, a very different matter. Different traditions interpret it in all sorts of ways: pure Self, Being, Emptiness, Suchness, the Ground of nature, and God, to name just a few. Such interpretations all embed the experience in distinct metaphysical systems, and amount to ontological claims tying it to the objective world in often-conflicting ways. We will return to such claims in a later section. For now, let us turn to some common claims of psychological effects of meditation in general, and the pure consciousness experience in particular.

IV

Perhaps the most common psychological claim about meditation is that it can help relieve tension. Intuitively speaking, this claim is not implausible. In most meditation systems, one sits quietly, with little or no gross muscular movement, and one's attention is withdrawn from its ordinary outward orientation and the problems of daily living. And as we have seen, meditation can produce reduction of somatic arousal significantly greater than one gains in simple eyes-closed rest. Thus it is only natural that the effects of meditation on relaxation and anxiety were among the first psychological variables to be extensively studied.

Many studies have in fact shown reduction of anxiety. Once again, however, the question of whether meditation has any significant effect above and beyond simply sitting and relaxing with eyes closed naturally arises. Here again meta-analysis turns out to be an effective tool. An article by Eppley *et al.* analyzed studies of the effects of relaxation and meditation on trait anxiety (roughly, the ongoing background level of a person's anxiety) (Eppley *et al.* 1989). Nearly 130 relevant studies were located and included in the meta-analysis. Of the meditation-related studies, 35 examined TM, 12 examined Benson's Relaxation Response, 6 examined procedures using concentration, 8 (some modeled on TM) procedures using Sanskrit mantras and a "permissive attitude," and 8 "placebo" procedures (e.g., sitting quietly with eyes closed). As expected, the so-called "placebo" procedures did have a significant effect on trait anxiety. Benson's Relaxation Response procedure matched the placebos in effect size. The TM technique had roughly 170 percent the effect size of the placebos and Benson's procedure. The concentration procedures had no significant effect. And the procedures in the "Sanskrit mantras, permissive attitude" category had an effect size approximately half that of the placebos. The relative effect sizes remained essentially unchanged when the correlations for variables such as population, age, sex, experimental design, hours and duration of treatment, pretest anxiety, demand characteristics, experimenter attitude, type of publication, and attrition were factored in.

These results raise a number of questions. While it is not hard to understand why procedures that involve concentration might not tend to reduce anxiety, it is not so easy to see why the "Sanskrit mantras, permissive attitude" procedures, sometimes explicitly modeled on TM, were less effective even than placebo. Similarly, it is not obvious why the Relaxation Response, incorporating, among other things, relaxed repetition of a subject-chosen word (e.g., "one") and simple Buddhist-derived breath-observation, should produce results only at placebo level. On the other hand, differences of effectiveness of different procedures on random populations should perhaps not be so surprising. Meditation traditions often emphasize that their procedures will be more or less effective (or even sometimes harmful) for different individuals, and as a result they are often highly selective about which procedures they will teach to whom, and at what stage(s) of their development. And we should note that absence of a significant effect for randomly selected groups, and even for all the members of such groups, of course does not imply that a procedure will not have a significant effect on selected individuals.[6] To the contrary, as we saw earlier, the finding that one procedure produces significant effects on whole groups makes traditional claims of comparable effects on specific individuals from other procedures, too, if anything more credible.

In sum, all questions of relative effectiveness of different procedures aside, the above meta-analysis appears to corroborate a second major claim of meditation traditions, namely that meditation can have a significant positive effect on anxiety.

V

Meditation traditions, of course, generally go quite beyond such modest commonsensical claims. One further claim often made, for example, is that the experience of pure consciousness can promote the growth of universal, ordinarily dormant potentials of human consciousness. The association of this experience with psychological well-being and growth has also been discussed in Western psychology, especially since the work of Abraham Maslow. Maslow noted that psychology would be well served by incorporating knowledge of people functioning better than the norm, as well as knowledge of pathological cases. His studies of highly successful individuals ("geniuses," etc.) found that they often displayed a characteristic cluster of traits (e.g., increased spontaneity, superior perception of reality, high levels of creativity, increased acceptance of self, others and nature) now used in standard measures of what is called "self-actualization." Furthermore, as Maslow and others noted, the most highly self-actualized individuals were much more likely also to have "peak experiences" of transcendence, ecstasy, and cognition of what he called "Being." These "peak experiences," of course, are exactly the kinds of experiences with which meditation traditions are often centrally concerned.

Such parallels between the developmental and experiential claims of meditation traditions and self-actualization studies led researchers to investigate whether meditation could enhance self-actualization. In an article in the *Journal of Social Behavior and Personality*, Alexander *et al.* describe a meta-analysis of the 42 studies of meditation, relaxation and self-actualization their literature search located (Alexander *et al.* 1991). Because of the small number of studies of most of the individual techniques, the authors combined the studies into three groups: TM (18 studies), Other Meditation (6 Zen, 3 Relaxation Response, 9 miscellaneous), and Other Relaxation (6 studies). All the groups showed a statistically significant effect on standard measures of self-actualization, with the Other Meditation and Other Relaxation groups having effect sizes roughly one-third that of the TM group. Thus it appears that meditation can in fact contribute to growth of self-actualization (the most widely studied construct of positive psychological outcome in the meditation literature).

VI

Meditation traditions also often go beyond merely identifying the pure consciousness experience as a component of full self-actualization, and identify it as experience of "self" itself. Thus, for example, Yoga and Vedanta maintain that the experience displays the true Self underlying the psychological phenomena and processes we ordinarily think of as constituting "self." Essentially the same understanding is found in Medieval Catholic monasticism, where the experience is characterized as being of one's "simple, uncreated, 'unbegun' nature ... the self in its naked, unmade, unbegun state"

(Wolters 1978: 213). Indeed, even some Buddhist traditions, which usually emphasize "no-self" doctrines, maintain that the experience displays our true "self-nature" or "Self" (one's "original face before one was born") beyond the illusory everyday self we ordinarily identify with.[7]

Thinking of something completely devoid of empirical qualities as one's *self* might seem a bit odd. But quite independently of such ancient meditation traditions, modern Western philosophical analyses would appear to suggest a close connection between pure consciousness and "self" itself. Common sense, of course, holds that each of us is a single person, the same, at some deep level, throughout our lives. Indeed Descartes' seemingly commonsensical argument at the dawn of modern Western philosophy that the existence of each of us as a self-identical, continuing self is the most indubitable fact of our experience was enormously influential. Yet Hume's argument that we do not find anything in experience corresponding to the commonsensical notion of self has been even more influential. And Kant strengthened Hume by arguing that the self not only is not, but cannot, be given in experience. Interestingly, however, Kant's analysis of the nature of experience in general indicated that the only thing that could fulfill our common notion of self would be qualityless "pure consciousness." But, he added, agreeing with Hume, that no such experience can ever be found in our quality-filled experience.

The situation changes entirely, of course, if pure qualityless consciousness can in fact be experienced, as the research we have been discussing suggests. For the same philosophical arguments that have rendered the notion of self so paradoxical would then, as Kant himself noted, identify the experience as experience of self. Indeed, even common sense would suggest that what is left over after one removes everything that can possibly be removed (as in meditation) from one's awareness ought to be, or at least include, one's self. Much more needs to be said here, of course.[8] Nevertheless, these few remarks may suffice to suggest something of the potential significance of the meditation-related research we have been discussing for philosophical as well as psychological questions.

VII

All of this, of course, is just a beginning. The only specific meditation experience we have even mentioned, much less discussed, so far is that of pure consciousness (voidness, Being, etc.). While this experience, often referred to as the "central" mystical experience, is obviously an important one, many other experiences, especially those referred to as "higher states" of consciousness, are also commonly emphasized in meditation traditions. Gaining these latter experiences is why many people turn to meditation in the first place. And some of them are widely taken to corroborate major, perennial religious claims. Thus claims of their existence, too, clearly need to be evaluated scientifically.

Anecdotally, these sorts of experiences are, in fact, reported by contemporary meditators, as the following examples from contemporary American practitioners of Zen and TM illustrate. First, from Zen:

> A wondrous peace enveloped me. My belly seemed to expand into a balloon, and a fog which had shortly before enveloped me, slowly began to lift, until a sweet nothingness invaded my whole being ... A thousand new sensations are bombarding my senses, a thousand new paths are opening before me. I live my life minute by minute, but only now does a warm love pervade my whole being, because I know that I am not just my little self but a great big miraculous Self. My constant thought is to have everybody share this deep satisfaction.
>
> (schoolteacher, in Kapleau 1972: 242–5)

> The world ... [is] apprehended by the senses ... in a vast "geometry of existence" of unspeakable profundity, whose rate of vibration, whose intensity and subtlety are beyond verbal description.
>
> (ex-businessman, in Kapleau 1972: 267–8)

And from TM:

> One of the most regular experiences in my meditation is of expanded awareness, of no longer being confined to the inside of my head, but being as infinite or more infinite than the universe. Sometimes I feel the boundaries of the mind being pushed out, like the ever-widening circumference of a circle, until the circle disappears and only infinity remains.
>
> (meditator from Connecticut, in Chopra 1989: 233)

> The sense of having a small, isolated self disappeared, and in its place was the delicious sensation of flowing out into everything I beheld. I felt a sense of complete fullness contained in my own silence...
>
> Standing there on the lake, I saw directly into the reality where time really is timeless. The same power that raised these mountains was flowing through me ... The single adequate word to describe my sensations at that moment is bliss.
>
> (physiology professor, in Chopra 1989: 236)

It would of course be good to know, from a practical as well as a scientific point of view, how frequently such experiences occur, with what procedures, after what periods of time, and in what sorts of people. Here we need not in principle simply rely on the meditators' own assessments. It is possible, for example, that families of the reported experiences, grouped together in ways suggested by traditional schemata of "higher states of consciousness," will turn out to have specific physiological correlates, as in the case of pure consciousness experiences. Also, as the above accounts illustrate, many of the experiences are reported to have subjective contents (love and compassion, altered sense of "self," etc.) of the sorts psychologists are already accustomed to study. Standard research protocols could thus be used to determine how well the subjects' reports conform with their behavior and objective personality traits. This would serve as an indication both of the truthfulness of the reports, and the degree to which they were products of factors such as expectation and wishful thinking, rather than the experiences themselves. Very little seems to have been done here to date, however, whether from lack of interest, funding, or enough subjects reporting such experiences.

One other, very different sort of research also should be mentioned here. As the above examples illustrate, meditation-induced experiences often have objective content, and this content is often taken to ground all sorts of claims. The above experiences, for example, refer to perception of (1) a fine, vibratory structure underlying the objective world and (2) an underlying identity between one's consciousness and the rest of nature. Such perceptions are widely reported in meditation traditions, and they underlie all sorts of objective claims these traditions make. Claim (2) above, for example, is a basic thesis of the so-called "perennial philosophy," held to express common themes of the world's major mystical traditions and religions.[9] Much more extraordinary claims – levitation, invisibility, changing the properties of the fundamental constituents of the universe, etc. – are also found in canonical texts of many traditions, Eastern and Western (Patanjali's *Yoga Sutras*, Buddhaghosa's *Path of Purification*, etc.). What makes these claims mystical rather than scientific, of course, is not so much their extraordinary content, but the absence of anything like objective corroboration.

Their contents, of course, are not in principle incapable of objective corroboration. Claims such as levitation and changing basic properties of objective phenomena are obviously highly testable. Objective evidence is also relevant to claims of the existence of a reality underlying all of nature, objective as well as subjective. Thus, for example, suppose that experimental subjects were demonstrably able to levitate or to generate knowledge of distant events faster than the speed of light would allow (e.g., knowledge on earth of sunspot activity within eight minutes of its occurrence) by "going within" and "interacting with pure consciousness." This would give us reason to begin to take seriously their claims of "interacting with" something objective "underlying" the external world (as well as their own subjective awarenesses). In the absence of such evidence, however, belief in their relevant claims remains just that – mere belief.

It might be argued that the fact that people experience what appears to them to be particular phenomena, whether subtle vibrations, a ground of the universe or even God, should at least count as some evidence *for them* of the reality of the putatively objective phenomena experienced. This is of course true. But it is precisely here that the question of objective knowledge begins, and that intersubjective corroboration is required. For our experiences are products of our central nervous system, and any particular experience can presumably occur if one's nervous system is in the appropriate state, whether or not the thing experienced actually exists independently of the person's experience (as the existence of hallucinations makes obvious). And if such things as universal vibrations, underlying ground, and/or God actually exist, their existence is presumably independent of any particular person's experience (other than, perhaps, God's). This is why common sense and scientific method both agree that establishing the existence of something outside of a person's consciousness requires going beyond that person's consciousness. Indeed, common sense makes it clear that the person having an unusual, putatively objective experience would be well advised to look for objective evidence corroborable by others. And as we saw above, such scientific evidence is in principle possible in the cases under consideration – it is just that it has not been produced.[10]

VIII

Nevertheless, as we have seen, a number of striking, if more mundane, meditation-related claims already appear to be supported by the existing research. Many studies and meta-analyses show that meditation can, as widely claimed, produce deep physiological rest, reduction of anxiety, and growth of self-actualization. There is also evidence that meditation can produce episodes of respiratory suspension, correlated with reports of experiences of "pure" consciousness, as often described in traditional texts. This in turn allows us to take such traditional reports of pure consciousness experiences at face value. Together these results support connections between the pure consciousness experience and self-actualization described in both traditional meditation-related texts and the psychological literature. Thus the claim that meditation can be a useful tool for promoting unusual levels of individual growth, made by many religions, also appears to be increasingly corroborated by the existing research. Finally, we have suggested that philosophical analysis supports the widespread traditional understanding of the pure consciousness experience as experience of "self." These are all important results.

On the other hand, a great deal more needs to be done. The existing research indicates that different procedures vary greatly in their effectiveness on particular outcomes. Finer-textured research distinguishing what aspects of what procedures produce what (subjective and objective) results on what populations is clearly called for. Presumably such research will follow, as knowledge of the growing body of research showing that meditation can have significant, beneficial results becomes more widespread. There seems much less likelihood, of course, that future research will corroborate the more extravagant claims of supernormal abilities. Nor does it seem at all likely that it will corroborate the various (and often inconsistent) ontological claims about the existence of a universal source of the universe (Being, suchness, God, etc.) that meditation-related experiences have often been held to display.

In sum, it appears that the research on meditation lends support for claims that meditation can enhance important psychological and phenomenological aspects of what may be called the religious *life*, lived with growing equanimity and deepening mystical experiences. But it also throws into sharper relief the lack of corroboration for ontological claims central to the *doctrines* of the world's major religions. Research giveth, and it taketh away.

Notes

1 Strictly speaking, only *perceptible* respiration ceases, for imperceptible microscopic lung activity remains.
2 Roughly half the studies in a typical literature search examine this technique, either alone or with other techniques. Study authors often indicate that this is because the availability of trained teachers, the ease of the practice, and the reported consistency of results make the technique, derived from the tradition of Advaita Vedanta, particularly well suited to scientific protocols.
3 For a brief review of physiological indices of reduced metabolic activity associated with pure consciousness experiences, see the Appendix to Shear 1999.
4 Compare, for example, Chinese Zen:

> When the mind is reduced to impotency, it is compared ... to ... a stone girl and an incense burner in a deserted temple ... The mind, thus stripped of all its activities [thought, feeling, experiencing, etc.], will vanish sooner or later, leaving its place to the self-nature.
>
> (Luk 1961: 20–1)

And Medieval Catholicism: "Crush all knowledge and experience of all forms of created things, and of yourself above all ... Alongside this self-regard everything else is quickly forgotten ... And this awareness, too, must go, before you experience contemplation in its perfection" (Wolters 1978: 111).
5 For further analysis of these and other related issues, see Shear 1999.
6 If, for example, a given procedure produces significant results in one percent of the population, an enormous group of randomly selected individuals would be required for any overall effect to be detected, even though by hypothesis the procedure would generate significant effects on selected individuals.
7 See, for example, Luk 1961: 12.
8 See Shear 1998, reprinted in Gallagher and Shear 1999.
9 See, for example, Shear 1994.
10 For further discussion of these points, reflecting on a meditation-induced experience of my own of what would appear to be God and the ground of the universe, see Shear 1995.

References

Alexander, C.N., Rainforth, M.V., and Gelderloos, P. (1991) "Transcendental Meditation, self-actualization and psychological health: a conceptual overview and statistical meta-analysis," *Journal of Social Behavior and Personality* 6, 5: 189–247.

Badawi, K., Wallace, R., and Orme-Johnson, D. (1984) "Electrophysiologic characteristics of respiratory suspension periods occurring during the practice of the transcendental meditation program," *Psychosomatic Medicine* 46, 3: 267–76.

Buddhaghosa (1959) "Meditation," in E. Conze (ed.) *Buddhist Scriptures*, Harmondsworth: Penguin.

Chang, C.C. (1959) *The Practice of Zen*, New York: Harper & Row Perennial Library.

Chopra, D. (1989) *Quantum Healing*, New York: Bantam Books.

Dillbeck, M.C. and Orme-Johnson, D. (1987) "Physiological differences between Transcendental Meditation and rest," *American Psychologist*, 42: 879–81.

Eppley, K.R., Abrams, A.I., and Shear, J. (1989) "Differential effects of relaxation techniques on trait anxiety: a meta-analysis," *Journal of Clinical Psychology* 45, 6: 957–74.

Farrow, J.T. and Hebert, R. (1982) "Breath suspension during the transcendental meditation technique," *Psychosomatic Medicine* 44, 2: 133–53.

Gallagher, S. and Shear, J. (eds) (1999) *Models of the Self*, UK: Imprint Academic.

Hebert, J.R. (1977) "Periodic suspension of respiration during the Transcendental Meditation technique," in D.W. Orme-Johnson and J.T. Farrow (eds) *Scientific Research on the Transcendental Meditation Program: Collected Papers*, vol. I, New York: MERU Press: 396–9.

Holmes, D.S. (1984) "Meditation and somatic arousal reduction: A review of the experimental evidence," *American Psychologist* 39, 1: 1–10.

Kapleau, P. (ed.) (1972) *The Three Pillars of Zen*, Boston: Beacon Press.

Luk, C. (1961) *Ch'an and Zen Teaching, Series 2*, London: Rider.

Maharishi, M.Y. (1984) *The Science of Being and Art of Living*, Washington D.C.: Age of Enlightenment Press.

Murphy, M. and Donovan, S. (1997) *The Physical and Psychological Effects of Meditation: A Review of Contemporary Research with a Comprehensive Bibliography, 1931–1996*, Sausalito: Institute of Noetic Sciences: 45.

Patanjali (1957) "Yoga Sutras" in S. Radhakrishnan and C. Moore (eds) *A Sourcebook in Indian Philosophy*, Princeton: Princeton University Press.

Shear, J. (1994) "On mystical experiences as empirical support for the perennial philosophy," *Journal of the American Academy of Religion* 62, 2: 319–42.

—— (1995) "Mystical knowledge?" *Sufi* 27: 12–16.

—— (1999) "Pure consciousness: exploration of meditation techniques," *Journal of Consciousness Studies* 6, 2/3: 205–8.

Shear, J. and Jevning, R. (1998) "Experiential clarification of the problem of self," *Journal of Consciousness Studies* 5, 5: 673–86, reprinted in S. Gallagher and J. Shear (eds) *Models of the Self*, UK: Imprint Academic, 673–86.

Wenger, M.A. and Bagchi, B.K. (1961) "Studies of autonomic functions in practitioners of Yoga in India," *Behavior Science* 6: 312–23.

Wolters, C. (trans.) (1978) *The Cloud of Unknowing and Other Works*, Aylesbury: Penguin.

Section 3
Psychology "as" religion

16 Diving into the depths

Reflections on psychology as a religion

G. William Barnard

Beginning explorations

Writing an essay on the history and current status of "psychology as a religion" – that frequently maligned, vaguely disreputable child of religion and psychological studies – is not a project that one takes on lightly. Who would want to describe a set of beliefs and practices that gives off a faint scent of marginality, if by doing so he or she risks a type of academic pollution by association?

But perhaps this risk can be mitigated somewhat with sufficient academic clarity. Therefore, for the sake of accurate understanding, it seems important to ask: what exactly is meant by the phrase "psychology as a religion"? For the purposes of this essay, "psychology" in "psychology as a religion" refers either to a humanistically oriented psychotherapy (i.e., the therapeutic practices and beliefs designed to assist an individual not only to overcome symptoms, but also to become more whole, fulfilled, congruent, and aligned with his/her depths) or a descriptive, phenomenological psychology that attempts, through introspective philosophical analysis and comparative study, to explore the nature of the human psyche. In the same vein, "religion" in the phrase "psychology as a religion" does not refer to an institutionally structured and maintained set of ritual practices or to a set of authorized theological dogmas. Instead, the term "religion" refers to what is often called "spirituality" – i.e., "religion" here is understood as a vehicle for exploration of the depths of reality and consciousness; it is that which brings one back to the source; it is that which heals, enlivens, and fulfills via a dynamic, experiential, living contact with a cosmic "more" (to use William James's purposefully vague term). Therefore, "psychology as a religion" is what happens when these two specific approaches to religion and psychology merge to such an extent that they fulfill similar, if not identical, roles and functions.

Another crucial question arises when studying "psychology as a religion": who should be considered legitimate "players" in this amorphous sub-field? A strong case certainly could be made for inclusion of Carl Jung and various transpersonal theorists (e.g., Abraham Maslow, Ken Wilber, David Michael Levin). Similarly, while William James's work is not a direct example of "psychology as a religion" (in the sense that he did not explicitly, and forcefully, offer psychology as an alternative venue for gaining existential meaning, creating a sense of wholeness, and/or nurturing a deeper connection to the numinous depths of reality), nonetheless, James is referenced frequently enough by more "orthodox" adherents of the "psychology as a religion" perspective that his ideas can be said to be, at least indirectly, a significant catalyst for their thought.

But what about those less academically qualified contributors to the "psychology as a religion" way of thinking – the assorted mesmerists, theosophists, neo-pagans, and New Agers who populate the more overtly popular realm of discourse and who share many, if not most, of the understandings of the nature of reality and selfhood articulated by James, Jung, and the transpersonal theorists? Do they count as part of the "canon," or is their thought too "lowbrow" to be seriously considered?

This essay intends to demonstrate that the answer is clear: Mesmerism, Theosophy, neo-paganism, and the New Age movement are prime examples of the "psychology as a religion" perspective. Some scholars, consciously or not, seem to think that the creative insights of such thinkers as James, Jung, and various transpersonal theorists have trickled down in diluted, easily digestible versions to more mainstream, less academic audiences. However, I would argue that, in reality, the academically anointed, "proper" thinkers (e.g., James, Jung, and transpersonal theorists) often went slumming with their rough-and-ready cousins from across the tracks, and in the process learned many valuable tricks of the trade. In fact (continuing with this perhaps somewhat forced metaphor), the complex interaction between James, Jung, *et al.* and their pop culture kindred was often very "Prince and the Pauper-esque," in the sense that it is frequently exceedingly difficult to discern exactly who influenced whom, and when.

Mesmeric invocations

Scholars looking back in history in an attempt to discern significant starting points for the melding of popular and intellectual cultures that permeates "psychology as a religion" could benefit from a close examination of Mesmerism. Named after the Viennese physician Franz Anton Mesmer (1733–1815), Mesmerism was rooted in a quasi-scientific notion of energy, specifically an invisible, all-pervasive, cosmic lifeforce that Mesmer termed "animal magnetism." As a physician, Mesmer believed that all illness, both physical and mental, was the result of a depletion in this cosmic energy.[1] Mesmer argued that if the equilibrium of this etheric substance was thrown out of balance in the human body, then the body's organs would be more prone to various diseases. The cure for all diseases, therefore, could be found in infusions of this cosmic energy, passing from Mesmer (or later, his numerous disciples) into the body of the afflicted person, ideally in order to catalyze convulsions or other involuntary bodily movements in the patients, movements that were understood to be cathartic healing "crises" (Fuller 1982: 6; Ellenberger 1970: 64). (Even if no "crisis" occurred, many patients, nonetheless, frequently reported that they felt a mysterious energy coursing through their body, or felt rushes of heat, or saw a luminous "fluid" streaming from Mesmer's body into their own.)

By the 1780s, Mesmer was all the rage in Paris (Lafayette was an ardent disciple and even attempted to initiate Washington into Mesmerism). But arguably, his reputation would not have been so glowing had his theatrical healing sessions not resulted in numerous healings, both physical and mental. (Hysteria was an especially prominent complaint.) Eventually, the scientific community in Paris could no longer ignore Mesmer's work and a commission of famous scientists studied over a hundred patients of one of Mesmer's most distinguished disciples. What they discovered was that in diseases ranging from "spleen infections, rheumatism, asthma, headaches, skin diseases, as well as various nervous disorders," most of the patients had substantially improved (Fuller 1982: 7). In fact, "all but six had already evidenced marked progress; over one-half claimed complete cure" (Fuller 1982: 7). Apparently, Mesmer's technique was astonishingly effective. However, the commission, using the best instruments available at the time, could find no evidence of any transmission of electrical or magnetic force, so the cures – fully documented as they were – were simply said to be the result of the patients' overactive imaginations. This conclusion (which, surprisingly, did not instigate research into the astonishing healing powers of the human mind), was the beginning of the end of Mesmer's spectacular popularity.

But Mesmer's cause was taken up, in a revised fashion, by his disciples. One of the most important was the Marquis de Puységur. According to Puységur, the impetus behind a patient's cure was psychological, not physiological. In Puységur's therapeutic sessions, he sought to establish a rapport between himself and the patient. This rapport enabled him, through a subtle effort of will and directed thought, to affect the patient's vital energy, which, in turn, catalyzed a profound altered state of consciousness: the mesmeric state of awareness. Puységur discovered that in the mesmeric state of awareness, several of his patients gained amazing abilities. Not only could some accurately diagnosis their diseases (or the diseases of others) and even at times offer remedies for these illnesses, but a few of his patients, while mesmerized, even demonstrated telepathic and clairvoyant abilities. Not surprisingly, Puységur claimed that he had discovered, below the level of ordinary, day-to-day awareness, a superior level of human consciousness.

Mesmerism eventually made its way to America. As Mesmerism began to spread, it increasingly began to acquire religious connotations. When a patient was mesmerized, he or she was understood to ascend through various stages of awareness (e.g., withdrawal of consciousness from the external world, increased awareness of interior sensations, knowledge of external events without the use of the physical senses, experiences of waves of energy, and perceptions of colored lights surrounding people). This ascension of consciousness culminated, at least in some, in the highest state of lucidity: the mesmeric awareness. Here, it was said, the patient was united with the creative energy of the cosmos and, as a result of this mystical connection with the universe, gained the ability to cure others, even at a considerable distance, and frequently demonstrated telepathic and clairvoyant gifts.

As time passed, Mesmerism, while never abandoning its emphasis on healing, was increasingly understood to be a system of beliefs and practices designed to help individuals contact and establish a rapport with the most profound dimensions of their selfhood and reality. As such, it became, in effect, what Fuller terms "the nation's first popular psychology" (Fuller 1982: x). What Mesmerism provided were powerful demonstrations of the healing, regenerative effects of a direct connection with an unseen, but dramatically felt, spiritual power. However, crucially, it did so in a way that dispensed with the theological dogmas and ecclesiastical underpinnings of its Christian counterparts. As such, Mesmerism, especially in the 1830s and 1840s, became a source of empirical support for those who began to transfer their loyalties from Christian denominations of various stripes to alternative religious movements, such as Spiritualism, Universalism, and Swedenborgianism. Mesmerism appealed to those who yearned for a direct, experiential connection with the divine, yet who were nonetheless appalled by the seemingly lifeless dogmas and institutional rigidity of orthodox Christianity. In this way, Mesmerism can be understood not only as an early version of "popular psychology," but also as a mid-nineteenth-century locus of American unchurched religiosity, expressed in seemingly scientific terms. What Mesmerism offered was appealing to many: ecstatic experiences of unity with a higher power that were understood to offer empirical evidence that the human mind has potentials that science was just beginning to discover.

What is fascinating about Mesmerism, especially its manifestation in America, is that it did not remain static. In many ways mirroring, or responding to, the profound shifts that were taking place in American society between 1860 and 1885 (i.e., massive growth in cities, combined with an influx of immigrants and a surge in industrialism), Mesmerism shifted gradually from a religiously tinged healing ritual into an all-encompassing philosophy of life.

One of the primary catalysts for this change in Mesmerism was Phineas Parkhust Quimby (1802–66). Quimby was convinced that all illness was the result of the patient's deeply ingrained unconscious beliefs – incorrect ideas that blocked the cosmic vital force from flowing into the human body and mind. For Quimby, it was the patient's beliefs that were the root cause of their disease. In order to counteract these debilitating misconceptions, Quimby sat with patients, and while in a self-induced trance state, projected energetically charged images of health from his mind into the patient's subconscious. Later in his career, Quimby added to this therapeutic technique an ongoing re-education of his patients into the "correct" beliefs necessary to maintain and deepen one's alignment with the cosmic powers – an alignment that was understood to be the root cause of health and prosperity. It is with Quimby that Mesmerism finally lets go of its old title, becoming, instead, the mind-cure philosophy or as it was often called, the New Thought.

According to mind cure and/or the New Thought, right beliefs open the floodgates of spiritual power, which is then free to flow into the subliminal recesses of the patient's mind, in turn catalyzing the patient's recovery. Therefore, the only barrier that blocked spiritual and material abundance was, in essence, psychological. According to New Thought adherents, most people live habitually with a deep belief in their separation from others and from the universe and are, consequently, riddled with fear and mistrust. If, however, they could learn to open up to the recognition of their inner connection to the divine – the Self of the universe – then they would be filled with a rejuvenating, healing, and joyous vitality.

Several scholars have commented, correctly, that New Thought, Swedenborgianism, Mesmerism, as well as many other alternative forms of American spirituality (e.g., Spiritualism, Transcendentalism, and contemporary New Age thought) are varieties of a longstanding, multifaceted tradition. William Clebsch calls this tradition "esthetic spirituality," noting that it consists primarily of "a consciousness of the beauty of living in harmony with divine things – in a word, being at home in the universe."[2] Sydney Ahlstrom uses another term, "harmonial religion," to designate this alternative, if at times polymorphous, religious tradition. For Ahlstrom, harmonial religion "encompasses those forms of piety and belief in which spiritual composure, physical health and even economic well-being are understood to flow from a person's rapport with the cosmos."[3] The different religious traditions which together make up "esthetic spirituality" or "harmonial religion" might appear to be inconsequential, fleeting, and peripheral in comparison to mainstream religious life; however, upon closer inspection, the mind-cure movement, Swedenborgianism, Transcendentalism, Spiritualism, and eventually the New Age, are simply different branches of a crucially significant and influential religious river, a river in which "lowbrow" and "canonical" currents of religiosity are inseparably intermixed, a river that, in many ways, flows directly through the heartland of Western culture.

Jamesian suggestions

William James (1842–1910) was very much aware of the beliefs and practices of various members of this polyvalent religious river. James's father was a close friend of Ralph Waldo Emerson, as well as many other New England

Transcendentalists, and was strongly influenced by the thought of Sweden-borg. James himself was at one point the president of the Society of Psychical Research and, consequently, was very interested in the claims made by Spiritualists. He also spoke highly of authors of the New Thought in public talks, such as "The Energies of Men" and "The Gospel of Relaxa-tion," and devoted nearly two chapters in *The Varieties of Religious Experience* to exploring the central tenets of their system, carefully examining the implications of New Thought beliefs and the seemingly miraculous healings associated with the mind-cure movement.

Like the adherents of the mind-cure movement, James believed in the energizing, healing results that could occur as the result of an experiential, living contact with a spiritual power that could be discovered within the deepest dimensions of one's own being. While James was not a strict pantheist like many of the mind-cure practitioners, he was sympathetic to the New Thought's emphasis on the importance of coming to a conscious realization of one's connection with a cosmic "more," an emphasis that is readily apparent in a famous quote by one of New Thought's leading proponents, R.W. Trine:

> The great central fact of the universe is that Spirit of Infinite Life and Power that is back of all, that manifests itself in and through all ... He is the life of our life, our very life itself   [and therefore] *in es-sence the life of God and the life of man are identically the same, and so are one* ... The great central fact in human life is the coming into a conscious vital realization of our oneness with this Infinite Life and the opening of ourselves fully to this divine inflow. [With this opening] we make ourselves channels through which the Infinite Intelligence and Power can work. In just the degree in which you realize your oneness with the Infinite Spirit, you will exchange dis-ease for ease, inharmony for harmony, suffering and pain for abounding health and strength.
>
> (James 1985: 88–9)[4]

James was convinced that physical and psychological healings did take place as a result of the teachings and practices advocated by the mind-cure movement. He was not naive, however; he realized that many of their dramatic cures were the result of "suggestion." But the power of "sugges-tion" to James simply meant the power of the mind to catalyze physical healings – a not insignificant ability. He was also aware that there were, at times, failures to cure the illnesses of patients and that there were perhaps even instances of self-deception or outright fraud. Nonetheless, he was also willing to claim that the tenets of the mind-cure movement were, in his eyes, confirmed, not only by the "regeneration of character" and "cheerfulness" seen in mind-cure adherents, but also by numerous examples of physical healings in which "the blind [were] made to see, the halt to walk [and] lifelong invalids ... had their health restored" (James 1985: 84).[5]

Besides James's openness to the healing potential of mesmeric sessions and the transformative effects of an experiential connection to cosmic forces, there are a number of ways in which James's philosophical outlook is congruent with many of the beliefs held by those who are explicitly part of the "psychology as a religion" perspective (which undoubtedly is one reason why New Agers and transpersonal psychologists repeatedly list his name as a crucial catalyst for their thought). For example, James downplays the role of institutionalized religion; he stresses the primacy and power of mystico-religious experiences; he accepts the personal testimonies of converts, saints, and mystics of various religious traditions as raw data for research into the deeper strata of the human psyche; he is open to the possibility that there are many levels of reality; and he is fascinated with the philosophical implications of non-typical states of awareness.

One of James's quotes (based on his own experimentation with nitrous oxide) that repeatedly appears in anthologies of transpersonal psychology and New Age sources illustrates his deeply held conviction that there is more to reality than we suspect:

> Our normal waking consciousness ... is but one special type of consciousness, whilst all about it, parted from it by the filmiest of screens, there lie potential forms of consciousness entirely different. We may go through life without suspecting their existence; but apply the requisite stimulus, and at a touch they are there in all their completeness ... No account of the universe in its totality can be final which leaves these other forms of consciousness quite disregarded. How to regard them is the question, – for they are so discontinuous with ordinary consciousness. Yet they may determine attitudes though they cannot furnish formulas, and open a region though they fail to give a map. At any rate, they forbid a premature closing of our accounts with reality.
>
> (James 1985: 307–8)

James speculates (as does transpersonal/New Age thought) that our ordinary waking consciousness is only a small subset of the spectrum of consciousness. Drawing upon the work of Fredrick Myers, his friend and fellow member of the Society for Psychical Research, James postulates that beyond the margins of our typical waking consciousness is the "subliminal self," the "enveloping mother-consciousness in each of us" from which our everyday consciousness "is precipitated like a crystal" (James 1986: 196). This subliminal self, according to both Myers and James, appears to be complex and multi-leveled. In its "lower" levels are forgotten memories, dreams, ingrained habitual patterns of perception, and the distorted understandings which lie at the root of psychopathology. However, at the "higher" levels of this psychic spectrum are creative insights, the inspirations of genius, the supra-cognitive knowledge of clairvoyance and telepathy, as well as sublime states of mystical union.

The subliminal self, according to James, is what connects us to the regenerative and often salvific energy of an unseen, but powerfully felt, spiritual world, a dimension of reality that is experienced, from one perspective, as the deepest and truest level of our selfhood, and from another perspective, as an "objective" level of existence that is analytically distinct from our conscious personality. This spiritual world is not understood by James to be *ganz ander*, it is not a completely separate reality divorced from our everyday world. Instead, this unseen world is intimately connected with who we are; it is present in the deepest levels of our selfhood and can never be known except in-and-through our psyche.

But the frequently unacknowledged interface between the spiritual world and our psyche does not imply that this unseen world is therefore simply a creation of our mind. For James, this "deeper world" is as much discovered as it is created. Like the material world, it has a directionality; it can be found in particular "places" when we orient ourselves to its "magnetic" influence. Yet unlike the material world, the spiritual world appears to be both conscious and benevolent; it makes itself known as an influx of powerful, beneficent energy. In a sense, the spiritual world is the raw material of divinity which manifests itself within an almost infinite number of forms: the fallible, mutable vessels of our different psyches. For James, therefore, the categories of the psyche and the spiritual are complexly intertwined; to explore the unseen depths of the psyche is to make an explicitly spiritual journey – an understanding that echoes notions articulated by other, less academically respected, writers and lecturers who were popular in James's time, e.g., mesmeric healers and New Thought authors. The "canonical" James, in this respect at least, is not only a close cousin to his "lowbrow" contemporaries, but also a grandfather to later New Age practitioners.

An esoteric Jung

In much the same way as William James, Carl Jung (1875–1961) is frequently cited as an individual whose thought has deeply influenced contemporary transpersonal theorists and New Age practitioners. It is easy to see why. Both James and Jung wrote of the transformative personal effects of powerful contacts with unseen, spiritually charged dimensions of the psyche, both stressed the primacy of direct experience over the authority of scriptural revelation, and both were fascinated with the implications of atypical states of consciousness. Furthermore (as will become evident below), Jung, like James, was immersed in a rich conflux of alternative metaphysical perspectives.

Nonetheless, unlike James, who remained the academic, the professor, and the philosopher, Jung gathered a circle of devoted disciples around him, considered himself a prophetic figure who had been seized by godlike forces, and attempted to utilize his theories of the psyche to empower the spiritual explorations of others. While James's writings supported the perspective of "psychology as a religion," Jung practiced and embodied that perspective in his life (especially after his break with Freud).

For decades (particularly following the publication of Jung's supposed autobiography, *Memories, Dreams, Reflections*), several scholars have commented on the religious thrust of Jung's ideas.[6] For instance, Philip Rieff brilliantly contrasts Jung's "new message of salvation" with Freud's "anti-message" (Rieff 1966: 91), pointedly emphasizing how Jung had a "pro-phetic mission, viably designed for modern consumption as psychology" (Rieff 1966: 113). In addition, Peter Homans points out that, along with his outward identity as a therapist, Jung also took on the roles of moralist, social critic, and prophet (Homans 1979: 71). Nonetheless, two recent works by Richard Noll (*The Jung Cult* and *The Aryan Christ*) have dug even deeper into Jung's practice of "psychology as a religion" (Noll 1994, 1997). Situating Jung in his historical and cultural context and probing beneath the hagiographical literature produced by Jungian disciples, Noll's avowed purpose is to provide an historical exposition of how Jung, influenced by occult traditions active during that time in Europe, considered himself to be chosen by the gods to bestow a new spiritual dispensation to an ailing modernity. However, it also seems clear that underneath Noll's seemingly impeccable academic good intentions, other more emotionally charged motives are at work. Noll does not simply offer a neutral, detached depiction of Jung. Instead, in much the same way as other academics who are contemptuous of various "lowbrow" psychology-as-a-religion perspectives, it could be argued that Noll seeks to discredit Jung, simply because of his affiliation with a number of esoteric and occult movements active at that time in Europe. However, it is not so obvious that simply because Jung's work was more overtly esoteric and religious than was previously thought, that it should therefore automatically be discounted by scholars.[7]

It is not my task here to summarize the full range of Noll's thorough research and provocative findings. For the purpose of this essay, I will primarily focus on two crucial aspects of his work: his discussion of the vortex of counter-cultural movements active in turn-of-the-century Germanic Central Europe that directly or indirectly appear to have influenced Jung's thought and Noll's articulation of Jung's explicit (if publicly hidden) messianic mission.

Noll points out that *fin de siècle* Europe was bubbling with unorthodox ideas and practices. Especially by 1914 and beyond, there was an upsurge of interest in eroticism, mysticism, occultism, Theosophy, Spiritualism and psychical research. Christian beliefs were challenged as never before. Many important thinkers and cultural leaders, based on scholarly investigations of the historical Jesus as well as the rise of positivism, evolutionism, and scientism, were convinced that the Christian story was false. Into this religious vacuum there arose a surge of interest in neo-paganism as well as a fascination with *Lebensphilosophie* – life philosophy. Drawing upon a wide range of thinkers, such as Friedrich Nietzsche, Wilhelm Diltey, Oswald Spengler, Karl Jaspers, Martin Heidegger, and Henri Bergson, the life philosophy movement stressed the centrality of direct inner experience and the ability of intuition to penetrate into the depths of life itself. Jung's teachings, which emphasize the importance of intuition and immediate experience and which not only promote the value of comparative mythology but also offer a basis for understanding psychical and mystical phenomena, did not suddenly appear out of nowhere, gifts from some transcendental, archetypal realm. Instead, Jung's beliefs came to life as the alchemical by-product of this seething cauldron of *fin de siècle* Europe.

One especially prominent ingredient in the bubbling brew of Europe's occult revival was Spiritualism. From early in his life, Jung was fascinated by Spiritualism's claim that entranced mediums could contact one's dead ancestors. (Jung was also intrigued by the findings of psychical research – the academic study of not only spiritualist seances, but also such phenomena as precognition, clairvoyance, and telepathy.) In 1899 and 1900, after extensive reading on the subject of Spiritualism, Jung decided to pursue research in the area himself. Using hypnosis, he put his 15-year-old cousin Helly into trance states and took notes as different spirits would speak through her. These notes, as well as Jung's ruminations on Helly's hysterical symptoms, eventually became the basis, in 1902, for Jung's doctoral dissertation, "On the psychology and pathology of so-called occult phenomena."

Jung's association with Spiritualism gave him first-hand experience into how to catalyze a trance state, a skill which would become useful in 1913, after his break with Freud, when he began to have visions and hear voices. In order to give some structure and coherence to this overwhelming and frightening cacophony of strongly charged experiences, he chose to let a female voice (later to be known as the anima) speak through him, as he had seen so many spiritualist mediums do before. As Noll emphasizes, the Jungian therapeutic technique of the active imagination, which is the refinement of these early imaginal dialogues, can in this way be traced to Spiritualism far more readily than it can to Jung's psychoanalytic training with Freud.

However, even when Jung was still aligned with Freud, he already had a vision of psychoanalysis that was more esoteric than scientific. According to Noll, Jung believed that psychoanalysis should be modeled after secret societies or initiatory and hierarchically structured religious orders of the past, where a select few would gain, step by step, secret knowledge until they were allowed into the restricted, privileged ranks of the governing elite. As Noll comments, "such a sacred organization was to operate outside the usual conventions of society, offering an extraordinary experience of revitalization or rebirth to those brave enough to seek the challenge" (Noll 1994: 190).

Jung's vision of psychoanalysis (which later became actualized in his analytic institute in Zurich) was strikingly similar to that of other small groups of cultural elites forming around the turn of the century, in both America and Europe, who saw themselves as the vanguard of a spiritual awakening and who devoted themselves to metaphysical and spiritual training. Perhaps the most famous and influential of all of these groups was Theosophy. Founded in 1875 by a remarkable and intriguing woman, Helena Petrovna Blavatsky (1831–91) and an equally intriguing man, Henry Steele Olcott (1832–1907), Theosophy eventually became a widespread and crucially significant movement in turn-of-the-century Europe and America. With its focus on comparative religion, study of the occult traditions, and exploration of the latent potentials of human beings as a way to create unity among different religions and cultures, Theosophy attracted the attention of a wide variety of cultural elites, such as Lord Tennyson and W.B. Yeats, the young Mohandas Gandhi, Rudolph Steiner, and Thomas Edison. For the first time in history, Theosophical publications offered mass-market access to Eastern and occult thought and sparked scholarship in these areas (of varying degrees of quality), scholarship pursued not for its own sake, but for personal spiritual renewal and growth. Jung and his disciples avidly read these Theosophical tracts, along with the more intellectually reputable texts of *Lebensphilosophie* and various mystical tracts published by the influential publishing house, Eugen Diederichs Verlag (Noll 1994: 86).

During the heyday of Theosophy, people all over Europe were experimenting with esoteric philosophies and alternative lifestyles. For example, between 1900 and 1920, Ascona, Switzerland, was frequented by creative individuals such as Hermann Hesse, D.H. Lawrence, Isadora Duncan, Franz Kafka, Paul Tillich, Max Weber, and later, by Jung himself. Ascona, an early predecessor of New Age enclaves in California and elsewhere, was the home of "neo-pagan, sun-worshiping, nudist, vegetarian, spiritualist, sometimes anarchist, sexually liberated groups experimenting with new life-styles or a new experience-based philosophy of life" (Noll 1994: 104). Many of Jung's patients and friends frequently visited Ascona, and its numinous aura appears to have rubbed off on Jung as well. Jung may have started the century as a solid member of the bourgeoisie, but by 1933, the time he began his famous Eranos conferences in Ascona, Jung's lifestyle and beliefs were decidedly countercultural.[8]

Jung's views were also strongly influenced by völkisch utopianism. Beginning in the nineteenth century in Germany, as well as Austria-Hungary, and even Switzerland, nationalistic groups sprang up, united by the idea of common ethnic identity – the Volk. These völkisch groups rejected Christianity in favor of neo-pagan rituals invoking Norse and Greek gods; they practiced Spiritualism, Theosophy, nature worship, hiking, sun worship, and emphasized anti-Semitic beliefs. Noll points out that Jung was fascinated with his Aryan origins, and repeatedly quotes völkisch literature.

Noll argues that by 1912, psychoanalysis for Jung was no longer a science but a personal religion – one which he wished to share with others in order to catalyze a cultural revival or rebirth. Jung began to teach that via the secret, initiatory experience of death and rebirth catalyzed by analysis, using the visionary techniques of the active imagination, individuals courageous enough to explore their own depths could directly realize their union with the energy of life and ultimately be led to an experience of self-deification.

This understanding of the salvific nature of analysis only deepened in 1913, when after his break with Freud, Jung began to interact with seemingly autonomous, mythologically charged figures – encounters that Jung took to be real. (One figure, a wise old man called Philemon, acted as a teacher and guru for Jung, just as the "ascended masters" did for Blavatsky.) According to Noll, in one especially vivid inner experience that took place in December of 1913, Jung became a god. In an elaborate visionary initiatory self-deification, filled with complex interactions with a male prophet (Elijah) and a blind woman (Salome – who he later cures), Jung battled with snakes coiled around his body, underwent Christlike sufferings, and ultimately, was transformed into a Mithraic lion-god. Noll argues that, in 1925, Jung shared this experience with a group of close disciples during a series of weekly seminars, his first in English. Noll claims that by sharing this experience with his disciples, Jung was not only revealing his spiritual status, but was also letting them know that the way towards personal transformation was to be found via the active imagination, and a lived, experiential descent into the underworld of the unconscious, where one has powerful interactions with godlike beings, and ultimately merges with the god within, in the core of the self (Noll 1994: 209–17; Noll 1997: 120–47).

From 1913 until 1916, Jung continued to have visionary encounters with a variety of archetypal figures within – encounters that provided him with the raw material that he later formed into the tenets of Jungian analytical psychology. All through World War One, safe in the neutral sanctuary of Switzerland, Jung and his disciples continued working together, forming a cohesive elite, with Jung as their guiding prophet and charismatic leader. In his public writings, Jung continued, for years, to present his psychology as a scientifically based, therapeutically effective set of insights into the nature of the psyche. In his private interactions with his disciples and patients, however, if Noll is correct, Jung's psychology was consciously, and overtly, structured as a redemptive, all-embracing, religious worldview and system of salvific practices.[9] While the "highbrow" aspects of Jungian thought blossomed in the warm sunlight of academic respectability, the "lowbrow" dimensions of Jungian thought were hidden from view, deeply rooted in the rich, dark, nourishing soil of European occultism and religiosity.

Transpersonal visions and New Age realizations

Arguably, the split between the public presentation of Jungian psychology as scientific and empirical versus the private self-understanding among Jungians that their work was a vehicle for spiritual growth in psychological garb continues to this day. Contemporary transpersonal psychologists (who are, in many ways, indebted to Jungian thought) also manifest this split between scientific and spiritual self-understandings in their work, affirming a dual allegiance to both science and mysticism, but rarely seeming to recognize that there is any real conflict between these two seemingly contradictory outlooks on life.

Transpersonal psychology, founded in the late 1960s, can be thought of as a further development of humanistic psychology. Humanistic psychology, begun by theorists such as Carl Rogers, Fritz Perls, Eric Fromm, Rollo May, and Gordon Allport, sprang out of a perceived need to offer an alternative to both behaviorism and psychoanalysis. It had (and has) a strong emphasis on the value of human subjectivity and direct inner experience. It emphasizes the value and uniqueness of individuals, promotes the validity and worth of spiritual values, and stresses the need to unfold the innate potentials hidden within each person. Transpersonal psychology shares these themes with humanistic psychology, but as the name implies, it is primarily interested in aspects of the human psyche that seem to transcend personal boundaries.

The founding father of transpersonal psychology was Abraham Maslow (1908–70). Famous for his discussion of the "hierarchy of needs," Maslow claimed that after fundamental physiological and social needs are met in human beings, there still remains the need for "self-actualization" (i.e., the inherently rewarding need to unfold one's latent gifts and potentials). Maslow also argued that "peak experiences" (i.e., dramatic, if short-lived, openings of consciousness leading to feelings of awe, a sense of wholeness and connection or even union with the natural world) are frequent, and natural, human occurrences that typically lead to positive psychological transformations (e.g., spontaneity, the ability to live fully and joyously in the present, and a deep sense of fulfillment and peace).

Maslow, like James, sought to disassociate these peak experiences from institutional religion. Maslow believed that these mystical illuminations are the original insights that, taken together, form the "intrinsic core" of all religions. However, Maslow also thought that institutional, legalistic, dogmatic religious structures distorted the purity of these original mystical insights, and additionally, often attempted to suppress any further mystical openings within their members. For Maslow, what transpersonal psychology offered was just the reverse: a conscious attempt to cultivate peak experiences in individuals, but without the dogmatism and bureaucratic rigidity found in most religions. He believed that transpersonal psychology could, and should, create a naturalistic faith, one that was based on personal experience, not on the authority of religious custom or sacred revelations.[10]

It is not surprising that Maslow's work became popular in the ambiance of the 1960s in America with its rebellion against mainstream cultural standards and its openness to psychedelic drug experiences. Other psychologists, either inspired by Maslow's work or on their own, became interested in exploring alternative states of consciousness as well as other non-typical experiences that point towards a deeper, transpersonal aspect of human existence. Hypnosis, meditation, biofeedback, yoga, parapsychology, shamanism, alternative forms of healing, mystical awareness, lucid dreams, and near-death experiences were all understood by transpersonal psychologists (and increasingly, others in disciplines outside of psychology as well) to point to the latent, unexplored potential ability all humans have to access higher states of consciousness and the capacity to become more loving, wise, and free than anyone had previously imagined was possible.

Transpersonal theorists, from the beginning, attempted to integrate Western psychological and scientific understandings with Eastern spiritual insights (as well as, increasingly, beliefs and practices of various "primal" peoples; e.g., native North Americans, Australian aboriginals, etc.). Fascinated by the fact that non-Western traditions seem to describe in great detail different levels of mystical experiences and also appear to offer specific information as to how a person might induce these experiences, apparently at will, transpersonal theorists (with varying degrees of sophistication) sought to appropriate and synthesize these non-Western mystical understandings and spiritual practices in order to create a new, more overarching, paradigm of the nature of reality and selfhood. This "new paradigm" attempted to integrate a wide amount of material drawn from a number of different disciplines (e.g., psychology, anthropology, ecological studies, cognitive science, religious studies, philosophy, sociology, and the "new physics") in order to promote a vision of the self and reality that was understood to be conducive to human flourishing, harmonious social interactions, and ecological balance.

The "highbrow" world of transpersonal psychology is intimately intertwined with the "lowbrow" universe of New Age thought and practices. In order to uncover the complex interrelationships between, for instance, James and the harmonial religious tradition, or Jung and the esoteric movements of *fin de siècle* Europe, scholars have had to do some very meticulous research. However, the task of demonstrating the mutual interweaving between transpersonal theorists and the New Age movement is relatively simple. In fact, the cross-fertilization of ideas between transpersonal theorists and New Age thinkers is so evident that some scholars, such as Wouter Hanegraaff, have simply included transpersonal theory as an academic and professional subset of the New Age movement itself.

The primary difficulty in studying the New Age movement is that, as James Lewis notes, "large, amorphous movements" such as this have no clearcut boundaries (unlike groups with defined organizational structures such as the Hare Krishnas, Scientology, or the Unification Church) (Lewis and Melton 1992: 5). New Age ideas and practices can be observed in a wide variety of formats; e.g., workshops, management training seminars, utopian communities, therapeutic relationships, and the day-to-day life of solitary spiritual seekers. This plurality of "unchurched" venues helped the New Age movement to evade the lens of scholarly scrutiny for many years. Essentially, it has only been in the later half of the 1990s that several substantive, critically sophisticated academic studies of the New Age movement were published.[11]

One of the most important observations to make about the New Age movement is that it is not new. Although the New Age movement as a cultural force only began to emerge after the 1960s (populated primarily by baby boomers searching for alternative forms of spiritual meaning) and really only became an integral (if often unacknowledged) part of American (and European) religiosity by the 1980s, it is nonetheless, as Robert Ellwood notes,

> a contemporary manifestation of a western alternative spirituality tradi-
> tion going back at least to the Greco-Roman world. The current flows
> like an underground river through the Christian centuries, breaking into
> high visibility in the Renaissance occultism of the so-called "Rosicrucian
> Enlightenment," eighteenth-century Freemasonry, and nineteenth-
> century Spiritualism and Theosophy.
>
> (Lewis and Melton 1992: 59)

Other New Age "ancestors" are (as this essay has hopefully demon-strated), Mesmerism, Swedenborgianism, Jungian thought, and more recently, humanistic and transpersonal psychology, as well as Eastern spiritual traditions, channeling, neo-shamanism, and the holistic health movement. The New Age movement, in its diverse, pluralistic, decentralized fashion, has taken, often unknowingly, this rich heritage of ideas and practices and fashioned them into a mutable yet viable synthesis. While there is no universally agreed upon New Age common creed, the following beliefs and/or practices have been identified by scholars as centrally important:

• Most New Age thought is essentially neo-Platonic. For New Age adherents, all of existence is interconnected and all of the many levels of reality (believed to be populated by various spiritual intermediaries, such as angels, spirit guides, and ascended masters) are, in the final analysis, forms of an absolute Oneness – a Oneness which takes the form of both matter and consciousness. This belief in the interconnection of all of life, in turn, is what underlies the notion that intensely charged, focused states of mind (via various "psychotechnologies," such as meditation, ritual, trance states, and so on) can have quasi-magical effects on the external world, leading to healing, increased prosperity, and social har-mony. In theory, if all of life is a form of one cosmic Consciousness, then all that individuals need to do to effect changes in the outer world is to shift their own state of consciousness.

- The Oneness of life can be discovered, experientially, within the depths of one's own self. The essence of selfhood is, therefore, divine. This inner self (or true self, or higher self) is understood to be the source of all virtues: wisdom, love, energy, power, creativity, and peace. Most people, however, have forgotten this inner divinity. With a consciousness that has been deadened by the values and beliefs of mainstream culture, they live on automatic pilot, wrongly believing that they are individual egos cut off from each other and from the universe. These deeply ingrained unconscious beliefs distort perception, and lead to fear, isolation, and suffering.

- However, New Age adherents also stress that it is possible to overcome these limitations and wrong ideas. A wide range of spiritual techniques, such as meditation, shamanic practices, magic, fasting, taking drugs, chanting, bodywork, drumming, and dance, are available to help individuals to have a powerful, transformative experience of their true nature.

- For the New Ager, direct experience is what is authoritative, not the dictates of established tradition or the opinions of others – even (typically) charismatic leaders. Daily decisions are made, not by obeying externally imposed commandments, but by following one's intuition, inner guidance, or inner wisdom. Mistakes and wrong choices are inevitable, but every experience is understood to be a necessary part of the lessons life has to teach. In this way, life is seen as a school created to help everyone to evolve spiritually. Life's task is to assist individuals to recognize their oneness with the universe – even if this evolution of consciousness takes many lifetimes (whether on this earth or in "higher planes" of existence).

- Although New Agers are adverse to the authority of institutionalized or established religious traditions, they nonetheless feel free to draw upon these traditions as resources to create an eclectic and unique synthesis of various religious (and psychological) perspectives and practices. Most New Age adherents are perennialists; i.e., they believe that it is possible, indeed necessary, to penetrate beneath the external, superficial crust of religious dogmas and rituals – the differences that divide – in order to discover a universal core of hidden wisdom, a mystical essence that underlies all religions. Therefore, the New Ager can safely bypass the moral codes, the authoritative commandments, the exclusivistic dogmas, of particular religions, and nonetheless participate via mystical communion or gnostic insight in what is believed to be the pulsing heart of every authentic religion.

- New Age thought and practice is focused on transformation and healing (understood broadly), both for the individual and for the planet. By transforming and healing themselves, New Agers believe that they are helping to transform and heal the world around them, a world that they are intimately connected with and ultimately responsible for – a world understood to be a living, conscious being that should be treated with respect and care. This world, and everything in it, is thought to be permeated with an invisible, yet tangible spiritual lifeforce (e.g., *ch'i, prana,* or ether). Healing and transformation occurs when this energy flows freely and fully, when it is unobstructed by negative subconscious beliefs or destructive patterns of interaction. One of the primary functions of many New Age practices is to raise the vibrations of this energy, to open up energy centers in the body, or to balance and harmonize the natural flow of this lifeforce.

Given the above set of beliefs and practices, many scholars who have examined the New Age movement have attempted to explain, as Paul Heelas notes, "why apparently 'sensible' – almost entirely well-educated – modernists would turn to what the great majority of their peers would regard to be pretty implausible mumbo-jumbo" (Heelas 1996: 136). The range of explanations is wide. Heelas himself argues that New Agers are reacting against problems that are inherent in modernity (e.g., identity fragmentation, the "iron cage" of bureaucracy, and a deep sense of meaninglessness) while they simultaneously exemplify, at least implicitly, many core modernist values (e.g., emphasis on the autonomy of the individual, distrust of tradition, focus on the new) (Heelas 1996: 135–77). In a related vein, Catherine Albanese argues that the metaphysical tradition in America (of which the New Age is a recent manifestation) attempts to combat the nihilism that has arisen when traditional theism no longer is persuasive and acts as an attractive alternative for a culture where religion increasingly functions as a form of therapy (Albanese 1999a: 315–16). Finally, Robert Fuller, drawing upon ideas found in the Self psychology of Heinz Kohut and object relations theory, postulates that New Age practice and beliefs are not simply a symptom of a pervasive cultural narcissism, but, more importantly, offer powerful, transformative ways to overcome and heal narcissistic wounds (Fuller 1989: 135).

While the last decade has produced several excellent academic studies of the New Age movement, there are still many scholars who have difficulty taking New Age ideas and practices seriously as a legitimate, albeit non-mainstream, philosophical perspective. Admittedly, some New Agers may well be "dabblers" or "dilettantes," but the degree of contempt and scorn found in the (typically off-handed) comments made by some scholars is puzzling.[12] All too frequently academics will note especially vivid examples of New Age excesses or aberrations and then dismiss the entire movement with a condescending laugh or a knowing, superior wink. Ironically, these same academics might themselves hold beliefs that, while more acceptable within the cloistered halls they inhabit, could easily be seen by non-initiates as equally impenetrable, irrational, or problematic as New Age thought (e.g., the thought of Derrida or Lacan as well as other assorted academically fashionable philosophical trends).

It is important to emphasize that I am not saying that there are no valid criticisms of the New Age – or more seriously, that no criticisms are allowed. There are many areas of New Age thought and practice that are quite problematic (e.g., the common claim that all religions say the same thing; the frequently naive, simplistic, and overly romantic portrayal and appropriation of the beliefs and practices of different religions; the mistrust or devaluation of intellectual criticism and historical awareness that often permeates New Age discourse; the more egregious forms of commercialization; and finally, the potential danger of narcissistic self-absorption and consequent lack of social awareness). New Age thought could, arguably, benefit from exposure to careful, respectful criticism. Unfortunately, few scholars seem willing to grant that New Age thought might even possess enough depth to merit their serious critical attention.

Perhaps part of the reaction against New Age thought is not because it is shallow, "pop," or fringy (which it at times is), but rather because, at least unconsciously, there is the nagging suspicion that this type of perspective, if treated seriously and given sustained attention, might actually offer a powerful and persuasive alternative to both secular skepticism and mainstream theism, which are, arguably at present, the top two contenders for academic power and prestige in the academy. Admittedly the New Age movement is often, at best, a "middle-brow" phenomena. There is no theorist in the movement with the theoretical sophistication of, for instance, Freud or Marx (although the writings of Ken Wilber and the philosophically nuanced channeled "Seth" material of Jane Roberts might be strong contenders). Nonetheless, the accessibility of New Age thought is a crucial part of its popular appeal – and simplicity of expression does not automatically mean that the ideas are not coherent, appropriate to the situation, and based on sound insights. The New Age movement, after all, can claim an impressive pedigree: neo-Platonism, Transcendentalism, *Lebensphilosophie*, and the work of William James, taken together, offer at least the potential for a worldview that might have much to offer that is both valuable and valid.

A wholesale dismissal of an entire tradition, or perhaps more seriously, a condescending refusal to even examine it with any degree of open-mindedness and thoroughness, suggests that irrational, unconscious motivations may be at work. Perhaps the virulence of many academic attacks on the New Age is, in fact, symptomatic of a sense of feeling threatened. Anthropologists have long recognized that a culture is typically more threatened by the "other" that is within their own midst than by the (allegedly) totally foreign other. Therefore, scholars can and do study new religions in Brazil, Africa, or Japan with thoroughness and an open-minded attitude, but when they observe a similar degree of syncretism and eclecticism in the New Age movement (or even many identical practices), these same researchers might well revert to harsh criticism or shallow scholarship. It seems that the New Age movement is simply too close to home for its difference to be acceptable.[13] As a spiritual variety of humanism practiced by many educated, upper-class, creative people (who are so similar to non-spiritual humanists), New Age thought seems to generate something close to a sense of betrayal in many academics: one of us went over to the other side.

Diving into psychology as a religion

Scholarly aversion to the New Age is, in many ways, symptomatic of a similar range of methodological problems that arise when academics are confronted with the multifaceted area of "psychology as a religion." Ironically, the academy is willing to embrace practitioners of "psychology as a religion" as long as they do not actually embody that perspective for themselves. As long as Jung and transpersonal theorists, for example, write *about* religious life (i.e., as long as they practice the "psychology *of* religion"), they are accepted as part of religion and psychological studies. But the moment that these theorists cross that unseen, yet vividly felt boundary (i.e., the moment that they are not content to simply describe and analyze religious life from a psychological point of view, but also begin to attribute to psychology an overtly spiritual function), at that precise moment these theorists switch epistemological status. At the very moment when they become advocates for a specific normative understanding of human beings, when they take on a prophetic role for themselves, when they attempt to articulate a new vision of human potential or expound on the underlying spiritual depths of reality (i.e., exactly at the moment when they begin to practice psychology as a religion), their contributions are considered to be suspect.

Why is this the case? Is there really no place for mystical metaphysics, for inspired discourse, for (dare we say it?) wisdom in the academy? Historical overviews, literary analyses, philosophical deconstructions, or biographical descriptions are, admittedly, essential, but is there not also value in the quest to help others gain meaning or a sense of purpose in their lives? Can we in the academy not make any "room" for or, even better, actively encourage those thinkers who offer creative insights, who are on fire with a new vision of life's possibilities, or who seek to transform themselves and others? Do practitioners of "psychology as a religion" belong within the religion and psychological studies "fold" or do they always remain "outside," specimens of study and analysis by other, more academically approved methodologies?

Furthermore, is the only valid (i.e., academically acceptable) way of studying the "psychology as a religion" perspective that of an outsider (whether hostile or sympathetic)? It would seem, on the face of it, that a theorist could personally and professionally speak out of a context of belief and practice that is aligned with, let's say, many current New Age understandings, in the same way that many religion and psychological studies practitioners speak and write out of a Christian context, or a Freudian context, or a feminist context. It is not clear, at least to me, why a clear-headed, intelligent advocate of the "psychology as a religion" angle of vision should automatically be seen as somehow biased, "flakey," or simply odd, instead of as someone who brings a unique, creative, interesting position to the give-and-take of the arena of the academic exchange of ideas. It would seem that, with the embrace of postmodernism by many academics (with its suspicion of the hegemony of rationality, with its insistence that we all understand the world through the lens of our particularity, with its openness to normative discourse), New Age thought would get a fair, respectful hearing. Someone advocating the merits of African-American theology or proclaiming the validity of the gay/lesbian experience for religious studies is taken seriously in the academy – so why should the New Ager be excluded?[14] There is certainly a precedent for normative, quasi (or overtly) theological discourse in religion and psychological studies (e.g., the works of Don Browning and James Fowler). It would seem, on the face of it, that the "psychology as a religion" perspective could also be accepted as a viable contributor to the multitude of methodological outlooks which currently populate religion and psychological studies.

Hopefully it is clear that "psychology as a religion" is not being advocated here as the *only* viable methodological perspective within religion and psychological studies. There is a crucially important role for detailed historical work, for epistemologically neutral phenomenological investigations, as well as for hardnosed evaluative analyses. But I would also like to think that the academy, priding itself as it does on self-reflective, critical awareness, would be open to having its most cherished assumptions (whether normative, epistemological, and even metaphysical) challenged. Ironically, it might well be that those "black sheep" who practice "psychology as a religion" are among those who are the best equipped in the field for this arduous, yet critically important, task.

Notes

1 This discussion of Mesmerism is especially indebted to Fuller 1982 and Ellenberger 1970: 53–253.
2 Clebsch 1973: xvi, quoted in Fuller 1982: 83.
3 Ahlstrom 1972: 1019, quoted in Heelas 1996: 30.
4 This quote is from Trine's immensely popular *In Tune with the Infinite* (Trine 1897: 16–17).
5 James was not unambiguously in accord with all of the mind-cure movement's beliefs. His own philosophical stance was less buoyant and optimistic, more complexly textured. See Barnard (1997: 288–96).
6 Richard Noll makes it clear that while *Memories, Dreams, Reflections* is presented as Jung's autobiography, in reality only three chapters were written by Jung himself (and even these were heavily edited). The rest of the book was compiled and composed by Aniela Jaffé, one of Jung's closest disciples. In fact,

Memories, Dreams, Reflections was originally intended to be Jaffé's biography of Jung (Noll 1994: 13–15).

7 Wouter Hanegraaff makes a similar point in his massive, insightful, and even-handed scholarly study of the ideas and history of the New Age (Hanegraaff 1998: 497).

8 For instance, Noll describes at length how Jung adopted a belief in the value of polygamy due to the influence of one of his patients, Otto Gross (Noll 1997: 70–97).

9 However, an important recent book by Sonu Shamdasani, an historian of psychology, disputes these (and other) claims made by Noll (Shamdasani 1998). Shamdasani is particularly concerned to dispel the notion that Jung was the author of the text which Noll claims was Jung's inaugural address to the Psychological Club of Zurich, the text in which, allegedly, Jung discusses the theme of self-deification. While I would not go so far as Shamdasani, when he suggests that "were it not for this text and the claims made upon it, there is little in Noll's work that would merit further attention" (Shamdasani 1998), it does appear that Shamdasani raises numerous legitimate and important questions as to the accuracy of Noll's attribution of this text to Jung.

10 Maslow's theories are eloquently and tersely framed in the thin volume, *Religions, Values, and Peak Experiences* (Maslow 1964).

11 In my estimation, Hanegraaff's text is the best source on the New Age (Hanegraaff 1998). Other helpful academic texts on the New Age movement include Heelas (1996) and Lewis and Melton (1992) as well as the sections on the New Age in Miller (1995) and Bednarowski (1989). Catherine Albanese has also produced several important monographs and articles that deal either with the New Age movement or its historical antecedents. See Albanese (1977, 1990, 1999a, 1999b).

12 A typical example of academic aversion to New Age ideas can be seen in the following statement:

> The pseudoreligious potpourri found in Boston and across much of America during the late nineteenth century is clearly a predecessor of the "New Age" movement during the late twentieth century. Just as the New Thought movement represented diluted Emersonian Transcendentalism for the masses, the New Age movement pandered to a materialist interpretation of what originally were authentic traditional teachings.
>
> (Versluis 1993: 316)

Quoted in Hanegraaff (1998: 462). Brown comments that one psychologist friend of his, responding to his research on channeling, told him, "I don't know how you can spend time with these sickening New Age types. They're just rich people with too much time on their hands." Brown goes on to note that "her opinion was only slightly more caustic than those offered by other university colleagues" (Brown 1997: 8).

13 After I had written this section, I was pleased to discover that Brown makes much the same point, when he suggests that the hostile reaction of many academics to the New Age movement

> may also reflect the similarities, as much as the differences, between New Age ideology and contemporary academic work. The New Age, for instance, celebrates indeterminacy and moral relativism ... [as well as] the rhetoric of personal empowerment that characterizes writing in the humanities today. For many academics, the likeness may be too close for comfort.
>
> (Brown 1997: 10)

14 However, New Age practitioners also have to be willing to publish and speak in academic venues, to enter into an intellectually rigorous dialogue, a mode of interaction that, so far at least, many, if not most, New Agers have actively avoided.

References

Ahlstrom, S.E. (1972) *A Religious History of the American People*, New Haven: Yale University Press.

Albanese, C.E. (1977) *Corresponding Motion*, Philadelphia: Temple University Press.

—— (1990) *Nature Religion in America*, Chicago: University of Chicago Press.

—— (1999a) "The subtle energies of spirit," *Journal of the American Academy of Religion* 67, 2: 305–25.

—— (1999b) "Narrating an almost nation," *Criterion* 38, 1: 2–15, 44.

Barnard, G.W. (1997) *Exploring Unseen Worlds*, Albany: State University of New York Press.

Bednarowski, M.F. (1989) *New Religions and the Theological Imagination in America*, Bloomington: Indiana University Press.

Brown, M.F. (1997) *The Channeling Zone*, Cambridge, MA: Harvard University Press.

Clebsch, W. (1973) *American Religious Thought*, Chicago: University of Chicago Press.

Ellenberger, H.F. (1970) *The Discovery of the Unconscious*, New York: Basic Books.

Fuller, R. (1982) *Mesmerism and the American Cure of Souls*, Philadelphia. University of Pennsylvania Press.

—— (1989) *Alternative Medicine and American Religious Life*, New York: Oxford University Press.

Hanegraaff, W. (1998) *New Age Religion and Western Culture*, Albany: State University of New York Press.

Heelas, P. (1996) *The New Age Movement*, Oxford: Blackwell.

Homans, P. (1979) *Jung in Context*, Chicago: University of Chicago Press.

James, W. (1985) *The Varieties of Religious Experience*, Cambridge, MA: Harvard University Press.

—— (1986) *Essays in Psychical Research*, Cambridge, MA: Harvard University Press.

Lewis, J.R. and Melton, J.G. (eds) (1992) *Perspectives on the New Age*, Albany: State University of New York Press.

Maslow, A.H. (1983) *Religions, Values, and Peak-Experiences*, New York: Penguin Books.

Miller, T. (ed.) (1995) *America's Alternative Religions*, Albany: State University of New York Press.

Noll, R. (1994) *The Jung Cult*, Princeton: Princeton University Press.

—— (1997) *The Aryan Christ*, New York: Random House.

Rieff, P. (1966) *The Triumph of the Therapeutic*, New York: Harper & Row.

Shamdasani, S. (1998) *Cult Fictions*, London: Routledge.

Trine, R.W. (1897) *In Tune with the Infinite*, New York: Crowell Co.

Versluis, A. (1993) *American Transcendentalism and Asian Religions*, New York: Oxford University Press.

17 The death awareness movement

Psychology as religion?

Lucy Bregman

Psychology as religion: the critique

When Paul Tillich (Tillich 1957: 84) and Paul Vitz (Vitz 1994: xiii) separately accused psychology of "replacing religion," and making claims of ultimate meaning, they voiced a common complaint among twentieth-century religious thinkers. Is psychology arrogantly overstepping its bounds as empirical science, and becoming a "cult of self-worship"? At what point do psychological frameworks become themselves myth, functioning in ways so similar to traditional myth that all modesty, all empiricism and all humility is abandoned?

This essay asks the "psychology as religion" question differently: how have psychologies of dying and bereavement conveyed a spiritual dimension of life for those who make use of their ideas, images and practices? Using Peter Van Ness' definition of "spirituality," I begin by stating:

> Facing outward, human existence is spiritual insofar as it engages reality as a maximally inclusive whole and makes the cosmos an intentional object of thought and feeling. Facing inward, life has a spiritual dimension to the extent that it is apprehended as a project of one's own most enduring and vital self.
>
> (Van Ness 1996: 5)

A wide range of "non-religious" frameworks may potentially serve as the vehicles for spirituality, regardless of the overt intentions of those who constructed these. The psychological theories of Freud, the human potential movement, and transpersonal psychology, have all done so. The results need not automatically be a "cult of self-worship," although some concern for an "enduring and vital self" will certainly be present. What most certainly happens is that the empirical-scientific status of psychology gets de-centered as psychological frameworks become useful for spirituality. That psychological theories claim empirical validity is part of their appeal, but the wild success of theories which never met the criteria of testability, falsifiability or publicly documented results, reveals how marginal the actual "scientific-ness" of psychology can be. It was never empirically proved that anyone dies in five stages, but the famous Kübler-Ross sequence is an example of apprehending "one's most enduring and vital self" as a spiritual project, using a psychological language to portray a human experience. Ideas such as this give form and direction to experiences surrounding death, to offer guidance, inspiration and the promise of understanding.

Note that our definition substitutes the word "spirituality" for "religion." Today, the former term has triumphed, reserving "religion" for the communal, organized tradition within which many but not all expressions of spirituality thrive. Therefore, any claims about psychology as religion focus on the personal meaning-making process, in encountering ultimate reality and coming to terms with "the cosmos [as] an intentional object of thought and feeling." No claims will be made that psychological institutional activities – the annual meetings of Association for Death Education and Counseling (ADEC), for instance – duplicate the organized communal activities of religious groups. There are many venues for the psychological perspectives on dying and loss; some are those of the human potential movement – weekend workshops – while others occupy "religious" spaces such as chaplaincy programs. In this area, at least, chaplains and other explicitly religious experts have been enthusiastic advocates of the psycholo-gies of dying and death, most often allies of the social worker, hospice coordinator and bereavement counselor and rarely their critics. I focus on the discovery and advocacy of ultimate meanings, rather than on the institutional contexts within which these make sense. The one major exception is to place psychological perspectives on dying within the contemporary context of health care, patients' advocacy and calls for dignity and humanity within medical settings.

This statement of the issues avoids the built-in animus against "psychol-ogy as religion" which fuels rhetoric such as Vitz's. There is no claim that the death awareness movement "conspired" to introduce new, anti-religious understandings of dying and death. In the case of "death and dying" as a topic, there already existed a vacuum in language and imagery, so that death awareness advocates say that "American culture denies death," and point to this silence in regard to illness, dying and bereavement as human experiences. As sociologist of religion Thomas Luckmann put it in 1967, "Death does not appear even as a subordinate topic in the sacred cosmos of a modern industrial society" (Luckmann 1967: 114). The death awareness movement spoke new words, created a language for us that now has become familiar, if not universally accepted. This language comes to function as a "spirituality" in the sense of our definition. It did not usurp religious language, it filled in what seemed a vacant niche (Bregman 1999).

Of course, religious traditions had contributed rich and complex ideas and imagery centered around dying and death. Yet these had already faded greatly from common awareness before the start of the death awareness movement, and from Christian theology as well. Even if we think that the psychological spirituality of dying, death and grief is less adequate than its religious precursors, this is a different judgment from that of Vitz and other opponents of "psychology turned religion." For the latter, in principle, psychology shouldn't supply ultimate meanings, no matter which particular ideas it offers for "spirituality." In this essay I allow that the death awareness movement has and does work in just this way, and base my assessment on examination of specific key images and meanings, such as death as "natural" and the problem of death as that of "coming to terms with loss." I am free to measure these against an ideal of adequacy grounded in a particular religious tradition, but in doing so I at least allow that psychology and Christian thought both can offer valuable ways to encounter death as spiritual reality. Indeed, given the prior vacuum and cultural silence, new images do not appear directly in conflict with older ones, and Christian pastoral writers have enthusiastically embraced the principal aims of the death awareness movement, simply because these spoke to issues and anxieties pervasive among contemporary persons.

The death awareness movement

The term "death awareness movement" is a label for the flood of popular, clinical and research writings covering topics of dying and bereavement, and for advocacy of the central themes of these writings. Although there were some attempts to start "scientific thanatology" as a sub-field of psychiatry before the late 1960s, the key date is probably the publication of Kübler-Ross' *On Death and Dying* in 1969. The phenomenal success of *On Death and Dying* meant that a trickle of specialists' writings became a flood of books, workshops, support groups for the dying and their families, and applications of Kübler-Ross' basic ideas to other issues (divorce, bereavement). The fundamental ideas became accessible to ordinary persons such as hospital patients, their families, and mourners. Important to this literature are the numerous autobiographies whose central plot is the protagonist's struggle with terminal illness, or of nursing a loved one who died. Overwhelmingly, these first-person narratives make use of psychological perspectives, indirectly if not by explicit quotations from Kübler-Ross and other exponents of psychologies of dying and grief (Bregman and Thiermann 1995).

The central message of these writings is that dying, however terrifying, could be faced and "accepted." It can be integrated into one's conscious and unconscious, intellectual and emotional awareness. For Americans thirty years ago, and for many still, this is a radical claim. It challenged a pervasive assumption that death was too terrifying to face, was always and inevitably "unacceptable," and therefore total denial – and the social silence in regard to death – was normal. The radical claim was that not just the dying, but those near them can come to terms with loss, and need not hide from death or block it out. Therefore, our society denied and repressed death, and this was a *problem*, not normal and universal (Kübler-Ross 1969: 11–18). It made the experience of dying, particularly for long-term hospital patients, isolating and more painful psychologically than it had to be. Thus, the psychology of dying and bereavement began as an advocacy language, and has continued so until now.

Kübler-Ross simply assumed that just as the dying go through five stages to acceptance of impending death, so the families of the dying also move from denial, through anger, bargaining, depression to final acceptance. The orderly nature of this progression was always an ideal, one that even its originator refused to pin down sufficiently with empirical data to make it stick. The point is not to insist that the five stages must occur in invariant sequence, or that everyone must follow the same pathway, but that clinicians, counselors, medical staff, etc., must recognize that a dying person is experiencing an impending loss, and is trying to accommodate and accept this loss. The goal of counseling is not to hurry the poor patient into acceptance, but to meet the person at whatever stage he or she is at (Kübler-Ross 1969: 62–6). No matter, therefore, that no empirical study ever showed a "five-stage progression," and that except for denial and depression, it was very hard to find "hard evidence" for any of the so-called stages. Moreover, once this real message was grasped, it was a short step to say that the only "correct" way to die was to follow one's own way, to express one's own style right up until the last moment of life.

Here, those familiar with the work of Bellah and associates, *The Habits of the Heart*, will recognize the theme of "expressive individualism," so closely linked to psychology by the authors of that volume (Bellah *et al.* 1985: 47). The "first language" of most middle-class Americans, expressive individualism, grounds all language of value and meaning in the self's urges and desires, the self's striving to become itself as a unique individual. No wonder some of the 1970s death awareness titles read like posters for expressive individualism: *To Die With Style, A Death of One's Own,* and Kübler-Ross' own edited anthology *Death: the Final Stage of Growth.* The "five stages" may have been widely employed to establish norms for "successful dying," but the net result was probably to open dying as another arena where "expressive individualism," the self as the measure of meanings and values, could flourish. (Vitz's critique of psychology as "self-worship" is actually a critique of this psychological expressive individualism, as it permeates theory and the "helping professions.")

A word should be added about the "expressive" dimension of this form of psychologically validated individualism. No value or practice has come under more attack by death awareness advocates than the "stiff upper lip" with which Anglo-Americans were told to meet tragedies of all kinds. To express one's sorrow, grief, fears, anger, outrage is important, in order to accept the reality of one's feelings. Screaming in privacy, pounding a pillow, crying: these suggestions are repeated endlessly, although the benefits of "blowing off steam" are often balanced against the social cost of doing so directly to others. Theologically oriented authors also advocate this view and deplore the "stoicism" that passes for Christian strength in the face of loss. Typically, pastoral care experts state: "We find it difficult if not impossible to imagine a situation of genuine loss or sadness in which crying makes anything worse" (Mitchell and Anderson 1983: 122). Moreover, speaking to an empathetic listener or support group about one's loss also helps, while keeping one's sorrow to oneself – as American society demands that the bereaved do – is seen as an obstacle to real acceptance. To some extent, this represents a generational divide; the "baby boomer" values are encoded in the psychologies of growth that have shaped the death awareness movement, so that the reticence of the elderly, for example, is never idealized even when honored as the way *they* maintain their deepest values and selves through crises.

Which psychologies have triumphed within the death awareness movement? One could argue that continuing research and new theorizing about bereavement shows a changeover from the initial individualistic human potential movement bent to a far more interpersonal, relational perspective. Freud and psychoanalytic perspectives, while honored up to a point (Freud's essay on "Mourning and melancholia" is constantly cited in reviews of the literature on mourning) do not control the themes of the death awareness movement. Speculations about the "death instinct" are entirely absent, as perhaps they have been from American psychoanalysis all along. Yes, patients deny and repress impending death: but the whole focus of Kübler-Ross *et al.* is that denial is not the last word, but the first stage. Defense mechanisms flourish, and can be identified and described using psychoanalytic terms, but the deeper implications is that people *can* face reality, *can* accept death and loss.

The more fundamental break with the psychoanalytic worldview is a different one. Getting beyond repression and denial to accept reality is, for the death awareness movement, very unlike the "education for reality" recommended by the Freud of *The Future of an Illusion*. For death awareness advocates, reality will not be bleak, cruel and ruthless, but filled with unexpected riches, a vivid appreciation of life's meanings, and loving ties among persons, even at the very end of life. It is impossible to overstate this thesis. Death can be accepted not because it is good in itself, but because in the process of acceptance, something of true worth, meaning and even peace is discovered. Love and hope do not die even when the sick person never recovers. This is the central inspirational message behind almost all the autobiographies, those with titles such as *A Death with Dignity*, *Thanksgiving: An AIDS Journal*, and *The Light Around the Dark*. The intent is not to deny sadness and the reality of loss, but to discern in their midst some vision of the total cosmos within which death and loss are relativized. It is the accomplishment of the death awareness movement to have offered a language and imagery to suggest this, while neither glorifying death nor repudiating life.

Bereavement: coming to terms with loss

This message continues, as does the psychological framing of the basic issues, through the 1980s and into the 1990s. The death awareness movement remains psychological in its perspective, defining the central problem posed by death as "coming to terms with loss," emotional coping and adaptation. Denial, repression, grief, depression, defenses and overcoming defenses, coping strategies: this is the vocabulary of the new language. Emotional conditions, with the dying or bereaved person as the experiencer of these, continue to hold center-stage. Books on counseling the dying or bereaved written in the late 1990s will be, in this respect, direct continuations of the books written in the 1970s. However, there is one significant change during this three-decade period. Kübler-Ross simply assumed that just as the dying patient goes through "five stages," so the family of the patient replicates this process as they prepare for the death. The process of dying and the process of anticipatory mourning are one and the same (Kübler-Ross 1969: 168). The model of "coming to terms with loss" could be applied to a range of situations, including bereavement after the death.

Today, no one makes this assumption. Studies of bereavement have progressed, have advanced within the paradigm of "coming to terms with loss," so that the debates are not "how much does dying resemble grieving?" but "what model specific to bereavement is most appropriate?" Loss implies attachment, and contemporary discussion of bereavement is grounded in attachment theory, developed by John Bowlby and continued by Colin Parkes in works such as *Bereavement: Studies of Grief in Adult Life* (Parkes 1972). The original model here begins from a relationship, unlike the "death the final stage of growth" psychologies. When a loss occurs, the attachment continues, and the bereaved individual must search for the lost beloved, experiencing intense misery and anxiety as a normal and predictable response to loss. Parkes and other 1970s and 1980s theorists took for granted that the final outcome of "coming to terms with loss" was letting go of the past attachment, and forming new ones. Or, in the words of one autobiographer, the "widow's journey" is "a return to the loving self" (Rose 1990). To remain a perpetual mourner was to fail in accomplishing this "return," to remain stuck in the past and its pain. Given this framework, it seemed natural to set time-frames and limits for "normal" mourning, and to distinguish between normal and "pathological" on the basis of how "stuck" the mourner remained.

In the early 1980s, Worden began to replace this model with one of tasks: "To accept the reality of the loss," "to experience the pain of grief," "to adjust to an environment in which the deceased is missing" and "to withdraw emotional energy and reinvest it in another relationship" (Worden 1982: 11–

16). Mourning is completed when these tasks are. More recently, Rando's expanded list of "six R-processes" furthers this approach:

1 Recognize the loss.
2 React to the separation.
3 Recollect and reexperience the deceased and the relationship.
4 Relinquish the old attachments to the deceased and the old assumptive world.
5 Readjust to move adaptively into the new world without forgetting the old.
6 Reinvest.

(Rando 1993: 45)

Mourning is no longer a "stage-based" process, and it is no longer grasped as if it were a medical disease. The term "complicated" has replaced "pathological" to label cases where the mourner gets into deep misery and stays there. These R-processes involve the whole person and the person's "assumptive world." Bereavement is still a loss, but it is very unlike dying. Note that permission is given to remember and retain the old, even when the emphasis is still on moving forward and "reinvesting." More and more theorists and clinicians recognize that the loss is never forgotten, that moving on does not require us to deny our pasts and our continuing bonds with the deceased (Klass *et al.* 1996). Those who stress this note how American society gives little space to mourners, and no space at all to the continued presence and relationship with the dead. What is intended is a richer, more nuanced picture of what it means to "move adaptively into the new world," for the bereaved. For parents of dead children, for example, it is simply inappropriate to tell them "you'll get over this, and have another child," even when that is physically possible.

What is interesting is not so much these particular developments within the psychological study of bereavement, but how *loss* remains the abiding, central category. Death is one kind of loss, but the loss model of coming to terms with another's death simply dominates all attempts to conceptualize the area. "Growth through loss," "coming to terms with loss," *All Our Losses, All Our Griefs*: these phrases show how loss as a category gives shape to the landscape of death for the death awareness movement. If there is a spirituality of the death awareness movement – and I believe there is – it takes the form of focus on "Grief: a sacred sadness" (the title of a lecture by Gerald May at the National Conference on Loss and Transition, 1998). Death in and of itself may be too metaphysical for psychologists to say much about. Dying can be spoken of, as impending loss. And bereavement, where the loss is an empirical fact already in the world, is easiest of all to discuss using this motif. What began as "thanatology" has actually, for the most part, turned into the study of bereavement, and the practice of therapies to help the bereaved.

Death as a natural part of life

It is not true to say that "death is not spoken of at all" in the death awareness movement. What is said about death, and said over and over and over, is that it is natural, "a part of life." It should and can be accepted because as a natural part of life, it is real and predictable. We flee from it at the risk of endless lies, self-deceptions, defensive maneuvers and denials. Something as natural as death may not always be acceptable to us in each particular case, but the starting point for psychological thinking on coming to terms with it, is that we do not fulfill our own humanity by denying something so basic. It is healthier to accept the inevitable and the natural, than it is to deny, repress or ignore it. "Death with dignity" is possible, is more desirable than total refusal to make room for death. This was the original Kübler-Ross message, and it really hasn't changed in the thirty years since *On Death and Dying* was published.

This message that "death is natural" was one of the features of "psychology as religion" that Vitz found detestable (Vitz 1994: 145–6). It represented to him a naturalistic, reductionist view of humankind, and a direct challenge to all Christian hope for resurrection. By this theological standard, the death awareness movement expresses the militantly secular kingdom of psychology colonizing territory that had previously belonged to faith. Some thanatologists agreed with this, and would have accepted Vitz's hostility as the sign of backlash against the advance of scientific thinking about natural processes. In the eyes of this author, both these positions seem to be misreadings of the actual situation, and – if I may put it this way – the party has moved to another room.

The "death is natural" theme undoubtedly continues within death and dying literature, and remains very central. But the contrast intended by those who use this is not to exclude "death is a prelude to resurrection." Chaplains and pastoral care writers find both assertions compatible, when the first is properly contextualized. It is meant to protest the continued denials practiced by high-tech health care, and the ethos for which the death of the patient is the doctor's "defeat." What Kübler-Ross found when she first began her study may still be true today: in a huge research hospital no patients were "dying." In the ICU, intensive care can mean incessant, relentless treatment, long after it is privately recognized as futile by doctors and nurses. Although many changes have occurred within health care, somehow unwillingness to face up to death and reluctance to stop treatments continue. Fundamentally, the one language publicly acknowledged in our society for dying and death is medicine, and within this the human experiences of the dying get squeezed out and silenced. "Death is natural" aims to overcome this. "Death is natural" is a slogan arising within this context of medical care at the end of life, and a protest against the overwhelming focus on technology at the expense of persons.

However, when this is understood, it is still possible to claim that "death is natural" carries its own spiritual rather than strictly "secular" scientific meaning. This spiritual reading claims that death, like birth, is part of life's cycle, it is what unites us with other living beings in an ecosystem that operates with harmony, if not with purpose. Nature here is neither "red in tooth and claw" nor as cold and indifferent to our hopes as Freud's use of it in *The Future of an Illusion*. This imagery of a "natural system" that operates benevolently, and within which all individual interests may be balanced out, is very widespread within psychology, and has led to ethical confusions, especially since the assumption is rarely stated so plainly. One confusion is that although the total ecosystem may work harmoniously, the experiences of any one participant in it can be filled with danger, anxiety, pain and violence, all of which are excluded when death awareness advocates evoke "nature."

What "nature" does here – and it really should have a capital N, for Nature functions as a god-term – is anchor the individual's struggle within a wider, more universal cosmic vision. Although "expressive individualism" may reign when it comes to practical advice and therapy, there is a sense in which "Nature" grounds and unites all of us. It is foolish, undignified and arrogant to set one's ego against "Nature," and Freud is not alone in questioning this ideal. The death awareness movement advocates a vision of human life that leaves room for death and loss, and the ultimate cosmic context for this is a bio-spiritual immanence, holding our myriad of individual selves into a greater whole. Expressions of this permeate the psychological writings of advocates, whether the topic is pastoral care for the families of the terminally ill, or psychological counseling for the bereaved. It appears within a wide range of autobiographical writings, some formal and professional, others by sufferers who are writing their narratives as self-therapy.

At this level, one may say that this implicit vision of Nature allows the death awareness movement to acknowledge an objective face to spirituality. The self may indeed experience loss, but what is gained is connection with the universe of Nature, which medical technology and the worldview behind it excludes. Is this vision anti-Christian? Post-Christian? Compatible with Christianity? For that matter, is it Jewish? Is it Buddhist? These questions are the right ones, because at this point, the death awareness movement's psychology is functioning as "religion," and needs to be addressed as such. But its relation to spiritualities that remain within any of the religious traditions is complex. Even though no Christians, Jews or Buddhists want to deify "Nature," all of these faiths find themselves allied to the death awareness movement's attempt to restore dignity and humanity to hospital patients, to raise awareness of the human situation rather than solely the medical condition of such patients, and to question the ethos of death denial within which much medical practice still flourishes.

Religious concerns: what is left out?

The death awareness movement translates the fundamental human fact of universal and inevitable death into issues of loss and acceptance of our ultimate place within Nature. The new words for death and dying – developed by psychologists but adapted by autobiographers, by bereavement support groups, by many others in American society today – may not be the only words spoken, and may compete with older, more religiously traditional words and images among certain populations. In this section, I briefly discuss some traditional concerns omitted, questions not asked, or if asked at all, immediately translated into the vocabulary of death awareness concepts. The purpose of this is to follow up on the idea of "psychology as religion," by looking at how religious concerns of primary importance in the past are excluded from the psychological spirituality of the death awareness movement.

First among these concerns is the one actually highlighted by Vitz: what happened to resurrection, or indeed, any references to an afterlife, a continued existence of the soul/mind/person after death? Anyone familiar with Christian guidebooks on "holy dying" will find that their entire understanding of dying as human situation is grounded in expectation that it precedes a personal encounter with God, who will judge one's deeds and character. Within this framework, death is expectable and ought to be accepted, but its meaning are very different than what the death awareness movement posits. This "eclipse of eternity" (Walter 1996) preceded the death awareness movement, so that no one can blame Kübler-Ross *et al.* for conspiring to wipe out references to heaven, life after death, or survival of the soul. This had occurred within Christian theology by mid-century, according to McDannell and Lang in their *Heaven: A History* (McDannell and Lang 1988: 322–52). Although personal beliefs of ordinary Christians may be closer to nineteenth-century theologies here, the lack of attention to afterlife is not confined to psychological spiritualities. As for themes of judgment, these had, in popular descriptions, also vanished or greatly receded, so that the fears of Kübler-Ross' dying hospital patients did not seem to include post-death divine wrath or punishment. Patients grieve missed opportunities, poor relationships, and previous, unmourned deaths – but without explicit reference to any form of afterlife.

An interesting twist to this is the attempted return of interest in afterlife on the part of "New Age" advocates, including Kübler-Ross herself by the mid-1970s. Tales of near-death experiences, Raymond Moody's *Life After Life* (Moody 1975) and its countless imitators, reveal fascination with this topic. But here the death awareness movement refuses to follow. The near-death experiences (NDEs), which are very often used to support some post-death continuation of an experiencing consciousness become contested ground for scientific sceptics to battle "New Age" advocates while some conservative Christians see such experiences as satanic deceptions. But the death awareness movement's mainstream hasn't taken the bait, has not entered these debates, has neither excluded the possibility of NDE nor taken up the cause. Why not? Is it a case of scientific credibility, concern with what is empirical and testable? Or is there another reason why the literature of the death awareness movement, and that of NDEs, remain on two separate tracks?

For the death awareness movement, the central core image is of death as loss. Some visions of after-death existence leave room for this image, while for the advocates of NDEs there is no place at all for imagery of loss. Death is a transition "from life to life" without real rupture, destruction or separation. There is no loneliness or abandonment, no depression, no need for anyone to relearn the world, let alone engage in six R-processes in order to come to terms with change. As Kübler-Ross, who became an advocate of this view herself, said it in a public lecture, "There is no death."

No wonder that, to the mainstream of the death awareness movement, this entire message reeks of denial. Whether or not death is "the end," a wall or a gateway is less the issue than the absolute denial of the loss image all the way through the near-death experience accounts. Those who report NDEs may not be rebuked or automatically considered pathological by their therapists, but neither do the latter encourage exploration of this mode of paranormal experience. Significantly, classic Moody-type NDEs are extraordinarily absent from the many autobiographies of terminal illness, for the latter express the mainstream concerns of the death awareness movement. It is the mission of death awareness advocates to persuade Americans that growth through loss is possible, that loss is an intrinsic part of life, and that our societal denial of this has burdened us all unbearably. From this perspective, a whole message that claims to be about death but that leaves absolutely no room for loss is humanly false. It is wiser to accept that loss is real, and can become "a sacred sadness," than to seek for reassurance that life and death can be loss-free. This is a spiritual conflict but not the same as the more publicized debates over the validity of NDEs, nor the exact conflict perceived by Vitz.

A related "left out" topic is the continued presence of the dead, after their deaths, among the living. Here, we encounter a "translation" of this topic from one focused on the ontological status of dead people's spirits to the psychological states of the bereaved. A widely reported phenomena among widows is the "sense of the presence" of the late husband, reassuring, consoling, guiding the lonely woman as she must do the work of grief. Other mourners as well report the presence of the recently beloved dead, sometimes visible, most often just "there," at least for the bereaved. For theorists who focus on mourning as a process of attachment, loss, search and letting go, these inner experiences assimilate into "search;" the presence of the deceased is an hallucinatory method of restoring them to the living. Those who focus on "continuing bond" take these experiences as evidence of the necessary relationship that persists yet changes, even after the death of one party (Conant 1996: 179–96). The sense of the presence of the dead becomes one mode of keeping these people psychologically "there" for the mourner, and this is not a pathological stance but part of maintaining the past while moving into the future.

What is *not* suggested is that the dead continue to have an active role as ontological agencies in and of themselves. Although many psychological writers cite customs of other cultures where it is definitely believed that the dead *do* have such a status, no one among death awareness thinkers actively champions this view. On the other hand, therapists and counselors freely recommend exercises that seem to require interaction between the living and the dead – or that ask for a suspension of disbelief about the issue discussed above. The family gathers, and the therapist sets an empty chair in the middle of the circle, and says, "This is X [the deceased] sitting here. What do you all need to say to him?" In turn, each person speaks, yells, cries, apologizes and so on. Under these conditions, no American will believe that the spirit of X is "really" sitting there. It is only someone from another culture, one for whom the rules for how the living and the dead interact are different, who will be confused by this technique. The same is true of another therapeutic practice. A widow writes *Letter to My Husband*, but who is the actual intended reader? Compare this to cultures where letters are left on the graves of deceased saints, and we sense the translation between old and new frameworks for meaning.

Survival of transcendence: psychology and spirituality in the death awareness movement

At this point, a religious critic of "psychology as religion" may step in and say: "You have just provided evidence for why psychology is *bad* religion, *impoverished* religion. It may not be 'self-worship,' but it has trivialized a profound metaphysical concern into managing feelings. Who cares how well a family has dealt with tasks or R-processes, compared with the momentous question of survival after death? If the dead truly exist, independently of the wishes and memories of the living, that is the Big Secret. Anything else is small-time."

If we add together the voices of Tillich and Vitz, we can construct a further step to this critique. Traditional faiths view dying as a setting to teach transcendence: the ultimate reality of God, or of Buddhist emptiness, dwarfs the foolish everyday concern with material possessions, personal goals, the world's standards of success. Meditations on skulls or skeletons encourage this awareness among the not-yet-dying. The point of heaven is God, and it is toward God that the dying person is to direct attention. Even the hope for personal "survival" is less central than this. Psychology over-reaches itself when it functions as religion, but it does worse damage by remaining silent about the ultimate reaches of faith, by teaching us to keep our eyes watching anything less than God. By presenting to us the language of "R-processes" or of "five stages of dying," we are forgetting the gospel or the dharma as they point us toward a cosmos that is truly full-sized, awe-ful and ultimate, magnificently above all of the concerns so dear to the death awareness movement.

This critique is not aimed solely at the death awareness movement, or solely at psychology. It is the stance of those who advocate what McDannell and Lang call a "theocentric" view of Heaven (McDannell and Lang 1988: 30), and these include just about every major religious figure they survey. It is the mark of being a major religious figure, it seems, to cleanse Heaven as Jesus cleansed the courtyard of the Jerusalem temple, throwing out all the human clutter that distracted from its status as a house of prayer. Within twentieth-century liturgies, particularly funeral services, this same move has been made: the funeral should focus on resurrection, the saving message of hope in Christ. From this stance, other, lesser stuff, including explicit attention to the particular experiences of the deceased, or the emotions of the bereaved, is just clutter.

But is it? The death awareness movement might not state its reply in these terms, but advocates could say that human beings, at least as we know them, are interested in things and persons other than God. We are beings of embodied attachments, of memories and feelings that include more content and contexts than the radically "theocentric" vision allows. These attachments aren't "clutter," they are the stuff of life. To say this is not to dishonor God, and at funerals to focus on death as loss is to honor both the stuff of life, and the God who creates it. Using this argument, which is explicitly theological but phrased in a way that many death awareness advocates would intuitively accept, one may say that the movement filled in a space for the stuff of life, when theology had emptied this out of one-sided theocentrism. To celebrate the uniqueness of an individual life at a funeral is more true to the character of God as creator of nature and persons, than to disallow particularities and focus exclusively on a universal, theocentric but excessively abstract message. Tillich's "God above God" couldn't possibly be interested in how miserable the mourners feel at or after the funeral, and that is precisely what the death awareness movement finds meaningful. Grief can be transformed into "sacred sadness," a deeper and more complex vision of life's totality. With our loves and losses given words, what can result is a spirituality inclusive of life's stuff without trivialization.

The death awareness hasn't therefore closed off transcendence, but it has left open ways for persons to discern it in new, close-to-the-bone and close-to-home places. Its focus on loss does not aim to debunk Christian or other hopes for something beyond death, nor is its use of "nature" really a militantly reductionist biologism. That is the mode of the hospital, of medicine, whose tyranny the death awareness movement aims to break. The latter's continuation over thirty years' span has yielded new words for coming to terms with death, words adopted by many who are neither psychologists nor outside of traditional religious spiritualities. It offers an example of psychology functioning as religion, while doing so in ways that actually revitalize religious attention to human experiences around which cultural silence and denial reigned.

References

Bellah, R.N., Madsen, R., Sullivan, W.M., Swidler, A., and Tipton, S.M. (1985) *Habits of the Heart: Individualism and Commitment in American Life*, Berkeley: University of California Press.

Bregman, L. (1999) *Beyond Silence and Denial: Death and Dying Reconsidered*, Louisville, Ky.: Westminster John Knox.

Bregman, L. and Thiermann, S. (1995) *First Person Mortal: Personal Narratives of Illness, Dying and Grief*, New York: Paragon House.

Conant, R. (1996) "Memories of the death and life of a spouse: the role of images and *sense of presence* in grief," in D. Klass, P. Silverman, and S. Nickman (eds) *Continuing Bonds: New Understandings of Grief*, Philadelphia: Taylor & Francis.

Freud, S. (1961[1917]) "Mourning and melancholia," *The Standard Edition of the Complete Psychological Works of Sigmund Freud*, vol. 14, trans. J. Strachey, London: Hogarth Press.

—— (1961[1927]) *The Future of an Illusion, The Standard Edition of the Complete Psychological Works of Sigmund Freud*, vol. 21, trans. J. Strachey and W.D. Robson-Scott, London: Hogarth Press.

Klass, D., Silverman, P., and Nickman, S. (eds) (1996) *Continuing Bonds: New Understandings of Grief*, Philadelphia: Taylor & Francis.

Kubler-Ross, E. (1969) *On Death and Dying*, New York: Macmillan.

Luckmann, T. (1967) *The Invisible Religion*, New York: Macmillan.

McDannell, C. and Lang, B. (1988) *Heaven: a History*, New Haven: Yale University Press.

Mitchell, K. and Anderson, H. (1983) *All Our Losses, All Our Griefs*, Philadelphia: Westminster.

Moody, R. (1975) *Life After Life*, New York: Bantam.

Parkes, C.M. (1972) *Bereavement: Studies of Grief in Adult Life*, New York: International Universities Press.

Rando, T. (1993) *Treatment of Complicated Mourning*, Champaign, Il.: Research Press.

Rose, X. (1990) *Widow's Journey: A Return to the Loving Self*, New York: Henry Holt.

Tillich, P. (1957) *Dynamics of Faith*, New York: Harper & Row.

Van Ness, P. (1996) "Introduction," in P. Van Ness (ed.) *Spirituality and the Secular Quest*, New York: Crossroad.

Vitz, P. (1994 [1977]) *Psychology as Religion: The Cult of Self-Worship*, Grand Rapids: Wm. B. Eerdmans.

Walter, T. (1996) *The Eclipse of Eternity: A Sociology of the Afterlife*, Houndsmills: Macmillan Press.

Worden, W. (1982) *Grief Counseling and Grief Therapy: A Handbook for the Mental Health Practitioner*, New York: Springer Publishing Co.

Index